D0203808

INTERNATIONAL HANDBOOK OF TRANSPORTATION POLICY

INTERNATIONAL HANDBOOK OF TRANSPORTATION POLICY

Edited by
TSUNEO AKAHA

Greenwood Press
New York
Westport, Connecticut
London

Library of Congress Cataloging-in-Publication Data

International handbook of transportation policy / edited by Tsuneo Akaha.
p. cm.
Includes bibliographical references
ISBN 0-313-25372-2 (lib. bdg. : alk. paper)
1. Transportation and state—Handbooks, manuals, etc.
2. Transportation—Handbooks, manuals, etc. I. Akaha, Tsuneo.
HE193.I65 1990
388'.068—dc20 90-2758

British Library Cataloguing in Publication Data is available.

Library of Congress Catalog Card Number: 90-2758
ISBN: 0-313-25372-2

First published in 1990

Greenwood Press, 88 Post Road West, Westport, Connecticut 06881
An imprint of Greenwood Publishing Group, Inc.

Printed in the United States of America

The paper used in this book complies with the Permanent Paper Standard issued by the National Information Standards Organization (Z39.48-1984).

10 9 8 7 6 5 4 3 2 1

CONTENTS

INTERNATIONAL HANDBOOK OF TRANSPORTATION POLICY

INTRODUCTION

Tsuneo Akaha

This is a survey of the public transportation systems and policies of twelve countries including five advanced industrial countries with market economies (France, Japan, the United Kingdom, the United States, and West Germany), three countries with centrally planned economies (China, East Germany, and the Soviet Union), and four developing or newly industrialized countries with market economies (Brazil, Korea, Mexico, and Zaire). The survey is concerned with the selected countries' experience with the development, maintenance, and use of publicly provided transportation infrastructure for both public and private (commercial or individual) purposes.

The diversity of the countries surveyed, both in terms of the type of economic systems (i.e., market and centrally planned economies) and the level of economic development, provides rich and varied national experiences from which lessons are to be learned. It also allows the reader to compare and contrast the different as well as similar needs and policy responses in the public transportation sector of the countries selected.

All modes of transportation are covered by the survey: railways, roadways, inland and coastal waterways, air transportation, and, in some cases, pipeline transportation. Both passenger and freight/cargo transportation are included. Narrative descriptions of the transportation modes are accompanied by quantitative indicators of the volume of transportation and other related data. Thus, some quantitative, as well as qualitative, cross-national comparisons may be made in terms of the relative importance of each mode of transportation or the changes in intermodal balance and distribution over time.

Equally important, most chapters present five sets of information about the selected countries that represent dimensions along which cross-national comparisons may be made:

1. *Background* (historical and geographical factors influencing the development and maintenance of the country's public transportation system and policy);
2. *Socioeconomic dimensions* (the impact of socioeconomic changes in the country upon its public transportation infrastructure and services and the resulting changes in government policy in this sector);
3. *Political dimensions* (the impact of political and ideological factors and considerations upon the country's public transportation system and policy);
4. *Recent trends and future prospects* (the major trends in public transportation in terms of the characteristics of the public transportation infrastructure and services, socioeconomic, technological, and political factors affecting government policy, and projected future trends and problems); and
5. *Transportation policy organization and process* (major government agencies and other entities which directly participate in the formulation and/or implementation of public transportation policy and notable characteristics of the process of policy formulation).

The country chapters are organized alphabetically in the following order: Brazil, China (People's Republic), East Germany (Democratic Republic), France, Japan, Korea (Republic of), Mexico, the Soviet Union, the United Kingdom, the United States, West Germany (Federal Republic), and Zaire. The survey covers the post–World War II period up through 1988–89, depending upon the availability of the most recent information. Some references to prewar developments are found insofar as such information is directly relevant to the understanding of postwar developments. The conclusion offers an overall assessment of the experience of public transportation development and policy in the advanced market economies, the centrally planned economies, and the developing market economies. It also provides a brief overview of the global transportation trends since the 1970s.

The appendix provides statistical tables that present some key transport statistics that allow for cross-national comparisons in terms of the scope of transportation activities in (1) gross domestic product (for market economies) and net material product (for centrally planned economies) in transport, storage, and communications; (2) gross domestic product and net material product (to be compared with that which is accounted for by transport activities); (3) the number of motor vehicles in use and the production of passenger cars; (4) railway passenger and freight traffic; (5) merchant shipping fleets; (6) goods loaded and unloaded in international maritime transport; (7) air passenger and freight transportation; and (8) employment in transport, storage, and communications.

The country chapters are followed by a bibliographical essay that introduces a selective collection of English-language materials on the public transportation systems and policies in the twelve countries surveyed, as well as general (non-country-specific) works on public transportation. The coverage is not meant to be exhaustive but suggestive of the rich array and increasing volume of works on this important public-policy sector.

The remainder of this introduction will present a brief summary of the major characteristics, as identified by the contributing authors, of the public transportation infrastructure, services, and policy in the twelve countries surveyed. Readers who wish to review a detailed account of the transportation system and policy of a particular country or countries may skip this section and go directly to the relevant chapter or chapters.

FRANCE

Government involvement in postwar public transportation development has been substantially more extensive in France than in the United States but less so than in Japan, the United Kingdom, or West Germany. At the end of World War II, centralized, elaborate administrative-technical bureaucracies were established. Market forces alone were simply insufficient to reconstruct the war-devasted national economy. In the earlier postwar decades, strategic (military) considerations heavily influenced the construction of roads, canals, and railroads, producing some imbalances of economic investment. In more recent decades decentralization trends have emerged and continue today. The public entity Autoroutes de France administers all mixed (public-private) autoroute (four-lane highway) projects. The state owns the interior waterway infrastructure which is utilized by private vehicles, but this sector is losing ground to other modes of transportation because of the high terminal (cargo transfer) cost. France is the third largest aircraft manufacturer in the world. Air France, created by statute as a national company and 99.38 percent state owned, has the dual character of a commercial enterprise and a public service.

LOTI (La Loi D'orientation des Transports Intérieurs) of 1982 sets the principal direction for French transport policy through the end of the current century. It provides that the state will give its financial support to the SNCF (La Société Nationale des Chemins de Fer Français) by virtue of the latter's essential contribution to the social and economic welfare of the nation. The Ministry of Equipment oversees the SNCF. Policy coordination has been difficult among government agencies, across modes of transportation, and between levels of government (from the national to the Régions and Départements). At all levels elaborate planning is conducted by elite bureaucrats with input from nongovernmental entities (i.e., employees, employers, and users).

France does not accept a general government responsibility for providing regular public passenger transportation throughout the country. As a result, there has been a marked urban bias in the development of public transportation. The geographical span of the country and the fact that the majority of the people live in sparsely populated rural areas have been further disadvantages for rural passenger services.

France's central location in economically dynamic Western Europe adds another challenge to the French transportation authorities. Transit traffic through the country imposes increasing burdens of infrastructure cost and investment on the nation. On the other hand, the nation's geographical location, along with its advanced high-speed train technology (the TGV or Trains Grande Vitesse), may turn out to be a blessing once the currently proposed high-speed European rail network becomes a reality.[1]

Decentralization of planning and management has continued, with Régions and Départements increasing their respective roles. However, little significant impact is expected for countrywide roadway, waterway, and railway transportation. Another main feature of French public transportation is its aggressive technological research and development. Examples discussed by Mitchell Strohl include the TGV, the 50-kilometer tunnel across the English Channel now under construction,[2] and the highly advanced aircraft manufacturing, which ranks third in the world.

JAPAN

Development of public transportation in Japan, before and after World War II, has been characterized by extensive government involvement. Public transportation infrastructure and services required extensive government involvement in the period of national reconstruction in the post-1945 period. In response to the rapid socioeconomic changes and technological advances that occurred during the following decades, the government undertook successive, five-year infrastructure development programs. However, socioeconomic changes have been so fast and so enormous that the management of public transportation has become an extremely difficult and prohibitively expensive enterprise for the government to maintain. The debt crisis and eventual privatization of the Japan National Railways (JNR), detailed by Tsuneo Akaha, is quite telling in this regard.

Aggressive technological innovation has been another main feature of Japanese public transportation. The development of a network of *shinkansen* (''bullet train'' lines), the construction of underwater tunnels connecting the main island of Honshu and the northern-most island of Hokkaido and large-scale suspension bridges to link the islands of Honshu and Shikoku, and the development of one of the largest and most modern merchant fleets in the world exemplify both the technological and financial capabilities of the Japanese and the political support behind them. In one area, namely, civil aviation, Japan's indigenous technological development has lagged behind other advanced industrial countries.[3] Potential exists in this area, however, and concerted public-private sector cooperation can be seen today.

As in the other advanced industrial countries, socioeconomic changes in Japan have created numerous problems: transportation-induced environmental degradation, urban traffic congestion, falling ridership in rural areas, declining trainborne freight, rising fuel costs, and increasing labor costs. The perennial problem of scarce land space continues to worsen as economic activity intensifies and competing uses of space press on valuable real estate. There are also increasing demands for quality of transportation services—such as accessibility, price competitiveness, convenience (regularity and frequency), reliability (dependability), and safety.

Intermodal balance in Japanese public transportation has followed the pattern seen in other advanced industrial countries. That is, railroad passenger and freight transportation has lost substantial ground to automotive transportation and, more recently, to air transportation as well. Intermodal policy coordination has been attempted but proven difficult because of the vertical (hierarchical) organization of the central government. Moreover, as the Osaka International Airport construction project illustrates, the government-initiated liberalization of foreign trade and opening up of the domestic market will increase foreign competition against domestic industries, including transportation.

UNITED KINGDOM

Public-sector involvement has historically been extensive in the United Kingdom as well. As exemplified by the Transport Act of 1947, which nationalized inland transport and the 1962 establishment of the British Railways Board to manage the rail system, the national government has expanded its role in public transportation development and operation in the postwar period.

Inland waterways were developed in the eighteenth and early nineteenth centuries, followed by the building of railroads by the turn of the twentieth century. The construction of highways has been relatively slow in the United Kingdom due to both the scarcity of resources and the widely held belief that roads are a local responsibility. As the national economy began to face difficulties in the 1970s, public funding for national transport activities was reduced across the board. The reorganization of local government since 1974 has increased the tension between the current government preference for private-sector services and the long-standing political support for public-sector involvement to provide essential services. More recently, Prime Minister Margaret Thatcher has vigorously pushed for the deregulation and, in some cases, privatization of the transportation sector. Her overall strategy has been to eliminate government subsidies of freight service and intercity passenger service and to reduce the subsidies for other passenger services. The most important example of this has been the Transport Act of the 1981 which privatized the non-railroad activities of the British Rail. Air transport, which has experienced a phenomenal growth in the postwar period, with substantial government aid and involvement, has also been touched by the privatization wind. William Waugh and Jane Sweeney provide ample examples of the ongoing privatization process.

As in the other advanced market economies, rail freight and passenger services have declined in recent decades. In contrast, roadway freight and passenger transportation, inland waterways, and pipeline freight service have gradually increased. The most dramatic expansion of any mode of transportation has taken place in the private automotive sector. Bus service has declined, particularly in rural areas. British sea transport is dominant in the European Economic Community (EEC). Britain has been less than enthusiastic about the proposed integration/coordination of rail, roadway, and inland waterway networks within the EEC.

UNITED STATES

In the United States, as Frank McKenna and David Anderson point out, extensive private-sector involvement in the development of transportation systems (particularly in railroad construction) in the prewar period has continued since the end of World War II. The role of government has been to encourage development of improved transportation by fostering a favorable business climate to induce private-sector activity.

Automotive transportation has expanded phenomenally and replaced railway transportation as the most important means of transportation for both private and commercial purposes. In contrast, inland waterways, important in the nineteenth century, have since declined. The transcontinental railroad network, developed by generous state land grants and speculative private investment in the nineteenth century, has remained virtually unchanged since the turn of the century.

Not all modes of transportation have strictly followed the private-sector-centered development pattern. Public funding for interstate highway construction in the postwar period, for example, has been justified in the name of national defense. The military use of aircraft during and after World War II has assisted the civil aircraft and avionics industries in becoming the most advanced in the world. Commercial aviation is now the predominant mode of intercity transportation in the United States.

Under the Reagan Administration (1981–88), federal government's role in public transportation was diminished, and deregulation in all modes of transportation has proceeded. Government ''disengagement,'' including federal funding cuts, has taken place at the very time when infrastructure needs of both urban and rural communities are growing.

Although the Department of Transportation was established in 1966 as the federal agency principally concerned with public transportation, a host of other agencies and regulatory agencies exist with authority over various aspects of transportation. As a result, overall policy coordination is complicated. Lack of a cohesive national policy that has characterized the market-driven development of public transportation continues today.

WEST GERMANY

In West Germany, postwar public transportation has been operated essentially as a mixed (public and private) economy. As before the war, the postwar policy has been to maintain public administration of transportation infrastructure and services through market regulations. Tariffs and market access have been regulated in all modes of transportation. Federal government programs are based on ten-year plans and are regularly assessed. The German Federal Railways, local public passenger transport, and Lufthansa are public property. Mixed transportation economy has resulted in distortions in competition at the expense of private transport firms.

Major government budget shortfalls following the oil crisis of 1973–74 have necessitated consolidation of public transport services and forced greater reliance on the private sector. These trends are further assisted by the ongoing deregulation of transport markets in anticipation of the full integration of the EEC in 1992. East-West transportation and, with it, transit traffic through West Germany have also increased in recent years, and further growth is expected. As the trends continue, state intervention in and subsidization of shipping firms in Eastern Europe will pose a greater problem to policymakers in the market economies, and the impact will be the greatest in West Germany, given its geographical location.

As in the other advanced market economies, changes in commodity structure have effected a modal split in West Germany, with the railroad and inland shipping gradually losing out to automotive transportation. A further increase in individual automobile travel is expected and so is traffic congestion in urban areas.

There is in West Germany a strong ideological support of the public goals of full employment, price stability, economic growth, reduction of regional disparities, and social equality. The extensive and far-reaching policy decisions of the federal government have resulted in a high degree of politicization of public transportation policy in West Germany. While the conservatives have preferred a more market-driven transport economy that favors private automobiles and roadways, the socialists have emphasized ''public'' transportation and favored railroad and urban public passenger transport. As well, the federalist structure of the political system has often resulted in inconsistencies among federal, state, and local priorities. Particularly problematic are the declining demands in sparsely populated regions of the country and increasing transportation-induced environmental problems in urban areas.

CHINA

In China, despite its massive efforts to expand its transport capacity since 1949, transport infrastructure and services have persistently been inadequate and remain underdeveloped today. The postwar history of transportation development clearly demonstrates the centrality of state control over public transportation as a means of national economic development, often with a degree of political commitment unparalleled elsewhere in the world.

The reconstruction of railroads and roads that had been destroyed during World War II and the subsequent civil war required massive infusion of labor and capital. The second (1958–62) and third (1966–70) five-year plans during the Great Leap Forward and the Great Proletarian Cultural Revolution, respectively, saw an almost total national commitment to heavy industry and its companion, freight transport. Passenger transport was neglected and intercity passenger travel declined; water transport continued to deteriorate; and civil aviation remained badly wanting.

Since the death of Mao Zedong in 1967 and the purge of the Gang of Four, more pragmatic economic policies were instituted. Impressive economic gains have been recorded after 1978 under the pragmatic leadership of Deng Xiaoping. This has put a heavy burden on the nation's railroads and ports. Inadequate transport infrastructure has threatened to become a major bottleneck for the economy. Since the early 1980s, transport and energy have been singled out as the two highest priorities for investment and modernization.

Road transport has experienced the most drastic growth of all modes of transportation since 1978. Long-neglected inland waterways are reviving, and river transport, inland water fleets, dams, and canals are being improved. Coastal shipping has also increased rapidly in recent years, particularly in southern China; coal loading facilities have been built and improved in most northern ports; and port construction has been expanded at an unprecedented rate to meet the nation's growing export needs.[4] Air transportation took off in the early 1980s, and diversification of the civil air fleet has proceeded since the early 1970s, when the entire fleet was Soviet-made. However, the railways remain the most dominant mode of transportation. But modernization needs are great in this mode of transportation as in all others.

The seventh five-year plan, adopted in September 1985, calls for an expansion and improvement of all modes of transportation for both passengers and freight, and improvements in the manufacturing of motor vehicles, locomotives, aircraft, and ships.[5] The current plan indicates a move toward decentralization in some segments of public transportation. Jacques Yenny reports that government policy is to give up direct management and operation of public transportation enterprises and to concentrate instead on indirect guidance through economic management tools—for example, taxation, banking, wage and labor rules, and integration of planning with competition and market regulation.

EAST GERMANY

Public transportation infrastructure and services in the German Democratic Republic are fairly extensive but grossly inefficient. Prewar private enterprises in roadway transportation, inland shipping, warehouses, and travel agencies have been extensively nationalized after the war. All modes of transportation at all levels (from national to local) are under the authority of one agency, the Ministry of Transportation.

Although public transportation has been given absolute priority, it has been neither efficient nor reliable. Instead, the demand for personal, namely, automotive production and transportation, has increased. Despite the high cost of automobiles (due to low domestic production and limited imports), the demand for them is steadily increasing. However, the government simply cannot respond adequately. Furthermore, inadequate road construction and repair and increasing personal transportation have resulted in mounting bottlenecks.

During the 1970s, trends were away from railway and toward roadway transportation, but the drastic increases in oil prices in the early 1980s forced a reversal in policy. In order to reduce the consumption of oil, the government raised inland freight tariffs, and, as a result, roadway freight costs shot up by 80 percent. Passenger transport policy also is dictated by the need to conserve energy and lower transport costs.

The preeminence of the railroad continues today, accounting for one-third of the volume and three-quarters of the performance (ton-kilometer). Roadway freight has been substantially cut since 1980. Inland waterways, well constructed by 1945, lost considerable importance in the postwar period and are insignificant today. Maritime shipping is holding its own. Major seaports have been rebuilt and expanded. The volume of air travel has been comparatively low throughout the postwar period, and in 1980, because of energy efficient needs, inland air transportation was totally discontinued.

SOVIET UNION

John Willerton notes that political priorities and geographical realities have guided the development of the Russian and Soviet public transportation sector. Transportation has served the need for unification and integration of the various regions, peoples, and economies of the Soviet Union.

Given the unfavorable natural climate and the vast land territory that is the Soviet Union, railroads have played a leading role. Inland waterways and highways have served mostly as feeders to the railroad system. During the Soviet period, that is, since 1917, rail transportation has served the important purpose of linking the industrial centers in the European area and the rich resources located to the east. An emphasis on the heavy industrial sector in the postwar economic development has also favored the railways.

Despite the post-Stalinist diversification of public transportation, the dominance of railways continues. Pipelines play a substantially more important role in the Soviet Union than in any other country, East or West. Inland waterways are of diminishing significance. Marine shipping has grown in importance in the past two decades, and the state-owned Soviet merchant marine today ranks fifth in the world in the volume of goods transported.

Expansion of motor and highway transportation is a very costly enterprise given its labor-intensive character and the great distances it has to cover. As a result, roadway freight accounts for only 2.2 percent of the total freight turnover. Private automobiles do not sit well with the Marxist-Leninist ideology and have been slow in developing in the Soviet Union. Since the Brezhnev era, however, massive investment has been made in the auto industry. Unlike other sectors, there is no national ministry in charge of the motor vehicle industry.

Urban transportation suffers from overcrowding, overuse, underfunding, equipment breakdowns, absence of repair and maintenance facilities, delays, and unreliable scheduling. Metro (subway) transport is increasing in importance in urban transportation. Aviation is a recent transport sector in the Soviet Union, but the demand in this sector is increasing, particularly for cargo transport linking distant production, processing, and consumption centers.

All-union (national) and republic Party organs oversee and guide policy, and specific all-union and republic governmental bureaucracies are separately responsible for funding the major types of public transportation. The compartmentalized and autarkic development of each sector and intersector competition for scarce resources have made effective planning and coordination difficult. Since transportation problems are seen as a major obstacle to the ongoing revitalization of the national economy under *perestroika,* a plan is underway to establish a single national state committee for transportation with broad supervisory authority over all transportation services. Nearly all modes of transportation are currently being changed over to full economic accountability and self-financing.

BRAZIL

Geographical barriers have long hindered the development of a national public transportation system. The forbidding interior, the massive Amazon River basin and tropical forest, the steep falls and rapids in many rivers, and the high-quality soil along the coast have understandably led to concentrated development in the country's coastal areas. What inland movement that took place beginning in the early eighteenth century was for the export of minerals and coffee. Export needs dictated the development, first, of coastal shipping and, second, railroads.

As Dale Krane points out, Brazil today has the most advanced railway, roadway, and air transportation systems in Latin America. The postwar expansion of public transportation has been driven by the private sector but with much government encouragement. Transportation has been a component of national and regional planning throughout the postwar period, even under the military rule from 1964 to 1985.

The central focus has been on the development of highway transportation and a major domestic automotive industry for import substitution, that is, substituting domestic production for automotive imports. Today Brazil's road network is the most extensive in Latin America. However, the highways are overburdened, with 70 percent of all automotive traffic using them. The railroad system remains poor in terms of geographical coverage, efficiency, and cost-effectiveness. Particularly problematic is the lack of railways that link regional capitals, each of which serves as the center of a regional railway system. Water transport has historically been neglected although maritime navigation has received occasional government attention, primarily for external trade. Airports remained dilapidated until the early 1970s but have since been maintained with some success.

Urban transportation was overtaxed by the chaotic growth of metropolitan populations in the 1950s and 1960s. As a solution, the government began building subway and street car systems in the mid-1970s. However, heavy dependence on foreign capital for the costly project ($1 billion annually) has contributed to the country's deepening external debt crisis.

The federal system of government requires regional (state) governments' support of the federal government, and federal public transportation programs have served as an important ingredient in this crucial political relationship. Corruption has often resulted. During the military rule (1964–85), traditional bureaucrats were replaced with technical experts, and the latter expanded use of ''autonomous agencies'' to manage different transportation sectors. This has led to a fragmentation of public transportation policy and planning.

The 1988 constitution transferred a number of transport-related taxes (e.g., gasoline and lubricants) from the national government to the states and municipalities. The decentralization effort is largely a response to the debt crisis that has gripped the federal government. Brasilia is strapped under the mounting weight of domestic and external debts and finds it difficult to undertake massive public projects, including public transportation programs.

KOREA

The impetus for modern transportation development in prewar Korea came from Japanese colonial rule of the country from 1910 to 1945. Much of the Japanese transportation was geared toward the export of raw materials to Imperial Japan. The devastation done by the Korean War (1950–53) delayed the postwar development of public transportation in the newly independent Republic of Korea. As Young Khil and Mary Khil point out, however, since 1961 vigorous, systematic, and continuous efforts to expand its public transport network have taken place as part of successive national economic development plans.

Extensive government control of the transport economy serves as an important tool to stimulate economic growth. Since the early 1960s, funding priorities have shifted in accordance with the national development plans, from railways to highways, to air transportation, and to harbors. Most recently, transportation infrastructure has been expanded in the northeastern section and the agricultural southwest.

Changes in intermodal balance have generally followed patterns observed in the advanced market economies. Roads have been dominant in the volume of passenger travel and freight haulage; railroads have declined in freight transport; shipborne freight has increased; freight trucking has remained steady; and the increase in private automobiles has been phenomenal.

Centralized sectoral management and government direction have effectively minimized private-sector involvement in transportation activities. The central government in Seoul fixes all prices in the transport industry, but the degree of government regulation varies from sector to sector. A separate government agency has been established to manage each mode of transportation, and interagency and intersectoral coordination has been rather loose. Decentralization of governmental functions has recently begun, but the Korean presidential system still remains highly centralized, and most policies continue to originate from the top.

MEXICO

George Guess characterizes Mexico's public transportation development throughout most of its history as ''dependent development.''

The development of rail transportation in Mexico from the early sixteenth century to the mid-nineteenth century depended largely on European capital. Mexico then turned to the United States for additional investment in railroad construction. Foreign dependency continued even after the rails were nationalized in 1937. Rails and roads continued to be used for the export of raw materials, steel, cement, and textiles. More recently, they have additionally been used to export automobiles and trucks to the United States.

Throughout the pre- and postwar period, development of transportation services was characterized by a heavy urban bias. As a result, transportation in rural areas is quite underdeveloped, preventing the development of an integrated national economy. Intermodal imbalance is a visible feature of the public transportation system in Mexico. For the last two decades, highways have been the mainstay of Mexican transportation policy. Although investment in the deteriorating railroads has significantly increased since the early 1980s, the bias toward roads continues.

Today, public transportation is part of a highly centralized political structure with the executive branch dominating the scene. Transportation policy is determined by the revolutionary authoritarian party (known as the PRI) through the powerful executive. The PRI organizes or co-opts functional groups such as labor and industry to control their participation and to mobilize them for political support.

The economic crisis in the early 1980s aborted López Portillo's ambitious plan to put substantial new investment in both rail and road transportation. Roads are decaying and railways are no longer able to handle their load efficiently. With a debt service export ratio of more than 50 percent, there is little capital available for new investment at home.

ZAIRE

Like Mexico, foreign penetration in Zaire has deeply affected the development (or lack thereof) of a public transportation system. Kendall Stiles notes that the system is weak in every respect, structurally, institutionally, financially, and technically. The problem has been compounded by widespread internal corruption and chronic mismanagement.

British exploration and Belgian investment in the last quarter of the nineteenth century led to the development of a railway in Zaire that was unequaled elsewhere in Black Africa. Railway construction centered on the export of rubber in the north and gold and copper in the southern region of the country. The four-year civil war following the June 1960 independence decimated the country's economy. Ever since then, infusion of foreign capital has become a central feature of public transportation in Zaire. Policies of promoting local control of foreign investment led to rampant cost overruns, corruption, and inefficiency during the early 1970s. By the late 1970s, massive borrowing of foreign capital and declining copper earnings caused the country to fall into severe debt (amounting to half of Zaire's gross national product). Mushrooming external debts resulted in greater export pressure, particularly copper and diamonds.

The Zairian transportation system is almost totally controlled by either the ONATRA (National Office of Transportation) or the SNCZ (National Corporation of Zairian Railways). The two organizations have essentially split the nation's land and water transportation geographically, with a north-south division just east of Kinshasa. Air Zaire is a special case. Management of this state enterprise is essentially taken over by European consultants. Underfunded and deteriorating road transportation is managed at the provincial level, with the central government remaining largely apathetic.

Overall, there is a glaring lack of basic day-to-day maintenance of the transportation infrastructure. Facilities and equipment are in general disrepair and are shrinking in size and effectiveness. The only exception are the railways, which are the largest in Africa, excluding South Africa. National transportation planning favors short-term private financial gains over long-term public benefits.

NOTES

1. The proposed rail network, approved by the transportation ministers of Europe in 1987, would link major cities of the twelve European Economic Community members and Switzerland and Austria with 19,000 miles of special track for trains running at more than 150 miles per hour. With the TGV, currently in operation between Paris and Lyons, the French lead the rest of Europe in the manufacturing and operation of high-speed trains and hope this will give them an advantage in the $100 billion project. Obstacles that must be overcome before the idea can become a reality include the enormous cost involved, agreement on a profit-sharing arrangement, establishment of uniform technical standards, competition between French and German high-speed train builders, and environmental impact. (See *The Economist,* March 11, 1989, p. 69 and April 29, 1989, p. 69; *New York Times,* January 5, 1989, pp. 1 and 25.)

2. On the English Channel project, a private company with a monopoly franchise granted by the British and French governments has raised $1.7 billion in equity finance and five times as much in loans. It is required to give what it expects to be a highly profitable operation of passenger and freight transportation across the channel back to the two governments in 2042. The tunnel is expected to become operational in 1993. (See references in note 1.)

3. The domestic development of the twin-prop YS-11—albeit by faithfully borrowing foreign designs—in the 1960s has been the only minimally successful experience that the Japanese can claim in this area. The few dozen of the sixty-four-seat YS-11s are now nearing the end of their lives. The Asuka, a second airliner designed and built wholly in Japan, was a failure. The prototype 80- to 100-seater, after devouring $120 million of taxpayers' money over the past twelve years, is now scheduled to go into a museum. The Ministry of International Trade and Industry (MITI) now wants to have a preliminary design for a short-haul seventy-five-seater code-named the YS-X worked out by 1990 and to have the aircraft in service four years later. (See *The Economist,* April 8, 1989, p. 72.)

4. The merchant marine consisted of only twenty ships in 1961 but has grown to about 1,000.

5. Historically, decision making in railways, civil aviation, and pipelines has been highly centralized, and subnational levels of government from provinces to cities, towns, and villages, as well as production enterprises and collectives, have all played a role in road and water modes of transportation.

1

BRAZIL

Dale Krane

As the world's fifth largest country, Brazil dominates South America. Half of the continent's area and more than half of its population are encompassed within Brazil. This country of 8.46 million square kilometers (kms) is so vast that all of Europe west of the Ural Mountains fits inside (Figure 1.1).[1] Brazil's size constitutes the primary obstacle to the country's integration. Size alone is not a detriment to an integrated transportation system, but size combined with difficult terrain can pose immense obstacles to the establishment of an efficient transportation network. The cycles and pace of national development, the investment strategies of various national administrations and state governments, and the character of the transportation agencies themselves have shaped Brazil's incomplete progress toward an integrated transportation system.

BACKGROUND

The tropical paradise that dazzled the early explorers also stymied the rapid penetration and utilization of much of the country. For example, Brazil's Atlantic coastline which extends for an uninterrupted 7,408 kms is punctuated with a number of fine, natural harbors. Unfortunately, the great escarpment of the Brazilian Highlands parallels about two-thirds of the coastline below the

Financial support for this research was provided by the Fulbright Commissions of Brazil and the United States. This chapter is a revised version of a paper presented at the national conference of the American Society for Public Administration, Boston, Massachusetts, March 28–April 1, 1987.

Figure 1.1
Brazil and Neighboring Countries

Source: E. Bradford Burns, *A History of Brazil* (2nd ed.; New York: Columbia University Press, 1980), 11. Copyright © 1980 Columbia University Press. Used by permission.

mouth of the Amazon. This mountain barrier, which in many cases comes right to the ocean's edge, slowed movement into the interior. As a consequence, the Portuguese explorers ''scratched along the sea like crabs'' (Torloni: 53) building ''a loosely connected series of coastal settlements'' (Roett: 4). Even today, almost 90 percent of the population (1986 estimate: 137 million) lives in one-third the national territory and within 250 kms of the Atlantic coast.

Another transportation obstacle is, of course, the Amazon River basin and tropical forest, which covers 42 percent of Brazil's land surface. In addition to the Amazon, Brazil possesses an abundance of rivers, but these rivers "all flow to the ocean over steep falls and rapids, which seriously impede navigation" (Roett: 2). Finally, the coastal plains, which were composed of high quality soil, provided little incentive to push agricultural operations into the interior.

Population distribution and transportation routes followed economic opportunities. For 350 years (1500–1850), the Brazilian economy rested solely on agricultural and mineral products. Sailing vessels connected the relatively isolated coastal towns to each other and to Lisbon. As mule trains and wagons pushed into the interior to open farm lands and to channel raw materials to the nearest port, transportation networks grew in a fanlike fashion from plantation to port. Unlike other Latin American nations, Brazil's development was not dominated by a single national center; instead several competing "archipelagos" of economic and political activity evolved.

Two major events opened the interior. First, the discovery of gold (1700) and diamonds (1729) northwest of Rio de Janeiro caused a population explosion in the province of Minas Gerais and forced the colonial government to control the transportation of these treasures. To insure the crown's 20 percent share of the mineral wealth, Portuguese authorities acted to funnel the gold and jewel trade to Rio and to close routes to other locations. It was no coincidence that the first effort to build a stone paved road was along the route to the mines.[2] The expansion of coffee cultivation from the old sugar areas in the northeast to the virgin lands of Minas Gerais and Sao Paulo provinces fostered the second opening to the interior. With the surge in world demand for coffee, plantations spread across the plateau west from Sao Paulo to Mato Grosso and south into Parana. The importance of coffee as well as other agricultural exports prompted state and federal governments to make major improvements in the country's harbor and port facilities beginning in the early twentieth century (Burns: 313).

Steamships began sailing along the coast in 1819 and ushered in the industrial age. Railroads appeared in the 1850s, but construction lagged until the coffee plantations moved to the interior provinces. Railroads then expanded at an accelerating rate; in 1889, total track equaled 9,650 kms and fourteen of Brazil's twenty provinces had some rail service. These early railroad lines replicated the fanlike pattern radiating from the regional ports to the interior farmlands. The direction of these rail lines was often determined by the demands of the Brazilian landed nobility who insisted on connecting their estates to each other despite the costs of circuitous routes (Wirth: 58).

Government concessions to private companies financed the pre-1900 era of rail construction. The federal government from 1900 to 1930 acted to rescind most private rail concessions and dominated rail construction until the 1920s when some state governments also built their own lines (Wirth: 58). The even faster construction of the early twentieth century—by 1914, 25,750 kms of track had been laid—did not change the basic pattern of plantation-to-port routes

(Burns: 312–313). River traffic, however, remained confined primarily to the largest rivers (the Amazon, the Sao Francisco, the Parana, and the Paraguay) and failed to develop at the same pace as the railroads.

Modern transportation modes and routes emerged very late in Brazil's history. Although General Motors sold automobiles in Rio as early as 1925, no serious campaign to build paved highways was undertaken until after World War II (*Rodovia:* 23). Encouraged by President Getulio Vargas' import substitution campaign in the 1930s, a domestic automotive industry quickly grew to become the largest in Latin America. President Kubitschek's movement of the national capital to Brasilia, 1,160 kms to the northwest of the old capital at Rio, was accompanied by "an ambitious program to build 'highways of national union' " (*Rodovia:* 460). By 1970 Brazil accounted for two-thirds of all the roads in Latin America and also owned the largest network of paved roads in Latin America (40 percent of the total).

The one form of modern transportation that did develop early in Brazil was the airplane. With its limited system of highways and railroads, Brazilians turned to the airplane as a means for overcoming the vast distances of their land. Commercial aviation began when a private company, VARIG Airlines, started operations in the southernmost state of Rio Grande do Sul (Brazil, 1965: 215). By 1939, nine commercial companies had built routes over 69,200 kms, and with modest government support "soon handled three-quarters of all commercial air traffic in South America" (Burns: 418).

After World War II, the number of cities served by airlines increased very quickly in an era of cutthroat competition. The advent of jet transport forced a drastic increase in airfares and a concomitant decrease in passenger volume. Only four companies survived this period of economic and technological change in the 1960s—three private companies (VARIG, CRUZEIRO, and TRANSBRASIL) and one company (VASP) operated by the government of Sao Paulo state.

Throughout most of its history, transportation in Brazil evolved as a function of the economic exploitation of the land's potential. Population movements coupled with changes in technologies and economic activities fostered expansion and diversification of transportation. Because the government played primarily a subsidiary role, the spread of transportation facilities and routes followed the impulses of private activity rather than any coordinated effort on the part of the national government to develop an integrated transportation network. One of the most serious consequences of this history is the severe traffic imbalance among the relative shares of the various transportation sectors (Table 1.1)

SOCIOECONOMIC DIMENSIONS OF THE TRANSPORTATION SYSTEM AND POLICY

Today Brazil is recognized as a global economic power. Since the end of World War II, Brazil has grown from an underdeveloped exporter of raw ag-

Table 1.1
Relative Shares of Traffic by Mode of Transportation, 1980

	CARGO	PASSENGERS
Highways	70.0%	96.7%
Railroads	17.0%	0.9%
Waterways	10.2%	0.1%
Aviation	0.2%	2.3%
Pipelines	2.6%	--

Source: Brazil, *Anuario Estatistico dos Transportes* (Brasilia: Empresa Brasileira de Planejamento de Transportes (GEIPOT), Ministerio Dos Transportes, 1980).

ricultural commodities to an aggressive exporter of widely diversified products. As the world's eighth largest free market economy, Brazil surpasses many developed European nations (e.g., Italy and Spain) in world trade. This economic expansion occurred in the short space of thirty years (1950–80) and at a pace similar to that of industrialization in Japan or the United States. Following practice common to other Third World nations, Brazilian governments after World War II adopted rational and highly technical approaches to development planning. Transportation policy has been a component of these plans from the beginning.[3] The Dutra Administration in 1950 devised the first national plan that specifically emphasized the transportation sector. This effort was followed by President Kubitschek's Program of Goals (1956) that included the ''highways of national union'' that were necessary to connect the new interior capital of Brasilia with the major economic and political centers of Rio, Sao Paulo, and Belo Horizonte.

With the 1964 coup d'état, control of the economy (and the polity) passed into the hands of a highly professional military officer corps that had extreme faith in and extensive practice with technical solutions to problems (Stepan; Nordlinger; Krane: 53). Six national development plans were adopted and vigorously implemented in the twenty-one years of military rule.[4] In addition to comprehensive national development plans, the military-civilian technocrats also conceived a separate plan for national integration and a number of regional development plans, all of which contained transportation projects. The contributions of these plans to the expansion and renovation of Brazil's transportation networks cannot be ignored.

In response to the catastrophic drought of 1970, a National Integration Plan (PIN) was formulated to open the north and northwestern areas of the country for colonization and to connect these areas with new highways to encourage migration away from the drought-ravaged northeastern area of plantations and subsistence farms. This plan called for "immediate action without regard for inflationary impact," and the funds were drawn from resources, both internal and external, earmarked for the regional development authorities already in charge of the Northeast and the Amazon. Among the new roads were the TransAmazon, the Cuiaba-Santarem, and the North Perimeter routes (Torloni: 60–68). Two examples of regionally targeted transportation projects include the PRODOESTE (southwest and center-west regions) and PROVALE (Sao Francisco River valley) plans. In addition to new highways, these regional projects incorporated new bridges, canals, and dams as well as new port and rail facilities.

As long as Brazil's economy was expanding at a breathless pace, the military regime was able to finance its transportation improvements from user charges or foreign loans. The 1973 oil crisis dealt a severe blow to the economic boom and forced the Geisel Administration in 1975 to (1) curtail the ambitious highway and vehicle investments of the previous administrations; (2) close all service stations on Sundays; and (3) inaugurate the PROALCOOL program to substitute alcohol (derived from domestic agricultural sources) to reduce gasoline consumption by 25 percent (Mello & Fonseca). At the same time, the national government poured funds into oil exploration along Brazil's coast.[5]

The oil crisis also undermined one of the main pillars of Brazil's import-substitution strategy, the automotive industry. In 1950 Brazil had a total of 409,486 registered motor vehicles; by 1979, the number of motor vehicles had expanded to 9,692,000, almost all domestically produced. This meteoric growth in cars, buses, and trucks had exactly the same consequences in Brazil as did the growth of vehicles in the United States: (1) increased mobility for all sectors of the population; (2) growth of suburbs; (3) traffic congestion on available roads; (4) increased smog; and (5) abandonment of the old urban trolley systems. As oil price rose, the overdependence of Brazilian cities on auto and bus transportation led to unacceptable congestion and costs. The last two military administrations altered national transportation plans to deemphasize the popular preferences for cars, buses, and trucks and to redirect investments to mass urban transit, suburban rail lines, and water transport. The shift in funds was dramatic: the First National Development Plan (1972–74) allotted 53 percent of its transportation monies to the highways of national integration; by contrast, the Second National Development Plan (1975–79) only allotted 24.1 percent of transport funds to continue the new regional programs. At the same time, railroad investment jumped from under 10 to 22.3 percent (Torloni: 378–379; Mello & Fonseca). By 1980, national government investments in the various transportation sectors had a very different appearance than they did at the beginning of the boom.

POLITICAL DIMENSIONS OF THE TRANSPORTATION SYSTEM AND POLICY

Three important features of Brazilian government influence the country's transportation policy. First, the basic organization of governmental levels, the contests for political power, and the execution and implementation of public policy all reflect Brazil's federal character. Second, Brazil exhibits a significant variation in regime types often in relatively short periods of time. And third, the administrative structure of Brazilian government has grown into a complex labyrinth of organizations, many of which possess considerable autonomy from either national or state governments. These three facets of the Brazilian policy process account not only for the basic characteristics of transportation policy, but also for the major problems faced in the policy area.

The impact of federalism on transportation policy has been strongest in the areas of railroads and highways.[6] During the First or Old Republic (1889–1930), "railroad credits and equipment led the list of economic favors required from the federal union" to insure state political support for the president (Wirth: 179). The larger state governments such as Sao Paulo and Minas not only invested state funds in rail networks, but also through their congressional delegations obtained federal support for railroads serving the coffee plantations. As a result of large state politics, more than half the trackage laid by World War I was located in just three coffee producing states—Sao Paulo, Minas Gerais, and Rio de Janeiro (Burns: 312). Similarly, since most Brazilian state capitals are located on the Atlantic coast, federalism interacted with geography to reinforce and replicate in steel the old plantation-to-port transportation pattern. These fanlike patterns emanating from each state capital to its associated hinterlands still exist today, and the lack of rail connections among different capitals and other parts of the country still cause serious transportation bottlenecks (Camargo: 20). Many state-operated railroads went bankrupt during the great depression, and the national government was forced to take over their operations and liabilities.

As mentioned earlier, the national government did not begin extensive highway construction until after World War II. Again, leadership in the larger, richer states acted first; for example, a Sao Paulo association opened an auto road from Sao Paulo to Rio in 1919, and in 1922 the Brazilian Automobile Club started construction on a road from Rio to Petropolis (*Rodovia:* 23). These two routes are noteworthy because they were the first highways to be paved by the national government's 1927 program based on the new national tax on imported gasoline. The National Highway Department (DNER) was created in 1937, and in 1940 federal taxes on combustible fuels were used to begin a state-municipality highway fund administered by the National Petroleum Council. As with railroads, highways developed as much from state and local initiative as from national government action. Second, the funding and operation of highways was divided among the levels of government. This, in turn, meant that the larger, wealthier states were able to build a highway infrastructure that was separate, but not necessarily complementary, to the national system. With the very late inauguration of a national highway program, Brazil's roads have also replicated the basic pattern from farm areas to the state capitals. The national government began to link different sections of the country with paved highways only during the Kubitschek Administration (1956–61).

As is typical with many Latin American nations, Brazil has experienced several changes in its form of government. Brazil began as a Portuguese colony (1500–1822) and with independence became Latin America's only monarchy (1822–89). A limited, republican democracy emerged in 1889 and lasted until 1930. After a period of political turmoil, an authoritarian government headed by Getulio Vargas ruled until 1945 when democracy was restored. This second democratic period failed after nineteen years and was replaced by a military-civilian dictatorship in 1964. During the military regime's twenty-one years of rule, five different army generals served as the national president, and each of their administrations exhibited a unique character. Civilian government returned in 1985.

Each of these political periods had a particular goal or interest that influenced the evolution of transportation policy. For example, neither the Portuguese nor Brazilian emperors took significant actions to foster transportation development, thus transportation networks in Brazil languished in very primitive conditions until the late 1800s. Twentieth-century governments likewise did little about transportation until after World War II. Vargas despite his establishment of a national petroleum monopoly and the aggressive pursuit of heavy industry "did not pave one meter of road . . . in almost fifteen years of discretionary power" (Guimaraes, 1985: 11). Post–World War II democratic administrations finally utilized the power of the national government to build transportation networks, but these new initiatives were driven by the larger goal of "developmental nationalism" (i.e., to make Brazil into a global power both economically and politically) (Burns: 454–466). As part of their import-substitution strategies, the four presidential administrations from 1945 to 1964 emphasized highways over all other forms of transportation, concentrating between 70 and 80 percent of all transportation investments in highways. The results, however, were not impressive as total highway mileage barely doubled from 258,390 kms in 1939 to 548, 510 kms (*Survey:* 190–196) in 1964. For the same period, railroad trackage declined slightly from 34,252 kms in 1940 to 33,596 kms in 1964.

The 1964 military regime pursued economic growth to make Brazil into a tropical superpower. Significant increases in transportation investments were an integral part of the military government's induced economic boom. Table 1.2 shows both the change in investments by mode of transportation and the absolute increases for each mode made during the "Brazilian Miracle." Two policy shifts clearly stand out. First, the military's dramatic program to link all parts of the nation with roads accounted for the almost 60 percent increase in high-

Table 1.2
Changes in Transportation Investment and Transportation Facilities, 1960–80

Investments

Period	Highways	Vehicles	Railroads	Water	Pipelines	Air
1960-63	16.7%	61.9%	9.3%	7.2%	--	4.9%
1964-67	29.0%	52.7%	9.7%	5.9%	--	2.7%
1968-73	27.0%	51.7%	8.2%	7.8%	1.4%	3.9%
1974-77	21.7%	51.0%	12.2%	10.6%	2.0%	4.1%

Source: Fernando Homem De Mello and Eduardo Gianetti Da Fonseca, *Proalcool, Energia E Transportes* (Sao Paulo: Livrara Pionera Editora, 1981), 120. Courtesy Enio Matheus Guazzeli & Cia, Ltda.

Facilities

Period	Highways (in kms)	Paved Roads (in kms)	Railroads (in kms)	Total Motor Vehicles
1960	476,938	13,357	38,287	1,035,887
1970	1,039,779	49,263	32,102	3,062,778
1980	1,270,333	87,213	30,105	10,190,000

Source: Armin Ludwig, *Brazil: A Handbook of Historical Statistics* (Boston: G.K. Hall & Co., 1985); Brazil, *Anuario Estatistico dos Transportes* (1984).

way investments. This money was used to build ''roads of penetration,'' such as the 2,132 km Belem to Brasilia highway, the 2,000 km TransAmazon road, the 1,500 km Cuiaba-Santarem Highway, and the still incomplete 4,000 km North Perimeter road around the northwestern quarter of Brazil. This massive new highway program had several purposes: (1) to connect and integrate all the Brazilian states; (2) to open vast areas of Brazil's western interior to migration in order to relieve the population pressure on the metropolitan areas of Rio and Sao Paulo; and (3) to facilitate the movement of military forces to undefended areas of the country (Torloni: 64–68). The second policy shift evident in Table 1.2 appears in the decline of highway investments in 1974–77 and in the increase in non-highway investments in this period. As Table 1.1 indicated, Brazil's transportation of freight and passengers is heavily dependent on its highway network. This situation became especially costly to Brazil, a country that imports about 90 percent of its petroleum, when the 1970s oil price shocks hit the world economy. The last two military presidents were forced to slow the

Table 1.3
National Government Investments in Transportation, 1980

Water Transport		32.7%
Ships (Merchant Marine)	22.5%	
Maritime Ports	8.8%	
Riverways and Ports	1.4%	
Railroads		29.8%
Highways		27.3%
Aviation		5.8%
Pipelines		4.4%

Source: Brazil, *Anuario Estatistico dos Transportes* (1980).

penetration of the interior and to switch investments to transportation modes that were less fuel consumptive (see Tables 1.2 and 1.3).

A third influence on Brazilian transportation policy is the elaborate administrative structure that exercises authority over the planning, construction, and maintenance of transportation networks. Superficially, Brazil's government is modeled after that of the United States.[7] The Brazilian bureaucracy, however, differs significantly from the American model, and its various components make for a complicated division of labor among administrative entities. Below the office of the president are located the ministries of state which are part of Brazil's traditional bureaucracy that has been burdened with a three-centuries-old heritage of patronage and corruption. Typical practice for an ordinary action, such as a license application, requires the use of a "dispatcher," who for a fee will expedite one's paperwork through the layers of *burocratas* (traditional bureaucrats—see Graham; Daland).

Beginning in the Vargas era, efforts to eliminate the spoils system and to create a cadre of elite civil servants were tried time and again with little positive results other than to add an occasional layer of technically trained personnel *(tecnicos)* to the traditional ministries (Roett: 138). These reform movements also gave birth to an occasional "autonomous" agency, often dominated by *tecnicos* rather than *burocratas*. The 1964 military regime targeted the traditional spoils system for a widespread purge that had the effect of allowing "the tecnicos free rein to plan the future economic transformation of the nation" (Roett: 139). One of the main organizational changes emerging from the displacement of the old bureaucrats and the transference of program planning and management to the new technically trained (and politically safe) experts was an increased use of "autonomous" agencies to perform new and innovative activities (Martins: 41–72).

At least seven types of autonomous administrative agencies exist ranging from foundations and research institutes to various forms of mixed public-private enterprises to ''pure'' government corporations to agencies with financial independence based typically on a dedicated tax.[8] Although a subsequent section will provide more detail about these autonomous agencies and especially about their roles in the policy process, some observations about the impact of Brazil's bureaucracy on the evolution of transportation policy are appropriate at this point. First, transportation policy is scattered among a number of very diverse agencies that exhibit particular legal, financial, and operational norms and procedures. Second, this fragmentation is compounded by Brazil's federalism which reproduces many counterpart agencies at the state and local level. Third, outside of commercial aviation, which is essentially a private industry in Brazil, the other transportation sectors are controlled primarily by government corporations and other autonomous agencies. Fourth, given the organizational fragmentation, coordination does not come easily and requires major initiatives coupled with substantial increases in funds. Fifth, each sector, because it has been treated differentially and independently, has evolved as a function of its own political-administrative dynamics. The overall result of governmental structure on transportation policy is twofold: (1) the absence until recently of integrated transportation programs; and (2) the lack of balance among the major transportation sectors.

RECENT TRENDS AND FUTURE PROSPECTS

The ''developmental nationalism'' of Brazil's post–World War II leadership has produced impressive gains in transportation infrastructure and its contribution to the quality of national life. No other Latin American country possesses the extensive automotive and aviation sectors found in Brazil. On the other hand, the Brazilian love affair with cars has encouraged an overreliance on road transport to the detriment of railroad, inland waterway, and mass transit sectors. In order to better understand the accomplishments and the shortcomings of Brazilian transportation, it is necessary to examine in more detail each of the principal transportation sectors.

Brazil continues to be a country poor in railroads. The national system is composed primarily of rail lines owned and operated by the Federal Railroad Network (RFFSA). Other significant rail companies are (1) the railroads owned by the state of Sao Paulo (FEPASA); and (2) railroads controlled by public enterprises in the mining industry.[9] Table 1.4 and Figure 1.2 provide an overview of the total railroad system in Brazil. A majority of the RFFSA and FEPASA lines were built anywhere from 60 to 100 years ago. Only the rail lines built to connect the new mining areas such as the Carajas line are efficient, modern systems (Galache & Andre: 307). Most of the federal government's system (RFFSA) is concentrated in the southeast and south, the regions of highest economic development and the largest urban areas, and in the old sugar

Table 1.4
Status of Railroad System, 1980

Railroad	Extension	Electrified
RFFSA	23,897km (79.4%)	1,055km (4.4%)
FEPASA	5,107km (17.0%)	1,524km (29.8%)
Others	1,101km (3.6%)	68km (6.0%)
TOTAL	30,105km (100%)	2,645km (8.8%)

Source: Hilario Torloni, *Estudos De Problemas Brasileiros* (16th ed.; Sao Paulo: Livrara Pionera Editora, 1983), 380. Courtesy Enio Matheus Guazzeli & Cia, Ltda.

plantation areas of the northeast. Few lines connect Brasilia to other parts of the country or connect one section of the country to another.

Brazilian railroads exhibit several administrative and managerial problems. First, the two main systems (RFFSA and FEPASA) suffer from very dense traffic; for example, from 1973 to 1984, tonnage on the RFFSA trains expanded (139 percent) from 14 billion tons to 33.5 billion tons. Obviously, this rapid increase in cargo placed an enormous strain on existing equipment. It is estimated that 15,000 kms of track are in need of restoration and 60,000 new cars are required (Camargo: 18–19; Torloni: 381). Second, the Brazilian rail network still suffers from the lack of uniform track gauge. One of the main sections of the federal system—the Central do Brasil lines—and almost one third of the Sao Paulo lines have gauges different from the rest of the system (Guimaraes, 1976: 29). Third, the federal system functions as a traditional bureaucracy. While progress has been made in decreasing the proportion of labor costs from 73 to 40 percent (1965 to 1980), labor costs still absorb all direct revenues, thus forcing the government to continue subsidies for capital equipment. Finally, the large debt of the Sao Paulo system, which annually equals the debt of the entire federal system, has yet to be solved (Torloni: 380).

An allied problem to the rail system is the high cost of domestically manufactured rail equipment. Annual domestic capacity is approximately 330 locomotives, 9,000 freight cars, and 800 passenger cars, but current production is only 70, 1,100, and 160 units, respectively. As long as the government fails to invest in new rail equipment, the unit cost of domestic equipment will remain prohibitive. Only the oil price shock forced the national government to upgrade rail equipment and move away from diesel engines to electric ones (Torloni: 381).

Without a doubt, one of the great successes of Brazilian transportation is its new and rapidly growing national highway system. Three important policy de-

Figure 1.2
Railway Network, 1977

Source: Brazil, *Anuario Estatistico dos Transportes* (Brasilia: Empresa Brasileira de Planejamento de Transportes (GEIPOT), Ministerio Dos Transportes, 1980).

cisions propelled the highway program to the point where it became Latin America's largest paved road system. First, during World War II, a national commission headed by Professor Mauricio Joppert recommended that the National Highway Department (DNER) be granted financial autonomy from the existing Ministry of Transportation and also recommended the establishment of a National Highway Fund supported by revenues from taxes on liquid fuels and lubricants derived from petroleum. These recommendations became law in 1945 and the "Joppert Law" enabled the newly autonomous DNER to distribute financial resources to both states and municipalities as well as to begin work on national highways. The second forward thrust in expanding the road system came with the movement of the national capital from Rio de Janeiro on the coast to the new inland location at Brasilia. President Kubitschek's "march to

Table 1.5
Status of Road Network, 1980

Road System	Extension	Paved
Federal	62,515km (4.9%)	39.695km (63.5%)
State	27,445km (2.2%)	7,792km (28.4%)
Municipal	1,180,373km (92.9%)	5,906km (0.5%)
TOTAL	1,270,333km (100.0%)	53,393km (4.2%)

Source: Hilario Torloni, *Estudos De Problemas Brasileiros* (16th ed.; Sao Paulo: Livrara Pionera Editora, 1983), 383. Courtesy Enio Matheus Guazzeli & Cia, Ltda.

the interior'' made it necessary to connect the new capital with the major economic and political centers that were more than a thousand kilometers away from Brasilia. The administration of General Medici (1969–74) provided the third principal impulse to the national highway program. Acting on plans already developed by technocrats in DNER and in the Transport Ministry, the Medici government launched a massive program to build the ''highways of national penetration,'' the PIN highways, and the highways associated with the regional development programs. This effort to ''construct Brazil the giant'' was formalized in 1973 as the National Highway Plan (Guimaraes, 1976: 48).

The success and the shortcomings of these three policy decisions can be seen in Table 1.5. Only 5 percent of Brazil's roads are part of the national highway system and of these only 63.5 percent are paved. Unpaved municipal roads constitute almost 90 percent of the total road system. On the other hand, approximately 70 percent of all traffic uses the national highway network. Consequently, the Special Construction Fund for road repair established in 1970 cannot keep pace with necessary maintenance. Current estimates put the number of kilometers in bad condition at 12,000, and when one adds the paved state roads in need of repair, the total comes to 20,000 kms (Camargo: 17). New construction outpaces repair; from 1980 to 1985 paved roads lengthened from 53,393 kms to 83,965 kms (a 57 percent increase).

Brazil possesses approximately 50,000 kms of navigable rivers, yet only 10 percent of all freight travels by inland waterways (Figure 1.3). Although the exploration and colonization of Brazil depended largely on water transportation, comprehensive planning and management of this sector has been ignored for most of the country's history. Water transport has always had the lowest investment priority among the various transport modes, and thus fluvial navigation has remained in a state of almost total deterioration.[10]

The first National Water Transport Plan, designed to resurrect the most underutilized sector of national transportation, appeared only in 1971. Its pur-

Figure 1.3
Waterway Network, 1977

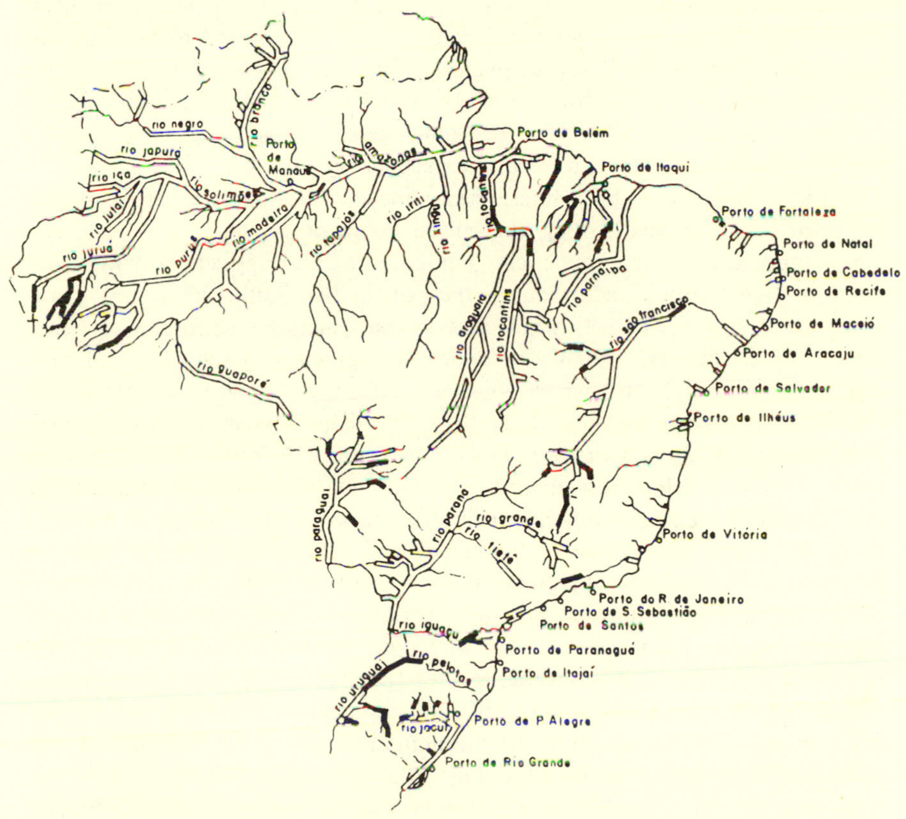

Source: Brazil, *Anuario Estatistico dos Transportes* (Brasilia: Empresa Brasileira de Planejamento de Transportes (GEIPOT), Ministerio Dos Transportes, 1978).

poses included (1) the adoption of new administrative methods; (2) accelerated construction on rivers, harbors, and ports; (3) renovation of shipping fleets; and (4) a new national policy of expansion in maritime shipping on an international scale (Torloni: 387). The plan inaugurated several new projects, among which are (1) the construction of locks and dams on four principal rivers (the Jacui, Parana, Parnaiba, and Tiete); (2) the acquisition of new tugboats and barges, especially designed to haul strategic ores, such as aluminum, iron, and tin; (3) the development of river ports to link the TransAmazon Highway with the major tributaries of the Amazon; and (4) improvements in the navigability of lakes behind large power dams. Although the Water Transport Plan stresses conventional infrastructure improvements, there are two clear threads in the current river transport policy. First, the benefit/cost logic of water transport has been driven home to policymakers by the technocratic planners in government agencies. The catalyst in converting this logic into actual policy was the 1970s oil price shock. Second, many of the most impressive new projects are driven by the country's mineral export policies. That is, new locks and dams, fleets of new tugs and barges, and port improvements are located to facilitate the movement of ore to the coast for overseas shipment. It makes good economic sense to transport bulk ore by water; however because these fluvial navigation improvements follow rather than lead other economic activities, it is obvious that river transport policy still receives a secondary priority.

Maritime navigation, by contrast, has gained occasional attention from government. As mentioned earlier, the coffee boom of the late 1800s and early 1900s prompted the new republican administrations to upgrade port facilities. Because of the coffee trade, Santos, the port of Sao Paulo state, grew to become the third largest (in tonnage) port in the Americas. Unfortunately, Brazilian ports by the early 1960s were antiquated, plagued by robberies and damage to cargos, weighted down by abusive tariffs, and slowed by extremely low productivity. It was estimated, at the time, that ships passed two-thirds of their port time waiting to be unloaded. These conditions moved the national government in 1966 to adopt new maritime policies that concentrated primarily on new port equipment and new administrative organization. The basic thrust of the 1966 policy was to lower operational costs and to raise the competitive position of Brazilian ports (Torloni: 387).

The 1966 program did not, however, make significant innovations in management because the ports continued under the administration of the National Department of Ports and Navigable Routes (DNPVN), which was a traditional bureaucracy. To break out of the DNPVN's bureaucratic restraints, the national government in 1975 replaced the traditional department with a new mixed public-private corporation, the Brazilian Port Enterprise (PORTOBRAS). This new entity was given responsibility for port operation and was charged with the task of raising port efficiency. The port of Santos, previously operated by Sao Paulo state, was similarly transferred to mixed management in 1980 (Torloni: 390). One of PORTOBRAS's first projects followed traditional policy toward port improvement—more than 200 West German high-speed derricks were purchased for the port of Rio de Janeiro. Since 1966, Brazilian port policy has concentrated on the construction of new ports along the entire Atlantic coast. These new ports have been designed for specific products and have been equipped with the latest technology.

To complement these port developments, the national government in 1971 acted to reverse the decline in the country's merchant marine fleet. One program rejuvenated thirty-six domestic shipyards, including the three largest—Maua and Ishikawajima in Rio and Verlome in Angra dos Reis. Construction was financed by a Merchant Marine Fund supported by a percentage tax on coastal and international freight. When one compares the 230,000 tons of new shipping built between 1958 and 1967 to the 5,300,000 tons built between 1975 and 1980, this program stands out as a clear success. The refurbished shipyards have attracted orders from around the world and have moved Brazil into second place in shipbuilding, only behind Japan in annual tonnage constructed.

This rapid expansion of ship construction was also linked to a larger global strategy adopted in 1969. With the economic "miracle" heavily dependent on export earnings, the heavy costs of shipping Brazilian-made products in non-Brazilian flag carriers became a significant addition to the nation's external debt. Official opinion traced the cause of these onerous freight charges to oligopolistic price fixing by an international cartel of powerful shipping companies. The federal government, in an exercise of nationalism, announced the Brazilian Doctrine which stated that, while the high seas continue to be free and Brazilian ports are open to ships of any flag, access to cargo of Brazilian origin must obey the regulations of SUNAMAM (the National Superintendency of the Merchant Marine). The most important of these regulations were (1) shipping companies that operate in Brazilian ports must utilize Brazilian-made transport; (2) cargo fees and other charges must be approved by SUNAMAM; and (3) Brazilian cargo destined for the exterior must be carried jointly and divided equally on ships of exporting and importing nations at a fixed minimum ratio of 65 percent, with the ratio to be increased to 80 percent over ten years, with the remaining proportion available to third-party flag carriers.[11] Two direct consequences flow from this new cargo policy. First, the demand for Brazilian ships increased which created conditions that permitted Lloyd-Brasil, the national fleet, to replace its antique vessels with new Brazilian-built ships. In the process, Lloyd-Brasil and the national tanker fleet have expanded to become Latin America's largest merchant marine. Second, the increase in cargo carried by Brazilian flagships led to a sharp drop in the balance of payments caused by shipping charges. During the early 1970s Brazil ran annual shipping cost deficits of approximately $35 million. By 1980, this deficit had been transformed into a $36 million surplus *(Relatorio)*.

Brazil's economic boom supported a resurgence of the nation's domestic air industry. Increased passenger and freight volume provided the capital to eliminate deficits and to modernize equipment. To help the airlines recuperate, the Department of Civil Aeronautics (DAC) redrew domestic routes and introduced new rate structures. Despite these changes, the number of domestic carriers dropped to three in 1975 when CRUZEIRO was sold to VARIG.

The dilapidated state of many Brazilian airports caused serious convenience, efficiency, and safety problems for the growing air traffic. A public corporation, the Brazilian Enterprise for Airport Infrastructure (INFRAERO), was created in 1972 to build, finance, and operate the industrial and commercial infrastructure of Brazilian aviation. INFRAERO launched a program to modernize and upgrade existing airports and to build major new airports that could handle present and future traffic. Among INFRAERO's accomplishments are the 1977 renovation of Rio's Galeao Airport for international traffic including supersonic planes and the opening in the early 1980s of new international airports for Sao Paulo and Belo Horizonte. Of Brazil's 42,000 airfields, 152 have permanent surface runways, and 10 are designated as international airports.

Throughout the postwar period, private ownership of aircraft increased to the point that by 1963, over 2,000 small planes were being imported annually at a cost of $300 million. Brazil's only aircraft maker, Neiva Aeronautic Construction Corporation Ltda., produced about 500 light planes per year. Economic factors and then the needs of the military led to the establishment in 1969 of the Brazilian Aeronautic Enterprise (EMBRAER), a mixed public-private corporation. The national government purchased 50 percent of the company's assets which had the effect of attracting over 100,000 individuals to buy EMBRAER's stock. The new firm, with its goal to develop a line of aircraft that could be marketed internationally, moved quickly. EMBRAER's first plane was a twelve-passenger, twin turboprop, with a speed of 400–600 kms per hour. It has been sold in twenty countries including the United States. By 1980, EMBRAER produced eleven different models and sold over 2,600 planes.

Essentially, Brazil has adopted a "nationalist" solution to air transport. As EMBRAER's technological and manufacturing capabilities have grown, it has been able to build larger, more sophisticated aircraft. The 1984 Brasilia, seating thirty, sold over 120 units even before the first commercial model came off the assembly line. Most recently, EMBRAER has entered into a joint production agreement with an Italian firm to build Brazil's first jet fighter (Torloni: 397–399).

With the industrialization campaigns of the 1950s and 1960s, several Brazilian cities soon became huge metropolises with wide expanses of industrial zones and suburban residential/commercial areas. This often chaotic urban growth exceeded the capacity of the traditional trolley systems and led to their swift substitution by a large number of private bus companies. By 1971, Brazil had 4,711 municipal bus lines, 7,861 intercity lines, 3,455 interstate lines, and 30 international lines (Brazil, 1974). The consequences, as expected, were extreme traffic congestion, dangerous pollution, and expensive oil imports. One of the most serious social impacts of these changes was a politically unacceptable cost of transportation for the average urban worker. In many cases, the costs of mass transit in metropolitan areas exceeded 20 percent of the minimum salary set by the national government (Camargo: 28).

In 1973 a new unit of government, the metropolitan region, was created in nine large urban areas to serve as a planning and management body which would work toward solutions of urban problems and encourage economic and social development in the metropolitan regions.[12] In 1976, as part of the Second National Development Plan, a new public corporation, the Brazilian Urban Transportation Enterprise (EBTU), was instituted to coordinate technical plans, programs, projects, and finances for urban mass transit. EBTU's early projects started construction of subway systems for Sao Paulo and for Rio. Under pressure to reduce the cost and the other consequences of urban traffic strangulation, EBTU relied heavily on foreign capital to finance these projects. By 1983, the first line of the Sao Paulo Metro carried over a half million riders per day. Work continues not only on the rest of the Sao Paulo and Rio Metro systems, but EBTU has also fostered the installation of modern streetcar systems, similar to those found in European capitals. While these large and urgent projects have made a dent in the congestion, unfortunately, the enormous short-run capital requirements, exceeding over $1 billion per year (Mello & Fonseca: 147), have contributed significantly to Brazil's external debt crisis (*The Economist:* 6).

TRANSPORTATION POLICY ORGANIZATION AND PROCESS

Public responsibility for the management of transportation in Brazil rests primarily with the two ministries of Transportation and Air Force. Three other ministers—the Ministry for Planning, the Ministry of Finance, and the Ministry of Administration—are important to note because of their cross-cutting authority to establish norms, rules, and standards, to develop and approve plans, to control certain funds, personnel, and equipment, and to provide technical supervision of financial and management affairs for the other ministries. The locus of policymaking resides not in the traditional bureaucratic departments, but rather it is exercised by several technically oriented "autonomous" agencies, especially those that link the president to the traditional ministries.

Civilian aviation falls under the aegis of the Air Force. In particular, the Departamento de Aviacao Civil, or Department of Civilian Aviation (DAC), is a traditional bureaucratic subunit of the Air Force Ministry and is directed by a military officer. The DAC performs many typical functions in regard to the coordination, control, planning, and support of commercial and private aviation. Five "autonomous" agencies are also associated with the Air Force's role in civil air policy. Two of these five are public enterprises described earlier, that is, EMBRAER and INFRAERO. The other three public enterprises include the Rio de Janeiro Airport Corporation (ARSA), the Aeronautical Telecommunications Corporation (TASA), and the Electromechanical Company (CELMA). TASA, it should be noted, operates an international service network for aviation communications, airplane security, and meteorology (*Perfil:* 50–53).

The principal national agency with responsibility for transportation administration is the Ministry of Transport created in 1967 to replace the ancient Ministry of Transportation and Public Works. The previous department was a classic example of the flaws and vices of traditional Latin American bureaucracies (Guimaraes, 1976: 18). The new department received a mandate from the Costa e Silva Administration to coordinate all forms of transportation (merchant marine, ports, rail, roads, urban, and water) except civilian air transport.[13] The Ministry of Transportation was mandated to coordinate its activities with the Air Force as prescribed by other laws (*Perfil:* 169).

The Transport Ministry contains a number of conventional units. The minister is directly served by the following offices (1) Gabinete do Ministro (minister's personal staff), (2) Consultoria Juridica (legal counsel), (3) Divisao de Segurança e Informaçoes (security and information division), (4) Coordenadoria de Assuntos Parlamentares (legislative affairs), and (5) Coordenadoria de Comunicaçao Social (press office). Two principal management officers compose the next layer. First, the Secretaria Geral (general secretariat) is in charge of administration, budget and financial planning, technical and special issues, and international affairs. At the same level is the Secretaria de Controle Interno (internal control secretariat) who serves as the ministry's auditing and accounting officer. Five main divisions report to the minister and to the two secretariats: administration, land transportation, water transportation, urban transportation, and personnel (*Perfil:* 170–171). These five units constitute the "direct administration" of the minister and function in conventional bureaucratic fashion.

Attached to the Ministry of Transportation are six "autonomous" agencies which implement major transportation programs. As pointed out earlier, a variety of "autonomous" units have been devised over time as an organizational mechanism for bypassing the traditional bureaucratic procedures, rules, and structures, thus giving new administrations the budgetary and personnel flexibility to launch new policy initiatives.

Three of the six "autonomous" transportation agencies pre-date the current organization of the Ministry. The National Superintendency of the Merchant Marine (SUNAMAM), dating from 1941, has responsibility for the administration and finance of the merchant marine, national navigation, and naval construction and repair. The Merchant Marine agency controls earmarked funds such as the National Port Fund and the Merchant Marine Fund. Four "associated enterprises" fall under SUNAMAM's jurisdiction: (1) Lloyd-Brasil, the national flag fleet; (2) FRANAVE, the Sao Francisco River Navigation Company; (3) ENASA, the Amazon Navigation Enterprise; and (4) SNBP, the Navigational Service for the Prata Basin (*Perfil:* 176).

The National Highway Department (DNER) is an "autonomous" agency that gained financial freedom in 1945 as part of the Joppert Law. This autonomy allowed DNER to construct and maintain the national highway system. DNER exhibits a standard internal administrative structure composed of bureaus for planning, construction, operations, personnel, administration, and purchasing. Like most highway departments, DNER possesses a field staff located at twenty-one regional offices. Also, the Federal Highway Police are part of DNER. DNER keeps a special office in Brasilia, called RODOBRAS, that has supervision over highway work in the Amazon region. Also attached to DNER is the Enterprise for Engineering and Construction of Special Works (ECEX) which built the Costa e Silva Bridge across Rio's Gaunabara Bay. DNER's projects depend on dedicated taxes levied on fuels, lubricants, and petroleum derivatives. It has also borrowed capital from international organizations such as the World Bank and the Inter-American Development Bank (*Rodovia:* 172).

Counterpart agencies to DNER exist at the state and municipal levels. These state highway and municipal road departments participate in various programs and funds managed by DNER. For example, highway funds are distributed among the Brazilian states according to a formula based on population, fuel consumption, motor vehicle registration, and geographic expanse (*Perfil:* 172).

The National Railway Network (RFFSA), is the third ''autonomous'' agency attached to the Transportation Ministry. Established as a mixed public-private corporation in 1957, RFFSA plans, finances, and operates the national railroads. It maintains the Fund for Railroad development and also operates three subsidiaries: the General Railroad Storage Corporation, the Porto Alegre Urban Train Corporation, and the Brazilian Urban Train Company (CBTU). CBTU was formed in 1984 to coordinate all metropolitan rail systems with special emphasis on service to low-income populations, who often live on the margins of the metropolitan area and must commute great distances for employment (*Perfil:* 178). To summarize, SUNAMAM, DNER, and RFFSA are, in many ways, similar to usual transportation divisions within any Ministry of Transportation. The importance and the power of the three agencies can be traced to their control over a major sector of transportation. Their control originates in their legislative mandates that provide these three agencies with legal ''autonomy'' from the ministry and its bureaucratic procedures, and with legislatively specified sources of revenues independent of the ministry. As a consequence, while these agencies report to the minister, they possess a significant voice in the development and implementation of their particular programs.

The other three ''autonomous'' agencies associated with the Ministry of Transportation all reflect the administrative reforms of the 1964 military regime and all are ''pure'' public enterprises. Two (PORTOBRAS and EBTU) manage major transport facilities and programs, and the third (GEIPOT) is an engineering and technical consulting firm. PORTOBRAS, its subsidiaries, and EBTU (described earlier) are governed by statutes pertaining to private corporations as well as their own legislative mandates. In essence, PORTOBRAS and EBTU are typical government-owned corporations common to many Western nations (Sharkansky).

The Executive Group for the Intergration of Transportation Policy (GEIPOT), has a complicated but short history that is interwoven into the basic character of Brazilian policy formulation. In 1965 GEIPOT was formed as an interministry committee with members representing the old Ministry of Transportation and Public Works, the ministries of Planning and of Finance, and the chief of staff of the Armed Forces. Its original function involved research and analysis of two types of transportation issues: (1) planning methodologies used by the various transportation sectors and agencies; and (2) the financing and engineering of specific highway projects. GEIPOT became an ''autonomous'' federal agency in 1969 reporting to the new Ministry of Transportation. GEIPOT's analytic tasks were enlarged to include research necessary to support the formulation of national transportation policy and to study the function of transportation in the national development process.

GEIPOT was transformed once again in 1973 into the Brazilian Enterprise for Transportation Planning. While GEIPOT retained its old acronym, its tasks were expanded further to plan national transport policy; to support the president in the formulation, orientation, coordination, and execution of national transport policy; and to advise the Minister of Transportation, by way of studies, research, opinions and information, about transportation policies for use in the minister's own decision processes. And finally GEIPOT was given responsibility to coordinate and oversee multimodal transportation programs. GEIPOT, as a public enterprise, provides its analytic services on a contract basis to public and private entities in Brazil and overseas (*Perfil:* 176).

GEIPOT has links to two other important administrative units that appear on the organization chart of the Ministry of Transportation—that is, the Conselho Nacional de Transportes (CNT) and the Comissao Coordenadora de Implantacao e Desenvolvimento do Transporte Intermodal (CIDETI). All three of these agencies (GEIPOT, CNT, and CIDETI) are part of the central core of policymaking bodies that surround the Brazilian presidency. In order to describe the work of these three agencies and, more importantly, to explain the policymaking process as it operates, it is necessary to leave the Ministry of Transportation and to examine the policy relationship between the president and the ministry.

Simply put, the president of Brazil is the "center" and the "motor" of policymaking. The president's signature, for example, is required for the implementation of all decrees, the appointments to all high offices (including ministers), and the "liberation" of budgeted and appropriated funds. Robert Daland describes the president's powers in this fashion: "The Bureaucracy can only move toward developmental goals when the presidency is viable, since he is virtually the sole channel through which the bureaucracy is energized" (Daland: 73).

The president directs the principal ministries and other administrative agencies via a network of "connecting entities" that bear various names: working group, advisory group, executive group, fund, board, council. These entities "are not merely interagency committees or ad hoc commissions such as appear in U.S. or British administration"; rather these entities perform several critical policy formulation and implementation functions.[14] This arrangement between the president, the "connecting agencies," and the ministries is not unlike the operations of the executive office of the President in the United States.

The National Transportation Council (CNT) acts as the connecting entity for transportation policy. It is presided over by the Minister of Transportation and its membership includes representatives from the ministries of the Army, the Navy, the Air Force and from SUNAMAM, RFFSA, the National Development Bank, and the director of civilian aviation (Daland: 79). Since 1964 CNT has formulated and coordinated national transportation policy. GEIPOT has served CNT as its research agency for the development of policy alternatives and options. GEIPOT also monitors the progress of the transportation sectors and prepares statistical information for use by CNT in its decision making.

The Coordinating Commission for the Introduction and Development of Intermodal Transportation (CIDETI) is another connecting entity that since 1974 has formulated policy for intermodal methods of freight movement. Its membership includes representatives from the ministries of Transportation, Finance, Industry and Commerce, Navy, Air Force, Foreign Relations, and Planning (*Perfil:* 170).

The transportation policy system in Brazil, then, can be conceived as a set of decision points, emanating from the presidential "center." The "center" develops and manages "connecting entities" (e.g., CNT and GEIPOT) that link the chief executive to the mainline ministries and the autonomous agencies. The ministries which are represented in the connecting entities participate in policy formulation. The ministries and the autonomous agencies implement policies formulated by the president and the members of the connecting entities. Most distant from the center are the government corporations and the mixed public-private enterprises that can raise capital in private markets and thus act with considerable discretion. This extended policy system evolved from the intractability of the traditional bureaucracies. Its evolution has given various national administrations a technical capacity and an administrative flexibility to undertake rapid advances in transportation development over the past quarter century.

CONCLUSION

Comprehensive and integrated transportation planning and management arrived late in Brazil's development. As a consequence, transportation policymakers have had to initiate and to finance massive projects in relatively short time spans. Without a doubt, the results of these urgent programs have been impressive and even spectacular. But at the same time, the national transportation system exhibits serious imbalances among the various sectors, caused particularly by an overreliance on motor vehicle transportation. The price paid for the neglect of rail and water transport has been a heavy drain on Brazil's export earnings.

Recent policy decisions now aim at correcting the previous imbalances. The success of the new policies from a technical standpoint can be expected, given the level of planning, engineering, construction, and management of public works in Brazil. What is in doubt, however, is the political volition and the economic capacity to pay the price necessary to build new projects. With large internal and external debts contributing to a serious economic crisis, the national government cannot easily afford to begin a new round of massive projects. Yet, without some new projects such as mass transit, bottlenecks and congestion will remain.

Future transportation policy in Brazil will be shaped by the decentralization created by the new constitution. The 1988 document transferred to the states and municipalities a number of transportation-related taxes (e.g., taxes on gasoline and lubricants) that previously were collected by the national government. Similarly, the distribution of national revenues on income has been altered to transfer a large percentage of funds to the states and localities. Even before the new constitution was promulgated, the Sarney Administration announced sharply smaller budgets for transportation agencies. Conversely, one can expect subnational governments to exercise more initiative in transportation policy. In Minas Gerais state, for example, 1,206 kms of new roads were opened in 1987 as part of a five-year plan to pave 6,000 kms of highways. A potential danger under the new constitution could emerge if the national government reduced its aid to the less developed regions, especially in the northeast.

Brazil's transportation policy remains a captive of the country's campaign to rid itself of hyperinflation. Management of the internal debt requires hard choices among public programs. It appears that transportation programs will be one of the policy areas targeted for retrenchment by the national government. Without some external aid, however, improvements in the critical north-south linkages or in the extension of transportation networks into the booming center-west will be delayed, President Sarney's decision to impose restrictions on the exploitation of the Amazon forest, including a significant slowdown in road construction, signals Brazil's willingness to negotiate with international development agencies. For the immediate future, Brazil's transportation system will be shaped not only by the progress made in resolving the economic crisis, it will also be shaped by the policy choices among the competing demands of economic growth and social justice made by representatives popularly elected since the return to democracy in 1985.

NOTES

1. The territory of Brazil exceeds the territory of all countries from Scandinavia on the north to Malta in the south, from Iceland in the west to the European parts of Russia (i.e., White Russia and the Ukraine). Burns, 16.

2. Burns (202) points out that Brazil's first ''paved'' road was started in 1856 and completed in 1861. It connected Petrapolis with Juiz da Fora and had a length of ninety-one miles. The road was constructed of crushed rock with roadside ditches of brick.

3. Brazil's first development plans were devised during the Vargas Administration in 1939 and 1943. According to Torloni (134), neither of these plans devoted special treatment to transportation.

4. There is no doubt that the military-civilian policymakers and administrators who engineered the ''Brazilian Miracle'' should receive credit for their accomplishments. However, two important points must be made. First, as Robock (189–191), demonstrates, a military-authoritarian regime was not a necessary condition for this growth.

Second, the price paid by the average worker was a 25 percent decline in real wages (Robock, 134–138).

5. The oil exploration eventually paid off with the discovery of Brazil's first large oil field off the coast of the state of Bahia.

6. It is important to note that the national government's assumption of state government railroad liabilities produced Brazil's first external debt.

7. At a national level, legislative, executive, and judicial branches have constitutionally distinct functions. These independent branches are also found at the state and municipal levels. The National Congress is composed of a Chamber of Deputies, elected from territorial districts based on population, and a Senate, composed of three senators from each state. The Brazilian president is a strong executive with budget-making powers, both subject to congressional review. State government basically repeats national government in form. The Brazilian court system is composed of four parallel hierarchies "which deal with matters pertaining to civil, labor, electoral, and military law," the state courts, and the Supreme Federal Tribunal. See Wesson and Fleischer (84).

8. This current list of types of administrative agencies and their respective powers is drawn from Daland (1981) and from *Perfil* (1985: 50–53).

9. Examples include the Vitoria and Minas Line (EFVM), the Carajas line (EFC), and the Ampa line (EFA).

10. The reasons for this official neglect of water transport are listed in Camargo (21–22). Also see Torloni (387).

11. This doctrine, if applied by other developing nations, would be very beneficial to them at the expense of the shipping cartel. It was adopted by UNCTAD in May 1970. See Valente.

12. These nine metropolitan regions are Belem, Fortaleza, Recife, Salvador, Belo Horizonte, Rio de Janeiro, Sao Paulo, Curitiba, and Porto Alegre.

13. Decree-Law 200, 15 March 1967.

14. The "connecting agencies" in the Brazilian executive branch carry out activities such as (1) definition of the contours of the problem; (2) technical planning followed by programming of the plans; (3) definitive formulation of policy, meaning the commitment of relevant authorities to implement their various programs which together constitute the policy; and (4) coordination of programs as between agencies concerned. See Daland (73).

REFERENCES

Brazil, *Anuario Estatistico dos Transportes* (Brasilia: Empresa Brasileira de Planejamento de Transportes, 1978, 1980, 1984).

Burns, E. Bradford, *A History of Brazil*, 2nd ed. (New York: Columbia University Press, 1980).

Camargo, Affonso Alves De. *Transportes: Novo Republica, Novos Caminhos*, Lecture delivered at Superior War College, Rio de Janeiro, July 1985.

Daland, Robert, *Exploring Brazilian Bureaucracy: Performance and Pathology* (Washington, D.C.: University Press of America, 1981).

The Economist, March 12, 1983.

Galache, G., and M. Andre, *Brasil: Processo E Integracao Federal 1985* (Sao Paulo: Edicoes Loyola, 1984).

Graham, Lawrence, *Civil Service Reform in Brazil: Principles versus Practice* (Austin: University of Texas Press, 1968).

Guimaraes, J. C. De Macedo Soares, "Transportes e Economia," *Jornal Do Brasil,* Nov. 11, 1985, sec. 1, p. 11.

———, *Transportes No Brasil: (Suas Grandes Metas)* (Rio de Janeiro: Editora Lidador, Ltda., 1976).

Krane, Dale, "Opposition Strategy and Survival in Praetorian Brazil, 1964–1979," *The Journal of Politics,* vol. 45, no. 1 (February 1983), p. 53.

Ludwig, Armin, *Brazil: A Handbook of Historical Statistics* (Boston: G. K. Hall & Co., 1985).

Martins, Luciano, *Estado Capitalista E Burocracia No Brasil Pos 1964* (Sao Paulo: Editora Paz E Terra, 1985).

Mello, Fernando Homen De, and Edurado Gianetti Da Fonseca, *Proalcool, Energia E Transportes* (Sao Paulo: Livrara Pionera Editora, 1981).

Nordlinger, Eric, *Soldiers in Politics: Military Coups and Governments* (Englewood Cliffs, N.J.: Prentice-Hall, 1977).

Perfil: Administracao Federal 1985 (Sao Paulo: Editora Visao, 1985).

Relatorio de Banco Central do Brasil (Rio de Janeiro: Banco do Brasil, 1981).

Robock, Stefan, *Brazil: A Study in Development* (Lexington, Mass.: D.C. Heath and Co., 1975).

Rodovia, Special Edition, "A Construcao Do Brasil Gigante" (Rio de Janeiro, Brazil: Departamento Nacional de Estradas de Rodagem, Ministerio Dos Transportes, Federal Republic of Brazil, 1972).

Roett, Riordan, *Brazil, Politics in a Patrimonial Society* (Boston: Allyn and Bacon, 1972).

Sharkansky, Ira, *Wither the State? Politics and Public Enterprise in Three Countries* (Chatham, N.J.: Chatham House Publishers, 1979).

Stepan, Alfred, *The Military in Politics* (Princeton, N.J.: Princeton University Press, 1971).

Survey of the Brazilian Economy (Washington, D.C.: Embassy of Brazil, 1965).

Torloni, Hilario, *Estudos De Problemas Brasileiros,* 16th ed. (Sao Paulo: Livrara Pionera Editora, 1983).

Valente, Murillo Gurzel, *A Politica de Transportes Maritimos do Brasil: Cronica de uma Batalha,* 2nd ed. (Brasilia: Ministerio dos Transportes, 1972).

Wesson, Robert, and David Fleischer, *Brazil in Transition* (New York: Praeger Publishers, 1983).

Wirth, John D., *Minas Gerais in the Brazilian Federation, 1889–1937* (Stanford: Stanford University Press, 1977).

2

CHINA

Jacques Yenny

BACKGROUND

Despite massive efforts since 1949, the transport system of China is still underdeveloped. This chapter traces the evolution of the various modes of transport in modern China. It focuses on the impact on the transport sector of policy decisions made by the central government. These decisions have sometimes been purely political and ideological and sometimes based more on economic considerations including, in recent years, market forces. The final section presents a brief description of the major actors involved in policy making for the transport sector.

Water transport played a key role in the historical development of transport in China, like in many other countries that are well endowed with rivers, lakes, and a long coastline. To complement natural waterways, the Chinese built canals, starting well over 2,000 years ago. The most famous example is the Grand Canal, connecting Beijing to Hangzhou, over a distance of 1,750 kilometers (km). Commenced in 486 B.C., it was completed in 1293 A.D., linking the rich agricultural area of the lower Changjiang (Yangtze River) with the capital of Beijing. Many smaller canals crisscross the fertile areas of South China, particularly in the Changjiang and Pearl River basins. With the advent of railways, however, water transport fell on hard times, and waterways were allowed to decay.

Railways, which now dominate so overwhelmingly both freight and passenger transport in China, had a rather bumpy start. Pushed by the Western powers occupying treaty ports, they were strongly resisted by the decaying imperial government and public opinion. Indeed, the first ten-mile line, laid in 1876 by the British outside of Shanghai, was bought a year later by the Chinese governor of the region and dismantled, with the equipment shipped to Taiwan (Hueneman: 3).

The next attempt was to be a Chinese one, in connection with coal mining in the Tangshan area, east of Beijing. Started as a mule-drawn tramway, the line was soon converted to steam and became the embryo of a future line from Beijing to Mukden (Hueneman: 63). By 1894, China's rail lines totalled 320 miles. In the remaining few years of the century, foreigners pushed more decisively for rail concessions, and many were granted to the British, French, Germans, Belgians, Americans, and Russians. The latter were even granted the right to construct a direct connection to Vladivostok through Manchuria, a major short-cut from the trans-Siberian route. Attempts by the Chinese to build railways were seldom successful as they had to depend on the foreigners for technical know-how as well as capital. Last but not least was Japan's involvement in rail construction, mainly in the northeast which it occupied from the end of the Russo-Japanese war, in 1905 to the end of World War II. To date, northeast China remains the region with the densest rail network in the country.

All transport modes suffered greatly during World War II and the subsequent years of civil strife. The first task of the People's Republic was to rehabilitate as quickly as possible the remnants of the old system. This priority task took three years, from 1949 to 1952, laying the foundation for the first five-year plan 1953–57. Albeit from a very low level in 1949, freight traffic, measured in ton-kilometers (tkm), tripled in three years, while passenger traffic increased 60 percent. In 1952, rail handled 79 percent of freight traffic, waterways 19 percent, with a mere 2 percent by road. The situation was hardly different for passengers, with 81 percent being carried by rail and the rest equally divided between road and water.

The first five-year plan was a period of reasonably well-balanced development of the various sectors of the economy. Within the transport sector, a good balance was struck between rehabilitation and overhaul of equipment and extension of the network. As a result, availability of locomotives increased from 82 to 92 percent and that of road vehicles from 67 to 72 percent of the fleet. For railways, the ratio of investments in new line construction to existing line improvement was only 1.3:1 (Foreign Broadcast Information Service: 279). Total transport investments reached the high level of 17.4 percent of all national investments—a level that would be reached again only during the fourth five-year plan, 1971–75.

Railway route kilometers increased 20 percent; highways 100 percent; and many waterways were rehabilitated. Motive power and rolling stock increased substantially as well as motor vehicles, ships, and airplanes. Construction of the first automotive factory began in 1953 in Changchun, and with the help of the USSR, the first Chinese built vehicle came out in 1956. Enough capacity was held in reserve and good intermodal coordination developed. Between 1952 and 1957, freight traffic increased from 73 to 173 billion tkm and passenger traffic from 25 to 50 billion passenger-kilometers (pkm) at annual growth rates of 19 and 15 percent, respectively.

POLITICAL DEMANDS ON THE TRANSPORTATION SYSTEM AND POLICY

Unfortunately, the balanced development achieved during the first plan period was not to continue. For the next twenty years, politics rather than economics would determine China's path toward development. It started with the second five-year plan in 1958 and the period known as the Great Leap Forward. A number of broad and not so coherent national policies affected the Chinese economy in general and also impacted the transport sector.

The leading policy decision was to concentrate on heavy industry under the motto "taking steel as the key link." In agriculture, the focus was exclusively of "taking grain as the key link." Grain was planted in areas that would be better used for some other crops including, for example, Mongolian pastures. All stops were pulled to meet unrealistic quotas, and, after a brief surge in output for two years, the economy collapsed and famine returned to China.

In the transport sector, the emphasis was also to produce rapidly new equipment at the expense of maintaining the existing stock. Locomotive maintenance depots were turned into manufacturing plants, and the availability of motive power and rolling stock fell. To palliate the need for more capacity, 1,000 steam locomotives were imported from the Soviet Union.

The output of the transport system shot up, with freight and passenger traffic more than doubling in three years, from the end of the first plan to 1960. After peaking in 1960, freight transport fell dramatically—40 percent in two years. The 1960 level was not exceeded again until 1970. These few figures illustrate the effect of broad policy decisions on the transport sector.

The heavy industry policy had another effect on the transport system, namely, the continuous emphasis and primacy of rail transport over other modes. Rail is indeed the most suitable mode for the massive movement of bulk commodities such as coal and ores. Also, China was following the Soviet model of development, and trucking was not well developed in the USSR. Furthermore, oil had only recently been discovered in China and accounted for only 1 to 2 percent of energy production in the 1950s, with coal making up 94 to 95 percent and hydro-power the rest. While road and water transport would generally require oil based fuels, rail could continue to operate with coal-burning steam locomotives. China is now the only country in the world still manufacturing large numbers of steam locomotives—up to 300 a year.

After 1949, China's foreign trade was primarily with the USSR and Eastern Europe, as trading ties with the West were generally severed. This trade was

Table 2.1
Length of Transport Routes (in 1,000 kilometers)

YEAR	RAIL	ROAD	INLAND WATERWAYS	DOMESTIC AVIATION	PIPELINES
1952	22.9	126.7	95.0	22.1	
1962	34.6	463.5	161.9	30.9	0.1
1965	36.4	514.5	157.7	34.9	0.4
1970	41.0	636.7	148.4	36.2	1.2
1975	46.0	783.6	135.6	47.1	5.3
1980	49.9	888.3	108.5	110.5	8.7
1985	52.1	942.4	109.1	171.2	11.8
1986	52.5	962.8	109.4	216.7	13.0

Source: Statistical Yearbook of China, annual.

mostly over land by rail, and ocean shipping and port construction received low priority at that time.

Another national policy called for the moving of industry away from the coast. This policy had two objectives: regional income distribution and also the development of self-sufficiency of various parts of the country for strategic reasons. A consequence of this decision to move to the interior, combined with the fear of aggression from the sea, was the considerable limitation of the role and development of coastal shipping.

In 1958, as part of the drive for regional self-sufficiency, the entire system of highway administration at the national level was abolished. Responsibilities for roads were devolved to local governments. The resources applied by the central government were minimal and consisted mainly of emergency funds to repair major roads or bridges that suffered damages from natural calamities. Due to the shortage of funds, most roads were built by labor-intensive methods with little equipment and local materials. These materials, obtained near the worksite, were not always the most suitable for road construction, and hand compaction did not always reach desirable standards. Bitumen was always in short supply; residual oil was used instead. The length of the network doubled from 1957–60, from 250,000 km to 510,000 km. This pace could not be sustained, and some of the roads were later abandoned. The 1962 statistics indicate a network of only 460,000 km, a 10 percent decrease from the 1960 figure (Table 2.1). Many roads remain substandard and cannot withstand today's increasing traffic. The automobile industry also proliferated in every province and is still very dispersed today with over 300 plants. A similar construction drive, with local labor, increased waterway length 70 percent from 100,000 to 170,000 km in a few years. It was also impossible to keep all these waterways passable, and the network shrank again.

The dispersal policy affected transport volumes in two opposite ways. On one hand, transport distances were shortened, but on the other, the need to distribute raw materials widely increased transport demand for bulk commodities. A typical case is that of iron and steel. Every province except Tibet produces steel, although iron ore resources are found only in a few provinces. Since iron smelting is a highly weight-reducing process—four to five tons of input for one ton output—it would be far more efficient to distribute steel than to transport iron ore and coking coal to all provinces for smelting.

A consequence of the suboptimal location of industry combined with a highly bureaucratic distribution system is the high amount of freight transport generated by the Chinese economy in comparison with other countries. Using a ton-kilometer (tkm) as a standard measure of freight output, China generates three tkm per dollar of GNP compared to well under two in India, Brazil, and the United States. Only the USSR has a higher freight intensity than China—over four tkm per dollar of GNP (Yenny & Uy: 2).

From 1963 to 1965, there was a need to readjust from the excesses of the second five-year plan (1958–62). Under somewhat more balanced policies, the economy improved, and in the transport sector, equipment was reconditioned to reach earlier levels of availability. For instance, twice as much was spent during these three years than during the previous five years on rehabilitating and repairing railway equipment. A movement was launched for the safe and punctual operations of trains, and, in 1965, the number of accidents had decreased 75 percent compared to 1960, and punctuality of freight trains was the highest ever. While much effort was made to restore the system's productivity, investment levels reached a low point, both absolutely and relatively. They accounted for less than 13 percent of total national investment compared to 17.4 percent during the first plan period.

In 1966, the formal planning process was resumed with the third plan (1966–70). Its first year (1966) coincided with the start of the Cultural Revolution. The transport sector was not spared, at least in the beginning, and many of the technical cadres were taken away from their jobs. Overall, however, the transport sector continued to grow. More emphasis was placed on expanding the networks than on maintaining existing ones. In the railway subsector, the proportion of investment funds allocated to the upgrading of existing lines decreased throughout the period. From 25 percent during the first plan period, it dropped to 19.4 percent from 1963 to 1965 and to only 10 percent during the fourth and most of the fifth plan periods. About 80 percent of the new construction took place west of a Beijing-Guangzhou line.

Foreign trade started growing in the 1970s, but ports were woefully inadequate. The proportion of total national investment in port construction had fallen from 0.4 percent during the first five-year plan to 0.2 percent during 1963–72.

In 1972, Premier Zhou Enlai made an appeal for a "three year change in the appearance of the ports" and the proportion of investments going to port construction jumped to 0.6 percent in 1973 and to over 1 percent from 1974 to 1978 (Foreign Broadcast Information Service, 1984: 283)

Low levels of transport investment are also made possible by the disregard for passenger transport demand. Priority is given to freight, and only the residual capacity, if any, is left for passengers. As a result, intercity passenger travel in China is much lower than in other countries at similar per capita income levels. In India, with the same per capita income, people travel three times as much as in China. In Brazil and the USSR, the figure is fifteen times greater, and in the United States, fifty times greater (Yenny & Uy: 24). A typical illustration of the neglect of passenger demand is the lack of development of civil aviation in a country the size of China. The total volume of passenger transport remained virtually constant, around 220,000 people per year for the entire decade of 1960 to 1970.

SOCIOECONOMIC DIMENSIONS OF THE TRANSPORTATION SYSTEM AND POLICY

Chairman Mao Zedong's death in 1967 and the subsequent purge of the Gang of Four opened the way to reform-minded leaders who were more concerned with pragmatic economic choices than political activism—hence the often quoted slogan, "It does not matter whether the cat is white or black as long as it catches mice." While policies started shifting almost as soon as the Gang of Four lost power, the start of the reform era is usually associated with the Third Plenary Session of the Party's Eleventh Central Committee held in December 1978.

Reform has not been a smooth process. But, so far, temporary setbacks have been more than compensated by the next upturns. There are many examples of see-saw policy changes or corrections between 1978 and today. The latest three to date were the crushing of student demonstrations and related downfall of General Secretary Hu Yaobang in early 1987; the 13th National Congress of the Communist Party in October of 1987, which largely vindicated economic reforms and opened the door for more; and the violent crushing of a pro-democracy movement at the Tiananmen Square in Beijing in June 1989, followed by economic sanctions by the United States and other western countries.

The result of the reforms undertaken since 1978 has been impressive. All sectors of the economy have been growing very rapidly. In a few years, grain production rose from 300 to 400 million tons per year; coal output from 600 to 850 million tons; and steel from 32 million tons in 1978 to 47 million tons in 1985, a 50 percent increase. Growth rates have been even more staggering in light industry, which had been neglected in the earlier periods. Typical consumer durables, always cited as an example of this development, are watches, bicycles and sewing machines—sometimes refered to as "the three rounds":

	1978 Production -in millions-	1985	1985/78
Bicycles	8.5	32.4	3.8 times
Sewing machines	4.9	9.9	2.0 times
Wristwatches	13.5	41.7	3.1 times

Source: Statistical Yearbook of China, 1978, p. 281.

This first generation of consumer durables has long been replaced by the next set of "big ticket items" for which annual production is growing even faster, albeit from very low levels. These are TV sets, washing machines, and refrigerators.

Accompanying internal reforms of the economy, the policy of "opening to the outside world" has resulted in similarly high growth rates in foreign trade. From some US$20 billion in 1978, it reached almost $70 billion in 1985, a 3.5-fold increase in just seven years.

Living standards of the population also increased dramatically since 1978. Per capita consumption increased almost 80 percent in constant terms. Average per capita income of farmers almost doubled bringing visible prosperity in the rural areas. Housing construction in cities and in villages surged. The yearly construction of housing for workers and staff was 811 million square meters during the period 1979–85 compared with an average of 183 million square meters between 1950 and 1978. The first private car was acquired by a female farmer in 1985.

All these developments had profound repercussions on the transport sector. The effects were both quantitative and qualitative. The surge in output of traditional sectors such as agriculture and heavy industry placed a tremendous burden on rail transport, while the development of light industry called for fast door-to-door delivery, which can only be done by road. The jump in foreign trade congested the ports and promoted the rapid growth of shipping.

These demands on the transport sector suddenly highlighted the effects of underinvestment in the sector in previous decades, and transport threatened to become a bottleneck for the economy. For example, by 1983, some 30 million tons of coal had accumulated at mine heads in Shanxi for lack of transport, and some of it was being destroyed by auto-combustion. Some coal even moved by truck up to 700 km at high cost, because of capacity constraints in the rail system. Similarly, it is estimated that ships waiting in ports incurred up to US$100 million in demurrage charges in 1978 alone.

Recognizing the seriousness of the situation, the government increased the

Table 2.2
Investment in the Transportation Sector Including Post and Telecommunications (yuan billion)

	1st FYP 1953-57	2nd FYP 1958-62	3rd FYP 1963-65	4th FYP 1966-70	5th FYP 1971-75	6th FYP 1976-80
Railway	5.916	10.416	3.395	11.250	17.308	14.047
Highway						
Waterway						
Aviation						
Pipeline						
Transp. Handling						
Subtotal						
Post and Telecommunications						
Total	9.015	16.330	5.378	15.001	31.759	30.245
Total Capital Investment	58.847	120.609	42.189	97.603	176.395	234.217
Transport (incl. Post&Telecommunications) as % of Total Investment	15.3%	13.5%	12.7%	15.4%	18.0%	12.9%

	1980	1981	1982	1983	1984	1985	1986	1987
Railway	3.044	1.445	2.637	4.221	5.852	7.715	8.466	
Highway	1.086	0.799	0.887	0.722	1.196	2.314	2.684	
Waterway	1.391	1.295	1.545	1.937	2.629	3.666	3.688	
Aviation	0.275	0.070	0.145	0.299	0.263	2.061	1.352	
Pipeline	0.054	0.018	0.017	0.006	0.010	0.145	0.505	
Transport Handling								
Subtotal	5.850	3.627	5.231	7.185	9.950	15.929	16.731	
Post and Telcommunications	0.384	0.420	0.490	0.619	0.896	1.166	1.351	
Total	6.234	4.047	5.721	7.804	10.846	17.095	18.082	20.400
Total Capital Investment	55.889	44.291	55.553	59.413	74.315	107.437	117.611	132.400
Transport (incl. Post&Telecommunications) as % of Total Investment	11.2%	9.1%	10.3%	13.1%	14.6%	15.9%	15.4%	15.4%

Source: Statistical Yearbook of China, annual.

percentage of investment going to transport every year during the sixth five-year plan, from 9 percent in 1981 to 16 percent in 1985 (Table 2.2). While not directly mentioined in the plan document, the main issues with which the government is concerned are (1) the shortage of capacity for freight and passenger; (2) the relative role of the various modes and in particular the allocation of short distance traffic; (3) the management of the system including policy formulation, planning and coordination and pricing of transport services; (4) the choice of technologies for infrastructure as well as for vehicles; and (5) the formation and development of staff in respect to all of these matters. Following are some specific policies or decisions which have guided development of the various modes since the early 1980s.

Railways still dominate the scene and were allocated over 60 percent of the 1981–85 plan's investment in the sector. The development policy, however, has shifted back to the improvement and capacity increases of existing lines and the construction of new lines in already congested corridors of eastern China. A large portion of the investment is addressing the critical energy supply problem and particularly improving coal transport from Shanxi province. This includes a plan to almost triple the capacity for coal movements to east coast cities and ports from 90 million tons in 1980 to some 250 million tons in the early 1990s. Capacity will be increased in seven major corridors through electrification, double tracking, new connections between existing lines and, finally, the construction of an entire new line of 650 km between Datong and the port of Qinhuangdao. This line will be electrified and incorporate new technology to carry trains of 6,000 to 10,000 tons—two to three times the present average load of coal trains.

Another objective of the railways is to replace steam by diesel and electric traction. The percentage of freight carried by the various modes of traction would just be inverted between 1980 and 2000, from 80 percent steam, to 20 percent steam, with diesel and electric about equally sharing the other 80 percent. Figure 2.1 shows the nation's railroad network.

Rail tariffs were increased in 1983 for the first time in sixteen years. In order to free the railways of short distance freight and passenger traffic which can more economically go by road, short distance freights and fares were increased again in 1985. China railways continued to be very profitable financially. In recent years, profits increased gradually to exceed 5 billion yuan (US$2.2 billion) in 1984. Profits have been close to the amounts invested each year in the railways by government. Therefore, Chinese railways are not the drain on public finances which many railways have become in other countries.

Road transport is the mode which has gone through the most drastic changes since 1978. At the national level, the road bureau has regained some of its former importance in planning for the nation's highways. A network of over 100,000 km has been officially designated as nation roads, connecting the national and provincial capitals, major seaports, rail nodes and important economic and tourist areas. Construction and improvement of 4,000 km of "missing links" in this network are receiving priority for investment. At the other end of the spectrum, rural roads are being extended to reach still isolated villages in remote and often mountainous regions.

The bureaucratic transport bureaus under the provincial transport authorities were unable to respond to the sudden increase in demand, and villages and, in the last few years, even private owners have entered the market. Changes in controls and regulations, combined with interprovincial agreements about fuel

Figure 2.1
Railroad Network in China

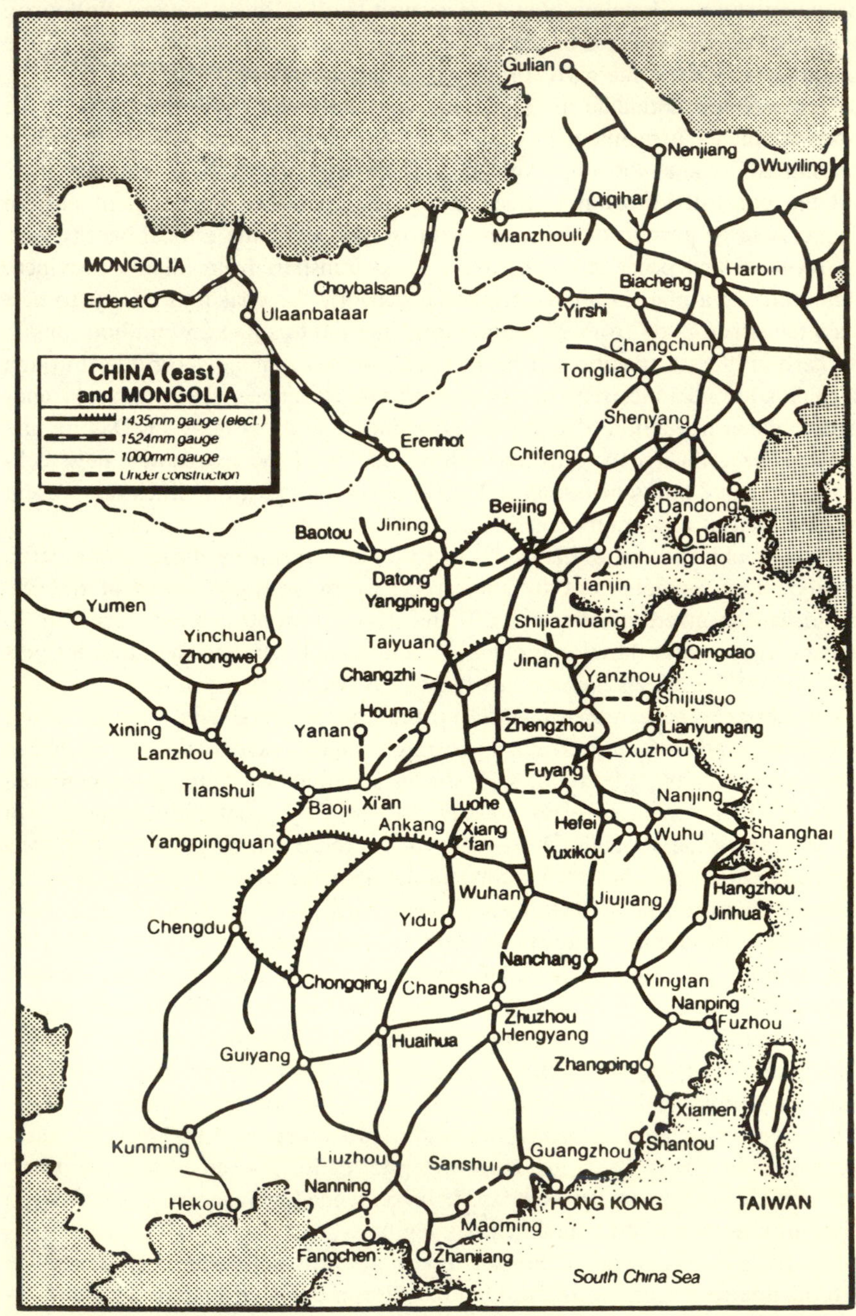

Source: Chris Bushell, *Railway Directory & Year Book 1989* (Surrey, England: Reed Business Publishing, 1989), pp. 352–353. Courtesy Reed Business Publishing, Ltd.

purchases, have opened the way to long-distance trucking. Until recently, the difficulty of obtaining fuel in a neighboring province forced the few trucks that ventured beyond their borders to carry enough fuel for the return trip—a less than optimal use of their loading capacity. Other jurisdictional barriers are gradually being abolished, thus permitting door-to-door transport and avoiding trans-shipments which greatly increased the cost of road transport in earlier years.

The result of all these changes is that the traffic carried by the state transport companies has grown very little over the last few years—16 percent between 1982 and 1985—while other trucks more than doubled their traffic in the same period. In 1985, state trucks performed 35.4 billion tkm, only 20 percent of the total estimate of 177 billion tkm. Tariffs are still regulated by government, but certain margins have recently been allowed to provide more flexibility and to attract return loads. Bus services have also greatly expanded, particularly since railway tariffs for short distance were increased.

Some progress has been made in improving the technology of trucks, by reducing their fuel consumption and introducing more diesel engines. However, the automotive industry remains widely scattered and inefficient with some 130 plants. Among these, only two produce 90,000 to 100,000 vehicles per year, mostly trucks. Besides these two plants, another two produce 20,000 to 30,000 units annually and the rest make fewer than 5,000 units per year. The industry is generally backward and inefficient because of the size of plants and the policy of self-sufficiency in parts production, which completely ignores economies of scale. Most models are still based on Western design of the 1950s with very high fuel consumption and gasoline engines. Total motor vehicle production reached 400,000 in 1985 (*People's Republic of China Year Book,* 1986: 375). A large number of trucks and private cars, many of which provide taxi services in the major cities, were imported in recent years, mostly from Japan. It is estimated that over 350,000 vehicles were imported in 1985.

The long-neglected waterways are experiencing revival. After steadily declining in percentage of total transport, inland water freight recently regained a little ground. In 1985, traffic exceeded 80 billion tkm, a 50 percent increase since 1980. About 85 percent of this traffic occurs on the Changjiang (Yangtze) and its tributaries. Ships still carried 20 million passengers in 1985, just below the figures for 1980 and 1981. But competition from all other modes is inevitable because of travel speed and time.

Major projects were started in the last few years, such as the upgrading of a section of the Grand Canal north of the Changjiang, to move coal to the industrial areas of Jiangsu province of Shanghai, and the deepening of the West River in Guangdong province to improve access to mineral deposits in western Guangdong and Guangxi. The inland water fleet is being modernized by the introduction of imported 6,000 horsepower push tugs, and large barge trains for coal can now be seen on the lower Changjiang. Greater attention is being paid to navigation when planning the use of water resources. In the past decades, many dams were built for irrigation and hydro-power without regard for transport potential of the rivers.

Coastal shipping traffic has also increased rapidly. In coordination with the rail plan for coal just described, coal loading facilities have been built in most northern ports. Expansion at Qinguangdao and a new coal port at Shijiusuo were partially funded by the Japanese Overseas Economic Cooperation Fund, (OECF). Large tonnages of coal now move to south China by coasters, thus relieving the pressure on highly congested north-south railway lines. Growth of coastal shipping has been particularly rapid in the southern reaches, between Shanghai and Guangzhou, through the Taiwan straits, where navigation had been cultivated after the establishment of the People's Republic.

To deal with the booming foreign trade, China engaged in an unprecedented effort of port construction. Over fifty new deep-water berths were built in major ports between 1981 and 1985, increasing cargo handling capacity by some 20 million tons per year. By the end of 1985, China had about 200 deep-water berths in the fifteen major ports under the control of the Ministry of Communications (MOC). Traffic at these fifteen ports increased over 50 percent, from about 200 million tons in 1978 to over 310 million tons in 1985 (Table 2.3). Container wharfs were built at major ports of Tianjin, Shanghai, and Guangzhou with the assistance of loans from the World Bank.

In 1961, China's merchant marine counted only twenty ships and carried 800,000 tons of cargo. Today, it ranks ninth in the world with more than 1,000 ships. China took advantage of the depressed world shipping market to build up its substantial fleet. Lately, it bought modern container and Roll on/Roll off (Ro-Ro) vessels. The fleet is calling at over 600 ports and has regular container services to Japan, Hong Kong, London, Hamburg, the United States, Southeast Asia, and the Persian Gulf. The China Ocean Shipping Company (COSCO), the largest shipping enterprise in China, has established offices and branches in major countries. China is pursuing a policy of importing free on board (FOB) and exporting cost, insurance, and freight (CIF), thus greatly reducing its former reliance on foreign shipping. The domestic fleet now carries over 70 percent of the country's seagoing foreign trade. Shipbuilding has followed the development of trade and shipping, and Chinese yards built over 1.6 million dead weight tons (DWT) in 1985. China also entered the export market with orders up to 1.2 million DWT received since 1980. Again, like the automotive industry, shipbuilding is dispersed in over 500 yards.

Air transport literally took off in the early 1980s. In 1985, the Civil Aviation Administration of China (CAAC) carried almost 7.5 million passengers. Many new domestic and foreign routes were opened, including thirty-four new domestic routes in 1984 alone. CAAC now operates internationally to twenty-five cities in twenty-one countries.

The fleet which was originally entirely made of Soviet aircraft has undergone great diversification. In the early 1970s, China purchased British Trident and ten Boeing 707s, mainly for use on international routes. In 1980, CAAC ac-

Table 2.3
Cargo Handled at Principal Seaports (in millions of tons)

YEAR	
1952	14.4
1957	37.3
1965	71.8
1978	198.3
1980	217.3
1981	219.3 0.9%
1982	237.6 8.3%
1983	249.5 5.0%
1984	275.5 10.4%
1985	311.5 13.1%
1986	344.1 10.5%
1987	397.0 15.4%

Note: Percentages indicate a growth from previous year.

Source: Statistical Yearbook of China, annual.

quired three long-range Boeing 747SPs to be used mostly on routes to the United States and Western Europe. Further diversification in the early 1980s included MD-82s, Airbus A 310s and Soviet TU-154s (*The China Business Review,* July–August 1986: 37–42). More than thirty airports were upgraded or built during the last plan period.

RECENT TRENDS AND FUTURE PROSPECTS

From the early 1980s, transport and energy have repeatedly been singled out as the two highest priority sectors for investment and modernization. Great progress has been made to increase transport capacity, and China ranks third in the world, after the USSR and the USA, for the throughput of domestic freight in terms of ton-kilometers. Much remains to be done, however, to keep up with transport demand and prevent transport from constraining economic growth, to modernize the system, to increase efficency and reduce transport costs, and, finally, to train staff to operate a modern transport system.

China has set for itself the goal of quadrupling the growth value of industrial and agricultural output (GVIAO), between 1980 and the end of the century. Annual growth rates achieved since 1980 indicate that this goal is quite feasible, providing that prevailing economic policies continue to be implemented smoothly. What will be the impact of such growth on the transport sector?

Freight elasticity with respect to GVIAO, which averaged 1.1 in the period 1952 to 1977, fell to 1.0 from 1977–82 and to only 0.67 from 1979–84 (World Bank, 1985b: 38). In 1984 and 1985, however, freight traffic grew again at the same rate as GVIAO, increasing by more than 12 percent each year. Chinese planners feel that economic reforms will help reduce freight transport demand. They predict that the expected quadrupling in output will generate only a doubling in freight transport demand. This means that between 1980 and 2000, every additional unit of output would require only a third as much transport as one existing unit of output. This assumes that the restructuring of the economy away from heavy industry and into light industry and services will further reduce freight elasticity (Table 2.4).

This scenario is far from assured, as contradictory forces pull on the transport sector. For the reduction in transport demand, one can cite the potential for reducing energy consumption in industry. Unit energy consumption in China is much higher than in any other major industrial country. This would greatly reduce the need for coal transport which is the largest component of Chinese freight. Increase of the share of the service sector in total output would also reduce transport demand. On the other hand, rationalization of industry and spatial location combined with increased specialization for economies of scale would tend to increase interregional exchanges and therefore transport demand. These contradictory forces affecting transport demand can best be illustrated in the case of coal. Coal consumption may well increase less rapidly than industrial output, but it may be more economical to increase the proportion of coal coming from north China, where mining costs are considerably lower than elsewhere in the country, thereby increasing transport distances. Indeed, average coal transport distance has already increased from 370 km in 1978 to 480 km in 1984. Depending upon the progress of structural changes in the economy and improvements in the distribution systems, transport demand in the year 2000 could range from 2.5 to 3 trillion tkm, versus 0.9 trillion tkm in 1980 (World Bank, 1985b: 39).

In contrast to freight, passenger transport has no way to go but up and, unless arbitrarily constrained again, very rapidly so (Table 2.5). Passenger traffic has increased at double-digit rates each year since 1980. The year-to-year increase reached 17 percent overall in 1985, with an 18 percent increase for rail passenger and a 41 percent jump in air travel. Trains are overcrowded, carrying up to one and a half times their seating capacity while plane tickets are often unavailable to the general public. Domestic as well as foreign tourism are booming. Rising incomes have led to higher demand for travel in most coun-

Table 2.4
Freight Traffic (in millions of tons)

YEAR	RAIL	ROAD 1	WATER 2	PIPELINES	AVIATION	TOTAL	OCEAN SHIPPING
1952	132.1	131.6	51.3	--	--	315.1	0.1
1960	672.2	707.9	324.8	--	--	1704.9	0.8
1965	491.0	489.9	227.5	--	--	1208.4	2.5
1970	681.3	567.8	249.5	--	--	1498.6	5.0
1975	889.6	725.0	325.6	60.3	--	2000.5	24.2
1980	1112.8	760.2	383.8	105.3	--	2362.1	42.9
1981	1076.7	715.1	369.6	109.3	--	2270.0	45.3
	-3.2%	-5.9%	-3.7%	3.8%		-3.9%	5.6%
1982	1135.3	787.8	397.2	108.6	0.1	2429.0	46.1
	5.4%	10.2%	7.5%	-0.6%		7.0%	1.8%
1983	1187.8	790.8	403.0	116.2	0.1	2497.9	47.6
	4.6%	0.4%	1.5%	7.0%		2.8%	3.3%
1984	1240.7	788.7	413.5	125.4	0.2	2568.5	55.5
	4.5%	-0.3%	2.6%	7.9%		2.8%	16.6%
1985	1307.1	762.3	434.0	136.5	0.2	2640.1	65.6
	5.4%	-3.3%	5.0%	8.9%		2.8%	18.2%
1986	1356.4	785.5	452.2	148.3	0.2	2472.6	72.3
	3.8%	3.0%	4.2%	8.6%		3.9%	9.0%

(in billions of ton-kilometers)

YEAR	RAIL	ROAD 1	WATER 2	PIPELINES	AVIATION	TOTAL	OCEAN SHIPPING
1952	60.2	1.4	11.8	--	--	73.4	2.8
1960	276.7	13.2	65.0	--	--	354.9	11.8
1965	269.8	9.5	43.3	--	--	322.6	23.7
1970	349.6	13.8	51.2	--	--	414.6	41.9
1975	425.6	76.4	152.1	49.1	0.1	849.4	353.2
1981	571.2	78.0	150.7	49.9	0.2	850.0	364.3
	-0.1%	2.1%	-0.9%	1.6%		0.1%	3.1%
1982	612.0	94.9	170.8	50.1	0.2	928.0	376.9
	7.1%	21.7%	13.3%	0.4%		9.2%	3.5%
1983	664.6	108.4	181.1	52.4	0.2	1006.7	397.7
	8.6%	14.2%	6.0%	4.6%		8.5%	5.5%
1984	724.8	153.6	196.1	57.2	0.3	1132.0	437.4
	9.1%	41.7%	8.3%	9.2%		12.4%	10.0%
1985	812.6	177.0	225.5	60.3	0.4	1275.8	532.9
	12.1%	15.2%	15.0%	5.4%		12.7%	21.8%
1986	876.5	195.8	248.9	61.2	0.5	1382.9	548.9
	7.9%	10.6%	10.4%	1.5%		8.4%	11.6%
1987	947.1	240.9	280.0	62.5	0.7	1531.2	660.0
	8.1%	23.0%	12.5%	2.1%		10.7%	11.0%

Note: Percentages indicate growth from previous year.

1. Road tons include only transport by highway transport departments.
   Road ton-km from 1980 include freight not managed by highway departments.
2. Water transport includes inland waterways and coastal shipping.

Source: Statistical Yearbook of China, annual.

tries, and China is no exception. By the year 2000, passenger travel demand could easily be five to six times greater than it was in 1980.

Although the share of rail freight and passenger transport has fallen from over 80 percent in 1952 to, respectively, 66 percent and 57 percent, rail remains the dominant mode and is expected to be so well into the next century.

Table 2.5
Passenger Transport (millions of passengers)

YEAR	RAIL 1	ROAD 2	WATER	AVIATION	TOTAL
1952	163.5	45.6	36.1	--	245.2
1960	618.2	325.2	123.3	0.2	1066.9
1965	412.5	436.9	113.7	0.3	963.4
1970	524.6	618.1	157.7	0.2	1300.6
1975	704.7	1013.5	210.2	1.4	1929.8
1980	922.0	2228.0	264.4	3.4	3417.8
1981	953.0	2615.6	275.8	4.0	3848.4
	3.4%	17.4%	4.3%	17.6%	12.6%
1982	992.1	3006.1	279.9	4.5	4282.6
	4.1%	14.9%	1.5%	12.5%	11.3%
1983	1060.4	3369.7	272.1	3.9	4706.1
	6.9%	12.1%	-2.8%	-13.3%	9.9%
1984	1133.5	3903.4	259.7	5.5	5302.1
	6.9%	15.8%	-4.6%	41.0%	12.7%
1985	1121.1	4272.3	270.0	7.5	5670.9
	-1.1%	9.5%	4.0%	36.4%	7.0%
1986	1085.8	4409.0	252.9	10.0	5758.5
	-3.1%	3.2%	-6.3%	33.3%	1.5%

(billion passenger-kilometers)

YEAR	RAIL 1	ROAD 2	WATER	AVIATION	TOTAL
1952	20.1	2.3	2.5	--	24.9
1960	67.4	14.6	6.2	0.2	88.4
1965	47.9	16.8	4.7	0.3	69.7
1970	71.8	24.0	7.1	0.2	103.1
1975	95.5	37.5	9.1	1.5	143.6
1980	138.3	72.9	12.9	4.0	228.1
1981	147.3	83.9	13.8	5.0	250.0
	6.5%	15.1%	7.0%	25.0%	9.6%
1982	157.5	96.4	14.5	6.0	247.4
	6.9%	14.9%	5.1%	20.0%	9.8%
1983	177.6	110.6	15.4	5.9	309.5
	12.8%	14.7%	6.2%	-1.7%	12.8%
1984	204.6	133.7	15.4	8.4	362.1
	15.2%	20.9%	0.0%	42.4%	17.0%
1985	241.6	157.3	17.4	11.7	428.0
	18.1%	17.7%	13.0%	39.3%	18.2%
1986	258.7	168.6	17.1	14.6	459.0
	7.1%	7.2%	-1.7%	24.8%	7.2%
1987	284.3	212.9	19.2	18.6	535.0
	9.9%	26.3%	12.3%	27.4%	16.6%

Note: Percentages indicate growth from previous year. The figures:
1. Includes passengers carried by state and local railways;
2. Includes only passengers carried by highway transport departments.

Source: Statistical Yearbook of China, annual.

Coal will remain the major commodity, accounting for 40 percent of all freight transport, and rail loadings could be between 800 and 900 million tons annually by 2000. Massive investments will continue to be required in all aspects of rail operations (i.e., infrastructure, motive power, and rolling stock). In recent years, provincial governments have taken upon themselves the construction of new railways, and more of this can be expected in the future.

New economic policies are creating a rapidly growing demand for road transport. Light industry products require quick distribution and careful handling, while agricultural and side-line products need good access to urban markets. Road density in China is still low in comparison with density in other countries. Many existing roads in the coastal provinces are already congested and deteriorating under the heavy and rapidly growing traffic. A major effort of road maintenance, strengthening, improving, and construction is needed. The question is how to finance this effort.

Even increased central government investment—which rose from 0.7 billion yuan in 1983 to 2.1 billion in 1985—cannot cope with the magnitude of the task. Greater reliance on local government financing, toll roads and joint ventures with foreign capital, like the Hong Kong to Guangzhou expressway, are all devices now being used to promote road infrastructure development.

Much remains to be done also to increase the efficiency of the automotive industry, diversify output, and reduce fuel consumption of the trucks and buses. Most of the production consists now of four- to five-ton trucks. There is a need for larger trucks to bring down road transport costs. These are now fifteen to twenty times the line haul costs of rail compared to ratios of five to seven times in other countries. At the other end, small pickups are needed to replace the ubiquitous walking tractors. Generally referred to as "oil tigers," they consume up to three quarters as much fuel as a four-ton truck, while carrying only one ton. Furthermore, since they travel at only 10–15 kilometers per hour, they greatly add to road congestion.

Further development of water transport will be mainly through greater reliance on multi-modal transport. The best example is the transport of coal, first by rail to northern ports or to Changjiang and then by ship or barge to south or east China. Containerization is another example of multi-modal systems which has a great potential in China. Small one- to five-ton containers have been used for a long time on the railways and waterways. The international containers used in foreign trade have only recently appeared on the scene. Most of them still stay in the ports or their vicinity. Their movement inland to final destinations has yet to be organized better. Potential for containerization of trade and some domestic traffic is still large. Achieving this goal would greatly increase port throughput as one container berth can easily handle over 1 million tons per annum versus the 400,000 tons typically handled at break bulk berths in China.

The potential for air travel is enormous. Currently, 110 million rail passengers per year travel over 800 km, spending sixteen hours and more on the train.

In comparison with this number, CAAC carried 7.5 million domestic passengers in 1985, equivalent to the level of U.S. air traffic in the late 1940s.

Again, decentralization is the adopted policy to stimulate development. Some steps are being taken to get CAAC out of operations and transform it into a regulatory agency for civil aviation. Two types of companies will take over operations. First, regional airlines will evolve out of CAAC's six regional bureaus and operate CAAC routes with former CAAC aircraft. Second, new regional and local companies will be formed. By the end of 1985, six such new airlines had been approved, and two of them, in Xiamen and Xinjian, had gone into operation.

The seventh five-year plan (1986–90) allocated 57 billion yuan (US$19 billion) or 15 percent of the state capital construction budget to the transport and communications sector, a 25 percent increase over the 45.5 billion yuan invested during the 1981–85 period. Slightly over half or 30 billion yuan went to the railways. Since the resources of the central government are limited, the instruments described here will be used to increase investment in the sector.

TRANSPORTATION POLICY ORGANIZATION AND PROCESS

Policy in general is formulated by the leadership of the Communist Party and particularly its Central Committee. The five-year plans for national economic and social development embody these policies. The proposal for the seventh such plan, since the founding of the People's Republic, was prepared by the party's Central Committee and adopted in September 1985 at the National Conference of the Communist Party. The plan has to be approved finally by the government and its main executive body, the State Council, but party membership is a prerequisite for assuming influential positions in government and particularly in the State Council. The State Council is an enlarged cabinet including the premier, two vice-premiers, the ministers, and heads of state commissions, bureaus, and offices.

The statement on transport of the seventh plan can be summarized as follows: Give priority to the development of transport and telecommunications by continuing railway construction; stepping up development of road, water, and air transport and rational coordination of the different modes. Freight transport in 1990 was expected to be 30 percent higher than in 1985. Passenger transport should be improved as well as the manufacturing of motor vehicles, locomotives, aircraft, and ships. The state should increase investment in the sector, focusing on major projects and infrastructure projects. The construction of local roads, railways, and inland waterways should be carried mainly by local people and authorities with their own funds. Local authorities and departments should be allowed to undertake air transport.

The direct management of the sector is basically under two ministries, the Ministry of Railways and the Ministry of Communications dealing with road

Table 2.6
Staff and Workers in Transport and Telecommunications Sectors
(in millions)

YEAR	STATE OWNED UNITS	COLLECTIVES	TOTAL
1952	1.12	--	1.12
1960	3.31	0.91	4.22
1965	2.45	1.73	4.18
1970	2.96	2.08	5.04
1975	4.00	1.90	5.90
1980	4.79	2.16	6.95
1981	5.02	2.19	7.21
1982	5.15	2.18	7.33
1983	5.26	2.15	7.41
1984	5.37	2.14	7.51

Note: This table has not been updated since 1984.

Source: Statistical Yearbook of China, annual.

and water transport. Civil aviation has its independent administration, CAAC, directly under the State Council. Its impending reform was already mentioned. Pipelines come under the Ministry of Petroleum.

Decision making in the railways, civil aviation, and pipelines is highly centralized, but, in the road and water subsectors, local governments at all levels play a role, including provinces, autonomous regions, municipalities, prefectures, counties, cities, townships, and villages as well as production enterprises, collectives, and, recently, specialized households. Transport policy decisions have to be coordinated horizontally among central ministries and agencies and vertically between central ministries and local agencies.

Coordination at the central level is done primarily by the State Planning Commission (SPC) and the State Economic Commission (SEC). Each has a transport bureau. SPC deals with long-term planning and has to approve major projects requiring central government investment and large regional projects. SEC deals with the implementation of the annual plan, including the allocation among transport modes and routes of the output of major planned commodities such as coal, iron and steel, grain, and the like. A Comprehensive Transport Institute, reporting administratively to SEC, is in fact the think-tank and research arm of the sector, working on major sectoral issues as well as long-term development alternatives.

The Ministry of Railways employs 3.1 million people, of which 1.7 million deal with operations (Table 2.6). The remainder are employed in the numerous other activities of the ministry, namely some sixty factories producing motive power, rolling stock, and other railway equipment; nine construction companies to carry out civil works; eleven universities; twenty staff colleges and more than 2,000 schools; and hospitals and housing facilities for the staff. The ministry also has a number of design institutes for the project preparation and ten research institutes which make up the Chinese Academy of Railway Sciences.

In recent years, great changes have taken place in the organization of the railways. The number of regional administrations has been reduced from twenty to twelve. At the same time, the administrations have been given more responsibilities and also more autonomy by being organized in the form of state-owned enterprises, with some authority over their retained earnings. For instance, the Beijing region was extended to include the coal mining area of Shanxi province, thus making it easier to organize through unit trains under one jurisdiction, between the mines and the ports. Locomotives are owned by the regional administrations, while freight cars are held in a national pool. Construction bureaus have been transformed in construction companies, who now have to bid competitively for work and can also bid for projects outside the railways.

The Ministry of Communications (MOC) manages directly only some major national roads and a national trucking company, fifteen major seaports, two coastal shipping bureaus, the shipping line COSCO, and the main streams of a few large waterways. Most of the extensive road and water transport systems, including infrastructure and equipment such as trucks, buses, ships and barges, and their operations are managed by provincial and local authorities. Each province has a Transport Bureau acting, in fact, as a provincial ministry of transport, with separate road and waterways administrations.

In the case of roads, the Ministry of Communications' role is primarily to establish construction standards for infrastructure and rules, regulations, and tariffs for the state transportation companies. The waterways are administered partially by MOC, partially by the provinces, and this has led to irrationalities in the past. For instance, the main course of the Changjiang was restricted to MOC's fleet, therefore necessitating cargo trans-shipment between the main course of the river and its tributaries. Many of these problems have been solved in recent years, and there are now more than 800 shipping companies in the Changjiang basin. All channels and all ports have been opened to all ships.

More autonomy is also being granted to major seaports. Starting with Tianjin a few years ago, this autonomy was extended recently to Shanghai and Dalian and will probably reach other ports, if the experiment proves successful. Various degrees of autonomy are being tested, particularly allowing ports to retain earnings in exchange for an increased contribution to their investment needs. Shipping companies, formally under the direct management of the ministry, are given greater autonomy and responsibilities. Also, collectives and specialized households are assuming a greater role for both road and water transport. The rural reforms have been authorized to acquire trucks and boats and to operate them virtually on a free market basis.

In summary, the government's policy is to give up direct management and operation of enterprises and to concentrate on indirect guidance through economic management tools such as pricing taxation, banking, wages, and labor rules and the integration of planning with competition and market regulation. Changes in structure, organization, responsibilities in the whole economy and in the transport sector have been so frequent in the last five years that it is very difficult to give a picture of the situation which would be still valid six months later. The 1980s were years of great experimentation in China to introduce more flexibility in a very rigid and bureaucratic system. Results of the reforms conducted so far have been very promising

CONCLUSION

Because China is a centrally planned economy, all decisions are made by the government rather than by the market place. The previous analysis shows the impact that certain broad political and economic choices, over the last thirty-five years, have had on the transport sector in particular. It illustrates the danger for the economy of insufficient levels of investment in the sector over too many years. Transport infrastructure is very capital intensive and requires many years of study, design, and construction before becoming operational. When the economy grows at the pace experienced in China since 1978, transport can become a serious bottleneck. The importance of transport has now been fully recognized in China, and great efforts are being made to develop and improve the system.

As the economy develops and grows, it is more and more difficult to plan for everything centrally. China, following the example of Hungary, has been experimenting with reforms including decentralization and small amounts of privatization. How far the reforms will go is difficult to predict. Privatization has already introduced sharp income differences in rural areas. Reforms of industry in urban areas are encountering difficulties as they threaten established privileges. Such developments raise questions among certain party members regarding the merit of reforms, and the threat of a return to ideology cannot be fully dismissed. The remaining years of the century will determine whether China can emulate the development of its neighbors in Asia.

REFERENCES

The China Business Review, Washington, D.C.: July–August 1986: 37–42.

Editorial Department of the PRC Year Book in Beijing, ed., *People's Republic of China Year Book 1986* (Beijing: Xinhua Publishing House, 1986).

Foreign Broadcast Information Service, *China in the Year 2000* (Arlington, Va.: Joint Publication Research Service, March 6, 1986).

Hueneman, Ralph William, *The Dragon and the Iron Horse: The Economics of Railroads in China, 1876–1937* (Ann Arbor, Mich.: University Microfilms International, 1982).

Joint Economic Committee, *Chinese Economy post Mao* (Washington, D.C.: Government Printing Office, 1978).

———, *China Under the Four Modernizations* (Washington, D. C.: Government Printing Office, 1982).

———, *China's Economy Looks Toward the Year 2000* (Washington, D. C.: Government Printing Office, 1986).

Ma, Hong, and Sun Shangin, ed., *Studies in the Problems of China's Economic Structure* (Arlington, Va.: Joint Publication Research Service, Foreign Broadcast Information Service, China Report Economic Affairs, August 3, 1984).

Radiopress, Inc., *China Directory in Pinyin and Chinese 1986* (Tokyo: Radiopress, Inc., 1985).

State Statistical Bureau, People's Republic of China, *Statistical Year Book of China 1986* (Hong Kong: Economic Information Agency, 1986).

World Bank, *China: Long-Term Development Issues and Options,* A World Bank Country Economic Report (Baltimore, Md.: The Johns Hopkins University Press, 1985a).

———, *China: The Transport Sector,* Annex 6 to *China: Long-Term Development Issues and Options* (Washington, D. C.: World Bank, 1985b).

Yenny, Jacques, and Lily Uy, *Transport in China: A Comparison of Basic Indicators with Those of Other Countries* (Washington, D. C.: World Bank, 1985).

3

EAST GERMANY

Rainer Hopf

In the transportation sector of the GDR (German Democratic Republic [East Germany]), all branches of public transportation as well as the industrial concerns, commercial enterprises and Combines with which they are associated are under the direction of the Ministry of Transportation. They include rail transportation, maritime transportation, inland shipping, waterways, roadway freight transportation, vehicle maintenance, local city transportation, roads, civilian air transportation, oil pipelines, and transportation oriented services. In a narrower sense, individual and occupational transportation are not counted in this category. In view of their significance in mass and freight transportation, however, both branches are included in the transportation sector.

The transportation sector, with its considerable economic implications and ramifications, reveals itself consistently as a weak point in the economic structure of the GDR. This is surprising above all because, as in other sectors of the economy, the opportunities for the state to influence supply and demand in the transportation sector have been considerably broadened. Even prior to the founding of the GDR, state-owned enterprises were predominant in their administration of the railways and the postal service, local city transportation, air transportation and harbor administration. Nevertheless, before the war there were pronounced centers of privately owned middle-class firms, particularly in

This chapter was originally written in German by the author and translated into English by Karen Fletcher, Alan Mitchell, and Amy Thomson, graduate assistants at Bowling Green State University, Bowling Green, Ohio.

the areas of roadway transportation, inland shipping, warehouses, and travel agencies. These areas too have been extensively nationalized in the GDR, to the point where transportation services are now almost exclusively (98.2 percent) furnished by publicly owned firms or firms associated with the state.

In the GDR, the state's exercise of influence goes substantially further. Until late-1989, when the Communists' one-party rule of the country was challenged and then terminated amidst a peaceful revolution in the GDR and elsewhere in Eastern Europe, there were many state-imposed restrictions on personal travel outside the country's borders. However, even in those days, neither the individual's choice of means of transportation nor the desired amount of travel within the country were restricted by the state. This continues today. In the shipping sector, however, the state prescribes for the enterprises and Combines upper limits on the volume of transportation, the means of transportation, and transportation routes. The adaptability of the carriers vis-à-vis the transportation needs of the economy is highly limited through state expenditures and the pervasive planning of transportation. As consumers of transportation, enterprises and Combines are unilaterally required to meet levels of performance set by carriers. Because state expenditures in the ways and means of transportation have been seriously neglected, the level of performance of the available transportation is qualitatively as well as quantitatively insufficient.

Despite the sweeping opportunities for directing or ''steering'' at the disposal of the GDR, a satisfactory division of labor among the carriers has yet to be realized. This is complicated further—depending on current economic expediency—by frequently changing ordinances and orientation guidelines that revise, remove, or even reverse those that went before. In the 1960s and 1970s, for example, carriers crucial to the business of foreign exchange (e.g., long-haul trucking) were especially subsidized. Today, on the other hand, emphasis is being put on cutting expenses and conserving energy. Hence follows the pronounced shift in emphasis from roadway freight transportation to inland shipping and rail transport.

An optimal division of labor among the carriers would also require a solution to the transport costs problem (ascertainment of the total costs of a mode of transportation, including the transportation costs and external liabilities—accidents, noise, pollutants). In East Germany, as in most of the industrialized, market-economy states, a satisfactory solution to this problem remains elusive. All the same, for a planned economy like that of the GDR, the most urgent task would be ascertaining the total costs of a mode of transportation, above all in order to direct the division of labor between rail and roadway on the basis of economic criteria.

The GDR's transportation system today (excluding postal service and telecommunications and occupational and individual transportation) has a share of approximately 3 percent of the net product of the producing industry. This percentage reveals in the GDR—as in other industrialized nations—a slightly retrograde trend, which is determined by the proliferation of individual and

Table 3.1
Economic Index for the Transportation Sector[1]

Percentage of:

Year	Net Domestic Product[2]	Investments in the Nat'l Economy[2]	Gross capital Investments in the Industrial sector[2]	Total Workforce
1960	6.5	10.7	20.2	7.2
1970	6.2	8.9	16.9	7.5
1980	5.9	8.6	14.3	7.4
1981	5.9	8.8	14.2	7.4
1982	5.8	7.5	14.0	7.4
1983	5.8	7.3	13.8	7.4
1984	5.7	8.1	13.7	7.4
1985	5.6	9.1	13.5	7.4
1986	5.4	9.9	13.4	7.3

1. Transportation, postal and telecommunications systems.
2. In real terms.

Source: Statistisches Jahrbücher der DDR [GDR statistical yearbooks].

occupational transportation. Likewise as in other countries, in the GDR the economic sector of transportation provides its contribution to the gross national product with a disproportionately high share of the factors of production (Table 3.1). At present, the transportation sector accounts for 7.5 percent of the work force, approximately 9 percent of (gross) fixed assets, and roughly 8 percent of capital expenditures.

BACKGROUND

The essential elements of the prewar history of the transportation sector in the GDR—until 1945 known as the German Empire—are enunciated in Chapter 11 on West Germany. Therefore only a few supplemental observations shall be considered here.

Before World War II the railroad was the most important means of transportation for both cargo and passengers. Its services and its share of total transportation were considerably higher than the continental European average. Through the building and expansion of canals, as well as through the canalization of rivers, inland shipping was able to strengthen its competitive position, although it could not threaten the predominance of the railroad. The development of the railroad infrastructure in the area that is today the GDR was already concluded around the turn of the century.

After World War I the automobile, encouraged by the construction of an efficient automobile industry and, in the period of National Socialism, a forced building of roads—including 3,500 kilometers (km) of autobahns, 1,300 km of which are in the area that is now the GDR—became a serious competitor for railway transportation and inland shipping. The German Railroad, at that time already fully nationalized, received therefore political protection from competition to the extent that roadway transportation of cargo (over 50 km) was subjected to a strict practice of mandatory licensing. At the same time, tariff arrangements (the "Reichskraftwagentarif" of 1936) insured that the costs of railway transportation could not be undercut by roadway rates. Because the economically distressed inland shipping sector was also to be protected, it was likewise incorporated into the legal regulations. These regulations remain today in either German state in their elemental form, if in slightly different variations or of different motivations.

War damages and *Demontage* (through the Soviet Union) in the period directly following the war significantly impaired the performance capacity of the GDR's relatively dense transportation infrastructure. After the division of Germany, the GDR leadership saw the cultivation of an indigenous raw materials industry with heavy industry as its main task. A modernization and expansion of transportation routes was not forthcoming.

In the 1950s and 1960s this proved particularly disadvantageous, not least of all because the building of new industrial centers and the emergence of new population centers not only increased traffic visibly, but also because transportation routes shifted increasingly to a north-south axis. Up until war's end, transportation retained a predominantly east-west orientation with a correspondingly arranged transportation infrastructure. The current structure and performance capacity of the transportation infrastructure is still significantly determined by this legacy. Although this infrastructure is relatively dense—even when compared with those of Western industrialized countries—its structural constitution and its qualitative basis for expansion do not meet the needs now placed on it by the population and by the national economy.

The first comprehensive investments—like the construction of the Havel Canal and the railway beltline around West Berlin—were determined by political objectives. Despite the wholly insufficient capacities of the significantly more important main connections, these had absolute priority. Next to the desire for independence from Hamburg or Stettin (today Szczecin) in maritime shipping, hard currency considerations and the prospect of national prestige contributed to the outfitting of Rostock as an international port. The modernization and expansion of important rail and roadway connections did not begin until the 1970s. A considerable part of this was financed by West Germany (the Federal Republic of Germany), which provided the GDR with investment monies in the billions for the construction of the transit routes (West Berlin–federal territory) (Table 3.2).

In the 1960s and 1970s the conversion from steam to diesel power in the German Railroad (DR) had absolute priority. The main reasons for this trans-

Table 3.2
Transportation Routes (lengths in Ka)

	1960	1970	1980	1981	1982	1983	1984	1985	1986
Railway Lines	16174	14658	14248	14233	14231	14226	14226	14054	14005
Main Lines	7362	7365	7621	7639	7638	7634	7651	7539	7531
Electrified	708	1357	1695	1808	1930	2096	2321	2517	2754
Road Network	--	119931	120528	--	--	--	--	124615	--
Freeways	1378	1413	1750	1783[1]	1881[1]	1881[1]	1850	1850	1855
Highways	10957	11003	11356	11252	11240	11258	11314	11324	11330
County Roads	33144	33313	34369	34424	34340	34242	34097	34040	34025
Municipal Roads	--	74202	73053	--	--	--	--	77401	--
Inland Waterways	2644	2519	2302[2]	2302	2319	2319	2319	2319	2319
Main Waterways	1521	1521	1546	1546	1675	1675	1675	1675	1675
Pipelines	--	681	1301	1301	1301	1301	1301	1307	1307

1) Including freeway feeders.

2) Reduction of inland waterways starting in 1980 due to re-classification of waterways used for inland shipping.

Source: Statistisches Jahrbücher der DDR (GDR statistical yearbooks).

portation policy decision were the then low oil prices as well as the investment costs which, when compared to those involved in electrification, were considerably lower. Because, however, the overall investment in and development of transport capacities for public freight transportation did not meet the increasing demands, bottlenecks were repeatedly encountered with regard to transportation implementation and performance. Because industrial, long-distance roadway freight transportation was then strictly regimented, occupational transportation expanded above all. As firms added their own motor fleets, bottlenecks which appeared with the provision of public transportation—those carriers subject to direct state planning such as the railroad, inland shipping, and industrial roadway freight transportation—could be avoided to some degree.

The rapidly rising crude oil prices characterizing the end of the 1970s hit the transportation sector of the GDR particularly hard and led to a fundamental reconsideration of transportation policy. Since the transportation demands of the national economy and transport costs were also quite high when measured against other industrialized countries, it became the order of the day, beginning in 1980, to lower transportation expenditures and to conserve energy.

The immediate control of the state in freight transportation was subsequently increased considerably. Freight transportation ordinances enacted in the beginning of the 1980s prescribed for firms quantity ceilings (transport limits) depending on the means by, and the routes over, which freight was transported. Those in demand of transportation services had to unilaterally accommodate the qualitatively and quantitatively entirely insufficient level of the transport carriers, in this case, because of the available infrastructure, almost exclusively with the railway. Envisioned as an economic deterrent against unnecessary transports and deadheading, tariff increases averaging about 60 percent hit all carriers, although with differing degrees of severity, depending on existing economic situations. Many concomitant measures, such as the forced electrification of German Railroad arteries, were to support the displacement of transportation to the railway. More than half of the total transportation sector expenditures flow at present to the railway. Despite these investments, bottlenecks and disruptions in transportation implementation are on the increase.

In terms of personal transportation, public transportation has absolute priority. Bus, tram, and local express fares have remained constant in price for decades at about 20 pfennigs. The quality, reliability and punctuality of public transportation, however, could not be effectively improved. This, next to the rising standard of living, could be among the reasons for the considerable expansion of individual transportation in the last decade. Although purchase and maintenance costs of an automobile are relatively high in the GDR, and although the state-controlled auto-repair capacities have remained far short of their demand, the car retains a very high position on the GDR citizen's want list. Because the state keeps the indigenous production of automobiles (Wartburg and Trabant) at a low level and because the hard currency situation discourages much importing of Western makes, the waiting period between ordering a car and its actual delivery is now twelve years or more. The attempt, at least in cities, to grant public transportation absolute priority over individual transportation must be seen as miscarried.

As a result the following can be maintained: 98 percent of transportation services are furnished by publicly owned businesses or firms with state participation. Despite these thoroughgoing opportunities for state guidance, the transportation sector proves again and again to be an area in the economic structure of the GDR which is rich in bottlenecks. The realization of an optimal division of labor among carriers and of a smoothly flowing transportation arrangement is, according to given economic expediencies, discouraged further by frequently changing orientation guidelines which alter, abolish, or even reverse previous ones. A more efficient transportation system would also require a speedy and comprehensive modernization of transportation routes and structures and of the vehicle fleets of all branches of transportation. The investment resources for this are limited in availability, to the point that the transportation sector will remain for the future a weak point in the GDR.

The original railway network (18,500 km) was considerably reduced by war's end. The twofold task—the clearing away of the wreckage and accommodating the sharply increasing demand—could not, on account of a dearth of finances up until today, be satisfactorily fulfilled. The length of track (14,000 km) corresponds roughly to that of the Federal Republic of Germany with a density of 12.9 km per 100 square kilometers (km^2), though only about one-third are double and multi-track lines, and only one-fifth are electrified (in West Germany, roughly two-fifths for both). Because in the past this deficient state of affairs led repeatedly to bottlenecks and because the railroad is now more dominant than before in inland transport, about 40 percent of the total expenditures in the transportation sector are allotted to the railroad infrastructure (Figure 3.1). The primary objective is to improve the insufficient transmissivity of the lines and to shorten the longer-than-average travel times.

Funds apportioned for the road network were spent primarily on maintaining and renovating the existing infrastructure, although a scarcity of investment resources left this action wanting: The condition of road surfaces (too light and hence overly susceptible to frost), the outdated engineering of the thoroughfares as well as the comparatively high quantity of road-level railway grade crossings do not meet the demands of today's road traffic. The trend toward personal transportation—also rapidly increasing in the GDR—is resulting in an increasing frequency of bottlenecks, above all in the newly industrialized and populated South, despite the fact that road density there (overall length/1,000 km^2 of land) is up to four times that of the North. Today's freeway (autobahn) network of just under 1,900 km was for the most part already in existence by war's end. Added were the Leipzig-Dresden (74 km) and Berlin-Rostock (229 km) autobahns, as well as the final section of the autobahn beltline (28 km) around Berlin. With considerable financial assistance from West Germany, autobahns crucial to the transit-traffic between the Federal Republic's main terri-

Figure 3.1
Main Railway Lines

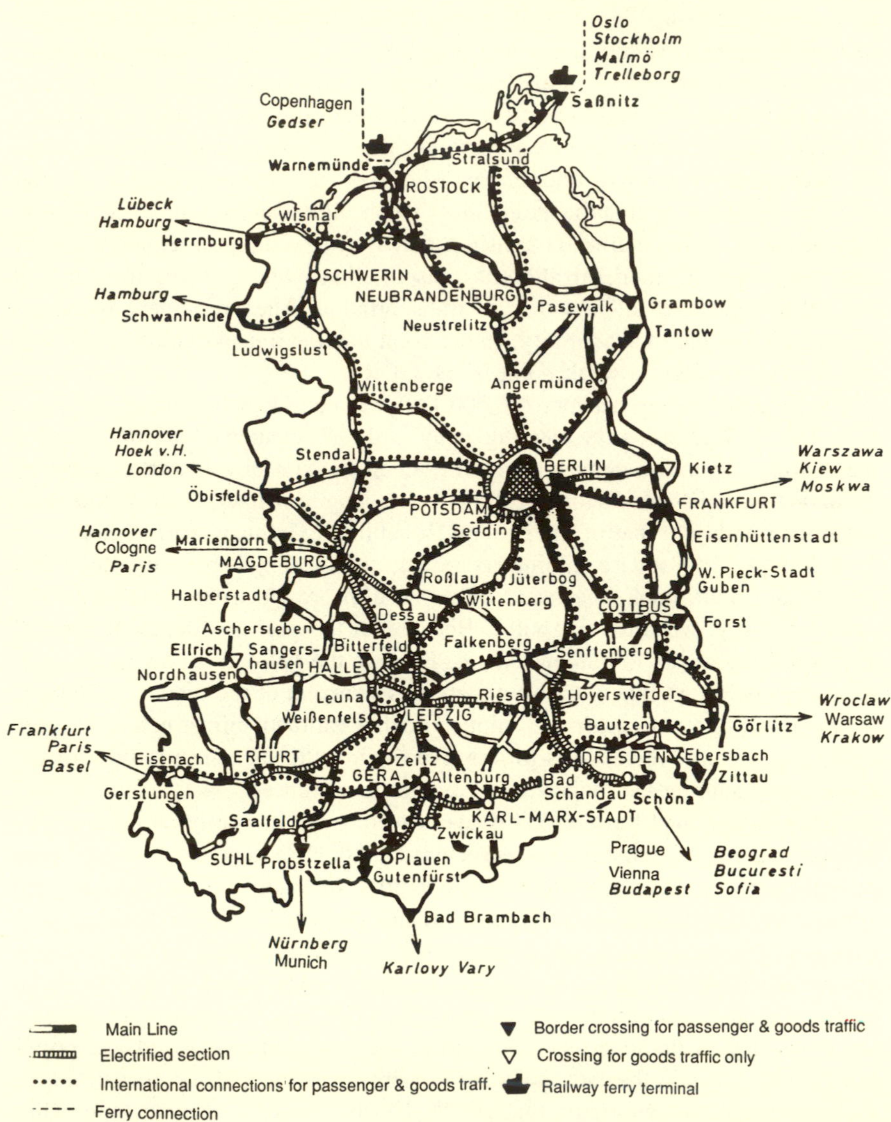

Source: Ökonomische Geographie der DDR [Economic Geography of the GDR]; *Internationale Transport Annalen* [International transportation annals]; *Statistisches Jahrbüch der DDR 1983* [Statistical yearbook of the GDR 1983]; *Kursbuch der Deutschen Reichsbahn 1983/84* [Course book of the East German Railways 1983/84].

Table 3.3
Transportation Route Density, 1986

	Length in km	Km Length per 1000 km² of Area
Railroad Tracks	14005	129
Main Lines	7531	70
Electrified	2754	25
Road Network	124611	1150
Freeways[1]	1855	17
Highways	11330	105
County Roads	34025	314
Municipal Roads[2]	77401	714
Inland Waterways	2319	21
Main Waterways	1675	15
Pipelines	1307	12

1. Including Feeders.
2. Figures from 1985.

Source: Statistisches Jahrbücher der DDR [GDR statistical yearbooks].

tory and West Berlin, which run through the GDR, were renovated, and a new autobahn was built connecting Berlin and Hamburg (Table 3.3).

In the local city transportation of the GDR, the tram *(Straßenbahn)* is the predominant mode of transportation. East Berlin has the only subway, and only a few cities have trolley-buses. The long-range goal orientation for city transportation, which grants electrified means of local transportation absolute priority, has, after decades of deferred renovation measures, led to the step-by-step reconstruction of the tram networks. In addition, in areas of overpopulation the railway has absorbed some of the increased burden on local transportation, although its lanes are in some parts wholly overloaded with long-distance travel and the transportation of freight. The general result is a poorer quality of transportation characterized by peak travel seasons, poor service, unpunctuality of passenger trains, and unreliability. Investment resources available to local transportation projects are required for the most part for the transportation engineering geared toward the opening of new subdivisions, primarily in East Berlin, to the point where hardly anything is left over for a fundamental modernization of the existing transportation infrastructure (Figure 3.2).

In order to supply the chemical industry as well as to cover the increased energy consumption in industrial and population sectors, a pipeline network of 1,300 km was built. However, changes in the energy market, along with the

Figure 3.2
Transportation Routes

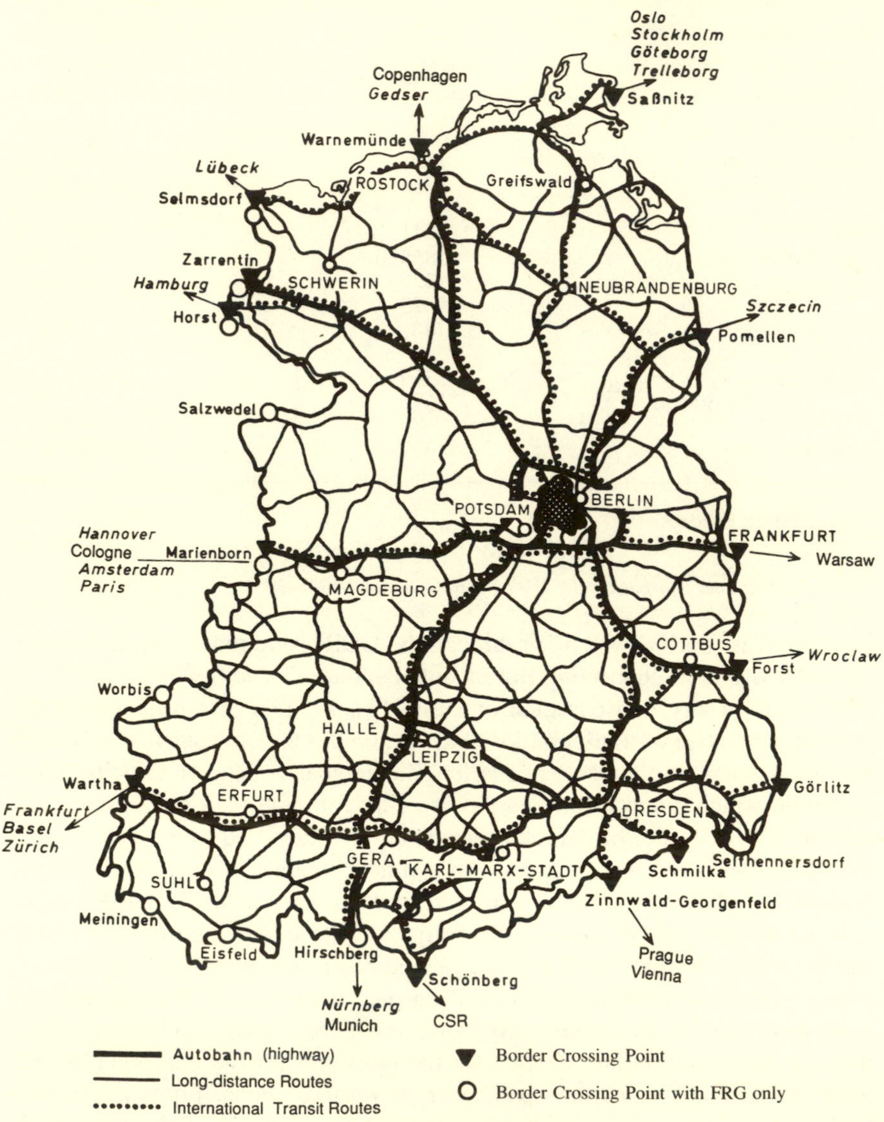

Source: *Ökonomische Geographie der DDR* [Economic Geography of the GDR]; *Internationale Transport Annalen 1976* [International Transportation Annals]; *Statistisches Jahrbüch der DDR 1983* [Statistical yearbook of the GDR 1983].

political target objective of substituting indigenous brown coal (lignite) for petroleum in the generation of energy, have led to the discontinuation of the expansion of the pipeline network.

Today's internal waterway system of approximately 2,300 km, which was already well-constructed in 1945, lost considerable importance because of the altered layout of Berlin and because the Oder and Elbe rivers became border-rivers for the GDR. The points of origin of the most important cargos, like the industrial district of Saxony and the seaport at Rostock, are not accessible by waterway. If inland shipping is to achieve greater significance, as is planned, then a corresponding north-south canal must be built; the network in the industrial districts must be expanded; the regulation of the depth of existing waterways must be maintained; the shipping fleet expanded; and harbor turnaround must be accelerated. The latter would of course require a modernization and expansion of inland harbors, for which—as for the other investment measures—the financial resources are not available.

The seaports of Rostock, Wismar, and Stralsund, which by war's end were totally destroyed or at any rate of no account up until then, were rebuilt and considerably expanded. First and foremost, between 1957 and 1970, Rostock was built with specially earmarked funds (700 million marks) into a modern, multi-functional harbor outfitted to handle bulk and packaged freight, chemicals, grain, oil, and Ro-Ro (Roll on–Roll off) containers. Aside from East Germany's desire for independence in maritime transportation from Hamburg (largest port in West Germany) and Stettin (Poland), foreign exchange considerations and the viewpoint of national prestige figured favorably in this construction. Today, with a yearly turnaround of around 20 million tons, Rostock has achieved front-line status among the Baltic ports (Table 3.4). All three ports in the GDR operate at maximum capacity. In order to reduce the currently still high foreign port turnover, for example via Hamburg, which is dependent on hard currencies, the wharf facilities at Rostock are being built up further.

Parallel to the expansion of the seaports, the merchant fleet was considerably expanded after the GDR's shipyards, which had been extensively decimated in the 1950s through reparation measures, had been employed predominantly toward repairing ships for the USSR (Table 3.5).

In air transportation, Berlin-Schönefeld alone was constructed as an international airport. Despite this concentration, in 1980, for reasons of energy efficiency, inland air transportation was fully discontinued, thus explaining the comparatively low number of aircraft passengers (3.1 million). Since there is no hard currency available for the purchase of Western-made airplanes, Soviet-made planes, which are technologically obsolete, consume high amounts of fuel, and no longer meet internationally accepted standards in terms of noise emission, are deployed. In 1988, however, Western-made airplanes (three Airbuses) were ordered for the first time.

Table 3.4
Cargo Turnaround

In 1,000 Tons								
By Port	1970	1980	1981	1982	1983	1984	1985	1986
Rostock	10138	15275	15563	15432	17730	18916	19674	20341
Wismar	1772	3285	3236	3985	4516	4851	4496	4120
Stralsund	866	719	704	817	881	931	953	1048
Totals	12776	19279	19503	20234	23127	24698	25123	25509
By Cargo Type								
Ores	1138	3753	3648	2567	3167	3652	3988	4091
Metals	1725	3271	3360	3291	3724	3934	3841	3962
Coal, Coke	1148	852	1050	1131	1184	1886	1492	1491
Petroleum[1]	3528	2521	2373	2968	3391	3112	3381	3423
Fertilizer		2984	2860	3211	3539	3677	4117	4332
Oth. Chem. Products	2889	426	353	497	447	524	533	564
Wood		397	499	580	787	818	902	686
Cement	356	435	551	495	555	445	800	794
Grains		2233	2088	2828	2890	2253	1022	1651
Perishable Goods	1046	537	802	577	580	682	866	920
Other Good Types	947	1871	1919	2089	2864	3715	4180	3595
Totals	12776	19279	19503	20234	23127	24698	25123	25509

In Percent								
By Port	1970	1980	1981	1982	1983	1984	1985	1986
Rostock	79.3	79.3	79.7	76.3	76.7	76.6	78.3	79.7
Wismar	13.9	17.0	16.6	19.7	19.5	19.6	17.9	16.2
Stralsund	6.8	3.7	3.7	4.0	3.8	3.8	3.8	4.1
Totals	100	100	100	100	100	100	100	100
By Cargo Type								
Ores	8.9	19.5	18.7	12.7	13.7	14.8	15.9	16.0
Metals	13.5	17.0	17.2	16.3	16.1	15.9	15.3	15.5
Coal, Coke	9.0	4.4	5.4	5.6	5.1	7.6	5.9	5.8
Petroleum[1]	27.6	13.1	12.2	14.7	14.7	12.6	13.5	13.4
Fertilizer		15.5	14.7	15.9	15.3	14.9	16.4	17.0
Oth. Chem. Products	22.6	2.2	1.8	2.5	1.9	2.1	2.1	2.2
Wood		2.1	2.6	2.9	3.4	3.3	3.6	2.7
Cement	2.8	2.3	2.8	2.4	2.4	1.8	3.2	3.1
Grains		11.6	10.7	14.0	12.5	9.1	4.1	6.5
Perishable Goods	8.2	2.8	4.1	2.9	2.5	2.8	3.4	3.6
Other Good Types	7.4	9.7	9.8	10.3	12.4	15.0	16.6	14.1
Totals	100	100	100	100	100	100	100	100

1. Including petroleum products

Source: Statistisches Jahrbücher der DDR [GDR statistical yearbooks].

Table 3.5
Merchant Fleet Ship Inventory[1]

Year	Number of Ships	Gross Registered Tonnage
1960	47	196898
1970	175	940060
1980	192	1305084
1981	177	1290265
1982	173	1171468
1983	174	1223865
1984	172	1201575
1985	171	1222410
1986	174	1344795
By Ship Type 1986:		
Dry Freighters	170	1294643
Mixed-Cargo Freighters	90	651792
Coastal Vessels	14	4905
Bulk-Cargo Ships	22	356357
Fruit Ships	10	56860
Ore/Oil Freighters	3	54810
Ro-Ro Ships	7	25769
Container Ships	23	122260
Tankers	4	50152

1. Excluding Ocean-going and Coastal passenger ships.

Source: Statistisches Jahrbücher der DDR [GDR statistical yearbooks].

SOCIOECONOMIC DIMENSIONS OF THE TRANSPORTATION SYSTEM AND POLICY

In the 1970s, a trend away from railway toward roadway transportation was discernible in the GDR, as in many other European countries. This development was fostered in that the transport capacities in the public freight transportation sector (excluding occupational transportation) did not meet the increasing demands of the economy. This resulted in a pronounced expansion of occupational transportation employing lorries, a mode of transportation that in the beginning did not widely lend itself to central planning in the GDR. The factory lorries are permanently available and have a flexibility in application significantly greater than that of the lorries owned by public transportation operations. Consequently, they demonstrate considerable operational advantages. On the basis of a lower spatial and temporal rate of utilization, and higher fuel consumption (kilojoule per gross ton-kilometer), however, occupational transportation is economically more expensive than rail transport, inland shipping, or public roadway freight transportation.

A further problem facing the GDR planning bodies results from the fact that firms registered an exaggerated transport demand—over and above the actual demand—in order to gain a margin of reserve in the face of continually stringent transport clearances.

These peculiarities led to prohibitive costs per transported unit of power (marks per ton and ton-kilometers [tkm]). In addition, in the late 1970s, the high transport expenses (and volumes) were criticized by politicians and scientists. In 1979 the figures for transported volume (ton and tkm respectively per unit of the gross social product) registered at 5.2 tons per 1,000 marks and 397 tkm per 1,000 marks. By way of example, the same figures for West Germany for the same year registered markedly less at 3.3 and 333, respectively.

Even if these characteristic figures provide no sufficient evidence of the efficiency of a transportation system, the GDR takes them as an incentive to lower transport expenses and volumes through optimization of the conditions of transportation and delivery. This is the major direction of the GDR's transportation policy in the 1980s, and, as a primary objective, it finds expression in all current one- and five-year plans.

At the same time, the GDR had great problems in the power industry in the early 1980s. The drastic increase in costs of petroleum products forced GDR planning bodies to reconsider previous transportation policy. The reevaluations centered on two questions: How can individual carriers transport more with less energy? How can more energy be conserved via a different division of labor among the various carriers involved with inland freight transportation? Since according to GDR estimates the ratio of fuel consumption (kilojoule per gross tonnage/km) among inland shipping, railroad and roadway freight transportation stands at 0.8:1.3, the railroad should assume more of the burdens of the roadway. Up until now, on the basis of natural preconditions—the Baltic ports and the southern industrial districts are not connected with viable waterways—inland shipping could not significantly assume more of the burdens of inland transportation.

The displacement of transportation to the railroad increased its problems considerably. The rail network's deficient state of development, the insufficient capacity of switching arrangements as well as the chronic dearth of manpower—the German Railroad (Deutsche Reichsbahn) continually lacks between 20,000 and 30,000 workers—led repeatedly to serious bottlenecks with negative economic implications in the 1960s and 1970s. The electrification of the railroads is now being hastened to increase its capacity for transmissivity and to insure its ability to assume more of the transportation burden. Here, in the context both of Europe and of the Council for Mutual Economic Assistance (COMECON) the GDR brings up the rear. A significant cause for the forced electrification is to be seen therein, that the electricity needed to power trains can be generated from indigenous brown coal (lignite); whereas the petroleum required for the still-predominating diesel-powered trains (60 percent) must be imported. Besides, the energy efficiency (kilojoule per tonnage/km) of an electric locomotive is nearly three times that of a diesel locomotive.

Many peripheral measures were used in the GDR to support the displacement of transportation burdens to the railroad and, at the same time, to lower transportation expenses (and volume). The inland freight transportation tariffs, which took effect in 1982, increased transport costs for the shipping economy on average between 60 and 70 percent. The tariff increases, intended as economic deterrents against unnecessary shipments and deadheading, applied to all carriers, if in varying degrees of severity. The tariff increases were, at the same time, to effect a displacement of transportation burdens among carriers. Accordingly, roadway freight transportation costs increased by roughly 80 percent, while inland shipping rates, for example, rose only approximately 47 percent.

The concrete goal of all measures was and is, in spite of rising value and quality of produced goods, to hold the total inland freight shipping amounts (tonnage) and capacities (volume) constant until 1990 and, where possible, to decrease them. Lorry service shall be limited more rigorously than before to local transportation, cross-border transportation, feeder service (to and from railway stations, rail connections and inland freight shipping installations) and special transports. In fact, 5 to 6 million tons per year were shifted to the railway until 1990. A proposed parallel to this is the yearly displacement of 1 million tons of rail and roadway cargo transports to inland shipping. This would increase the railway's percentage of transport service by almost four-fifths and that of inland shipping's by almost 5 percent, while the proportion of roadway transport service would diminish by nearly 50 percent.

The central direction of transportation policy for passenger traffic centers also on energy conservation and the lowering of transport costs. While a multifaceted apparatus can, as shown, be implemented toward the realization of these goals in the realm of freight transportation, such opportunities are much more limited vis-à-vis passenger traffic: More than half of the transportation capacity falls in the category of personal transportation. Even in a socialist country, personal transportation is not amenable to planning and is therefore left out of consideration. Although personal transportation is taken into consideration in the context of the longer-range planning (general transportation plan, general transportation layout) that coordinates development plans with cities and communities, it is no longer considered in the context of the one-year and five-year plans. In these, although performance data for the production of personal automobile tires as well as for the maintenance of automobiles are brought forth, information about the growth in the number of automobiles or other reference guidelines having to do with personal transportation are not to be had. Appeals to the ''socialist consciousness'' of GDR citizens not to overrely

Table 3.6
Vehicle Inventory

	Vehicle Inventory (in 1,000)			Vehicle Density (Vehicles per 1,000)		
Year	Autos[1]	Motorcycles & Scooters	Totals	Autos	Motorcycles &Scooters[2]	Totals
1960	299	848	1147	1.7	4.9	6.7
1970	1160	1374	2534	6.8	8.1	14.9
1980	2678	1305	3983	16.0	7.8	23.8
1981	2812	1304	4116	16.8	7.8	24.6
1982	2922	1302	4224	17.5	7.8	25.3
1983	3020	1307	4327	18.1	7.8	25.9
1984	3157	1315	4472	18.9	7.9	26.8
1985	3306	1319	4625	19.9	7.9	27.8
1986	3462	1322	4784	20.8	8.0	28.8

1. Personal and Pick-ups.
2. Excluding mopeds.

Source: Statistisches Jahrbücher der DDR [GDR statistical yearbooks].

on the automobile at least in city traffic cannot replace an integrated transportation policy that coordinates individual measures for the various modes of transportation with a comprehensive general concept embracing all carriers.

The development and structure of personal transportation in the GDR has been shaped by the rise in the standard of living, which goes along with increasing individual motorization and the rising number of citizens gainfully employed and of pupils and students. Aside from that, other factors, such as increasing leisure time, suburbanization, and concentration processes and tendencies in the health, social, and educational systems as well as in trade and industry, have had effects. The consequences of these changes are such that the distance covered per inhabitant has nearly doubled over twenty years. Considering the distances covered, the increase in mobility was even greater.

Although automobile transportation is very expensive in the GDR, its degree of motorization is far and away the highest in COMECON (cars per 1,000 inhabitants). Currently, almost half of all private households in the GDR own a car (Table 3.6). The average net income today amounts to about 900 marks. The least-expensive car, the Trabant, costs nearly 10,000 marks. The Wartburg, another GDR-made car which, since 1988, includes a VW Rabbit engine, costs about 30,000 marks. Neither make meets the Western automobile purchasers' standards for quality, comfort, or pollution control (in terms of exhaust emissions), which means that they cannot be sold in Western countries and that they are increasingly met with distribution difficulties within COMECON. Since imported automobiles are significantly more expensive, however, GDR citizens are dependent on makes indigenously produced.

Running an automobile is also comparatively expensive. One liter of ethyl fuel costs 1.65 marks, although the price has remained constant for years (regular grade: 1.50 marks). A further problem for automobile owners is maintenance. As a result of the long waiting periods and the high prices of new cars, available cars are kept exceptionally long and are accordingly in need of repair (average working life is fifteen years or more; many autos are over twenty years old). Vehicle maintenance capacity, however, lags far behind increased demands. Even if the increased performance levels in this service area provided for in the current five-year plan should be realized, there could still be potential bottlenecks.

As a final consequence it remains to be shown that even socialist countries like the GDR were not able to realize alternative transportation concepts. The price and tariff configuration for public and individual means of transportation alone satisfies the transportation policy goal prioritizing public transportation. Travel fares for inland transportation via train, bus, and local city transportation services have remained constant and very low for decades. The next-to-nothing fares, above all for local transportation, necessitate continually rising subsidization (almost 5 billion marks in 1986). This price configuration is particularly emphasized in the GDR as an important component of social policy. Nevertheless, the automobile has come to be used (also in the GDR) on a daily basis and has thus assumed the character of a means of mass transportation. In cities and areas of congestion, socialist transportation policy shapers limit themselves to promoting public transportation and making it more efficient. However, verbal testimonies aside, substantial improvements in local public transportation are not in sight.

Among many others, goals in this direction include the better coordination of public transportation (train, bus, city-local), the harmonizing of different networks, the elimination of parallel lines, the integration of development and control systems between long-distance and regional transportation, carpooling, and the creation of footpaths and promenades. The building of new subdivisions almost exclusively on the outskirts of cities necessitates at this stage the employment of some means of transportation along paths set aside earlier for pedestrian and bicycle traffic. The question as to how public transportation is to stabilize the demand recurrent in all one- and five-year plans for a safe, punctual, and reliable means of transportation to and from work without significant investments in local transportation is not answered by transportation policymakers in the GDR. Aside from many verbal commitments from politicians, substantial improvements in local public transportation are far from being realized.

RECENT TRENDS AND FUTURE PROSPECTS

Characteristic of the GDR transportation system is, as just suggested, the absolute preeminence of the railroad. Currently, the railroad contributes to a good one-third of transport volume (tons) and to nearly three-fourths of transportation performance (tkm). In 1986 the East German railroad reached statistically approximately the same level of performance as that of West Germany (1986: 305 million ton; 61 billion tkm). This is an astonishing achievement when one considers that the GDR's line network is only around half the size of that of West Germany, and more poorly outfitted. The German Railroad furnishes transportation for mineral oil, petroleum products, construction material, semi-processed and finished goods, and mixed cargo which, in Western countries, is being assumed more by inland shipping and trucking.

Roadway freight transportation, above all occupationsl transportation, which expanded in the 1970s also in the GDR, has been cut back strongly since around 1980 by way of legal, administrative, and tariff-oriented measures. The number of trucks at the disposal of firms for their own transport needs was sharply decreased. Concomitantly, in recent years the power of disposition enjoyed by firms over their own trucks has been drastically withdrawn. They will be needed to fulfill transport needs outside the firms. The truck transportation of freight sank between 1980 and 1986 from around 67 percent to 57 percent in terms of amounts of goods transported (tonnage) and from 25 percent to 19 percent in terms of goods transported over distance (tkm).

With percentages of 2 percent (tonnage) and 3 percent (tkm), inland shipping is an insignificant carrier. Because of the geographical situation of the waterways, these percentages will not change, even if this energy efficient means of transportation were to be involved more vigorously in the responsibilities of transportation (Table 3.7).

Because of the stagnating and declining use of petroleum and petroleum products, oil pipelines are losing in significance in terms of inland transport.

While transportation indicators (tkm) for maritime transport showed a retrograde trend up to 1985, 1986 saw a marked increase (Table 3.8). This was effected first of all by an expansion of the areas covered. The goods turnover in the seaports (Rostock, Wismar, Stralsund) increased continually to today's figure of 25.5 million tons. This is double the turnover of 1970. Rostock alone accounts for four-fifths of this. Rostock's turnover volume thus approximates two-fifths of that of Hamburg, the largest port in the Federal Republic in 1986.

In terms of personal transportation, the GDR registers—as do many Western states—an increasing stagnation and/or decline in the public transportation sector (train, bus, subway, rapid local transit, tram). Conversely, individual transportation registers high rates of growth. Although the GDR contributes considerable resources to public means of transportation toward insuring stable fares for local and long-distance transportation, this could not stay the advance of individual transportation. Although public transportation in GDR cities still outweighs other means of transportation (the tram is the primary means of transportation), the relationship there, parallel to increasing motorization, is reversing itself (Table 3.9).

For a period of fifteen to twenty years, long-range plans include transporta-

Table 3.7
GDR Transport Performance for Inland Shipping[1]

		1960	1970	1980	1981	1982	1983	1984	1985	1986
Commodity Volume	Million Tons	571	755	1099	1064	986	964	954	959	946
Railroad	Percentages	45.7	43.8	28.3	29.6	32.7	33.8	35.4	36.3	36.6
Inland Shipping		2.4	1.8	1.5	1.6	1.7	1.8	2.0	1.9	2.0
Road Freight Transport[2]		51.9	61.4	66.4	65.1	61.7	60.5	58.7	57.8	57.4
Local Transport		50.6	58.3	62.4	61.5	58.5	57.5	56.2	55.3	54.7
Long-Distance Transport		1.3	3.1	4.0	3.6	3.2	3.0	2.5	2.5	2.7
Pipelines		—	2.0	3.8	3.7	3.9	3.9	3.9	4.0	4.0
Transport Performance	Million tkm	40114	58260	84576	82805	77224	76986	78060	80661	80956
Railroad	Percentages	81.9	71.2	66.7	67.3	69.9	71.2	72.5	72.2	72.7
Inland Shipping		5.6	4.1	2.6	2.8	3.0	3.2	3.4	3.0	3.1
Road Freight Transport[2]		12.5	21.0	24.8	24.1	21.0	20.0	18.6	18.7	18.9
Local Transport		9.5	13.6	14.7	14.7	13.1	12.3	11.8	11.6	11.7
Long-Distance Transport		3.0	7.4	10.1	9.4	7.9	7.6	6.8	7.1	7.2
Pipelines		—	3.7	5.9	5.8	6.1	5.6	5.5	5.6	5.3

1) Excluding maritime shipping and air transportation.
2) Including occupational transportation (percentages of total transportation in 1960: 26.7% for commodity volume and 5.9% for transport performance; 1986: 42.4% and 9.3% respectively.

Source: Statistisches Jahrbücher der DDR [GDR statistical yearbooks].

Table 3.8
Volume of Commodity Transport for Maritime Shipping by Commodity Type (in 1,000 Tons)

	Total Goods				Dry Goods				Tank Goods			
Year	Totals	Ex-port	Im-Port	For Third	Totals	Ex-port	Im-port	For Third	Totals	Ex-port	Im-port	For Third
1960	1375	315	773	287	1188	315	617	256	187	--	156	31
1970	8511	446	4139	3925	6597	446	2578	3572	1914	--	1561	353
1980	12553	698	5030	6824	9758	698	3939	5120	2795	--	1091	1700
1981	12525	609	4008	7908	9951	404	4002	5545	2574	205	6	2638
1982	11018	1319	4941	4758	9144	691	3716	4737	1874	628	1225	21
1983	11923	1840	5245	4837	10348	885	4629	4832	1575	955	616	5
1984	12771	1395	6379	4996	10923	1232	4705	4984	1848	163	1674	12
1985	11403	1033	5700	4671	10336	885	4793	4660	1067	148	907	11
1986	11582	1020	6167	4395	11078	917	5776	4385	504	103	391	10

Source: Statistisches Jahrbücher der DDR [GDR statistical yearbooks].

Table 3.9
Personal Transportation Index[1]

Mode of Transportation	1960	1970	1980	1981	1982	1983	1984	1985	1986
	millions of persons transported								
Total Transportation	4388	5479	7594	7710	7787	8014	8254	8467	8617
	in percentages								
Public Transportation	82.0	63.5	54.0	53.1	52.1	51.5	50.4	49.4	48.5
By Rail[2]	21.0	7.5	5.5	5.3	5.4	5.3	5.1	4.9	4.6
By Bus[3]	16.0	20.8	16.2	15.8	14.8	14.2	13.8	13.4	13.1
City/Local[4]	45.0	35.2	32.2	32.0	31.9	32.0	31.5	31.1	30.8
By Plane	0.0	0.0	0.0	0.0	0.0	0.0	0.0	0.0	0.0
Individual Transportation[5]	18.0	36.5	46.0	46.9	47.9	48.5	49.6	50.6	51.5
	billion passenger-kilometers								
Total Transportation	52.3	80.2	111.8	113.5	116.0	119.0	123.1	128.9	135.0
	in percentages								
Public Transportation	74.4	53.6	49.9	48.5	47.0	46.2	45.3	44.0	42.5
By Rail[2]	41.0	17.7	17.3	16.7	17.2	16.7	16.3	15.4	14.5
By Bus[3]	19.0	21.6	18.7	17.7	15.6	15.2	14.6	14.2	13.8
City/Local[4]	14.0	12.2	10.3	10.4	10.4	10.8	10.9	10.9	10.7
By Plane	0.4	2.1	3.7	3.7	3.8	3.5	3.5	3.5	3.5
Individual Transportation[5]	25.6	46.4	51.1	51.5	53.0	53.8	54.7	56.0	57.5

1. Excluding inland and maritime shipping.
2. Excluding rapid city/local transport (S-Bahn).
3. Overland transportation including bus and occupational transportation.
4. Tram, bus, trolley bus, subway, rapid city/local transport.
5. Transportation with cars and pick-ups, motorcycles, scooters, and mopeds.

Source: Statistisches Jahrbücher der DDR [GDR statistical yearbooks].

tion development guidelines for the GDR territory at large and for smaller regional entities (districts, cities) and the subsequent consequences these plans may have for the existing transportation infrastructure. Growing out of these long-range objectives, the focal points for midrange planning—the five-year plans (like goods and passenger transportation demand, demand for investment, demand for manpower, materiel and energy, characteristic figures for transport expenses and volumes, measures for the economic integration with the socialist partner-countries)—are developed and passed into law by decree of the People's Congress (Volkskammer) (Figure 3.3).

The leading challenge in all these plans for the years up to the turn of the next century is to lower further transport costs and to conserve still more energy. This means a continued displacement of transportation to the railroad. In terms of implementation, however, this has been met today with great difficul-

Figure 3.3
Planning Organization

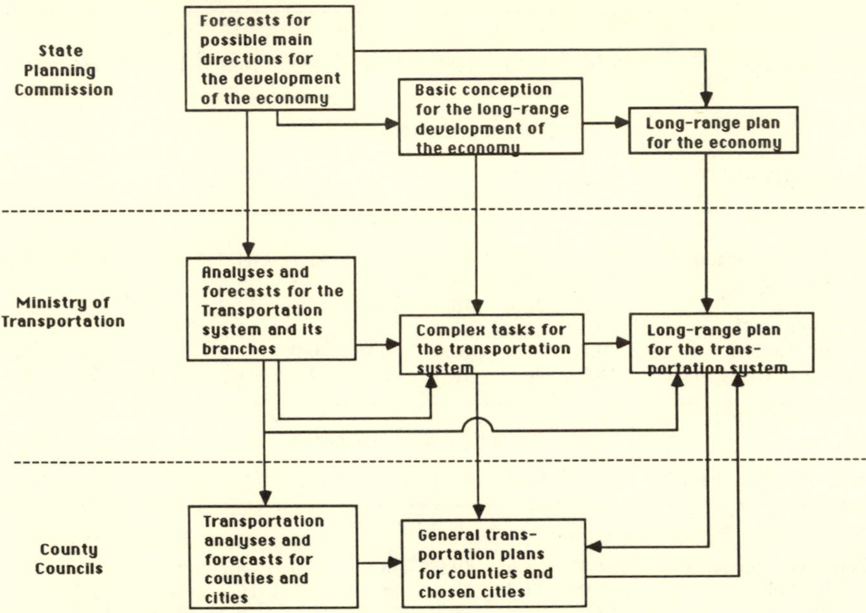

Source: Autoren Kollectiv, *Ökonomie des Transports* [Transport economy], Bd. 1, vol. 1 (Berlin, GDR: Transpress VEB Verlag für Verkehrswesen, 1977), p. 197.

ties. Although transportation displacements in the first half of the 1980s enabled the lowering of transport costs and energy consumption to a considerable extent, this policy of conservation led to a pronounced worsening of transportation services for the cargo industry. Transport times are too long; cargos may be delivered unpunctually or not at all and are often damaged through transportation. As an all-purpose means of transportation, the railroad is limited in its capacity to set aside the necessary transportation clearances even for specialty cargos of the chemical and construction industries. The GDR's economy pays for the administrative lowering of fuel demand and transport costs with considerable losses in productivity.

Since the GDR leadership recognized the fact that the previous approach to energy and transportation economizing has led to an impasse, innovation among the carriers and in the economy are now being emphasized. Envisioned is an overall economic approach designed to attain a lowering of transport costs and an increase in (work) productivity via an efficient organization of inner and interfirm transportation, turnover, and storage processes. Railroad bottlenecks in particular are to be eliminated through innovative measures. This will involve the enlargement of the electrified network of lines, the elimination of shortcomings in signaling and safety technology, the employment of efficient electric locomotives, increasing the efficiency of automobile operation, increasing container transportation as well as a heavier utilization of computer technology and micro-electronics in the "steering" or controlling of storage and turnaround processes as well as the actual transportation. The firms of the cargo industry shall reform the entire working process according to logistical criteria especially because it is hoped that the input and output processes of this industry still hold considerable resources for increasing efficiency. Since indigenous technologies for comprehensive innovations are not available, it is endeavored to keep abreast of transportation innovations of other countries, above all Western countries. It remains to be seen whether the GDR will be successful, at least on a mid-term basis, in developing more efficiently its transportation processes.

For the framework of planning in the economy, which, in view of problems facing the power industry, demands a marked reduction in the consumption of petroleum products, personal transportation remains a serious problem. In order to curtail the unlimited proliferation of personal transportation—as seen in Western countries—the improvement of the performance, punctuality, accessibility, comfort, and service of public means of transportation is sought. This demand has found expression, obviously without success, in all one- and five-year plans since 1950. Because available investment resources are scarce, it is doubtful that the quality of public occupational, school, and travel transportation can be distinctly raised. It is to be expected that, even in the GDR's cities, individual transportation will continue to expand.

The result can be counted on that the general scarcity of investment resources will henceforth stand in the way of a speedy, uninterrupted, and comprehensive modernization and expansion of both the traffic lanes and the vehicle fleets of all transportation sectors. Much points to the fact that planning for the carriers as well as the commitment of investment resources for the coming years will have to be oriented almost exclusively toward short-range development of demand and currently prevailing exigencies. It may well be the case that a significant increase in the efficiency of the transportation system in the GDR is not to be realized in the foreseeable future.

Of the approximately 490,000 people employed in the transportation sector (excluding postal and telecommunications systems), about 250,000 (51 percent) work for the German Railroad and about 175,000 (36 percent) in public roadway transportation, and here first and foremost for city local transportation firms (subway, bus, rapid local transit [S-bahn], and tram) (Table 3.10). Inland shipping (2 percent), maritime shipping (5 percent), civilian air transport (2 percent), and private transportation firms (1 percent) are insignificant by comparison (Figure 3.4).

The ascending scientific generation recruited for the transportation system comes for the most part from the "Friedrich List" College of Transportation (Hochschule für Verkehrswesen) in Dresden, founded in 1952. The college is divided into six scientific sections: Marxism/Leninsim; transportational and in-

Table 3.10
Manpower in the Transportation Sector[1]

Year	Trans. Total	State-Owned: Totals	Railroad[2]	Public Road Trans.[3]	Inland Shipping	Maritime Shipping	Civilian Air Trans.
1960	373355	358340	245914	55263	6869	4443	--
1970	435973	422141	258604	110445	5943	14950	4283
1980	469457	461660	241782	162150	7773	22035	6976
1981	470512	462821	242956	163694	7942	22276	7215
1982	478680	471318	247937	166325	8116	22276	7553
1983	483216	467067	252213	166460	8261	22198	7335
1984	485393	478394	252816	168633	8340	22928	7375
1985	488471	481427	251414	172085	8391	23346	7437
1986	487807	480834	248773	173723	8401	23732	7465

1. Excluding Postal and Telecommunications systems.
2. German Railroad.
3. Including shipping agencies and city-local transportation.

Source: Statistisches Jahrbücher der DDR [GDR statistical yearbooks].

dustrial management and vehicle technology; technical transportation cybernetics; transportation architecture; mathematics; computer engineering and natural sciences. Since 1971, a section for military transportation and communications has been affiliated with the college.

Of the total 620,000 employed in the transportation sector (including postal and telecommunications systems; a breakdown into both categories is not possible), roughly 85 percent have completed a course of vocational or professional training. Around 3 percent have graduated from a university, 6 percent possess vocational college degrees, 4 percent have earned professional master certificates (Meisterablschluß), and 71 percent hold skilled labor certificates.

TRANSPORTATION POLICY ORGANIZATION AND PROCESS

The highest administrative body is the Ministry of Transportation (MfV). By order of the GDR cabinet council (Ministerrat), it is responsible for the central administration and planning of the entire transportation system (Figure 3.5). Centrally administered above all are transportation sectors whose emphasis lies in long-distance or international transportation or which have some particular strategic significance: The German Railroad (DR) as the public railway transportation carrier (direct administration through the Ministry of Transportation); maritime shipping (Central Administration for Maritime Transport in the Ministry of Transportation); inland shipping (Central Administration for Inland Shipping and Waterways in the MfV); roads (Central Administration for Roads

Figure 3.4
Administrative Organization of the Transportation Sector

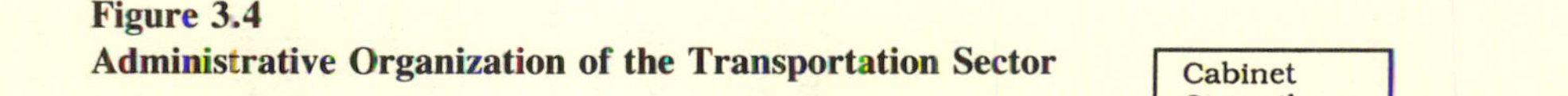

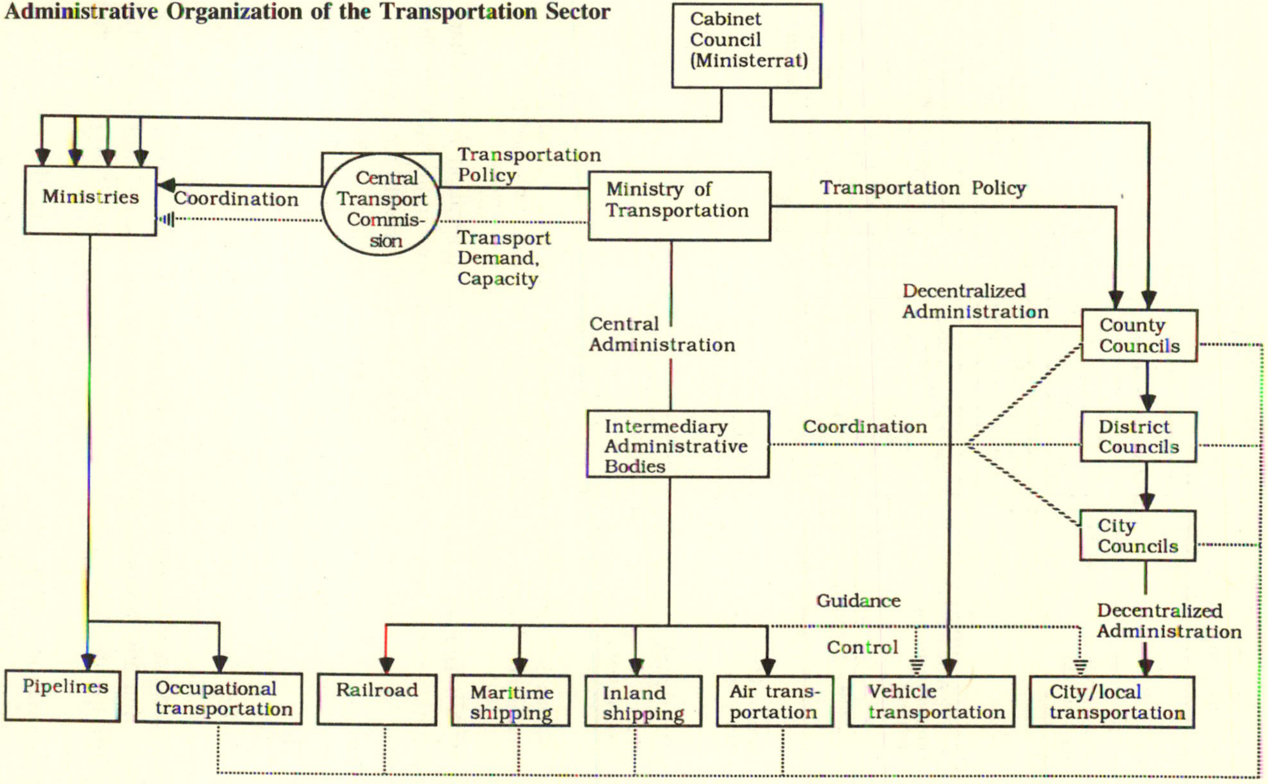

Source: Autoren Kollectiv, *Ökonomie des Transports* [Transport economy], Bd. 1, vol. 1 (Berlin, GDR: Transpress VEB Verlag für Verkehrswesen, 1977), p. 162.

Figure 3.5
Planning and Administrative Bodies in the Transportation Sector

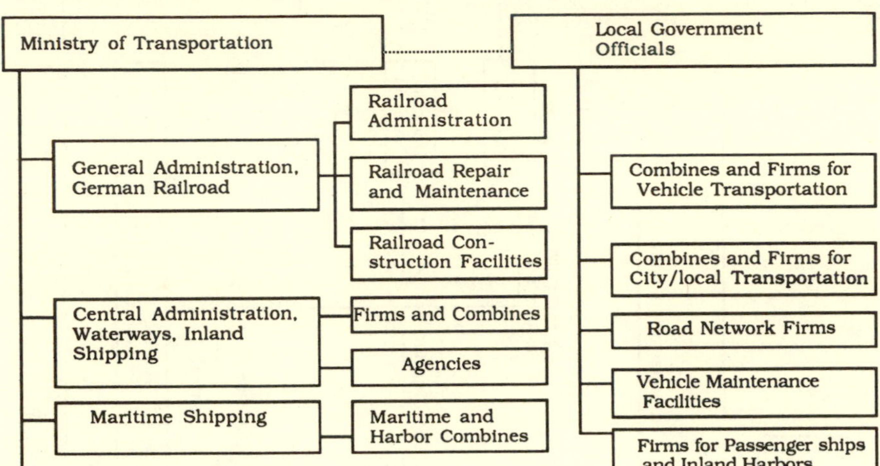

Source: Autoren Kollectiv, *Sozialistische Volkswirtschaft—Hochschullehrbuch* [Socialist economy—university text] (Berlin, GDR: Verlag Die Wirtschaft, 1989), p. 385.

in the MfV); and air transportation (Central Administration for Civilian Air Transportation in the MfV). The central administrations in the MfV are directed each by a deputy minister out of a circle of nine deputies to the minister.

A decentralized adminstration is used in those transportation sectors with a predominantly territorial significance (such as motor and local city transportation). Their Combines (Transportation Combines) are subordinate to councils at the county, district, and city levels. They are, of course, subject likewise to the guidance, control, and direction of the Ministry of Transportation. By way of transportation planning, balancing of accounts and other coordinating measures, occupational transportation is incorporated by the central and territorial transportation administrating bodies as well as the district-level transportation Combines toward the fulfillment of the totality of public (state) transportation obligations.

Transportation committees play an important role in the coordination of transportation-sector implementation as well as in the cooperation of all administrative organs, Combines, and firms. Members include colleagues from state agencies, industrial firms, Combines, and transportation carriers.

The transportation committees deliberate and decide on measures aimed at improving occupational transportation. They look at methodological questions involved in the investigation, planning, and balancing of transportation demand, on the division of responsibilities among carriers, on the development and utilization of transport capacities (including occupational transportation), and over short-range operative measures for transportation sector implementation.

In the interest of controlled management of the transportation sector, the GDR has developed, aside from the long-range plans, a variety of short-range plans (quarterly, monthly, ten-day, and day plans) as well as year plans. The year plans are significantly more precise than the middle- and long-range plans and contain the goals (transport performance for all branches and firms in the transportation sector) and the means necessary for their realization.

Toward the end of more direct implementation of transportation responsibilities in consideration of fluctuations in yearly transport demand, the year plan is broken down into operational plans (for quarters, months, days and for brigades, etc.). These play an important role above all with regard to the German Railroad. The most important legal regulation is the Freight Transportation Ordinance. This law embraces the fundamental principles for the planning, administration, and organization of public freight transportation, for the division of responsibilities and the joint operation of railroad, inland shipping, and trucking as well as the fundamental principles for the cooperation of transportation carriers and clients.

The Balancing of Transportation (*Transportbilanz Anordnung*, March 1982) is an important planning instrument. It contains decisions concerning the balancing of necessary transportation performance with the transportation capacities of the individual carriers. The working out of the national data in tons and transportation performance (tkm) contained in the one-year and five-year plans is based on these transportation balances and is calculated on the following levels of output: The MfV calculates the transport balance of the GDR, the councils of the counties for that of the counties (including the German Railroad and inland shipping), and the councils of the districts for that of the districts.

As far as personal transportation is concerned, only the areas of public transportation are included in concrete planning. This is all the more surprising in that this branch accounts for the greatest share of energy consumption and, as such, would present itself as most in need of energy-saving measures.

REFERENCES

Autoren Kollektiv, *Die Bauwirtschaft der DDR* [GDR construction industry] (Berlin, GDR: Transpress VEB Verlag für Verkehrswesen, 1984).

———, *Ökonomie des Transports,* Bd. 1 und 2, [Transport economy, vol. 1 and 2] (Berlin, GDR: Transpress VEB Verlag für Verkehrswesen, 1977).

———, *Ökonomische Geographie der Deutschen Demokratischen Republik* [Economic geography of the German Democratic Republic] (Gotha/Leipzig: VEB Hermann Haack, Geographisch-Kartolographische Anstalt, 1977).

———, *Reproduktion und Verkehr* [Reproduction and transportation] (Berlin, GDR: Transpress VEB Verlag für Verkehrswesen, 1982).

———, *Sozialistiche Volkswirtschaft—Hochshullehrbuch* [Socialist economy—University text] (Berlin, GDR: Verlag Die Wirtschaft, 1989).

Buck, H. F., "Rationalisierungsschwerpunkte im DDR-Verkehrswesen bis 1985" [Rationalization focal points in the GDR transportation system to 1985], *Deutschland Archiv,* nr. 5 (Köln: Verlag Wissenschaft und Politik, 1981).

Bundesministerium für innerdeutsche Beziehungen, "Materialien zum Bericht zur Lage der Nation im geteilten Deutschland 1987" [Materials for the report on the state of the nation in divided Germany 1987] (Bonn: 1987).

DDR Verkehr, Zeitschrift für Komplexe Fragen der Leitung und Planung des Verkehrswesens [GDR transportation, (monthly) periodical for complex questions of administration and planning in the transportation system] (Berlin, GDR: Transpress VEB Verlag für Verkehrswesen).

Deutsches Institut für Wirtschaftsforschung, *Handbuch DDR-Wirtschaft,* 4, Auflage [Handbook of the economy of the German Democratic Republic] (Reinbeck bei Hamburg: Rowohlt Taschenbuch Verlag GmbH, 1985).

Die Straße, Zeitschrift für Forschung und Praxis des Straßenwesens [The road, (monthly) periodical for road network research and practice] (Berlin, GDR: Transpress VEB Verlag für Verkehrswesen).

Franke, P., et al. *Transportpreise* [Transportation prices] (Berlin, GDR: Transpress VEB Verlag für Verkehrswesen, 1971).

German Institute for Economic Research, *Handbook of the Economy of the German Democratic Republic* (Westmead, Farnborough and Hampshire, England: Saxon House, Teakfield, 1979).

Günther, J., *Transportstatistik* [Transportation statistics] (Berlin, GDR: Transpress VEB Verlag für Verkehrswesen, 1970).

Hofmann, K., *Ökonomik, Organisation und Planung der Eisenbahn* [The economics, organization, and planning of the railroad] (Berlin, GDR: Transpress VEB Verlag für Verkehrswesen, 1968).

Hopf, R., "Transport- und Nachrichtenwesen" [Transportation and communications systems], *DDR und Osteuropa—ein Handbuch* [GDR and Eastern Europe—a handbook] (Opladen: Leske & Budrich GmbH, 1981).

———, "DDR-Güterverkehr zurück zur Schiene" [GDR freight transportation back to the rails], *Wochenbericht des DIW* [DIW weekly report], Nr. 8 (1981).

———, "DDR Individualverkehr nimmt weiter zu" [Individual transportation increases further], *Wochenbericht des DIW* [DIW weekly report] nr. 15 (1982).

———, "Verkehrswesen" [The transportation system], *DDR-Handbuch* [GDR handbook] (Köln: Bundesministerium für Innerdeutsche Beziehungen, Verlag Wissenschaft und Politik, 1985).

Internationale Transport-Annalen [International transportation annals] (Prague: NADAS; Berlin, GDR: Transpress; Warsaw: WkL, annual; appeared until the early 1980s).

Kramer, E., *Die Entwicklung des Verkehrswesens in der DDR* [The development of the transportation system in the GDR] (Berlin, GDR: Transpress VEB Verlag für Verkehrswesen, 1978).

Lexikon der Wirtschaft—Verkehr [Lexicon of the economy—transportation] (Berlin, GDR: Transpress VEB Verlag für Verkehrswesen, 1972).

Mieth, G., G. Teßmann, and J. Matthäi, *Transportpreise* [Transportation prices] (Berlin, GDR: Transpress VEB Verlag für Verkehrswesen, 1981).

Rehbein, G., *Ökonomie des Nachrichtenwesens* [Economy of the communications system] (Berlin, GDR: Transpress VEB Verlag für Verkehrswesen, 1979).

Schneider, R., ''Eisenbahngüterverkehr—Realisierung der Aufgabenstellung nach dem X. Parteitag der SED'' [Railway freight transportation—realization of objectives after the tenth party congress of SED (Social Unity Party of Germany), *FS-Analysen,* nr. 3, (Berlin: Forschungsstelle für gesamtdeutsche wirtschaftliche und soziale Fragen, 1985).

———, ''Innovationen auf dem Gebiet des Eisenbahnverkehrs in der DDR'' [Innovations in the area of railway transportation in the GDR], *FS-Analysen,* nr. 2 (1987).

Statistisches Jahrbücher der DDR [GDR statistical yearbooks].

Tismer, J. F., ''Wirtschaftspolitische Strategie der Intensivierung im Binnengüterverkehr der DDR in der 80er Jahren'' [Political-economic strategy of the intensification of inland freight transportation in the GDR in the 1980s], *FS-Analysen,* nr. 5 (1982).

Transpress Lexikon Eisenbahn [Transpress railroad lexicon] (Berlin, GDR: Transpress VEB Verlag für Verkehrswesen, 1981).

Weymar, T., ''Das Auto—Statussymbol auch im Sozialismus'' [The automobile—status symbol in socialism also], *Deutschland Archiv,* nr. 3 (1977).

———, *Im Trabi zur Sonne, zur Freiheit* [In the Trabi (''Trabant'') to the sun, to freedom] (Köln: Verlag Wissenschaft und Politik, 1985).

Wissenschaftliche Zeitschrift (WZ) [Scientific journal (quarterly)] (Dresden: Hochschule für Verkehrswesen ''Friedrich List'').

4

FRANCE

Mitchell P. Strohl

BACKGROUND

Down through the centuries the nearly constant size of France, as well as its physical and political geography, have heavily influenced centrality of political direction and public expectation. From a quite early time there has been the tendency toward a bureaucratic state, conferring high social regard upon the able administrator and the technically competent. There has developed a system of depersonalized control through public law and public oversight. But public ownership and operation have emerged much more recently, and that story is still unfolding at the present writing. Law making and decision making nearly always take place after study by nonpolitical experts as well as by consultative councils in which multiple and often conflicting interests are represented.

Within the last forty years there has been acknowledged the need for decentralization of some of the aspects of economic planning and public finance decision making. The highly rigid model of bureaucratic centrality no longer meets the more complex demand and expectations of modern French society. The first step toward decentralization, taken in 1955, was to superimpose on the map new geographical subdivisions, the Region, of which there are twenty-three. It is through the Region and the mechanics of the PLAN that most decentralization of economic decision making has evolved.

Lying on the western edge of the European maritime peninsula, France has a comparatively large and fertile land area relative to population. With nearly

20 percent of the country's inhabitants living in the Paris metropolitan commuting zone, the Ile de France, the population is indeed unevenly spread. Marseilles, the next largest city, is only one-fifth the size of Paris. The distance between them is 863 rail-line kilometers. The country is shaped like a hexagon whose maximum transportation dimension, from Calais on the Strait of Dover to the southeastern coastal city of Menton, is 1,419 rail-line kilometers. Distances in France can now usually be traveled in one day by air, highway, or rail, but the distances can be sufficiently great to generate the cost and management problems of medium- and long-distance movement.

Except for the Massif Central, most of the mountainous obstructions to movement lie along the eastern and southern borders: Ardennes, Vosges, Jura, Alps, and Pyrenees. Except for the Rhône and Garonne, most of the waterway systems are in the north and northeast of the country.

Important in the development of the French transportation system generally, and in the earlier orientation of policy, has been the strategic position of the country. For most of its history France has been concerned with rivalries and the possibility of armed conflict with its neighbors, most especially Germany to the east. Defeat in the Franco-Prussian war gave impetus to the first truly comprehensive transport policy in the near modern era, Le Plan Freycinet of 1878–79. Facilitating economic exchange, mobilization of armed forces, and subsequent movement of armed bodies and supplies therefore has played a most important part in the allocation of resources for construction of transportation superstructure: roads, canals, and railways, and in their geographical orientation. The strategic considerations heavily influenced the rail network especially, producing some imbalances of economic investment. International boundaries produced other phenomena such as gateways, with their fan and funnel effects, upon lines of movement. There has always existed a perceived need for boundary crossing controls for different purposes and usually administered by different ministries.

A factor that has had considerable bearing on the evolution of transport policy in France has been the vast destruction resulting from the last two European wars. Destruction in World War I was localized in the north and east. It was far more generalized throughout the country in World War II. Both wars caused a rapid and premature wearing out of equipment without timely replacement. Rapid replacement and restoration of transport facilities was imperative for the reestablishment of the nation's vitality. Market forces could not be relied upon to do this. Crucial decisions had to be made concerning the most effective use of limited capital. Some allocations might be delayed for a considerable time (e.g., those for four-lane autoroutes). This dramatic situation was what brought into being the PLAN.

As in most European countries, competition for possession and use of exploitable land has always produced land use policy problems, thus generating a large and complex body of administrative law. Until recently France could be classed as an agrarian country, having a large rural population. A remarkable feature of the French communications network is the high density of very old rural roads. A continuing problem in interior transportation has been the mobilization of capital for investment in projects where return has usually been problematic, at least snce the turn of the century. State ownership, state financing, and state guarantee of interest have been some of the measures taken to assure investment in transportation undertakings of perhaps undisputed social and strategic value.

A matter of increasing significance in present transport policy making is the economic necessity to reduce dependence upon imported petroleum fuel. Nearly all the oil consumed in France must be imported, as must an increasing amount of gas, all of which must be paid for in foreign currency exchange. France is nearly always in a deficit balance-of-payments position.

France is, along with Germany, Switzerland, and Austria, what is called a "transit state"—a country whose territory is crossed by traffic between two other states. A simple example is truck traffic originating in the United Kingdom and destined for Italy. The truck crosses the English Channel by ferry, travels down a continuum of French autoroutes and crosses into Italy, using the Mont Blanc tunnel. For the French railways, available figures show that transit rail traffic increased by 45 percent between 1970 and 1980. The increase in transit traffic is causing serious problems in assessing infrastructure costs and investments in France and in other countries.

The transit problem is only one aspect of what has come to be called the requirement for "harmonization," that is, the requirement to adhere to general transport policies established by international authorities for all European states west of the iron curtain, including Yugoslavia. But the economies are those of sovereign states, and the problems are those that national states are expected to solve. The state economies are comparatively small and more interdependent. One estimate has it that the crossing of the international boundaries, with the usual administrative obstacles, increases by as much as 20 percent the retail costs of some goods. The origins of some border crossing procedures and attendant delays and costs are to be found buried deeply in the social choices and administrative methods of the countries. It is not only a question of standardization of such things as axle weights, vehicle dimensions, insurance requirements, and sanitary regulations. The real problems are often grounded in the differing divisions of ministerial responsibilities in countries: transport, health, environment, finance, interior, and foreign affairs.

In France, as elsewhere among Western industrialized countries, the instruments of transport policy had to be profoundly altered because of one factor above all, the automobile. More accurately, pressures brought about by the automobile and truck placed excessive loads on the policy system, beginning about 1950 (see Tables 4.1, 4.2, and 4.3).

In the ten years from 1960 and 1970, priority was given to the privately owned car: Credit became easier, French car companies expanded their production for both domestic and export sales, housing with poor or no access to

Table 4.1
Road Network, 1986 (in kilometers)

Total	Motorway	Highway (National)	Secondary (Regional)	Others (Local)	% Paved
804765	6265	28500	350000	420000	100

Note: Total and others exclude 700,000 km rural roads.

Source: European Marketing Data and Statistics 1988/89, 24th Edition (London: Euromonitor, 1988). Courtesy Euromonitor.

public transport was constructed and sold in increasing amounts. Freight transport by truck increased enormously; railways closed branch lines with increasing frequency. Rural bus service diminished, and France moved into the era of the private car and, rather tardily in some eyes, into the era of four-lane highways.

A problem was that the policy formulating and directing system was too rigidly centralized and bound by administrative rules and style that were not sufficiently innovative in the face of the fundamental social changes wrought by the automobile. La Société Nationale des Chemins de Fer Français, or the SNCF (an autonomous publicly owned commercial establishment in charge of the nationwide railway network), was no longer the centerpiece of the system; trucks were more flexible in every way including rates charged, and market entry for them was easy. Automobiles were becoming part of French life, as well as a major feature of the industrial economy.

As in all present day public policy, the most pivotal ingredient is financing for new infrastructure. The problem here turns on the necessity to coordinate policies among modal systems that are nearly always in competition with each other. It could hardly be otherwise; the pressure of traffic forced the construction of highways, and the railways and waterways saw a reduction in their

Table 4.2
Trends in Car Traffic Volume, 1977–1986
(in millions of car kilometers)

Year	1977	1980	1981	1982	1983	1984	1985	1986
	226500	240000	246000	253000	255000	256000	262000	275000

Source: European Marketing Data and Statistics 1988/89, 24th Edition (London: Euromonitor, 1988). Courtesy Euromonitor.

Table 4.3
Trends in Total Goods Transported via Road 1977–1986

Year	1977	1980	1981	1982	1983	1984	1985	1986
	100100	115500	111000	108000	103000	105000	106000	110000

Source: European Marketing Data and Statistics 1988/89, 24th Edition (London: Euromonitor, 1988). Courtesy Euromonitor.

share of infrastructure funds. Infrastructure costs for an effective rail transfer for Paris airports was found excessive, and the load on the highways increased. The most recent legislation aims at a better control and coordination of Orientation of Inland Transport, La Loi d'Orientation des Transports Interieurs (LOTI), of December 30, 1982.

From 1914 until the era of four-lane highways, by law called autoroutes, there was little in the way of original road construction where roads had not previously existed. Following World War II, the policy direction and financial effort was toward the restoration of existing networks. In 1960, France had only 25 kilometers of autoroutes. The length of national roads (i.e., under national government responsibility) was an excessive 76,000 kilometers, and the central budget was the only source for investment and maintenance. Highway improvements were confined to re-grading, establishing bypasses, building some ring-roads around metropolitan areas, and widening existing roads to three and four lanes. Car ownership and use, as well as market entry into commercial transport, were already saturating some roads at certain times. By 1955, the foreseeable investment requirement was significantly greater than what could be provided for in the national budget. The tax on fuel was increased, and the revenue fed a newly created special fund for road investment. The special fund was to be used to supplement budgetary appropriations. There were annual variations and adjustments to the fuel tax and fund. But neither the First PLAN (1947–53), nor the Second PLAN (1954–57) provided for any priority on road construction. The Third PLAN (1958–62) called for an expansion in road capacity.

In 1958, the Fourth Republic constitutional regime was replaced by the Fifth Republic under the presidency of Charles de Gaulle. The executive power of government was considerably strengthened and that of the multi-party Assemblée Nationale (National Assembly) weakened. Henceforth, the head of government was in a far more effective position to lead the process of lawmaking. De Gaulle was quite positive about France's inferiority among countries with four-lane highways. Italy already had many more kilometers. But de Gaulle was in fact giving his imprimatur to a system whose technical and financial planning had already begun. In 1958, there was already in existence a master plan (Schéma

Directeur) for autoroutes. This master plan provided for 2,100 kilometers of specifically recommended toll-charging autoroutes, as well as relief roads and autoroutes near large cities (Autoroutes de dégagement). This plan was succeeded by a fifteen-year master plan, formulated in 1960.

By 1970, it was clearly evident that the original highway traffic forecasts had been too low. To meet the urgent requirement for autoroutes, the organization of private autoroute construction-operating companies was encouraged. These would truly be concessionary ventures, entirely responsible for financing, construction, and subsequent operating. By this measure, there were widened sources of financing, while reducing construction costs as much as 15 percent. Also, by 1970, the older mixed companies began to show a profit. But by 1974, and the oil-price crisis, some of the private companies were running into trouble: a reduced rate of traffic increase, higher interest charges on financing, and some inept management. The government advocated and pressed mergers, at the same time calling upon lower-level government echelons (the Régions and below) to take over part of the financing, spelling out specific allocations.

SOCIOECONOMIC DIMENSIONS OF THE TRANSPORTATION SYSTEM AND POLICY

The law of April 18, 1955, defined autoroutes and the future status of the autoroute. It permitted the state to construct autoroutes on its own account, and the result is 500 kilometers of autoroute free of toll. The law also provided that the state could concede construction and operation to a mixed (private-public) company in which the public interest must be in a majority position. The concession agreement and its table of rights and privileges (Cahiers des Charges) can authorize the concessionaire to collect tolls in order to finance payment of interest, liquidate loan principal, pay for repairs, and possibly pay for extension of the autoroute. From 1957 to 1964, five autoroute mixed companies were founded. They were organized by local public bodies, with a common partner in the investment institution, Caisse des Dépôts et Consignations (CDC), with its subsidiary, Société central pour l'équipement du territoire. These took over a part of the administration of the companies. But the decree of May 12, 1970, modified the 1955 law to permit the granting of concessions to private groups. Between 1970 and 1973, four such private companies were created. At this time there are eleven mixed companies and sixteen private companies.

A decree of the Council of State fixes the conditions of the concession: construction, operation with its own employees, and repairs, generally for a period of thirty years. Each company makes its own budget. Tolls and other public service prices are subject to state control (Economic and Social Development Fund). State supervision is centralized and direct. The 1981 socialist government undertook some changes looking toward an equalization of the financial situations of the companies, and a "harmonization" of tolls. Harmonization here means market intervention to equalize income.

The greater part of autoroute financing has come from long-term bond issues, of which government-guaranteed foreign ownership now amounts to 50 percent of the total debt. Bond issues were sold for all mixed companies by a state company called the Caisse Nationale des Autoroutes managed by CDC. The private companies are financed largely by their own banking institution participants. Tolls in general have not kept pace either with increased costs of construction or with prices generally. Environmental impact costs have risen very fast.

The law of Dec. 30, 1982, created a public establishment called Autoroutes de France whose function is to insure an equalization of the resources of all of the mixed companies. Those companies showing a profit will be required to reimburse the debts that the deficit companies have contracted with the state. If the amount is insufficient, the Autoroutes de France can ask for a new loan. By a later decree, all mixed company profits come under the control of this public entity. Eventually all autoroutes will come under its adminstration.

Regulations for freight transport by road are provided for by the decree-law of April 1, 1934; the law of July 5, 1949; and the decrees of Nov. 1, 1936, Jan. 12, 1939, Nov. 14, 1949, and June 20, 1973. The latter also describes the freight transport zones of the country: the "Short Zone" of 150 kilometer operating radius, and the "Long Zone" beyond. The directive of Oct. 20, 1980, fixes the rules for combined rail-highway transport and for vehicles loaded on railway cars. The decree of Nov. 14, 1949, as amended, contains the basic rules for highway public carriage of passengers. Highway mode labor rules are elaborate and detailed.

A very great problem in road transport operation as a public service lies with the decline in the quality of passenger transportation in rural areas. Unlike Switzerland (and to a lesser degree, Austria and West Germany), France does not have a tradition of transport policy that accepts a general government responsibility for providing regular public passenger transportation throughout the country. France is a much larger and less densely populated country than Switzerland, Austria, and Germany. Salvation for regularly scheduled bus services that are experiencing financial difficulties can only be expected with the full development of département Transport Plans. Départements are now responsible for all route authorizations within the département urban routings and passenger tariffs. When the largest of political pressure is less remote, it can be expected that the pressure will increase and be more concentrated with correspondingly greater prospects of success. Most oversight and control of firms engaged in the transportation business, issuance of authorizations for engaging in international traffic, and professional licensing is at the level of the Région.

A decree of August 8, 1978, placed a directorate of roads under a general directorate of interior transport in the Ministry of Transport, now Ministry of Equipment. There also exists at the national level a National Road Committee, composed of delegates from twenty-four regional professional transport groups, whose function is to participate in the coordination of all transport policy. The National Committee hears appeals from disciplinary decisions (usually against small operators violating labor and tariff rules). Its chief function is the establishment of tariffs and their enforcement in the trucking industry. In addition, there exist national committees of freight forwarders and of rental companies. There are twenty-four market exchange offices for brokerage of freight consignment operators.

The Ninth PLAN is most emphatic on improving road safety. France is third in the industrialized world in the number of people killed per 100 million vehicle-kilometers (behind Belgium and Austria), and second in the number killed per million inhabitants (only behind Austria). In France the cost of highway injuries is borne by the National Health Service, itself always in deficit. The PLAN points out that statistically one in six born today will be killed or gravely hurt in an automobile accident, and one in two will suffer some kind of injury on the highways.

The French interior waterways system, with a total length of 8,568 kilometers, provides the slowest of all means of transportation. As in all European countries, it is a state-owned infrastructure utilized by privately owned vehicles, many of which are owner-operated. An absolute constraint to the size of the user boat is the lock between two water levels. There is no common-carrier passenger traffic and very little noncommercial traffic, although pleasure boating on French waterways is increasing in volume. The French canals are usually frozen and out of use during the winter months. Because of the slow speed of travel, waterways are most apt to be used for bulky, low-value cargo: coal, some petroleum products, some agricultural products, and construction materials. Coal is of declining importance as a source of energy in France. The building construction industry is of reduced importance as well and is now generally sited away from waterways, thus reducing new trans-shipment costs.

The waterways system consumes the least amount of energy per ton-kilometer. Waterways in France, at least, enhance the environment more than they deface it. Waterways have the additional function of drainage, water management, and hydroelectric power. Occasionally, French waterways are a source of irrigation water, but often roads and railways are constructed over the same terrain as waterways: river valleys and relatively level ground. Thus, they are nearly always confronted with intermodal competition, even for the same cargo. And they lack the flexibility of the road certainly, but even of the railway. Some French waterways are affected by adverse weather. The Seine and other rivers are occasionally too high for bridge clearances.

The waterways in the north and east carry 90 percent of the waterways traffic and 95 percent of the ton-kilometers. Unlike much of the German waterways system, and certainly those of Belgium and the Netherlands, many French canals cut across watersheds (i.e., they are junction canals). With their consequent changes in levels, these canals require a great many locks, canal tunnels,

Table 4.4
Trends in Total Air Distance Flown (Scheduled) 1977–1986
(in millions of kilometers)

Year	1977	1980	1981	1982	1983	1984	1985	1986
	270.0	276.3	270.5	274.6	275.2	270.8	275.8	288.1

Source: European Marketing Data and Statistics 1988/89, 24th Edition (London: Euromonitor, 1988). Courtesy Euromonitor.

canal carrying bridges, and inclined plane installations. Waterways transported 4.3 percent of the total French freight traffic in 1984. The waterways are to be found in only thirty-four of the ninety-six Départements, but within those Départements, they transported 11 percent of the ton-kilometers. Where there are canals of European gauge, this figure attains 34 percent of the traffic. Along the large gauge Seine waterway, 50 percent of the traffic tonnage goes by water.[1]

Although the ton-kilometer cost for waterways transportation is very low, a great deal of this cost advantage can be lost in terminal costs, and most especially so for shippers not actually located on the shores of the waterway. Moreover, all costs of cargo handling must be borne by the shipping activity, and none by the state, the owner of the waterway. There is nothing like the ''private siding'' of the rail line, in which the SNCF assists in meeting the expense. The French maritime ports are poorly equipped to transfer cargo from ocean ship to canal boat. Because of handling equipment problems and stevedore labor practices, cargo transfer in maritime ports is twice as costly as in river ports. In France, there is must emphasis placed on the logistic approach, or transport stream, at the present time. Also, there is a new emphasis placed upon the marketing approach. Both are a bit late for saving the traditional waterways industry.

The air mode in France can be divided into five groupings: companies in international service, Air Inter, regional airlines, aircraft industry, and the airports and airways. Recent trends in air transportation in France are shown in Tables 4.4, 4.5, and 4.6.

The companies nearly entirely in international service are Air France (publicly owned) and UTA (Union de Transporte Aeriens), a private company. The general internal airline, Air Inter, is operated as a private company, but of mixed ownership. The regional airlines are sometimes called *le troisième rang* (third rank) or *les compagnies régionales.*

France is the world's third largest aircraft manufacturing country, employing 127,000 people in the aircraft industry. The Airbus consortium, of which the French government-undertaking Aerospatiale is the prime company and assem-

Table 4.5
Trends in Air Passenger-kilometers, 1979–1986
(in millions of passenger-kilometers)

Year	1979	1980	1981	1982	1983	1984	1985	1986
	32784	34128	36504	37608	38316	38472	39252	39240

Source: European Marketing Data and Statistics 1988/89, 24th Edition (London: Euromonitor, 1988). Courtesy Euromonitor.

bly builder, is the builder of the Airbus, the only real competitor of Boeing and Douglas in the wide-bodied aircraft business. Aérospatiale is 37.9 percent owner of Airbus Industrie. It is also a 50 percent partner with Aeritalia in the manufacture of the regional turboprop aircraft ATR 42.

The European tourist trade and the geographical position of France are favorable to the French air service industry. Paris is one of the two most important terminal points for the North Atlantic and polar airline runs to Europe, a major transit and transfer point for the tourist and business traffic.

Air France was created by statute as a national company having the dual character of a commercial enterprise and a public service. As a commercial enterprise, Air France is expected to cover from its own resources the costs of operation and financing. As a public service the company is subject to ministerial oversight and whatever operational constraints that are believed to be in the public interest. The company is currently a partner with the state in three operating contracts. One of these provides that the state will take over 90 percent of the deficit in operating the supersonic transport, Concorde, and all of the other financial charges in connection with it. Air France will receive no monopoly privilege on any routing and will receive no subsidy for operating a service in competition with any other French company. The state imposes on Air France the responsibilities of developing economic, social, and cultural exchanges; assisting in achieving a favorable foreign exchange position; enhancing the image of France abroad; and aiding in regionalization. The com-

Table 4.6
Trends in Air Freight Transport, 1979–1986 (in millions of ton-kilometers)

Year	1979	1980	1981	1982	1983	1984	1985	1986
	2031.3	2092.9	2239.9	2297.8	2596.6	2893.9	2980.5	3195.5

Source: European Marketing Data and Statistics 1988/89, 24th Edition (London: Euromonitor, 1988). Courtesy Euromonitor.

pany is owned 99.38 percent by the state. There are 35,232 employees, ninety-seven aircraft of all types, a 68 percent load factor for 1984. The company holds a financial interest in Air Guadeloupe, Air Djibouti, Middle East Air Lines, Air Inter, Air Madagascar, Tunis Air, Air Mauritius, and Royal Air Maroc. Air France operates in domestic traffic only to Nice and Corsica.

UTA is a private stock company, 92 percent of whose shares are held by the French forwarding and chartering organization, Chargers Réunis, and 3 percent by the airline's employees. The remainder of the stock is held by several French financial institutions. There are 6,560 employees, and eleven aircraft, all DC-10s or B-747s. The system has 254,935 route-kilometers with forty-six stations in thirty-eight countries. It is now making a new effort to expand its route coverage. There is no French domestic service, except the terminus in Paris. Load factor in 1984 was 60.3 percent.

Air Inter is the general internal airline, centered in Paris. It was created as a private corporation with the following participation: Air France, 24.97 percent; SNCF, 24.97 percent; UTA, 14.69 percent; Compagnie de Navigation mixte, 8.69 percent, various financial institutions and others, 26.68 percent. The company employs 7,025 workers and operates forty-four aircraft of four types. The system operates 26,554 route-kilometers. Passenger load factor in 1984 was 64.79 percent. Air Inter operates pursuant to a contract with the state, the latest one being signed in July 1985. The contract (for fifteen years) provides that Air Inter will operate fifty routes, twenty-seven radiating from Paris or Lyon and twenty-three transversals. The airline is given a monopoly of operation over these lines. The monopoly, designed for complete amortization of the purchase of the company's new Airbus 320s, allows Air Inter to continue its policy of covering the operating losses of certain lines by some of the profits made on others.[2]

There are currently six scheduled airlines in regional service, plus six more operating small local services. Altogether there have been forty-eight operators of this kind. There are forty-nine air charter and taxi services, and eighteen helicopter services. Ministerial authorization is required for all commercial air service.

France has seventy-eight regional airports and two airports under national statutes: Aéroport de Paris and Bale Mulhouse. Aéroport de Paris is a public establishment of the state which controls Roissy (Charles de Gaulle), Orly, and Le Bouget airports, plus eleven secondary airports and heliports. Aéroport de Paris employs 5,400 people, but it is estimated that 60,000 people work at various enterprises on airport premises. Fifty-two airports belong to the state, seventeen belong to départements or cities. Four belong to mixed ownership, and five to military installations.

French transport policy with respect to air transport is quite clearly separated into these areas:

- International operations to other countries outside of Europe, with the prospect of deregulation;

- International operations within Europe, and the prospect of deregulation pursuant to court action;
- Operations to French overseas Départements and Territories;
- Operations within metropolitan France; these can be seriously affected by deregulation in Europe;
- The export market for aeronautical equipment;
- Airports and airways; and,
- Charter traffic.

Primary responsibility for air transport policy formulation is in the Ministry of Equipment. Closely associated with it is the National Transport Council, whose composition is noted later. At the regional level are transport committees analogous to the National Council. Below the level of the National Transport Council are two other consultative bodies: the Higher Council for Infrastructure and Aerial Navigation and the Higher Council for Commerical Aviation. Within the ministry proper are the Inspector General of Civil Aviation and Meteorology and at the working level the General Directorate of Civil Aviation. There is a substantial body of law that bears directly upon policy formulation and execution called Le Code de l'Aviation Civile. The law will often specify the implementing administrative decrees to be issued by the Council of State (Conseil d'Etat).

Air France and UTA are both in excellent competitive positions in the world market, whatever may be the interim market disorder and end result of deregulation. Air France quite visibly has employees in excess of its needs, a difficult problem generally in France. Both companies have the imposed national requirement to share in serving overseas territories and Départements. France remains in an excellent competitive position in serving worldwide markets for aeronautical equipment. The airways problem is almost entirely a technical one, and currently one of modernization. The airport situation generally does allow for a number of policy options. But given the current French preoccupation with decentralization and territorial management, it is the French internal net that poses the kinds of policy choices that interest diverse actors in French public life.

The problems of the internal airlines begin with the facts of French geography. Approximately 20 percent of the population lives in the Paris commuting area. Most of the company home offices are in Paris as are the home offices of most of the banks and insurance companies. And, of course, the government ministries are in Paris. No other French cities or metropolitan areas are remotely comparable in size. The SNCF provides an excellent service to all parts of the country for those who do not want to use private vehicles and for whom expenditure of time is more discretionary, such as vacationers. The French telephone system now works well from Paris to any part of the country. What remains for the internal airlines are mostly out-and-back business travelers and others for whom time is an important consideration.

Regional airlines are a group promoted by local community action, each originally acting independently of the others. They do not benefit from any balancing out, either among each other or for that matter among the runs of a given airline. Each company tries to respond to the needs that local communities have considered the justification for their establishment and financial support. They live generally as a result of their public subsidies. Aside from the questions of mediocre management and some mistakes on aircraft purchases, and questions of labor law, the financial problem is to meet the need for this service at something like manageable cost. For the moment, no change can be foreseen, and subsidies will continue into the future. The regionals are shrinking in number. One alone, TAT (Transport Aérien Transrégional), now has two-thirds of the regional traffic.

There are many problems with French airports and policies. Most airports were originally created by the state, for reasons of defense or to support air transport when it began. In most cases, although owned by the state, the airports are operated by chambers of commerce and industry. According to a 1973 master plan for aeronautical equipment, airports are classified according to the size of the industrial zone and urban area being served. There are thirty-six airports in the smallest category (fewer than 50,000 passengers per year), handling only 4.4 percent of the passengers. They are most affected by the fortunes of the regional carriers. Only four in that category operate at a profit. With small airports, debt service takes a total of 48.9 percent of the financial turnover. Aéroport de Paris is financially independent, without significant aid from the state.

POLITICAL DIMENSIONS OF THE TRANSPORTATION SYSTEM AND POLICY

The development and evolution of the railway system and policy reflects the nature of intricate interactions between the political and economic forces in the society. Changes in the pattern of rail passenger and freight transportation (see Tables 4.7, 4.8, and 4.9) have, as elsewhere, forced some difficult decisions on the French rail transportation policymakers.

The convention of August 31, 1937, provided for the establishment of a Société Economique Mixte to be called, as mentioned earlier, the Société Nationale des Chemins de Fer Français (SNCF), with 51 percent ownership by the state and 49 percent with the previous concessionaire companies who would remain in existence until 1955 and who would be paid the guaranteed dividends on original capital. The convention was to remain in force for forty-five years, from January 1938 to December 1982. Given the inflation that had occurred between 1938 and 1955, shareholders got about 2 percent of the value of their original holdings. The railway was to be governed by a Council of Administra-

Table 4.7
Length of Public Railway Network Operated 1977–1986 (in kilometers)

Year	1977	1980	1981	1982	1983	1984	1985	1986
	34150	33886	34107	34108	34193	34688	34676	34639

Source: European Marketing Data and Statistics 1988/89, 24th Edition (London: Euromonitor, 1988). Courtesy Euromonitor.

tion having eighteen members: state, ten; private stockholders, three; and five designated on the proposals of the labor unions.

By the 1970s, the system of tariffs was coming nearer to meeting the needs of the country. But the SNCF was certainly vulnerable to the complaint that the management of its public service was too much subject to noncommercial obligations and direct oversight by the government. Movement had to be toward free users' choice, equal treatment of all modes on burdens and rules affecting operators, and autonomous management. As Dec. 31, 1982, approached—the scheduled date for the termination (or revision) of the 1937 convention—general agreement had emerged that closer coordination of all modes of transport was required, that the free market principle was by now the only one really feasible, that freight transport had to be looked at according to a logistical systems approach, that although there was a social responsibility toward deviation from the market principle in certain cases (elderly people, school children, and thinly populated areas), the transportation system could no longer be a source of palliatives for economic problems unrelated to transportation. Rates had to come closer to true costs. The advent of the computer had provided the possibility of enormous new operational efficiencies, savings in manpower, and corresponding financial savings. The organized and disciplined nature of the rail mode lends itself particularly well to large-scale computerization.

France is a participatory democracy. Notwithstanding a tradition of central-

Table 4.8
Trends in Railway Passenger-kilometers 1977–1986
(in millions of passenger-kilometers)

Year	1977	1980	1981	1982	1983	1984	1985	1986
	51828	54492	55656	56856	58428	60276	60780	59904

Source: European Marketing Data and Statistics 1988/89, 24th Edition (London: Euromonitor, 1988). Courtesy Euromonitor.

Table 4.9
Trends in Railway Freight Carried 1977–1986
(in millions of net ton-kilometers)

Year	1977	1980	1981	1982	1983	1984	1985	1986
	66216	69468	64392	61200	59376	60120	58488	52800

Source: European Marketing Data and Statistics 1988/89, 24th edition (London: Euromonitor, 1988). Courtesy Euromonitor.

ized and technocratic public service, there exist potent labor unions, a bundle of rising expectations set in motion by world prosperity, much technological innovation, and ready transfer of it among the interdependent western industrialized countries. The largest labor union is controlled by the French Communist Party. This is a powerful political mixture that rules out any easy transport policy solutions. The smooth institutional relationships of yesterday can become tomorrow's insoluble burdens.[3]

The then-forthcoming termination of the 1973 convention precipitated two studies and reports. The first of these—the Guillaumat Commission study—caused much objection when it established that fully half of the SNCF freight traffic was vulnerable to truck competition; it was the half where rates and costs were too high. It was shown that the rail-route transport, with its attractive aspect of energy saving, had to be exploited much further. As for passengers, it was stated that there is definitely a continuing market but that government intervention would continue to be necessary for public transportation in thinly populated areas.

Quite evident throughout the Guillaumat report is the central position of the railway in any transport policy: the functioning of the whole surface transport apparatus according to market principles is possible and socially preferable, and that supposes a complete but progressive liberalization of rates. The commission noted that the high cost of fuel would serve as an excellent stimulant for the achievement of overall efficiency.

The second was an interministerial study to recommend a new methodology for analyzing conditions of intermodal competition to arrive at a better understanding of future transport needs and the coordination of infrastructures. This was the Quinat Report of April 1980.

For the SNCF the overall policy document of greatest importance is La Loi d'Orientation des Transports Intérieur of 1982 (LOTI). Title II, chapter I of this law (effective since Jan. 1, 1983) embraces the statute for the railways to replace the convention of 1937. The new statute creates the SNCF as a public industrial and commercial establishment to operate, equip, and develop the national railway system according to the principle of public service, including the creation of subsidiaries and the participation in other complementary or connecting organizations. There is a provision for transfer of all property to the new company. A Council of Administration, of eighteen members, is created. From among them a president is selected and then confirmed by the government's Council of Ministers. Regional consultative committees can be instituted on the request of interested regional groups for the purpose of consulting on SNCF activities bearing upon the economic and social welfare of the region.

The SNCF is granted management autonomy. A table of articles and conditions of contract (Cahier des Charges), approved by the Council of State, fixes the parameters of functions, the operational requirements, and the operational conditions of its public service. There is required a contract between the state and SNCF for purposes of determining future objectives and the means to achieve them. The state and the SNCF took two years and four months to negotiate and sign the required contract. The contract (for 1984–89) called for contracts with all regions for railway services, for increased productivity for freight transportation, and for increased full train traffic in international services. According to the contract, the state is responsible for securing 45 billion francs (in 1985 value) to finance new infrastructure investments, for TGV Atlantique (see the next section), and for electrification in Brittany and to the Massif Central.

LOTI provides that the state will give its financial support to the SNCF by reason of the latter's essential contribution to the social and economic welfare of the nation, and taking into account SNCF's specific infrastructure responsibilities. The methods for accomplishing this support are set out in the Cahier, permitting and encouraging management improvement, productivity, and financial balance. The SNCF is to operate the accounting system required of commercial enterprises generally. It can conclude arbitration agreements for the settlement of disputes and claims. It is under the oversight of the state according to a decree of the Council of State. This oversight function is now in the Ministry of Equipment.[4]

A source of continuing concern is the enormous losses in productivity resulting from occasional strikes, the reasons for which seldom make any sense at all to the public. But a public company with a large number of employees and a clientele that is the nation itself is a natural target for labor unions who at this time are in difficulties generally. Moreover, no labor law fixing union responsibility and contracts exists such as in the United States.

A continuing problem for rural areas has been the steady closing of omnibus and branch line passenger services, simply because it did not pay. As a national company, SNCF can only be seen in terms of its overall responsibilities and costs. Many omnibus services never paid for themselves, but with mounting labor costs, deficits continually worsened. From a corporate point of view, the answer is obvious. But it is the local communities and their people who mostly bear the consequences. For a number of years it has been possible for communities to conclude with SNCF agreements to continue, to improve, or to reopen service under cost-sharing contracts. There now exists formalized machinery, including the regional transport master plan, to facilitate this, together with the possibility for some subsidy from DATAR (Délégation à l'Aménagement du Territoire et à l'Action Régionale), Commission for Land Use and Regional Action, explained further in the next section. There are now five such arrangements, with more likely to come.

A major problem in waterways policy is also political. There is the understandable motive to protect the owner-operator of the individual boat from the ravages of competition with the fleet owners—usually more capital-intensive owners—as well as from excessive competition from his fellow owner-operators. Generally, these are owners of the *péniche classique,* the self-propelled 300-ton boat that is specifically designed for operation in the Freycinet canals whose locks are 38.5 meters long and have a depth of 2.2 meters. Here is a classic case of government intervention in a service sector whose potential is already precarious. It is now a tenet of French transport policy that the user will be guaranteed a free choice of mode to select. The problem is exacerbated by the fact that the waterways fleet of France is composed of about 2,800 separate business enterprises operating about 3,400 active boats; 2,300 of the enterprises are in fact owner-operators of single boats. It is the owner-operators who own 90 percent of the self-propelled *péniches classiques* and 60 percent of the larger self-propelled boats. Owner-operators are practically nonexistent on the Rhine.

The political style of the country is such that there is a kind of commitment to a sector of society and to a mode of transport that in fact only marginally contributes to the economy.

The Grégoire Commission was directed by the Minister of Transport on March 5, 1982, to take into account the decline of the waterways system and to define priority improvement measures to be realized or to be scheduled in the Ninth PLAN. The recommended measures were to be written into an overall view for the long term. Thirty-eight members of the Grégoire Commission represented both houses of parliament, the committee of fleet owners, the national association of independent waterways workers, the chamber of waterways freight brokers, the international conference of users of transportation, all of the major trade unions, the National Office of Navigation, the association of chambers of commerce and industry, the chambers of agriculture, as well as the following ministries: budget, economy and finance, interior, industry, maritime, leisure time, agriculture, environment, plan, transport, economic and social council, higher transport council, and Ponts et Chaussées. Also on the commission were five technical experts and four rapporteurs. In short, it would appear that every possible viewpoint could be heard during the deliberations.

The commission was left in no doubt about the public attitude of the then socialist government: that far from being an out-of-date tool, the waterway system is indispensable to the good functioning of the transport market. The transport minister blamed the current problems of the waterways system on past policies and declared the transportation system as a whole a public service even though he also said that the problem of demand could not be separated from the need for a revival of the economy in general. He further stated that the owner-operator users of the waterways must not die but should be assured of a future that would allow them to modernize their equipment and access to the market. The commission's job was to find ways to bring that about. The commission's recommendations included, among others, the completion of projects already underway and two others for a large canal extension (including the large-gauge Rhine-Rhône canal); the creation of a fund for the promotion of waterways transport; the establishment of two new organizations to serve the owner-operators of river craft as well as several measures to improve existing services.

Some of the commission's recommendations have already been implemented. But the report of the Ninth PLAN was hardly encouraging, recognizing the weak position of the waterways in the country's economy and the meager prospects.

However humanitarian may be the expressed policies of government, there must be made a choice of priorities of expenditure. The French style leans toward thorough study, seemingly technologically grounded. And the studies certainly are illuminating, while at the same time protecting the government against accusations of high-handed and uninformed decision making. But the fact remains that the Grégoire study was dealing with a marginal activity of declining economic importance, and one that simply commands declining political clout even from the labor unions. The commission may be considered an advanced exercise in political cosmetics.

There is much excitement, both positive and negative, about the long existing project for a large-gauge junction canal connecting the Rhine with the Rhône. The project has been extensively studied and periodically considered. There is already a Freycinet gauge canal, in bad condition, and with little traffic. The large-scale canal is not likely to be built. Its prospective cost simply cannot be justified by any prospective economic gain. A further, unspoken concern of the successive governments is the possibility of utilization by Soviet waterways vessels financed and operated on other value structures and hence murderously competitive commercially. They can come up the Danube to the new Rhine-Danube canal, then up or down the Rhine—not a pleasant prospect.

RECENT TRENDS AND FUTURE PROSPECTS

The French road network is about 803,000 kilometers long, not counting rural paths and lanes. There are 6,160 kilometers of four-lane autoroutes of which 1,400 kilometers are urban expressways (no tolls). There are 29,000 kilometers of highways under national jurisdiction, of which three-quarters are two-lane, and about 12 percent are more than two-lane. There are 28,000 kilometers of national secondary roads, 347,000 kilometers of Département roads, and 421,000 kilometers of roads under community responsibility (that includes all city streets). Finally there are 700,000 kilometers of rural paths and lanes.

In 1985, there were 20,800,000 private and commercial vehicles operating. There are 380 cars for 1,000 inhabitants. In 1983, there were 79,664 buses, 2,809,995 trucks of categories, and 131,515 semi-trailer prime movers. In 1981, there were 812,000 people employed in automobile construction or subcontracting; 867,000 people worked in some form of road transport business, and 476,800 worked in distribution, repair, and filling station activities. In 1984 there were 24,238 road transportation businesses, of which about 86 percent were owner-operated.

A new master plan was issued in 1970 by DATAR, the Commission for Land Use and Regional Action. This plan reorganized the national road network into primary and secondary categories. National secondary roads were then reclassified as Département roads, and the national network was reduced to 43,000 kilometers.

Approved in 1984, the largest highway master plan was published by decree on Feb. 14, 1986. This master plan is described, not as a plan for imperative action, but as a plan for long-term objectives. It supersedes the autoroute program of 1977. The present autoroute system contains 6,085 kilometers of which 4,266 are concessionary. Not included are 1,320 kilometers of urban expressways. The 1986 master plan calls for ultimate provision of 6,760 kilometers of autoroutes. Altogether the master plan calls for 35,000 kilometers of national highways, autoroutes included. Of these, 2,700 kilometers are to connect autoroutes and 6,400 kilometers for purposes of better connections in certain areas.

Since 1955, French transport policy on road construction has had to respond to the dynamics of increasing demand. The initially overriding objective of simply increasing capacity has been supplemented by additional considerations: environmental protection, land use competition, decentralization of responsibility, and highway safety. Rates of demand were underestimated, especially as the economy expanded in the 1950s and 1960s. By the 1970s it became very apparent that efforts to improve road capacity could be never ending, reaching a point of incompatibility with other values in the social fabric. Sobering judgments had to be made; a four-lane autoroute takes a greater measure of safety. But every new autoroute project, besides costing more per kilometer with every passing year, raises new disturbing environmental problems. Toll collections have risen much more slowly than inflation. Further, financing will probably be through longer-term fixed loans. High toll rates are already causing truck operators to use parallel roads running through villages when they are not constrained by time limits. But, in fact, truck tolls on some autoroutes (notably to the north) do not compensate for the wear on the roads caused by very heavy trucks.

The railway network of France, or about 90 percent of it, belongs to the SNCF, the autonomous publicly owned commercial establishment founded in 1937. There are 34,688 kilometers of rail line, of which 11,335 kilometers are electrified in two separate electric power systems: the original 1,500-volt direct current system and the new system of 25,000 volts 50-cycle monophase current. The electrified lines haul 82.4 percent of the 60.84 billion ton-kilometers of annual freight traffic of the SNCF. There were 60.2 billion passengers handled in 1984. The on-time performance of trains is excellent, and main-line track maintenance is superb. There were 245,700 employees in 1984. Figure 4.1 shows the national railroad network.

The French interior waterways system has a total length of 8,568 kilometers, of which 3,955 kilometers are navigable or canalized rivers, and 3,413 km are canals, largely located in the north and east of the country. The canals are in seven classifications, according to the boat tonnage that can be accommodated. Only classes II through VII are commercially exploitable, and only classes V through VII, the European Scale Class and above, can be considered as having any long-term prospects of commercial viability.

There are actually in use 4,787 kilometers of class II through IV waterways and 1,925 kilometers of class V through VII waterways. Of the latter, none of the larger-scale waterways in France is connected to each other and only the Deule, Moselle, and Rhine waterways are connected to other European systems. Currently the waterways fleet numbers 4,831 barges, 3,695 self-propelled barges, 31 tugboats, and 216 pushers. The self-propelled barges are decreasing in number annually and none have been built in over twenty years. There are about 15,000 people employed in the waterways mode, of which 2,676 are owner-operators of one or more self-propelled barges which are generally in a state of obsolescence. This latter figure is in fact probably greater because many of these barges are family-operated ventures. The largest river ports are Paris, Strasbourg, Rouen, Le Havre, and Dunkerque, in that order.

Recent and continuing technological developments in French transportation are receiving international attention. An example is the high-speed train, known in France as *train grande vitesse* (TGV).[5] Because of some technical limitations to the capture of electric power from an overhead line while moving at very high speed, as well as the advanced developments in gas turbine power plants, the SNCF considered that the gas turbine installation had the greatest power plant promise for the new high performance vehicle, and research and new development proceeded with it. Active construction planning of the TGV line only began after operational feasibility of the vehicle was well established. Then came the oil crisis of 1973–74 and the consequent rise in the price of oil. France must pay for oil in foreign exchange at a price over which the French government can exercise little or no control. Moreover, it was agreed the world over at the time that the trend of the future oil prices was unpredictable. Given the fact of hydroelectric power in the east of France, as well as the prospective dimensions of France's nuclear power program, the shift of the TGV line to electric power was the logical answer.

The TGV line is not just a train path for a very high-speed train operating between Paris and Lyon. It is in fact a system of trains, with the highly prof-

Figure 4.1
Railroad Network in France

Source: Chris Bushell, *Railway Directory & Year Book 1989* (Surrey, England: Reed Business Publishing, 1989), p. 286. Courtesy Reed Business Publishing, Ltd.

itable Paris-Lyon path as the trunk of the system. The total viability of the TGV-Sud-Est rests in the fact that from the trunk are branches to Besançon, Berne, Lausanne, Geneva, Annecy, Chambéry, Marseille, Toulon, Montpellier, and St. Etienne. The whole system makes for efficiency both in travel time and in cost. The careful planning and design of the TGV trunk assured the necessary policy decisions for the project to proceed. Of course, the potential market has also played an important role in the development of the system. The TGV-Atlantique line (Paris to Tours and Rennes) was completed in 1989. The government has also announced final commitment for TGV-Nord, designed primarily to connect Paris to the Channel Tunnel. TGV-Nord will go through Lille, where there is to be a prospective connection to Brussels and Cologne. In addition, the plan envisages a kind of TGV belt line around the east of Paris to connect TGV-Sud-Est (Lyon) and TGV-Atlantique. The path of the belt is to pass Charles de Gaulle Airport at Roissy as well as the site of the soon-to-be-constructed Euro-Disneyland. TVG-Sud-Est is to be extended, with a branch to go around Lyon, to the east of that city, and to reach Valence.

The policy thrust of this government decision is that TGV system development must progressively pass from a scale strictly French to a scale of European dimensions. A somewhat more distant objective is a line, TGV-Est, to Strasbourg, undoubtedly looking toward connections to the north-south Frankfurt/Main-Basel path in Germany.

Another development receiving much international attention is the Jan. 20, 1986, agreement between France and the United Kingdom for the construction of the Channel Tunnel, with an anticipated operational date of 1993. The configuration will be a double rail tunnel for traffic plus a third and smaller diameter tunnel for service and ventilation. The total length is 50 kilometers. Two services are to be offered: through-train service from Paris to London, and a road vehicle carrying shuttle service between terminals that will take 35 minutes. It is anticipated that the tunnel will be used by Paris-to-London TGV trains for a minimum time passage, Gare du Nord to London (probably Waterloo) in three hours. The TGV trains for this purpose must be smaller in cross-section to accommodate the British loading gauge which is smaller than that of the Continent. Another technical problem is that on the British side the power feed is at 750 volts DC, on outside third rail—a factor tending to preclude best utilization of the speed characteristics of the TGV—although bi-current power systems now pose no technical problem.

The overall economic and transport implications of the tunnel are fundamental, even if the engineering problem is quite manageable as is the financing and prospective amortization of costs. In fact that amortization can be demonstrated as coming from the tunnel's substitution for the far more costly and less economically efficient services by air along with intermodal split surface service involving ferry traffic. Financing is to be entirely from private sources: the Eurotunnel consortium and the stock funding syndicates, France-Manche and Channel Tunnel Group.

Quite certainly, most of the shipborne cross-channel services will disappear, along with the principal economic supports for Calais, Boulogne, Ostend, and Zeebrugge on the Continent side, and Dover, Folkstone, and Harwich on the English side. Undoubtedly, there will be a considerable reduction in the traffic demand for London-Paris air service, now at about ten flights each way per day. Altogether the Channel Tunnel will bring about some significant economic orientations in each country and to some reduced extent also in Belgium. It is generally believed that the tunnel will lead to an increase in truck traffic across the Channel because of the reduced time of crossing. There are numerous policy modalities that can only be worked out through experience.

French transport policy, like the public policy of which it is an integral part, exhibits some of the outward appearances of undergoing fundamental change. The highly centralized bureaucratic-technocratic model, essentially distributive and rather paternalistic, is no longer thought to meet the values and needs of the body politic as a whole. The shift to more generalized participation has been under way for thirty years, but it was accelerated considerably during the five years of the Socialist Party government just past. But the whole centralizing bureaucracy of Paris remains in place, as big and seemingly as powerful as ever, and the distributive reins are all still there. It is that the Régions and the Départements are now encouraged to make master plans of their own for transport facilities and are allowed the privilege of formulating and contracting means of paying for them, including contracting with the state to subsidize some part of the costs. It seems inevitable that total tax supported costs will increase, but also that the Régions, Départements, and cities will have a far greater share in the determination of local priorities. In countrywide transportation, little significant change can be expected in most systems: SNCF, Air France, Air Inter, the whole waterways network, and control of the autoroutes and routes nationales. For reasons of scalar economics and general efficiency, it can hardly be otherwise.

Some weaknesses of the transport system are found in the services rendered to localities. First, there is the ever-decreasing quality of rural passenger services by omnibus trains of the SNCF or by highway bus service, mostly privately owned. This kind of service is very often deficitary, with little hope of making it pay. Second, some of the regional (third level) airlines, as well as most of the smaller airports continue to operate in the red. These services are absolutely required for the continued economic health of many outlying areas, but it is unlikely that they can become self-supporting in the near future. A third problem is the likelihood of a continuation of some maldistribution of passenger transfer service for the Paris airports, in the face of increasing highway traffic and increasing air freight and air passenger volume. Fourth, the impending deregulation of intra-European air passenger transportation will have a significant effect upon government-controlled Air France and Air Inter as well as upon the competitive position of the SNCF in international traffic.

Fifth, absence of interconnections between the several large-gauge waters in

France is a major problem. Sixth, some of the autoroutes continue to operate at a deficit, with the likelihood that shortfalls will become proportionally larger over time, because of increased maintenance costs. Seventh, the SNCF is faced with the requirement for further electrifications. And finally, the French government has refused to agree to Italian reelectrification of the Col de Tende rail line and failed to upgrade the branch from Nice to Breil-sur-Roya, thus denying true effectiveness of a more direct routing between northern Europe and the Mediterranean coast. Upgrading the Nice-Breil branch and electrifying it would be enormously expensive. And to do so would have the effect of reducing overall SNCF revenue from freight traffic moving from the center of Europe to the French Mediterranean seacoast.

These problems need to be assessed against the following achievements and successes in French transportation policy. First, there is the successful development of TGV. Second, the French transportation system has been assisted by an innovative and successful transport vehicle industry for highway, rail, and air modes. Third, the French can take pride in the superbly conceived and operated Paris regional transportation system, truly a model to be studied by others. Fourth, there is the well-conceived and operated interior airline connecting the major cities: Air Inter. Fifth, SNCF local service has been restored and upgraded in five instances through cost-sharing contracts with local authorities. There are likely to be more of these. And, finally, the SNCF is changing into an innovative, ever more logistically oriented railway system.

TRANSPORTATION POLICY ORGANIZATION AND PROCESS

In lawmaking, the government has the constitutional structure to pass precise legislation and to do so with outstanding speed, if that is desired. Political parties serve as the transmission belt of politics. As a vehicle for articulating people's concerns in transportation policy matters, political parties are not as impressive as are informed pressure and consumer groups whose views are treated rather seriously by the government.

The phenomenon of "decentralization," of decision, consultation, financial burden-sharing, and responsibility sharing has been an ongoing process for the last four decades. The recent socialist governments gave it a new face and a further thrust by the laws of March 2, 1982; Jan. 7, 1983; and July 22, 1983. Transport policy making in France involves two ultimate questions: What is the price? And who pays?

Today, policy initiation is in response to some expressed need to improve upon a policy already in existence or to improve upon the operation of some system or service that present policy provides, and that always against a background of social change and rising expectations. Ideological factors have had little influence upon the process, except insofar as the social program of nationalizations and spending have caused some subsequent problems in the financing of proposed infrastructure projects. But, in fact, there is little in the way of difference in the policy choices made between political *majorité* and another.

Certainly, the most important policy instrument in France today is LOTI, passed on Dec. 30, 1982. In the same government of Pierre Mauroy, the PLAN was placed under a Ministry of the Government, and the Commissariat du Plan was instructed by the prime minister to formulate the transport policy sector of the PLAN to conform with the provisions of the law. It is this law that is intended to be the principal transport policy directive for France until the end of the century.

The thrust and intent of LOTI are well set out: economic service as a whole; full attention to conservation of energy and to ecological input; the right of users to be fully informed; the full right of user choice; overall policy making by the state and territorial authorities, with the thrust toward planning that is decentralized geographically, contractual in law, and democratic in the scope of participation; with constant priority to be given to forms of collectives (e.g., common carrier, transport facilities). Public authorities have an absolute right to intervene in tariff schedules, but these are always fixed by the agency organizing and operating the transport facility. Tariff rules can be established by the state in concert with transport firms, professional organizations, and users. The "state" in this case usually means the Ministry of the Budget.

The law provides for the establishment of master plans by the state and by collectivities or various administrative units. These are to ensure coherent systems over the long term for the different modes. Rules and methods for master plans are to be set out in a decree of the Council of State.

The national-level policy flow in transportation is shown in Figure 4.2. There is established a National Transport Council, as well as regional and departmental transport councils, to be composed of representatives of transporters, their employees and representatives of users. The state determines the rules on the council's organization and functioning.

Chapter I, Title II of LOTI sets out the new statute for the railway system, replacing the convention of 1938. Chapter II deals with urban transport and defines the territorial perimeters for that transport policy as well as the approval required. All truck transporters must be registered with the state. LOTI, in addition, prescribes a number of rules of contracts, financing, cancellation of licenses, social conditions, and safety.

The master plan for each transport mode looks ahead to what should be or might be the extent and nature of the respective mode at some future date. It serves as a kind of hypothesis for long-range technical planning. This master plan is approved as a planning document by decree of the government or by public law. Master plans are also prepared and approved for the Régions and Départements. All are reviewed in connection with preparation of the transport policy section of the national PLAN. The PLAN then represents a set of priorities for financing and realization. The PLAN is ultimately presented to the parliament to be enacted into law. Even when so enacted, it does not have the

Figure 4.2
Transport Policy Flow (Airways)

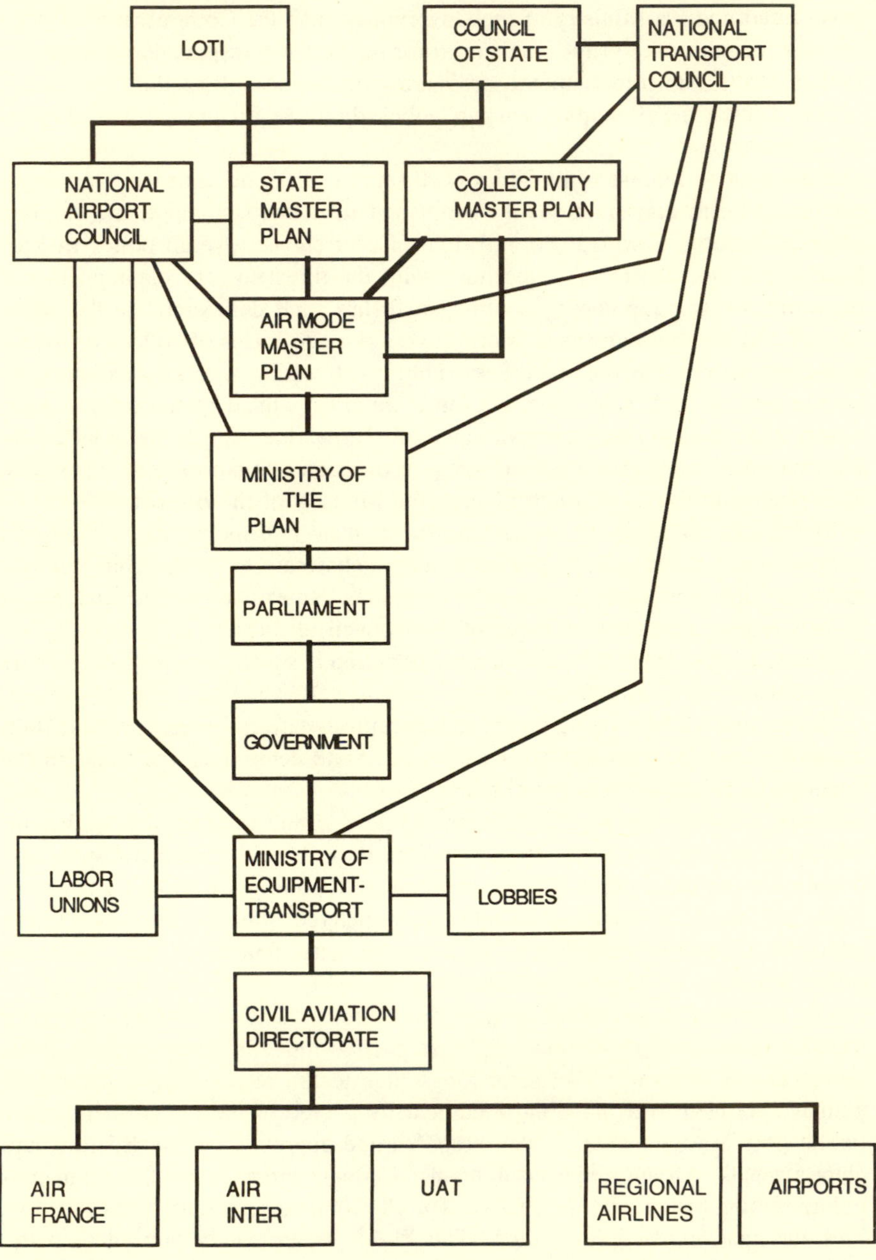

force of authorizing legislation. But its authority in connection with infrastructure budgeting and financing is profound. Thus, the PLAN's provisions and the reasons are accepted as transport policy requirements. Contracts binding transport organizations, and the state or Régions, or the state and lower levels of government, must facilitate the goals set out in the PLAN. LOTI and the PLAN are interlocking instruments. LOTI spells out more detailed rules on contracts as they deal with specific infrastructure projects and their financing.

One of the major purposes of the PLAN is to effect a choice in determining the economic principle under which a public commercial establishment shall operate: Is it to be according to the management rules for a private business, wherein it is expected to earn its way, and charges for service are fixed to that purpose? Or according to the principle of public institution management? In the latter case, the service agency is a management wherein tariffs are charged according to marginal social cost of the user's inclusion in the traffic being served, and the investments in facilities are decided on the basis of their benefit to the public as a whole. Either one of these can accommodate itself nicely to intervention by the state. In fact, no publicly owned service operates completely according to one principle or the other. It is for the commissariat of the PLAN to devise the most rational solution for each mode, and it is hoped that the implementation of LOTI will provide the appropriate coordination of investment and management among all modes of transportation. The problem is difficult: each mode has its partisans with their vested interests. The balance between what is conceived as an overall national requirement and what should be left to the judgment of regional authorities, with their increasing vested interests, is also very difficult to manage, most especially in a state with its traditions of centrality such as France.

The ministerial level is the next transport policy instrumentality. By a decree of April 12, 1978, transport was transferred from the Ministry of Public Works to a newly created Ministry of Transport. The independent ministry, whose structure and workings were relatively easy for the outsider to understand, continued until the advent of the Fabius government, of July 23, 1984. Then transportation was placed under the Ministry of Urbanism, Housing, and Transport. Since the March 1986 parliamentary election and a new right-wing government under M. Chirac, transportation has been put under a kind of super ministry called Ministère de l'Equipment (Ministry of Equipment). The term *Equipment* can be roughly translated here as public establishment. The new super ministry includes transportation, public works, housing, territorial improvement, environment, and urbanism. The objectives in the arrangements of the Fabius government, and the new Chirac government are to bring about greater policy coordination below the prime minister level. There is reason to doubt that transportation will be lodged in an independent ministry within the near future. Sea transportation is now also located in this ministry, but as a separate state secretariat.

As a practical matter, nearly all of the oversight, technical, and policy formulation offices identified with the pre-1984 Ministry of Transport remain in place. These are now in the charge of a sub-cabinet-level political appointee called the Ministre délégue chargé des Transports (simply translated to mean minister designated to represent the government's interest in transportation, with decision-making power). The activities over which he is responsible are in and coordinated with the Ministry of Equipment. De facto, the position is a rank below minister. The path of policy making within the new super ministry is still evolving.

The ministry carries out policies adopted by the government (i.e., the Council of Ministers and the prime minister), and implements and changes regulations as may be required by legislation. Naturally, the ministry represents France in international bodies, such as the important European Conference of Ministers of Transport. Although the SNCF is an autonomous corporation, as is Air France, the minister is required to review closing or organizing of rail services.

The administrative functions are carried out by six directorates: civil aviation, highways, highway traffic and security, meteorology, ground transport (railways, canals, and pipelines), and the directorate of economic (having to do with the PLAN), financial, and administrative affairs. Reporting to the ministry are these staff technical agencies: General Council of Points et Chaussées, and general inspectorates for environment and property, labor and transport manpower, civil aviation, and meteorology.

The directorate general of civil aviation has its responsibilities fixed by the decree of Oct. 26, 1978. These are to plan and carry out policies on the national and international levels, policies concerning infrastructure, air transportation, airways traffic, aircraft construction, and training of aeronautical personnel. Under this directorate are about 11,000 employees, including all of the civilian air controllers.

Highways are in two different directorates. One is concerned with design, construction, repair, and regulation of the road system, as well as the legal questions concerning it (land expropriations and property damage caused by construction). A subdivision of this directorate is responsible for economic and financial studies in connection with proposed construction plans. It is concerned also with the financial and administrative problems of the highway and urban master plans. Another subdivision exercises the government's oversight of the financing and contracting of autoroute concessionaire.

A full directorate of the ministry is responsible for operation of the highways, coordination and control of registration, driver education, highway signals, circulation planning, research activity, safety devices, highway pollution, consumption of energy, and also the furnishing of personnel for European Economic Community (EEC) and United Nations (UN) working groups, organization of highway information centers, and standards for drivers.

The directorate of surface transportation is concerned with the promotion and development of public transportation on waterways, highways, and rail. It attempts to regulate conditions of competition among modes and regulates working conditions, especially for bus and truck drivers. This is the office of oversight for the SNCF, the Régie Autonome des Transports Parisiens (RATP), the concessionary autoroutes, and various private city transport companies. This directorate participates directly in the waterways operation, and it is charged with regional, department, and city transport questions, and transport of dangerous materials.

Separately within that part of the ministry concerned with urbanism is a center for study of urban transportation. The directorate of economic, financial, and administrative affairs is charged with the budget, accounting, management, and transport statistics. The purpose of the meteorology directorate is rather self-evident and is fixed by decree of Oct. 31, 1978. But in France, special emphasis is placed upon the obligations arising out of international agreements. The meteorology directorate employs about 3,500 people.

At all modal and territorial levels, there are provisions made for nongovernmental inputs to transport policy. At the top level is the nongovernmental membership of the National Transport Council. Professional organizations consult officially in the making of rules for highway transport. In each Département there is a commission for highway security and working hours for transport employees. It is composed of representatives of employees' and employers' organizations. In addition, there is what might be called the transportation lobbies: Comité des transporteurs aériens complémentaires (third-level air lines association), Syndicat national du personnel navigant de l'aéronautique civile, among others.

NOTES

1. Of the exchange traffic tonnage with West Germany, 30 percent is by waterway and the figure is 44 percent with Belgium and the Netherlands.

2. The state does not contract to furnish any financial subvention. Forty-nine of the Air Inter services, carrying 22 percent of the passengers, are deficit operations. Fourteen lines carry two-thirds of the traffic and make a profit. Of these, the most important routings are from Paris to Marseille, Toulouse, Nice, Bordeaux, and Strasbourg, in that order. The anticipated deregulaton of intra-European airline service may seriously imbalance the financial operations of Air Inter. During the first year of full operation of the TGV rail line, Paris-Lyon traffic of Air Inter decreased 33 percent.

3. A major problem for the SNCF is labor legislation that requires retirement of operating employees at age 50 and of non-operating employees at age 55. The retirement pension payment is equal to 80 percent of the most recent six months of active salary, indexed. The rule no doubt had some merit when the operating employees were identified with the steam locomotive, whose last year on the SNCF was 1974. Now there are far more pensioners on the rolls than active employees. Currently, this matter is "under study." And objections to the study are loud and long, especially from the labor unions: the study might lead to similar reviews among employees of the post office and Electricité de France Gaz de France. For the labor unions, who have organizational and membership problems, this issue appears more viable than some others.

4. Oversight provisions can be onerous at times because they are the legally established conduit for the exercise of political pressure on the SNCF management. But they must be provided by law so that there exists an appropriate body to oversee the terms of the state-SNCF contract mentioned here. Often it is more symbolic than real. But the symbolism itself has a certain value and must not be discounted as simply "playing politics."

5. The spectacular photo-image and speed performance of the train tend to obscure the reasoning and carefully coordinated planning that brought it into being. It commenced revenue operation in 1981. The TGV was not intended to relieve pressure on the lines served, but to reduce travel times and improve the quality of service for the user. In the 1970s, transport investment became less oriented toward increasing capacity and more toward improving productivity and reducing costs.

REFERENCES

Les Aspects Socio-Économiques des Trains à Grande Vitesse [The socioeconomic aspects of high-speed trains], 2 volumes (Paris: Documentation Française, 1984).

Balat, R., and B. Peguilan, *The Network of Air Passenger Service in Europe* (European Conference of Ministers of Transport, 1983).

Bernadet, Maurice, and Gilles Joly, *Le Secteur des Transports* [The transport sector] (Lyon: Economica, 1978).

Bozin, Jean-François, *Les Défis du TGV* [The challenges of TVG] (Paris: Denoel, 1981).

Borg, P., J. R. Fradin, and M. Manheim, "Paris," *Managing Transport* (Paris: OECD, 1979).

Boyer, Albert, *Les Transports Routiers* [Roadway transportation] (Paris: Presses Universitaires de France, 1973).

Broussole, Denis, *Le Rail et La Route* [Railways and roadways] (Paris: Economica, 1981).

Caron, François, *An Economic History of Modern France* (New York: Columbia University Press, 1979).

Carré, J. J., P. Dubois, and E. Malinovash, *French Economic Growth* trans. John P. Hatfield (Stanford: Stanford University Press, 1975).

Chesnais, Michel, *Transports et Espace Française* [Transportation and French geography] (Masson, 1981).

Chimi, Leo W., *Competitive Position and Future of Inland Waterway Transport,* Round Table 49 (Paris, ECMT, 1980).

Commissariat, Général du Plan, *Aéronautique et Espace, IX Plan 1984–1988* [Air travel and geography, Ninth PLAN 1984–1988] (Documentation Française, 1983).

———, *Compétence Transferées aux Collectivités Territorials* [Delegation of tasks to territorial collectivities] (Documentation Française, 1985).

———, *Politique des Transports, IX Plan 1984–1988* [The politics of transportation, Ninth PLAN 1984–1988] (Paris: Documentation Française, 1983).

Cullon, R., and D. Schwartz, "Combined Transport: Technical, Economic, and Commercial Aspects," *Transport and the Challenge of Structural Change,* European Conference of Ministers of Transport, 1980, pp. 135–199.

de Santos, Gerard, and José Ranardo, *Le Chemin de Fer du Col de Tende* [Railways of the Col de Tende] (Menton: Edition du Cabris, 1979).

La Documentation Française, *Un Dossier: La Liaison Rhine-Danube* [A dossier: the Rhine-Danube linkage] (Paris: Documentation Française, 1979).

European Conference of Ministers of Transport, *Infrastructure Capacity Problems Raised by International Transport,* Round Table 45 (Paris: ECMT, 1979).

———, *The Interface between Air and Land Transport in Europe* (Paris: ECMT, 1983).

———, *International Road Haulage: Taxation Systems,* Round Table 71 (Paris: ECMT, 1986).

———, *Possibilities and Limits of Regulation in Transport Policy,* Round Table 42 (Paris: ECMT, 1979).

Fayard, Alain, *Les Autoroutes et Leur Financement* [Autoroutes and their finance] (Paris: Documentation Française, 1980).

Fruit, Elie, *Les Syndicats dans les Chemins de Fer en France 1890–1910* [Railway conglomerates in France, 1890–1910] (Paris: Editions Ouvrières, 1976).

Frybourg, Michel. *The Cost of Combined Transport,* "France," Round Table 64 (Paris: ECMT: 1984).

Funel, Paul and Jacques Villiers, *Le Transport Aérien Français* [French air transport] Paris: Documentation Française, 1982).

Grégoire, Roger, *Le Transport Fluvial* [Waterway transportation] (Paris: Documentation Française, 1983).

Guillaumat, Pierre, *Orientations pour les Transports Terrestres* [Objectives for land transportation] (Paris: Documentation Française, 1978).

Hanappe, P., and C. Bonte, "International Goods Transport: Regulation" (Paris, ECMT, 1985), pp. 157–181.

INSEE, *Les Transports en France en 1983–1984—XXIIe Rapport de la Comptes des Transports de la Nation* [Transportation in France in 1983–1984—The 22nd report of the National Transportation Accounting Board] (Paris: INSEE, November 1985).

Juillard, E., *L'Europe Rhénane* [Rhine valley Europe] (Paris: Armaud Colin, 1985).

Lorin, Philippe, *Le Train à Grande Vitesse* [The high-speed train] (Paris: Fernal Nulttain, 1981).

Malaurie, M. C., "Passenger Transport," *Regulations of International Transport* (Paris: EMCT: 1985), pp. 261–289.

Merlin, Pierre, *Les Politiques de Transport Urbain* [Urban transport policy] (Paris: Documentation Française, 1985).

Ministère des Transports, *TGV-Atlantique* (Rudeau Report) (Paris: Documentation Française, 1984).

Ministère des Transports, Ministère de l'industrie et de la Recherche, *Rapport de la Mission Transports Terrestres* [Report of the Commission on Land Transportation] (Paris: Documentation Française, 1983).

Morellet, O., R. Maulé, and X. Godard, "Passenger Transport," *Review of Demand Models,* Round Table 58 (Paris: ECMT, 1982).

Navailles, Jean-Pierre, *Le Tunnel sous la Manche* [The Channel Tunnel] (Champ Varrow: Epoques, 1987).

OECD, *Airports and the Environment* (Paris: OECD, 1975).

———, *The Future of European Passenger Transport* (Paris: OECD, 1977).

Pillet, J. Ph., *Les Economies d'énergie dans les Transports Ebertrans* (Energy economics in Ebertran transport] (Paris: 1980).

Quinet, E. R.; R. Marche; and C. Reynaud, "Assessment of Society's Transport Needs—

Goods Transport,'' *Ninth International Symposium on Theory and Practice of Transport Economics,* November 2–4, 1982 (Paris: ECMT, 1983), pp. 137–193.

———, *La Coordination des Infrastructures de Transport* [Coordination of transport infrastructure] (Paris: Documentation Française, 1980).

———, *Les Transports en France* [Transportation in France] (Paris: Documentation Française, 1982).

Reynaud, C., ''International Goods Transport: Investment,'' *The Evaluation of Past and Future Policy Measures* (Paris: ECMT, 1985), pp. 99–156.

Richard, Charles, *Les Autoroutes* [Freeways] (Paris: Presses Universitaires de France, 1984).

SECAP, *Système de Gestion Autonome du Réseau d'Autoroutes et Application du Péage a son Financement* [The self-management system of the freeway network and the use of toll revenues for self-financing] (Paris: SCET-Autoroute, 1984).

Strohl, Mitchel P., *Transportation Geography of Western Europe,* unpublished textbook (Paris: 1981).

Tarrino, A., *Public Transport in Rural Areas: Scheduled and Non-scheduled Services,* ''France,'' ECMT Round Table (Paris: ECMT, 1984), pp. 103–142.

Villette, J., *Transports Décentralisations 9th Plan* [Transportation decentralization Ninth PLAN] (Paris: Documentation Française, 1986).

5

JAPAN

Tsuneo Akaha

BACKGROUND

Japan today has one of the most developed domestic and international transportation networks in the world. In the development of the nation's modern transportation, the national government has played and continues to play a central role. This chapter briefly traces the development of land, sea, and air modes of transportation in modern Japan, focusing on the sometimes timely and effective and sometimes slow and inadequate response of the national government to the demands of economic and technological change in the country, as well as on the nature of those demands. The discussion will also introduce the Japanese government's recent decision to privatize the Japanese National Railways as a way of highlighting the impact of political forces on the national transportation policy. Finally, the study will present a brief overview of the transportation policy process and major participants in that process.

Under the national banner of *fukoku kyōhei* (enrichment of the nation and strengthening of military and industrial potential), the Meiji government (1868–1913) embarked on an aggressive program to develop the nation's transportation system (Transport Policy Council: 5). The building of railroads, port and harbor facilities, and roads was deemed particularly essential to the nation's modernization process. Through public investment, government aid for private

This study was supported in part by a research grant from the Association for Asian Studies/Northeast Asia Council.

industry, and government-assisted introduction of Western technology, the Japanese accomplished their task quickly. They ran their first train between Tokyo and Yokohama in 1872 and their first electric trolley in Kyoto in 1895; imported their first automobile in 1899; and introduced their first domestically produced airplane in 1911 and automobile in 1912. The imperial government also saw the development of maritime transportation as a matter of national security and, in addition to developing a modern world-class navy, took a direct hand in the development of a modern maritime industry by providing extensive subsidies for shipbuilding and shipping.

Government involvement quickly became one of the central features of transportation development in Japan, in peacetime and in wartime alike. The Sino-Japanese War of 1894–95 and the Russo-Japanese War of 1904–1905 contributed both to the rapid expansion of the transportation system, particularly maritime and naval transport, and to aggressive government involvement in the process. The latter culminated in the nationalization of major railroads in 1907 under the Japanese National Railways (JNR). Furthermore, the worldwide shortage of ships in the aftermath of World War I provided an opportunity to expand aggressively the nation's shipbuilding capacity, and by 1920 Japan had become the third largest shipbuilder in the world.

Following the depression of 1929 the government expanded its role in transportation development through extensive investment in public works, including the construction and repair of roads, ports, and harbors. Public assistance was also extended to the shipping and shipbuilding industries which were in a state of depression. Elsewhere the government maintained a regulatory function vis-à-vis the bus and trucking industries which had begun operating in 1910 and 1915, respectively, and rapidly expanded after the Tokyo earthquake of 1923. In 1928 the government entered the new business of air transportation by establishing a Japan Air Transport Corporation. The nationally owned company gradually expanded its operation as the government constructed more than twenty airports by 1941.

As the nation embarked on the path of militarism and imperialism, its transport capabilities were mobilized to serve national purposes. To ensure strategic supplies at home and abroad, the military-controlled government severely restricted civilian use of gasoline and other fuels beginning in 1937, totally banning the sale of gasoline for commercial passenger transport in 1940. Maritime transport was subjected to strict government regulation for national security reasons after the outbreak of the Sino-Japanese War and received a major boost by military procurement after the promulgation of the National Mobilization Law in 1938. Finally, in 1942 Japanese shipping was placed under total government control.

When Japan was defeated in World War II and placed under the authority of the Supreme Commander of the Allied Powers (SCAP), the nation had lost three-quarters of its shipping capacity. Destruction of the nation's railway system was also extensive: 1,600 kilometers, or 5 percent of JNR's total railroads had been destroyed or severely damaged, as had 1,400 kilometers of private railroads, 890 steam locomotive engines, 570 electric engines, 2,200 passenger cars, and 9,550 freight cars. Damage to the nation's automotive transportation was just as extensive, and much of what remained could not operate because of the fuel shortage (Seisakujihōsha: 13–14).

Under these circumstances and given the importance of transport-based infrastructure for Japan's postwar socioeconomic recovery, the government in Tokyo naturally assumed a central role in the reconstruction and rehabilitation of the nation's transportation system (Transport Policy Council: 5). During the first decade immediately following the war, the national government established the foundation of Japan's present-day transportation system and policy.

Under the new constitution the four-year-old Ministry of Transport (MOT) was placed under civilian control in 1949. Its basic structure remained the same until, later, a major reorganization in 1984. More 1949 legislation established JNR as a "public enterprise." JNR was the operator of the national railway network, but its ownership and control remained in the hands of the government. This arrangement, as will be seen later, had important implications for the management of postwar JNR. Also 1949 saw JNR lay off 9,500 of its employees as a cost-cutting measure. JNR workers, organized into labor unions, were barred from striking by the law on public enterprise labor, and their grievances could be settled only through mediation—a system still in existence today. Another pattern that was set early in the postwar period was that railroad construction was financed not by revenue expansion but by massive borrowing.

Japanese shipping and shipbuilding regained independence in 1952 as SCAP relinquished its control over those industries. A public corporation had been set up in 1947 through which private shipbuilders could borrow public funds. Starting in 1953 additional government funds were made available for shipbuilding through the three-year-old Japan Development Bank. The government assistance enabled the shipbuilding industry to develop what has since come to be known as *keikaku zōsen* (planned shipbuilding). Also, in 1953 the government initiated a program for partially subsidizing private shipbuilders' interest payments. This system has continued off and on to this day.

The construction and modernization of port and harbor facilities were slow in the period immediately following the war. Government investment in public works initially emphasized the expansion of food production and reconstruction of municipal infrastructures. As the Korean War increased the demand for coastal shipping, however, the construction of port and harbor facilities received increasing government attention. Authority to administer, operate, and construct such facilities was vested in local governments rather than in the national government. This pattern holds true today.

Administration of public vehicular transport was removed from the wartime control of the Ministry of the Army and placed under the reorganized, civilian MOT at the conclusion of the war, and soon thereafter the government agency undertook a series of legislative and administrative measures to liberalize automotive transportation. The dramatic economic expansion assisted by the Korean War was a boon to the trucking industry; the volume of non-rail freight transportation quadrupled within ten years of the end of the war.

In 1953 the government began 50 percent capital participation in the first Japanese civil airline, Japan Air Lines Co., Ltd. (JAL) founded in 1951. With the conclusion of aviation agreements with the United States and the United Kingdom in 1952 and with the Netherlands, Sweden, Norway, Denmark, and Thailand in 1953, and with the commencement of a Tokyo–San Francisco service, JAL entered the world of international aviation. The merger of two private regional firms led to the formation of All Nippon Airways Co., Ltd. (ANA). JAL and ANA have since become the two most important scheduled airlines in Japan.

Between 1955 and 1965 Japan experienced unprecendented economic growth, its GNP growing at a remarkable average annual rate of 9.8 percent. This growth facilitated and was sustained by the expansion of social capital such as port and harbor facilities, roads, and railroads. The government was again called upon to provide much of the necessary capital and technological input. Its role was not uniform across all modes of transportation, however. On land, the government continued to operate the nation's railroad system through JNR but offered only limited assistance and encouragement to the bus and trucking industries. The government also facilitated stable and regulated growth of air transport and provided important assistance and direction in stabilizing the fragile maritime transport industry.

In 1956, JNR formulated its first five-year Transport Capacity Expansion Plan. At an estimated cost of ¥598 billion ($1.66 billion),[1] the plan was to add 24,000 new freight cars to JNR, extend its railroads over a distance of 1,400 kilometers, and electrify 1,650 kilometers of railroads. The plan was succeeded by another five-year plan. The main purpose of the new plan was to modernize JNR's transportation system, including the construction of its first *shinkansen* (high-speed or bullet train) between Tokyo and Osaka, the doubling of tracks over a distance of 1,100 kilometers, the electrification of 1,800 kilometers of trunk railroad routes, and the introduction of 1,800 diesel engines. The whole plan was estimated to cost ¥1,350 billion ($3.75 billion). As a result of these two plans, the volume of passenger transportation and freight transportation on JNR jumped from 91.2 billion passenger-kilometers and 42.6 billion ton-kilometers in 1955 to 164.2 billion passenger-kilometers and 58.9 billion ton-kilometers in 1964, respectively (Seisakujihōsha: 27). The new high-speed line between Tokyo and Osaka was completed and started its operation in 1964, the year that the Japanese still fondly and proudly remember. The Internation Olympics were held in Tokyo that year.

The decade saw not only the dramatic quantitative expansion of the Japanese economy but also accelerated urbanization in large metropolitan areas of the country. Most typical in this regard were Tokyo, Osaka, and Nagoya, where fast population growth resulted in increasing traffic congestion and overcrowding. MOT responded by promoting the construction of subways and the expansion of rail transport capacity through subsidies, both public and private. Subways were extended to the total distance of 55 kilometers in Tokyo, 27 kilometers in Osaka, and 9 kilometers in Nagoya (Seisakujihōsha: 28–29).

The bus and trucking industries also expanded. Within twenty years of the end of the war the total distance covered by licensed bus operators more than doubled, and by the mid-1960s the expansion of regional bus networks had been completed.[2] During the same period, the total volume of cargos carried by trucks increased by 240 percent, while the volume for railroads and for coastal shipping increased by 30 percent and 130 percent, respectively.

Air transportation, both domestic and international, also experienced fast growth during the same decade. On the international side, Japan signed aviation treaties with fourteen countries, increased the number of scheduled flights from Tokyo to San Francisco, began flights to Los Angeles, and started scheduled flights to Hong Kong, Bangkok, and Singapore. In the early 1960s, JAL further extended its service to Paris and then to New York, thus realizing its long-cherished dream of "encircling the globe." Domestic passengers increased from 340,000 in 1955 to 750,000 in 1959 as the number of flights and destinations increased (Seisakujihōsha: 32–33).

The 1960s was also a period of increasing competition in civil aviation, and the government was busy finding a balance between healthy competition and stability in the industry. By 1964 six local, scheduled airlines had regrouped themselves into two main groups, the All Nippon Airways (ANA) group and the Japan Domestic Airlines (JDA) group. MOT, which had begun licensing airline routes and fares in 1951, served as intermediary in the reorganization of the domestic airlines and in 1964 decided that main domestic routes would be operated by JAL, ANA, and JDA.

The government was forced to take an even more direct role vis-à-vis the nation's unstable maritime industry. The booming U.S. economy and the closing of the Suez Canal in 1956 had brought an unprecedented boom to Japanese shipbuilding and shipping. As the Suez crisis ended and the demand for new oceangoing ships slackened, however, many Japanese shipbuilders and shipping companies ran into severe financial difficulties. As a result, by 1959 the government had to resume interest payment support for commercially financed shipbuilding activities. The National Income Doubling Plan (Kokumin Shotoku Baizō Keikaku) for 1961–70 helped push up the demand for Japanese-owned oceangoing ships. However, the shipbuilding and shipping industries were facing a deteriorating financial situation and could not be expected to meet the expanded demand on their own. Instead of offering free aid, in 1963 the government ordered a consolidation of shipping companies to place them on a sounder financial basis. As a result, eighty-eight companies were regrouped into six, representing 80 percent of Japan's total oceangoing fleet. The government did, however, suspend qualifying companies' interest payments on Japan Development Bank loans for five years. Through rationalization, consolidation, modernization, and technological innovation, Japan was able to maintain its position as the world's largest shipbuilder—the status it had attained in 1956.

SOCIOECONOMIC DIMENSIONS OF THE TRANSPORTATION SYSTEM AND POLICY

Despite the government's effort to expand the nation's public and commercial transport systems during the preceding decade, the effort could not adequately meet the growing demands of the times. Additional problems surfaced due largely to socioeconomic imbalances brought about by the accelerated economic growth. Shifts in population to major metropolitan areas created traffic congestion and overcrowding. At the same time, decreasing population in the more remote and rural sectors put an increasing financial strain on transportation operators, both public and private. With these developments came increases in traffic accidents and environmental problems, including noise and air pollution. Again the government took major initiatives, with an increasing emphasis on qualitative improvement in the nation's transportation systems.

JNR embarked on its third Transport Capacity Expansion Plan (1965–71) with two major tasks: expansion of passenger transport capacity on the trunk lines and improvement of safety measures. The plan called for government investment of ¥2,972 billion ($8.2 billion). After spending about half of this amount, JNR had to suspend this ambitious plan in 1968 because of its deteriorating financial situation. The extension of the high-speed line was continued. With the completion in 1975 of the Osaka-Hakata line (Sanyo Shinkansen), the total distance of the modern railroad reached 1,000 kilometers. According to the New National Comprehensive Development Plan of 1969, an additional 7,200 kilometers of *shinkansen* lines were slated for construction. The building of three such lines was planned in 1970 and subsequently started: the Tohoku Shinkansen (between Tokyo and Morioka), the Joetsu Shinkansen (between Tokyo and Niigata), and the Narita Shinkansen (between Tokyo and Narita, where the New Tokyo International Airport is located) (see Figure 5.1). Five other high-speed railroads were planned but their construction was frozen as a result of dramatic increases in construction costs in the aftermath of the oil crisis of 1973–74 (Seisakujihōsha: 39–40).

JNR's financial problem grew to serious proportions during this period. After recording its first real loss of ¥30 billion ($83 million) in fiscal 1964, the national corporation went into deeper and deeper debt, with its accumulated deficits standing at ¥53.6 billion ($147 million) at the end of fiscal 1966. The problem was largely attributable to the limited fare increases permitted for all JNR operations and to the loss of a major share of the freight market to commercial carriers. To cope with this problem, a Committee for the Fiscal Reconstruction of JNR was established as an advisory board to the transport minister. In 1968, the committee recommended that JNR fares be increased by about 10 percent at the beginning of the reconstruction period (1969–75) and that the

Figure 5.1
Main Transportation Networks

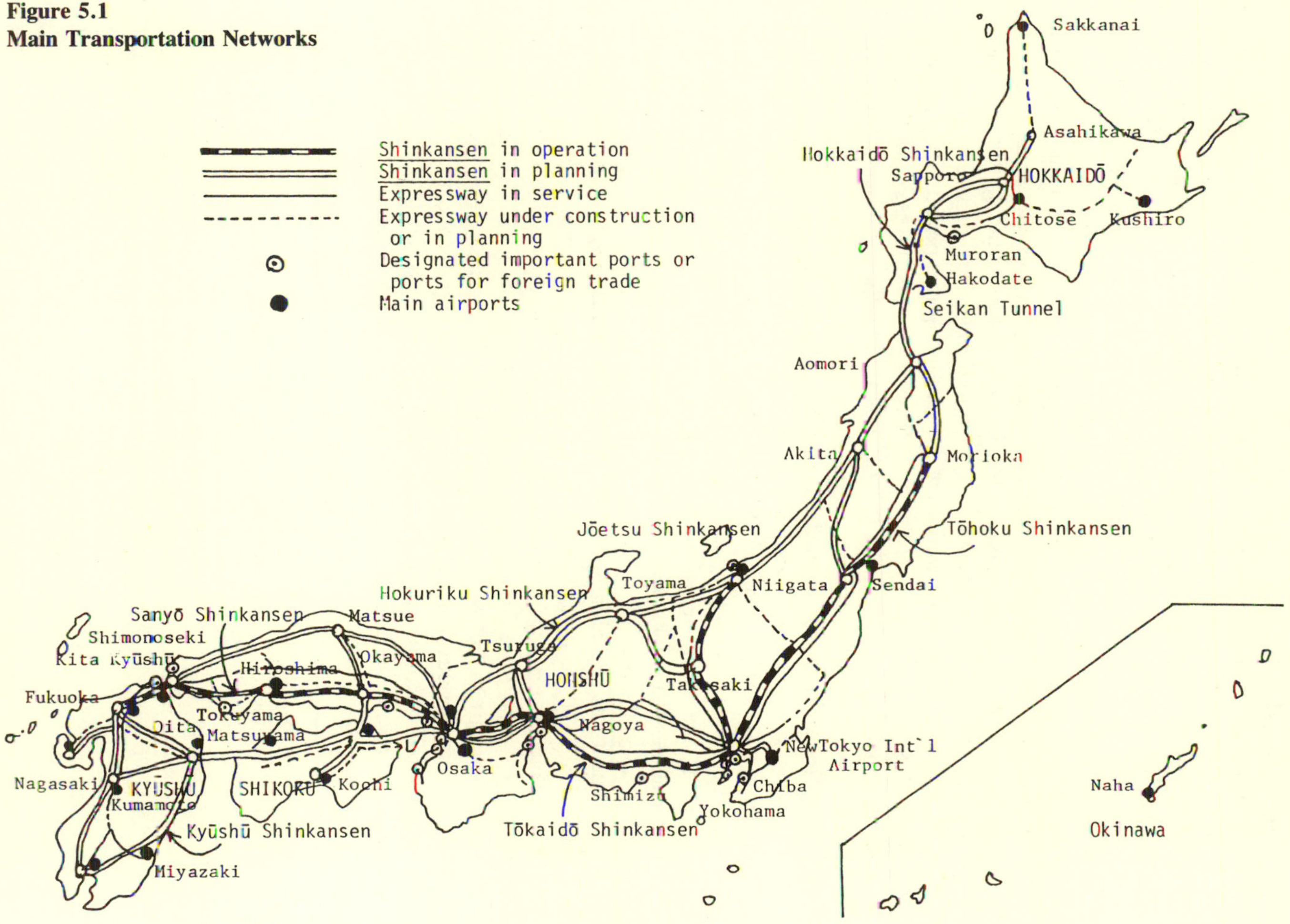

transport minister be empowered to approve additional fare increases thereafter (Seisakujihōsha: 41).

Urban population growth continued unabated throughout the 1960s and 1970s, further exacerbating the problem of traffic congestion and overcrowding of passenger transport systems. In response MOT increased its subsidies for the construction of subways in large metropolitan areas such as Tokyo, Osaka, Nagoya, and Sapporo. The government paid 10.5 percent of the subway construction cost over a five-year period starting in 1967. Government support was expanded in 1973; this time the national and municipal governments contributed 66 percent of the total cost of subway construction over eight years. The Railroad Construction Corporation, established in 1964 for building new JNR lines, was empowered in 1972 to assist in the improvement and expansion of private railroads. Private companies did not sit idle during this period. They prepared a Transport Capacity Expansion Plan (1967–1971) and invested 88 percent of its originally estimated cost of ¥297 billion ($8.2 billion) (Seisakujihōsha: 40–41).

Air transportation continued its expansion during this decade. Tokyo and Moscow signed a civil aviation agreement in 1966, paving the way for the extension of JAL services to Paris and London via Moscow in 1970. JAL's direct around-the-world service started in 1967, boosting the pride of the Japanese as one of the very few "national flag carriers" in the world. The normalization of relations between Japan and the People's Republic of China in 1972 paved the way for a civil aviation treaty between the two countries. The agreement was signed in April 1974 and the Tokyo-Beijing service started later that year. On the other hand, Taipei banned all JAL services to Taiwan in 1972, but after a new company, Japan Asia Airlines, was founded with 100 percent capital from JAL, Taipei permitted its service to Taiwan in 1975. In sharp contrast to JAL's bright future, all local domestic carriers except ANA were facing serious financial difficulties. Upon the recommendation of the Civil Aviation Council the government decided in 1966 to mandate a consolidation of local operators. Subsequently JDA and Toa Koku merged to form a new company—Toa Domestic Airline (TDA).

As the demand for air travel and freight transport grew and newer and larger aircraft were introduced, a need arose for enlarging airports and improving airport facilities. To respond to this need, MOT formulated in 1967 a five-year plan (1967–71) to extend the runways at the Tokyo International Airport (Haneda) and to build a new international airport near Osaka, as well as to extend the runways of smaller airports and build new ones, at an estimated total cost of ¥115 billion ($319 million). Additionally, a new plan was drawn up to build a New Tokyo International Airport (Seisakujihōsha: 45–46). The plan was succeeded in 1971 by yet another five-year plan (1971–75) with an estimated total cost of ¥560 billion ($1.56 billion).

Environmental pollution caused by various modes of transportation also became a major policy problem during this decade. Air and noise pollution from automobiles was particularly problematic. The government enacted the Basic Law for Environmental Pollution Control in 1967 and the Air Pollution Control Law the following year. Measures to reduce photochemical smog and lead contamination of the atmosphere were also instituted, as were regulatory standards for noise pollution and improved safety standards. As domestic and international air traffic increased, noise pollution became a serious problem and forced the government to adopt aircraft noise standards in 1973, but the results were mixed.

Maritime transport business had significantly improved after the consolidation of the shipbuilding industry into six groups. Four of them occupied the top positions in the world, and the other two were among the top ten. Planned shipbuilding between 1964 and 1968 had produced a total of 294 vessels at 9.29 million gross tons. The construction of container ships, automobile carriers, very large crude carriers (VLCC's), and 100,000-ton specialized ore carriers proceeded as well (Seisakujihōsha: 48).

Several developments in international shipping had an important bearing on Japanese maritime transport. The containerization phenomenon in international shipping for example necessitated and promoted the construction of container terminals at the country's major ports. Most importantly, negotiations in the United Nations Conference on Trade and Development (UNCTAD) over the entry of developing countries' shipping concerns into scheduled liner conferences and their share of the shipping market produced a Code of Conduct for Liner Operations in 1974. The Japanese were first concerned about increasing competition from less-developed countries, but as the treaty went into effect in 1983, they decided to accept the new code and are preparing for accession.

The government continued to promote the construction and expansion of port and harbor facilities to meet the fast growing import-export needs of the country. After the completion of the first five-year port and harbor expansion plan (1962–66), MOT issued three more five-year plans at an estimated cost of ¥650 billion ($1.81 billion), ¥1,030 billion ($2.86 billion), and ¥2,100 billion ($6.93 billion), respectively (Seisakujihōsha: 52).

Transportation is an energy-intensive business. It consumes about 15 percent of Japan's energy and 34 percent of the nation's oil supply. Privately owned automobiles, which account for about 40 percent of the total volume of passenger transport, consume 70 percent of the energy used for this purpose. By comparison, trains are far more efficient consumers of energy. While carrying almost as much passenger traffic as private vehicles, trains consume only about 10 percent of the energy used for passenger transport in Japan. The dramatic increase over the years in the number of privately owned cars has naturally pushed up the total energy consumption for transportation purposes.

The oil crisis of 1973–74 alarmed MOT and the transport industry. The government issued emergency oil use guidelines in November 1973 and placed large energy users under an oil and electricity use control in February 1974. Among other things, MOT regulated the use of fuel by railroad, bus, and trucking industries. Government control of oil consumption was gradually relaxed and eventually lifted in September 1974. The reduction of oil consumption during the oil crisis caused the first and the only negative economic growth that Japan has experienced since before World War II. Its GNP contracted by 0.2 percent in 1974.

Although non-transportation industries, including the power industry, have substantially reduced their dependence on oil since the crisis of 1973–74, transportation's dependence on oil has remained virtually unchanged to this day. Well over 90 percent of the total transport-related energy comes from oil (Unyushō, 1985: 9–13). Another oil crisis would be bound to have serious consequences for Japan's transportation system.

Since the oil crisis, the growth of demand for passenger and freight transport in Japan has generally lagged behind the GNP growth, a phenomenon unexperienced in the previous years when the former had closely followed the latter. This exacerbated the financial problem of JNR. By 1975 JNR's current accounts deficit had run up to an astounding ¥915 billion ($3.08 billion). That year the government adopted a guideline for JNR reconstruction designed to increase its efficiency and services and to balance its budget by 1977. The budget balancing act was unsuccessful, however, because, first, scheduled fare increases were delayed by five months and, second, when they finally went into effect in November 1976, the overall ridership on JNR lines had dropped sharply (Seisakujihōsha: 54). Consequently, the government was forced to postpone the target year for balancing JNR's accounts to 1979. The government introduced a major reform in the JNR fare policy in 1977 by amending the law on JNR fares to allow the transport minister to approve fare increases without parliament's approval until JNR's financial situation improved. However, neither the new policy nor the series of cost-cutting measures that followed had much impact on the overall financial standing of the public enterprise.

Air transport also experienced turbulent years following the oil crisis. The government adopted a third Airport Improvement Plan for 1976–80. The plan was to spend an estimated ¥920 billion ($3.10 billion) to prepare for the opening of the New Tokyo International Airport, to expand runways at the old Tokyo International Airport, and to introduce more jet planes to local airports. Of these, the opening of the new airport at Narita was the most problematic.

By 1973 about half of the construction work on the new airport had been completed, including a 4,000-meter runway and a passenger terminal. The opening of the airport, however, was delayed long beyond its originally scheduled date of March 30, 1978. There were several problems. First, the transport of fuel by pipeline from Chiba Harbor to the airport could not begin as scheduled because of disagreements between the Ministry of Finance and the local authorities over the financing of the latter's purchase of modern fire engines. Second, groups opposed to the new airport project, following earlier activities designed to block the construction of the airport, built two steel towers to obstruct the takoff and landing of airplanes. On May 6, 1977, a court order finally allowed the airport authorities to remove the structures by force. Four days before the rescheduled opening of the airport, however, a group of radical students and supporters broke into the control tower and destroyed some equipment. This further delayed the opening of the airport until May 20.

In 1974, the Civil Aviation Council issued a report recommending that a new international airport be built in the Osaka Bay, with two 4,000-meter runways and one 3,200-meter runway. In February 1977, MOT announced its study plan and began a feasibility study the following year. In September 1980, the Air Transport Council submitted a basic plan for the proposed airport to the transport minister. According to the plan, there would be two 4,000-meter runways and another 3,400-meter runway; these runways would handle 260,000 takeoffs and landings a year; the airport would be built on reclaimed land; and the total airport area would be 1,400 hectares. The airport was originally scheduled to open about 1990, but the $7 billion project is behind schedule and over budget. The first phase of the project is now supposed to be ready by spring 1993. Many expect it to cost 20 percent more than originally planned.

In 1974, the shipping industry recorded the largest profits ever in its history. Even though this resulted mostly from long-term contracts the industry had carried over from previous years, which did not reflect the industry's performance in 1974, the government decided the following year to suspend its subsidy program for shipping companies' interest payments. Ironically, 1974 marked the beginning of the long period of depression from which the maritime transport industry has yet to recover. The Shipping and Shipbuilding Rationalization Council recommended in 1978 that the government reinstitute the subsidy program, and the government responded favorably by implementing a three-year provisional interest subsidy program starting in 1979.

Japan's maritime industry faces many problems today. First, the size of the Japanese merchant fleet is increasing, but, at the same time, the Japanese-owned ships carrying Japanese crews are losing their international competitiveness. As a result, Japan's seaborne trade is increasingly dependent on foreign vessels and seamen (Figure 5.2). Second, as the size of ships has increased and the average size of a crew has decreased, there is a growing surplus of Japanese maritime labor. Over the last decade, reserve seamen have increased from 30 to 80 percent of all mariners in the country.

Third, the oil crises of 1973–74 and 1979 have caused a major surplus of tankers globally and a drastic reduction in the volume of new shipbuilding. This and the rising labor and material costs have placed shipbuilding companies in a difficult financial situation. The 1978 report of the Shipping and Shipbuilding Rationalization Council indicated that the major shipbuilding companies would have a 35 percent surplus capacity in 1985. Also in 1978 the shipbuilding industry was designated as one of the industries experiencing a depression and thus eligible for special government aid. The elimination of surplus shipbuilding capacity was achieved by March 1980. Although Japan continues to turn out about half of the new ships built in the world each year, the total

Figure 5.2
Trends in Japanese Seaborne Trade (percentage)

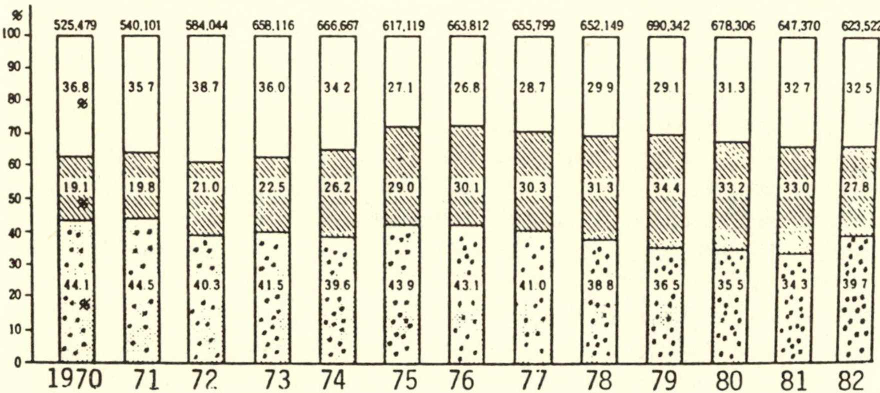

Source: Unyushō, ed., *Nihon Kaiun no Genkyō,* Tokyo: Nihon Kaiji Kōhō Kyōkai, 1984, p. 47.

volume of shipbuilding in the world and in Japan has contracted substantially since the 1970s. (Figure 5.3).

POLITICAL DIMENSIONS OF THE TRANSPORTATION SYSTEM AND POLICY

Japan's transportation system and policy have not developed in a political vacuum. Many political forces exist which influence the development of public transportation systems and the process of transportation policy. This is particularly apparent in recent developments concerning the privatization of the Japanese National Railways.

The series of measures that MOT and JNR had undertaken to improve JNR's financial standing in the 1970s had all but failed. By 1983 JNR's long-term accumulated debts had reached an astronomical ¥19,983 billion ($84.1 billion). What caused this?

First, JNR lost a good portion of its business to its commercial competitors. After reaching the record 215,289 million passenger-kilometers in 1975, as shown in Table 5.1, the volume of JNR's passenger transport declined to the low of 190,767 million in 1982. Although, thanks mainly to the expansion of *shinkansen* services, the volume has since recovered somewhat, JNR's share of the total domestic passenger traffic continues to decline. As shown in Table 5.2, JNR's cargo transport service has met an even worse fate. After experi-

Figure 5.3
Trends in the Volume of Shipbuilding in the World

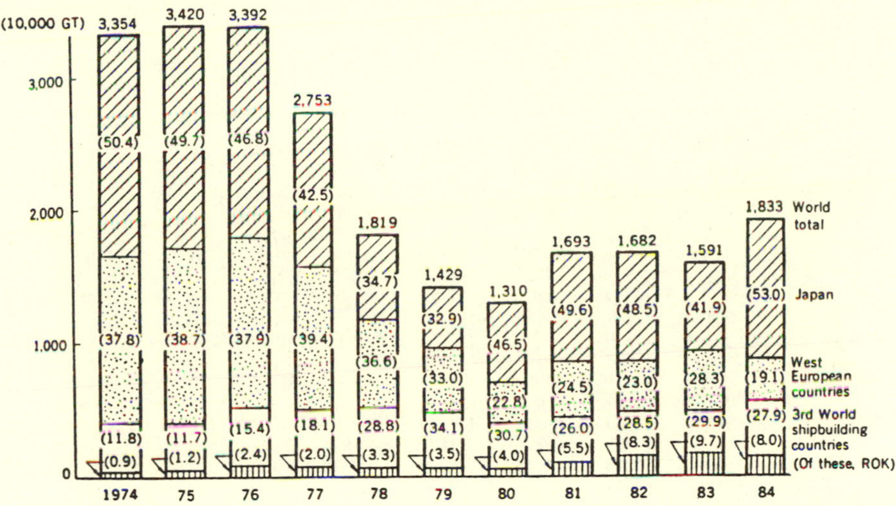

Source: Ministry of Transport, *Annual Report of Transport Economy, Summary (Fiscal 1985)*, Tokyo: Printing Bureau, Ministry of Finance, 1986, p. 13.

encing the best year in 1970, with 62,435 million ton-kilometers, the volume of cargo transported by JNR drastically dropped, standing at 21,625 million ton-kilometers in 1985. JNR's share of the total domestic freight transport consequently declined, from 39 percent in 1960 to 5.0 percent in 1984.

JNR's revenues from its passenger division steadily increased over the years; its income from freight service increased until 1979 but has since declined. As a result, revenues from transport services showed modest but steady increases. However, JNR's expenditures grew faster. Whereas its revenues and expenses stood at ¥1,993 billion ($6.7 billion) and ¥1,220 billion ($4.1 billion), respectively, in 1976, they changed to ¥3,299 billion ($13.9 billion) and ¥4,553 billion ($19.2 billion) in 1983, creating a deficit of ¥1,254 billion ($6.9 billion) in 1984.

Second, JNR's management suffered from the politicization of the process of JNR fare changes. Until 1977 all JNR fares had to be approved by the Japanese Diet (parliament). Members of the Diet, naturally hoping to increase their votes in their election bids, opposed any significant fare increases. The politically driven system caused serious delays in fare increases. The problem was compounded by JNR's aggressive investment in the expansion and modernization of its railroads and trains in the first part of the 1970s. JNR's construction expenditures had until then hovered around ¥300 billion ($833 million), but in 1972 they jumped to ¥500 billion ($1.65 billion). By 1978 they had more than doubled (Okada: 56–57).

Table 5.1
Domestic Passenger Transport by Transportation Mode (in millions of passenger-kilometers)

FY	Total	JNR	Shinkansen	Private railways	Buses	Passenger cars	Aircraft	Passenger boats
1965	382,481	174,014	10,651	81,370	80,133	40,622	2,939	3,402
1970	587,178	189,726	27,890	99,090	102,894	181,335	9,319	4,814
1975	710,711	215,289	53,318	108,511	110,063	250,804	19,148	6,895
1976	709,549	210,740	48,147	108,826	98,714	264,499	29,119	6,651
	(- 0.2)	(- 2.1)	(- 9.7)	(0.3)	(- 10.3)	(5.5)	(5.1)	(- 3.5)
1977	711,033	199,653	42,187	112,644	104,639	263,961	23,636	6,500
	(0.2)	(- 5.3)	(- 12.4)	(3.5)	(6.0)	(- 0.2)	(17.5)	(- 2.3)
1978	747,489	195,844	41,074	115,285	107,009	296,043	26,923	6,384
	(5.1)	(- 1.9)	(- 2.6)	(2.3)	(2.3)	(12,2)	(13.9)	(- 1.8)
1979	777,336	194,690	40,986	117,770	108,317	319,869	30,246	6,443
	(4.0)	(- 0.6)	(- 0.2)	(2.2)	(1.2)	(8.0)	(12.3)	(0.9)
1980	782,031	193,143	41,790	121,399	110,396	321,272	29,688	6,132
	(0.6)	(- 0.8)	(2.0)	(3.1)	(1.9)	(0.4)	(- 1.8)	(- 4.8)
1981	790,358	192,115	41,717	124,089	108,827	328,251	31,032	6,044
	(1.1)	(- 0.5)	(- 0.2)	(2.2)	(- 1.4)	(2.2)	(4.5)	(- 1.4)
1982	804,363	190,767	46,105	125,577	104,836	347,219	30,106	5,859
	(1.8)	(- 0.7)	(10.5)	(1.2)	(- 3.7)	(5.8)	(- 3.0)	(- 3.1)
1983	821,964	192,906	50,440	128,546	103,418	360,747	30,626	5,722
	(2.2)	(1.1)	(9.4)	(2.4)	(- 1.4)	(3.9)	(1.7)	(- 2.3)
1984	832,306	194,180	50,826	130,152	103,064	365,631	33,498	5,780
	(1.3)	(0.7)	(0.8)	(1.3)	(- 0.3)	(1.4)	(9.4)	(1.0)
1985	858,195	197,463	55,423	132,620	104,898	384,362	33,119	5,733
	(3.1)	(1.7)	(9.0)	(2.1)	(1.8)	(5.1)	(-1.1)	(-0.8)

Note: Figures in parentheses denote the rate of percentage increase over the previous year.

Source: Ministry of Transport, *Annual Report of Transport Economy, Summary,* Tokyo: Ministry of Transport, annual.

Third, JNR's finances were adversely affected in a similar way by a politically motivated investment policy. Of the 18.6 million passengers that JNR carried in 1981, 66 percent were within the two largest metropolitan areas around Tokyo and Osaka. Yet only 13.3 percent of the ¥108.5 billion ($492 million) government investment in JNR construction works that year went to the two areas with the greatest demands. The disproportionately heavy investment in rural areas was a consequence of the parliamentary system that favored (and continues to favor) the less populated areas of the country. Liberal Democratic Party (LDP) legislators from rural districts are naturally inclined to favor new construction projects in their communities (Omori: 74). New JNR construction works are reviewed and approved by the Railroad Construction Council headed by the powerful executive board chairman (Omori: 74).

Fourth, the Japanese Railroad Construction Corporation, a public corporation with government capital participation and oversight, added to the politicization of JNR. Since its foundation in 1964, the corporation had been a major contractor of many JNR construction works. The individual who had more to do

Table 5.2
Domestic Cargo Transport by Transportation Mode
(in millions of ton-kilometers)

	Total	JNR	Private railways	Automobiles	Coastal shipping	Aircraft
1965	186,346	56,408	890	48,392	80,635	21
1970	350,656	62,435	988	135,916	151,243	74
1975	360,779	46,577	770	129,701	183,576	152
1976	373,905	45,526	779	132,619	194,321	160
	(3.6)	(- 2.3)	(1.2)	(2.2)	(5.9)	(5.3)
1977	386,992	40,587	746	143,095	202,294	183
	(3.5)	(- 10.8)	(- 4.2)	(7.9)	(4.1)	(14.4)
1978	409,464	40,413	791	56,065	211,971	244
	(5.8)	(- 0.4)	(6.0)	(9.1)	(4.8)	(22.4)
1979	442,035	42,284	803	172,888	225,786	273
	(8.0)	(4.6)	(1.5)	(10.8)	(6.5)	(22.1)
1980	439,064	36,961	740	178,888	222,173	290
	(- 0.7)	(- 12.6)	(- 7.9)	(3.5)	(- 1.6)	(6.0)
1981	427,487	33,398	690	181,309	211,763	327
	(- 2.6)	(- 9.6)	(- 6.8)	(1.3)	(- 4.7)	(12.9)
1982	417,012	30,246	635	187,719	198,052	360
	(- 2.5)	(- 9.4)	(- 8.0)	(3.5)	(- 6.5)	(10.1)
1983	422,321	27,086	560	193,527	200,748	400
	(- 1.1)	(- 10.4)	(- 11.8)	(3.1)	(1.4)	(11.2)
1984	434,600	22,721	513	200,813	210,107	446
	(2.9)	(- 16.1)	(8.6)	(3.8)	(4.7)	(11.5)
1985	434,377	21,625	509	205,941	205,818	482
	(- 0.1)	(- 4.8)	(- 0.7)	(2.6)	(- 2.0)	(8.2)

Note: Figures in parentheses denote the rate of percentage increase over the previous year.

Source: Ministry of Transport, *Annual Report of Transport Economy, Summary,* Tokyo: Ministry of Transport, annual.

with the establishment of the semi-public corporation was former Prime Minister Kakuei Tanaka, who once said, "JNR is charged with a national mission and must construct new railroads [including those] that cannot be built by the private sector because they will lose money." Between 1964 and 1982, the corporation won government procurement worth over ¥1,517 billion ($6.08 billion) in connection with JNR construction projects. In addition, the corporation received ¥1,700 billion ($6.8 billion) in government funding for the construction of the Joetsu Shinkansen, which incidentally services the local district in Niigata Prefecture from which the former prime minister comes. Other major recipients of government contracts for JNR projects included major financial contributors to the ruling party (Omori: 74).

Fifth, the special status of JNR as a public enterprise proved to be problematic. The view, typified by Tanaka's statement, that JNR had a special responsibility for providing transportation services to the general public often led to demands for services and investment without sufficient thought given to the enterprise's financial health (Okano; Kato).

Finally, distorted, confrontational labor-management relations in JNR had a detrimental impact on the morale of JNR employees. The LDP-influenced JNR management and the leftist labor unions of JNR workers were often at odds with each other on major public policy issues. The influence of leftist political parties in JNR unions, particularly that of the Japan Socialist Party, virtually guaranteed JNR labor's confrontational approach to the management. The conflict-ridden labor-management relationship in JNR was further exacerbated by the government's policy not to allow public enterprise employees to go on strike. Between 1953 and 1977 more than 60,000 JNR employees received some penalties for striking or for other illegal acts. Seven hundred of them were fired (Takagi: 87). The proliferation of independent unions within JNR also increased conflict and weakened morale within the public corporation.

In July 1982, a number of recommendations were prepared for administrative reforms in JNR by a Provisional Commission on Administrative Reform, created at the initiative of the then Director General of the Administrative Management Agency and current Prime Minister, Yashuhiro Nakasone.[3] The commission recommended, among other things, the division of JNR into seven blocks within five years and the eventual transfer of JNR ownership to the private sector.

The government adopted the commission's recommendations, and in May 1983 the legislature mandated financial reconstruction of JNR and establishment of a supervisory committee for that purpose. The newly created committee submitted its report to the prime minister in July 1985. The committee's report recommended and the government agreed that effective April 1, 1987, JNR should be divided and privatized as follows: (1) JNR's passenger division would be divided into six companies, three in Honshu and one each in Hokkaido, Shikoku, and Kyushu; (2) the *shinkansen* lines would be collectively held by one company; (3) the freight division would be separated from the passenger division under an independent company; (4) a new communications company would be formed to succeed JNR's communication facilities; (5) JNR's research and development outfits would be consolidated into one research institute; (6) the railway policy system would be abolished; and finally, (7) JNR would first become a special company wholly invested in kind and eventually privatized by gradually selling its stocks.

In November 1986, over objections from the socialists and communists, the parliament approved a series of legislation to make the government decision a reality. First, the Law on the Reform of Japanese National Railways ordered that JNR be divided into six passenger transport companies, one freight service company, and one holding company for all the *shinkansen* lines, and that a public corporation be set up to assume and pay off a major portion of the existing JNR debts. The second legislation, the Law on Passenger and Freight Railroad Companies, envisaged the seven new corporations mentioned in the first legislation. Third, the Law on the Shinkansen Holding Organization would allow the government to lease the existing four high-speed railroad lines to a holding company to be set up.

The fourth legislation, the Law on the Public Corporation for JNR Debt Repayment, charged the organization to be set up with the task of repaying JNR debts and securing reemployment opportunities for surplus JNR employees and mandated open bidding for the selling of JNR real estate and other assets. Fifth, the Law on Special Measures relating to the Promotion of Voluntary Retirement and Reemployment was three-year legislation whose purpose was to promote voluntary retirement and to facilitate reemployment for former JNR workers. Sixth, the Law on the Implementation of JNR Reform amended all existing JNR-related laws and stipulated that the construction and operation of *shinkansen* lines now under construction or under planning be placed under the Japanese Railroad Construction Corporation and the six proposed passenger service companies. Finally, the Law of Revising the Local Tax Law accorded a preferential status to the seven new companies regarding tax on fixed assets (e.g., real estate).[4]

Thus, the government prepared the way for the most historic reform of JNR since its foundation. However, many problems lay ahead. Of the six new passenger transport companies (renamed JR), the ones that would be built for Hokkaido, Shikoku, and Kyushu were expected to start on a rocky financial basis even though the government was determined not to transfer existing JNR debts to them. According to government estimates, the three companies were expected to operate at a deficit of ¥49.5 billion ($350 million), ¥14.8 billion ($104 million), and ¥27 billion ($190 million), respectively, in 1987 (the first year of operation). In contrast, the passenger operations by the East Japan, Tokai, and West Japan counterparts were expected to bring in a net gain of ¥248.4 billion ($1,750 million), ¥26.4 billion ($190 million), and ¥80.5 billion ($570 million), respectively (Handa: 9). In actuality, the JR group of seven companies, including the freight company, performed better than expected, collectively bringing in a net profit of ¥50 billion ($333 million), about 2.8 times as large as had been anticipated (*Asahi Shimbun,* May 31, 1988, pp. 1, 9).

The Debt Repayment Corporation, whose funds were to be used to establish a foundation to keep the three fragile companies' accounts in balance, was itself expected to operate in deficit (*Asahi Shimbun,* August 3, 1986, p. 1). There was also fear that many local JNR services in the sparsely populated islands would be discontinued after the reform of JNR.

Also problematic was the future of the surplus JNR workers. After the new companies hired 215,000 of the current JNR employees, there would be a surplus labor of 61,000 persons, of whom 20,000 were expected to voluntarily retire. Of the remaining 41,000 workers, only 2,500 were slated to find permanent employment with the Debt Repayment Corporation, leaving 38,500 former JNR employees who would have to find jobs elsewhere.

Yet another controversy concerned the future construction of *shinkansen* lines.

In 1982, the construction of five high-speed lines, which were still in the planning stage, had been frozen for financial reasons. They were the Morioka-Aomori portion of the Tohoku Shinkansen, the Hokkaido Shinkansen (between Aomori and Sapporo), the Hokuriku Shinkansen (between Takasaki and Osaka), and the Hakata-Kagoshima and Hakata-Nagasaki routes of the Kyushu Shinkansen (see Figure 5.1). Full-scale construction of these lines, covering the total distance of 1,440 kilometers, was estimated to cost ¥5,320 billion ($22.34 billion) (*Asahi Shimbun,* Dec. 16, 1986, p. 4). The Finance Ministry argued such a large-scale project would defeat the purpose of the budget austerity measure the government had adopted to reduce its deficit. Political pressure was too much, however, and in December 1986 the government decided to lift the freeze and approved a ¥15 billion ($95.5 million) budget for 1987 for the construction of the Tohoku Shinkansen, the Hokuriku Shinkansen, and the Hakata-Kagoshima route of the Kyushu Shinkansen. The government approved an additional ¥3 billion ($19.1 million) to pay for preconstruction work for the other two lines (*Asahi Shimbun,* Dec. 30, 1986, p. 1).

RECENT TRENDS AND FUTURE PROSPECTS

In its 1981 *Report and Recommendations Concerning a Comprehensive Transport System,* the Transport Policy Council foresaw a rapid increase in the demand for transport capability and called for the expansion of public transportation (Transport Policy Council: 8–10). The quantitative expansion and qualitative improvement of Japan's various transportation systems that have followed the report place Japan among the most advanced countries of the world in terms of its transportation capabilities. The annual volume of passenger transport by all modes of transportation combined today exceeds 800,000 million-kilometers, more than a twofold increase since the 1960s. The total volume of cargo transport amounts to more than 400,000 million kilotons, or two and a quarter times as much as in the 1960s.

Since the 1971 report, Japanese society and economy have undergone some major changes, with important consequences for transportation policy. First, Japan's GNP, which had grown at the average annual rate of more than 10 percent in the 1960s, grew by only about 5 percent during the 1970s. After recovering from the immediate effects of the oil crisis, Japan's economy has shown a modest yet respectable growth rate, slightly below 5 percent. However, the growth has since slowed down, to only 2.5 percent in 1986.

Second, the rapid economic growth of the 1960s and 1970s has substantially increased personal income, making for changes and diversification of values. As a result, the demand for more individualized and personalized modes of transportation, particularly private automobiles, has grown. For example, private passenger vehicles have increased their share of the volume of passenger traffic from slightly over 10 percent in the mid-1960s to well over 40 percent in the middle of the 1980s; whereas during the same period the public and

Figure 5.4

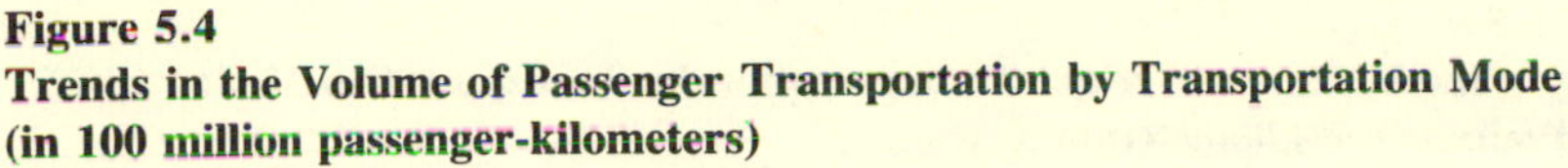

Trends in the Volume of Passenger Transportation by Transportation Mode (in 100 million passenger-kilometers)

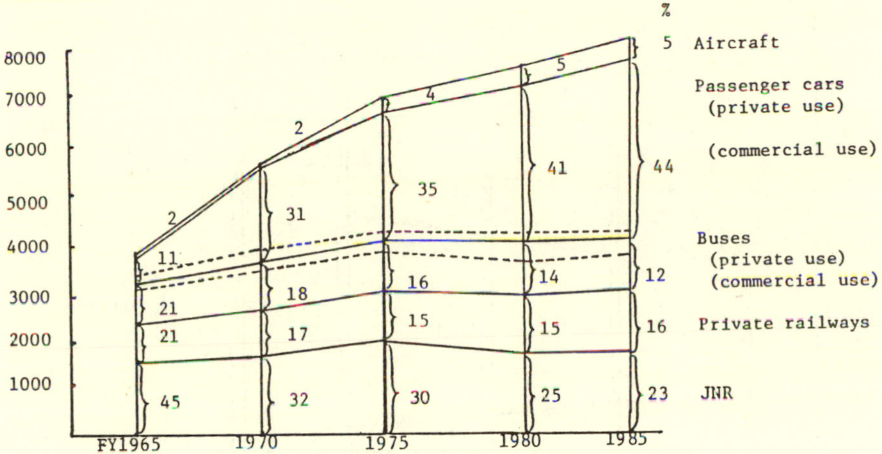

Source: Ministry of Transport, *Annual Report of Transport Economy, Summary (Fiscal 1985)*, Tokyo: Printing Bureau, Ministry of Finance, 1986, p. 1.

private railroads' shares dropped from 45 and 21 percent to 23 and 16 percent, respectively (Figure 5.4).

Similarly, significant changes have taken place in freight transport. The transport of bulk cargo in the earlier decades has given way to more diversified freight transport. For example, speedy and convenient door-to-door delivery of customized packages by trucks has grown substantially in the recent decades. As shown in Figure 5.5, JNR has been the biggest loser, its share of the volume of freight transport dropping from 31 percent in 1965 all the way down to 5 percent in 1985.

A third important trend today is the dispersement of population and industries to rural areas. The so-called U-turn phenomenon—reversing the earlier trend toward increasing concentration of socioeconomic activities in major metropolitan areas—provides a major challenge to public transportation policy makers. Increasingly sophisticated and diversified tastes and needs of the population require convenient, speedy, economical, safe, and environmentally sound forms of transportation that at the same time serve diverse and local needs and provide a convenient linkage between large metropolitan areas and more rural areas. The last of these needs is clearly recognized by the government. The fourth Comprehensive National Development Plan (1987–2000) calls for the establishment of a transport zone within which an easy one-day trip is made possible from any point to any other point (*Asahi Shimbun*, August 9, 1986, p. 1).

Another important demographic trend is the progressive aging of the popu-

Figure 5.5
Trends in the Volume of Freight Transportation by Transportation Mode (in 100 million ton-kilometers)

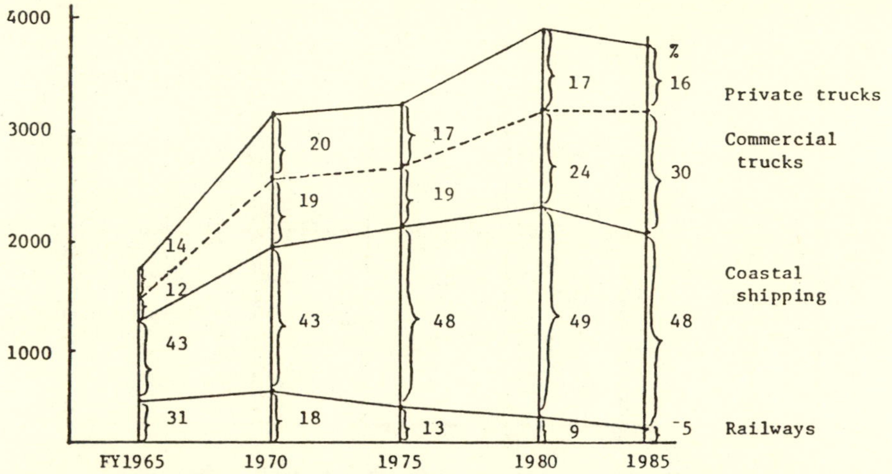

Source: Ministry of Transport, *Annual Report of Transport Economy, Summary (Fiscal 1985)*, Tokyo: Printing Bureau, Ministry of Finance, 1986, p. 1.

lation. The pyramidal structure of Japan's population in the earlier decades is expected virtually to disappear in the early twenty-first century. An older labor force will be a more expensive one. As the ridership gets older, furthermore, the need and the cost to improve the convenience, economy, and comfort of public transportation will also increase.

Fifth, requirements of the energy situation and concerns regarding the environment add to the cost of maintaining a sound public transportation system. Development of energy-saving measures is an especially important public policy responsibility in the small resource-poor Japan. A sixth, continuing trend relates to the changes in Japan's industrial structure. Steel, petrochemical, and other basic materials industries are giving way to higher value-added and information-based industries, such as industrial machinery, electric and electronic industries and service industries. The resulting shift in industrial products has generally favored nonrailroad modes of transportation.

Seventh, internationalization of Japanese society and economy has proceeded at an unprecedented rate in recent years, boosting the nation's international transport activities. The volume of scheduled air passenger transport in and out of the country stood at 6,290,000 persons in 1974, increased to 11,250,000 in 1979, and further increased to 16,060,000 (Figure 5.6) in 1984. By 1990, this number is expected to top 30,000,000. In June 1986, the Transport Policy Council made a number of recommendations regarding the expansion and improvement of air transportation, including pluralization of Japanese airlines in

Figure 5.6
Trends in the Volume of Scheduled Passenger Transport to and from Japan

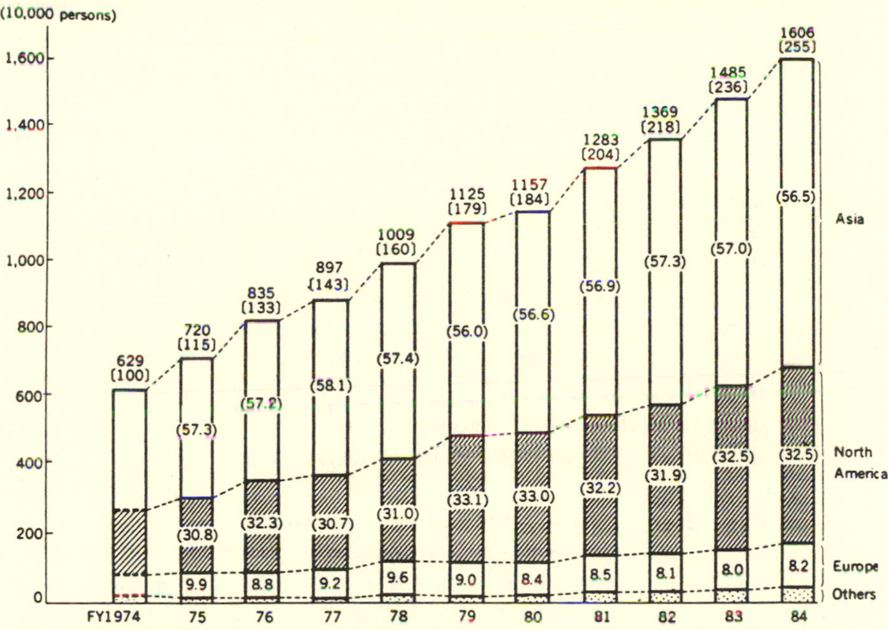

Notes: 1. Figure in brackets denotes index, assuming the volume of regular passenger transport departed from and arrived in Japan in fiscal 1974 is 100.
2. Figure in parentheses denotes each region's share (%) in the volume of regular passenger transport departed from and arrived in Japan in each fiscal year.

Source: Ministry of Transport, *Annual Report of Transport Economy, Summary (Fiscal 1985),* Tokyo: Printing Bureau, Ministry of Finance, 1986, p. 12.

international air services. The number of Japanese nationals traveling overseas has increased dramatically in recent years, particularly since the devaluation of the U.S. dollar and the continuing drop in oil prices. To meet the expanding needs in this area, Japan has vigorously sought new international air routes. Between May 1985 and October 1986 alone, for example, Japan Air Lines gained seven new regular routes to Europe, the United States, Guam, and Australia (Ministry of Transport, 1986: 12–13). All Nippon Airways, which started its first overseas service in 1986, plans to expand its international operations by gaining new routes to Honolulu, London, San Francisco, and New York by 1991 (*Asahi Shimbun,* May 20, 1988, p. 10).

In connection with the internationalization of Japanese economy and the growing role of Japanese air transport in the process, a major controversy has arisen. Japan's decision to build a new international airport in the Osaka Bay attracted American attention. The United States, intent on gaining access to slowly but steadily liberalizing Japanese markets, has demanded that American corporations be allowed to participate in the bidding on the airport construction project on an open and equitable basis with Japanese construction firms. Tokyo at first resisted Washington's demand, maintaining that the project was a private-sector activity and the government could not intervene. However, under U.S. pressure, Tokyo has assured that the project will be accessible to foreign corporations as well as domestic. The project is a part of the fifth five-year airport expansion program started in 1986. The construction, begun in January 1987, is expected to be completed in time for the scheduled opening of the airport in 1992 (Ministry of Transport, 1986: 7 and 15).

In 1979 the volume of seaborne and airborne cargo imports and exports stood at 610 million tons and 80 million tons, respectively, but is expected to grow to 920–1,000 million tons and 150 million tons by 1990 (Transport Policy Council: 11). These expectations led to the formulation of the seventh five-year port and harbor expansion program started in 1986. The plan, with the projected total investment amounting to ¥4.4 trillion (or $35.2 billion), is expected to contribute to the domestic demand expansion effort promoted by the Japanese government (Ministry of Transport, 1986: 20).

Structural changes in the domestic industries away from energy and resource-intensive patterns of development, along with changes in the international shipping economy, have created a large surplus of maritime transport capacity in Japan. In June 1986, the government instituted a special law for scrapping specified oceangoing vessels and continues to encourage cost-cutting efforts including personnel cuts. Likewise, the shipbuilding industry has also been experiencing enormous difficulties. A June 1986 recommendation of the Shipping and Shipbuilding Rationalization Council suggested disposing of surplus shipbuilding capacities (by as much as 20 percent), regrouping of shipbuilding companies, the scrapping of vessels, and creating new demands for shipping. The Ministry of Transport is currently studying these suggestions (Ministry of Transport, 1986: 3 and 5).

Japan's increasingly information-oriented and technology-intensive economy and society place a high premium on the research and development in the transport sector. Technological advances have had a major impact on the development of the transportation system in the country. The speed of rail-based transportation, for example, has improved from 32.8 kilometers per hour, when the first locomotive ran in Tokyo in 1872, to 210 km/h, the maximum speed of existing *shinkansen* trains. Safety is another feature that needs to be emphasized. Since the first *shinkansen* started its operation between Tokyo and Osaka in 1964, the high-speed lines have carried well over 125 billion passengers, but there has been not one accident-related death on any bullet train (Sugawara & Osawa: 41–42). A painful reminder of the importance of transportation safety occurred on August 12, 1985, when a JAL aircraft crashed in a mountainous region northwest of Tokyo, killing 520 people aboard.

Advances in electronics technology and new materials development are raising new hopes. An example is the JNR-JAL experimentation with magnetic linear motors. Vehicles being developed are lifted a fraction of an inch off a special track by magnetic forces, eliminating the friction of wheels. At the completion of this development, the new vehicles will be capable of operating at speeds over 480 km/h, with an energy cost less than that for airplanes (Unyusho, 1984b: 38–39; Lincoln, 1983a: 104). Technological improvements are also being made in satellite-aided ocean navigation, port and harbor construction, transportation safety, meteorological activities, and earthquake prediction.

Another spectacular example of the application of advanced technology to public transportation is the construction of the Seikan Tunnel that runs underneath the Tsugaru Strait (refer to Figure 5.1). When tunnelers from opposite sides of the strait met on March 10, 1985, more than twenty years after the first boring began, thirty-four lives had been lost, chiefly in transportation accidents, and ¥1.1 trillion ($8.5 billion) invested. Rail services through the 54 kilometer (thirty-four mile) tunnel, begun on March 13, 1988, are expected to provide a safe and fast alternative to the weather-dependent ferry across the strait (Igarashi: 24; Sugawara & Osawa: 44–45; *New York Times,* June 24, 1986, p. 17; *Christian Science Monitor,* March 14, 1988, p. 9).

Yet another spectacular example of Japan's modern technological application to transportation is the successful construction of a series of road-and-rail bridges connecting the Honshu and Shikoku islands. The six bridges totaling 37.3 km (twenty-three miles) in length, collectively known as Seto Ohashi (or the Seto Great Bridge), took ten years to complete and cost ¥1.2 trillion (over $9.2 billion). The longest of the bridges, Minami Bizan Seto Bridge, is a suspension bridge with a center span of 1,100 meters (3,608 feet) (*Christian Science Monitor,* March 14, 1988, pp. 9–10).

TRANSPORTATION POLICY ORGANIZATION AND PROCESS

Most major public policies are formulated on the basis of consensus among the "three pillars" (or "tri-pods") of the ruling Liberal Democratic Party, the administrative bureaucracy, and the private-sector interests and concerns typically represented by the business and industrial communities. Transportation policy is no exception. The process generally involves (1) the transportation industry and its associated business concerns; (2) the Liberal Democratic Party; and (3) the Ministry of Transport and other administrative bureaucracies (e.g., the Ministry of Construction). The opposition in the Diet provides a kind of political and policy check on the transportation "establishment" represented by the industry–LDP–bureaucracy coalition. In addition, the "public service" nature of transportation readily makes for policy input from local governments and the general public. The public works and other transportation infrastructure necessarily point to input from the construction industry. Finally, such policy matters as may require national legislation and/or government budget allocations necessarily involve the Diet. The general policy process is summarized in Figure 5.7.

Figure 5.7
Transportation Policy Process

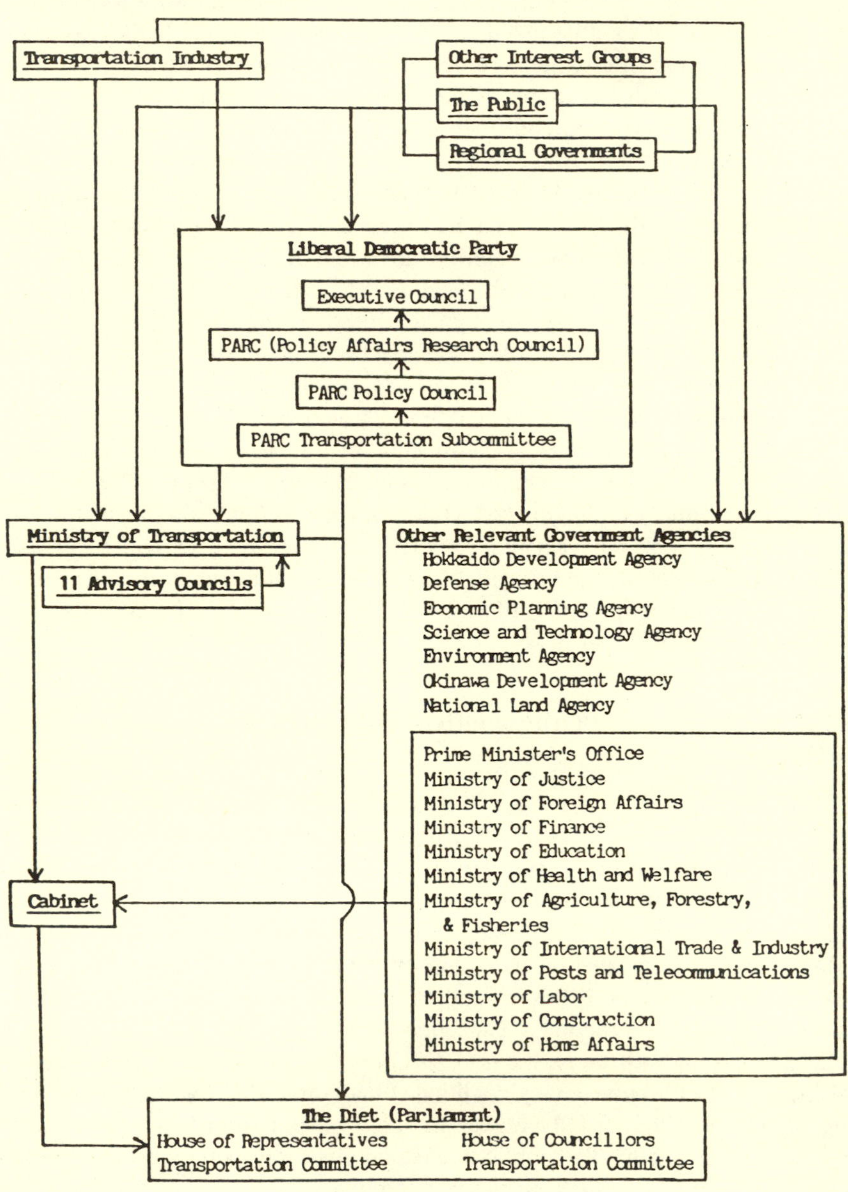

Note: The arrows indicate the direction of policy decision and influence.

Critical linkages among the major participants in the policy process are provided by the governing party, particularly those of its members who serve on the transportation subcommittee of the party's Policy Affairs Research Council. It is they who directly receive input from private-interest groups as well as from local governments and politicians regarding public transportation; it is they who, through negotiation with members of other subcommittees, formulate the basic policy demands of the party; it is they who apply overt and subtle political pressure on the administrative bureaucrats in charge of formulating legislative bills and government budgets in the transportation sector; and finally, it is they who, as members of the Diet, represent their party and "clients" in legislative deliberations.

The most important government bureaucracy in the transportation sector is the Ministry of Transport. Until 1984, MOT was organized as shown in Figure 5.8. One of the striking features of the system was its vertical organization, in which policy in each mode of transportation was formulated pretty much separately and independently of policy for other modes. The Maritime Shipping Bureau, the Ship Bureau, the Seafarers Bureau, and the Ports and Harbors Bureau were in charge of maritime transport policy, the Railroad Supervision Bureau and the Automobile Bureau were charged with the responsibility for land-based transportation policy, and the Civil Aviation Bureau looked after air transportation policy. Under this hierarchical policy system, development of long-term, comprehensive transportation policy integrating policy measures for all modes of transportation was largely lacking. Recent and continuing trends outlined above require comprehensive, flexible, diversified, and integrated transportation policy at the national and regional levels. Hence, the reorganization of the agency in July 1984.

The agency's new structure reflects a recognition of the importance of developing comprehensive and efficient policies in the areas of international transportation and tourism, regional transportation, and cargo distribution. The reorganization of local transportation administration, with the merger of maritime and land transport bureaus into a regional transportation bureau, reflects the same recognition.[5] The new transportation administration emphasizes policy based on more objectively assessed needs rather than the past approval and licensing system (Arino: 5). Politicization of the approval and licensing process had led to an uncontrolled and inefficient use of public resources for the development and expansion of transportation systems in the country (Kyoikusha: 31). Minor organizational changes were also made in transportation agencies external to but subject to MOT authority, including the Maritime Safety Agency and the Meteorological Agency.

MOT is aided by eleven advisory councils: the Council for Transport Technology, the Transport Council, the Council for Transport Policy, the Council for Rationalization of Shipping and Shipbuilding Industries, the Council for Maritime Safety and Seamen's Training, the Council for Ports and Harbors, the Council for Civil Aviation, the Council for Construction of Railways, the

Figure 5.8
Organization of the Ministry of Transport (MOT)*

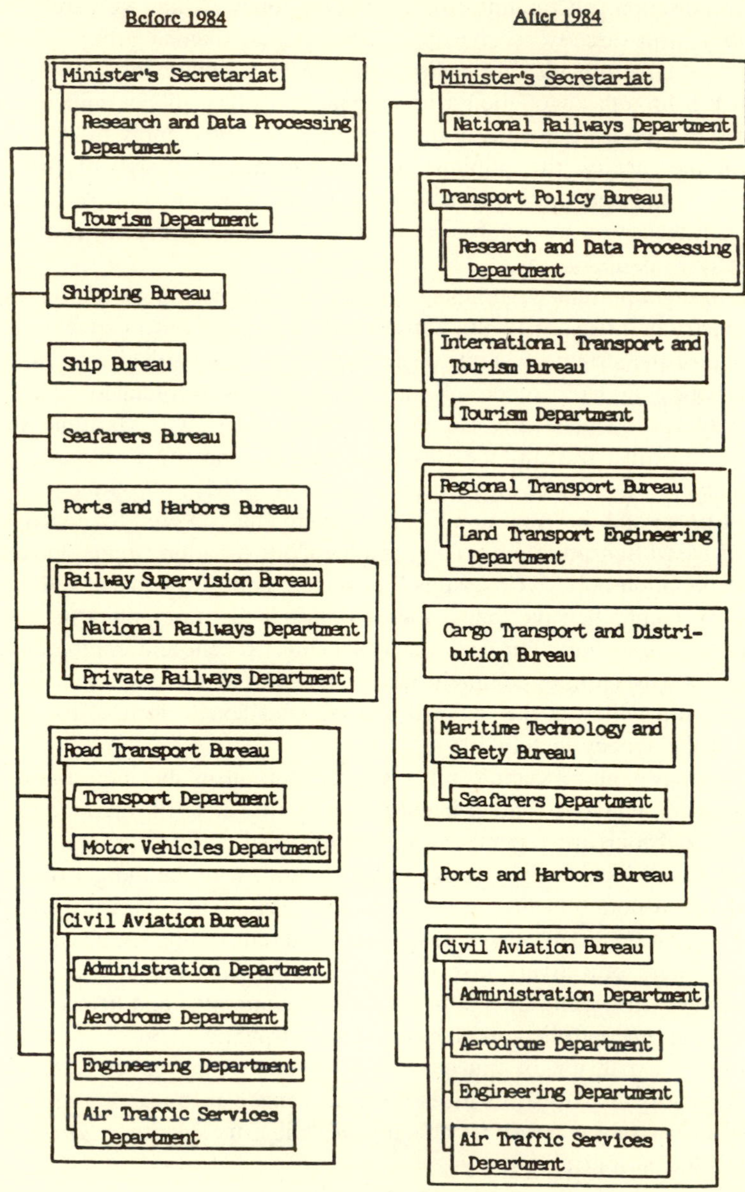

*Includes only units within MOT proper.

Source: Institute of Administrative Management, *Organization of Government of Japan,* Tokyo: Administrative Management Bureau, Management and Coordination Agency, Prime Minister's Office, 1983 and 1984.

Tourism Policy Council, the Compulsory Automobile Liability Reinsurance Investigation Committee, and the Aircraft Accident Investigation Committee. There is also the Meteorological Council advising the Meteorological Agency. Upon request from the MOT minister (and the director-general of the Meteorological Agency), the advisory councils provide recommendations based on studies and deliberations among their members made up of learned individuals and representatives of relevant bureaucratic units.

There are a number of so-called public corporations which have been established by special law and, under MOT authority, are engaged in the development and provision of various public transportation services. They are JNR, Japan Railway Construction Corporation, New Tokyo International Airport Authority, Honshu-Shikoku Bridge Authority (also under the authority of the Ministry of Construction), Housing and Urban Development Corporation (also under the authority of the Ministry of Construction), Japan Nuclear Ship Research and Development Agency (also under the authority of the Science and Technology Agency), National Space Development Agency (also under the authority of the Science and Technology Agency), National Space Development Agency (also under the authority of the Science and Technology Agency and the Ministry of Posts and Telecommunications), Teito Rapid Transit Authority (also under the authority of the Ministry of Construction), JAL, Japan Motor Terminals Co., Ltd., Japan National Tourist Organization, and Japan Shipbuilding Industry Foundation. Such entities have been created by the national government by special law as instruments for activities required by the state. A public corporation is established primarily when particular activities are better managed in the form of a profit-making enterprise, when efficiency in performance is more likely to result than under direct operation by the national government, or when more flexibility in financial or personnel management is required than is normally possible under the laws and regulations pertaining to government agencies (Administrative Management Bureau: 106).

Finally, government commitment to public transportation is indicated by the number of personnel on government payroll who devote all or most of their official time to public transportation policy formulation or implementation as well as by the size of budget it allocates to MOT and other government agencies in charge of various areas of public transportation (Table 5.3).

CONCLUSION

This study has highlighted the important role that the national government has played in the development of Japan's modern transportation system. It has also shown the demands made upon the nation's public transportation system by the changing needs of Japanese society and economy. The rather generous resource commitment to the quantitative expansion of all modes of public transportation during the period of accelerated economic growth gradually shifted

Table 5.3
Main National Government Agency Personnel and Budget

	Number of Full-time Personnel (in Agency Proper), FY 1984		General Account Outlays by Agency and Purpose, FY 1986 (in millions of US dollars)
Prime Minister's Office	605		42,115
Ministry of Justice	49,931	(47,959)	2,404
Ministry of Foreign Affairs	3,795		2,584
Ministry of Finance	76,114	(23,273)	77,626
Ministry of Education	136,452	(135,673)	28,173
Ministry of Health & Welfare	59,172	(58,270)	60,214
Ministry of Agriculture & Forestry	75,649	(25,449)	17,177
Ministry of International Trade & Industry	12,779	(9,688)	4,820
Ministry of Transportation	**35,066**	**(16,247)**	**6,255**
Ministry of Posts & Telecommunications	313,970		149
Ministry of Labor	22,679	(22,679)	3,012
Ministry of Construction	27,457		23,255
Ministry of Home Affairs	546	(386)	63,410

Source: The data for personnel are from Institute of Administrative Management, *Organization of Government of Japan,* Tokyo: Administrative Management Bureau, Management and Coordination Agency, Prime Minister's Office, 1984, pp. 4–27; the data for general account outlays are from *Japan: An International Comparison, 1987,* Tokyo: Keizei Kōhō Center, 1987, p. 81.

toward increasing commitment to the qualitative improvement of the transportation system during the following years.

As the Ministry of International Trade and Industry (MITI) has played a key "developmental role" (Johnson) in Japan's prewar and postwar industrialization at home and economic expansion abroad, so has the Ministry of Transport (MOT) played an essential role in the development of modern transportation in the country. Technological and financial investment for the quantitative expansion and qualitative improvement of the national railway system was generous. The political process also assisted in the expansion of the JNR network to increasingly rural and remote areas of the country, fulfilling its mission as a provider of an important public service. That very philosophy and the political support behind the public enterprise ironically caused its demise. The corporation's current account deficits and debts rose in alarming proportions. The government has finally decided that the only way to salvage the nation's railroad system is to break up and privatize JNR.

NOTES

1. The foreign exchange rate had been set at ¥360 to one U.S. dollar on April 25, 1949, and the Japanese government adopted the rate as the official exchange rate in

August 1952. The official exchange rate remained unchanged until August 28, 1971, when the government adopted a floating exchange rate system—the rate changing dramatically since. In the present study, Japanese yen figures are translated into dollar figures using the average exchange rate for any given year.

2. For a brief overview of the trucking industry in Japan, see Okano, 1982.

3. For an analysis of administrative reform efforts by the Japanese government, see Wright & Sakurai, 1987.

4. The English translations of the original Japanese legislation are the author's.

5. For a description of the functions of the major subdivisions of the ministry, see Administrative Management Bureau, 1985.

REFERENCES

Administrative Management Bureau, Management and Coordination Agency, Prime Minister's Office, *Organization of the Government of Japan, 1984* (Tokyo: Institute of Administrative Management, 1985).

Asahi Shimbunsha Chōsakenkyūshitsu, ed., *Kokutetsu Kaikaku—Kōsha kara Minei e* [JNR reform—From a public enterprise to private operation] (Tokyo: Asahi Shimbunsha, 1982).

Arino, Ikuma, "Unyushō no Soshiki Kaikaku" [Organizational reform of the Ministry of Transport], *Kōwan,* no. 61 (1984), pp. 5–13.

Asahi Shimbun, May 31, 1988, pp. 1, 9; August 3, 1986, p. 1; Dec. 16, 1986, p. 4; Dec. 30, 1986, p. 1; August 9, 1986, p. 1; May 20, 1988, p. 10.

Christian Science Monitor, March 14, 1988, p. 9.

Furuta, R., and Y. Hirai, *A Short History of Japanese Shipping* (Tokyo: Tokyo News Service, 1967).

Handa, Hiroyuki, "Privatization: Japanese National Railways: JNR, Jr., " *Look Japan,* no. 375 (1987), pp. 6–9.

Hosoda, Kichizo, *Kokutetsu o Kataru* [Speaking of JNR] (Tokyo: Rikuun Keizai Shimbunsha, 1981.

Igarashi, Hideo, "Transportation: Aomori-Hakodate Tunnel, *Look Japan,* no. 386 (1988), p. 24.

Japan: An International Comparison (Tokyo: Keizai Kōhō Center, 1987 and 1988).

Johnson, Chalmers, *MITI and the Japanese Miracle: The Growth of Industrial Policy, 1925–1975* (Stanford: Stanford University Press, 1983).

Kato, Hiroshi, "Gyōsei Kaikaku to Kokutetsu Saiken" [Administrative reform and JNR reconstruction], *Kokutetsu: Kōkigyo to Kōkyō Kōtsū* [JNR: Public enterprise and public transportation], Jūristo Zōkan Sōgō Tokushū, vol. 31 (1983), pp. 123–128.

Kōtsu Kyōryokukai, *Kōtsū Nenkan, 1984* [Transportation yearbook] (Tokyo: Kōtsu Kyōryokukai, 1984).

Kotsu Nenkan [Transport yearbook] (Tokyo: Kōtsū Kyōkai, annual).

Kyōikusha, ed., *Unyushō* [The Ministry of Transport] (Tokyo: Kyōikusha, 1979).

Lincoln, Edward J., "Transportation," in *Kodansha Encyclopedia of Japan,* vol. 8 (Tokyo: Kodansha, 1983a), pp. 98–104.

———, "Transportation and Communications," in Frederica M. Bunge, ed., *Japan: A*

Country Study, Area Handbook Series (Washington, D.C.: U.S. Government as represented by the Secretary of the Army, 1983b), pp. 176–178.

Ministry of Transport, *Annual Report of Transport Economy, Summary* (Tokyo: Printing Bureau, Ministry of Finance, 1986).

———, *The Current Situation of Japanese Shipping* (Tokyo: Japan Maritime Development Association, annual).

Murakawa, Ichiro, *Seisaku Kettei Katei* [Policy-making process] (Tokyo: Kyōikusha, 1979).

New York Times, June 24, 1986, p. 17.

Oda, Masao, *Kaiun Gyōkai* [The maritime shipping industry] (Tokyo: Kyōikusha, 1985).

Okada, Kiyoshi, "Kokutetsu Mondai o Kangaeru Yottsu No Shiten" [Four perspectives in considering the JNR problem], *Kokutetsu: Kōkigyō to Kōkyō Kōtsū* [JNR: Public enterprise and public transportation], Jūristo Zōkan Sōgō Tokushū, vol. 31 (1983), pp. 54–59.

Okano, Yukihide, "Kōkyōsei, Kōritsusei, Saisansei" [Publicness, efficiency, profitability], *Kokutetsu: Kōkigyō to Kōkyō Kōtsū* [JNR: Public enterprise and public transportation], Jūristo Zōkan Sōgō Tokushū, vol. 31 (1983), pp. 105–110.

———, *Rikuun Gyōkai* [The land freight industry] (Tokyo: Kyōikusha, 1982).

Omori, Kazuo, "Seiji to Kokutetsu. Riken to Shūhyō no Kōzō" [Politics and JNR. The structure of vested interests and winning of votes], *Kokutetsu: Kōkigyō to Kōkyō Kōtsū* [JNR: Public enterprise and public transportation], Jūristo Zōkan Sōgō Tokushū, vol. 31 (1983), pp. 73–77.

Seisakujihōsha, ed., *Nihon no Kanchō: Sono Hito to Soshiki, 1984-nenban Unyushō* [Administrative agencies of Japan: Their people and organization, 1984, The Ministry of Transport] (Tokyo: Kokudoseisaku Kenkyūkai, 1984).

Sugawara, Misao, and Nobuo Osawa, "Kokutetsu no Kijutsu: Sono Shakaikeizaiteki Yakuwari" [JNR's technology: Its socioeconomic role], *Kokutetsu: Kōkigyō to Kōkyō Kōtsu* [JNR: Public enterprise and public transportation], Jūristo Zōkan Sōgō Tokushū, vol. 31 (1983), pp. 40–46.

Takagi, Ikuro, "Kokutetsu no Rōshi Kankeishi to Genjō" [The history of JNR labor-management relations and their present situation], *Kokutetsu: Kōkigyō to Kōkyō Kōtsū* [JNR: Public enterprise and public transportation], Jūristo Zōkan Sōgō Tokushū, vol. 31 (1983), pp. 83–89.

Totten, George, "The Reconstruction of the Japanese Shipbuilding Industry," in Robert L. Friedheim et al., eds., *Japan and the New Ocean Regime* (Boulder, Colo.: Westview Press, 1984), pp. 130–172.

Transport Policy Council, *Basic Direction of a Comprehensive Transport Policy Based on Long Term Perspectives: Laying the Groundwork for Tomorrow's Needs under Conditions of Trials and Adversity (Excerpts)* (Tokyo: Transport Policy Council, 1981).

Transportation Research, Part A: General, vol. 23A, no. 1 (January 1989), Special Issue: Transportation Research in Japan.

Unyushō [The Ministry of Transport] (Tokyo: Kyōikusha, 1979).

Unyushō, ed., *Nihon Kaiun no Genkyō* [The current condition of Japanese maritime shipping] (Tokyo: Nihon Kaiji Kōhō Kyōkai, 1984a).

Unyushō, *Shōwa 50-nenban Unyu Hakusho* [1983 Transport White Paper] (Tokyo: Ōkurashō Insatsukyoku, 1984b).

Unyushō Unyuseisakukyoku Jōhōkanribu, ed., *Unyu Kankei Enerugii Yōran, Shōwa 60-nenban* [Summary of transport-related energy, 1985] (Tokyo: Unyushō Unyuseisakukyoku Jōhōkanribu, 1985).

Wright, Deil S. and Yasuyoshi Sakurai, ''Administrative Reform in Japan: Politics, Policy, and Public Administration in a Deliberative Society,'' *Public Administration Review,* no. 2 (1987), pp. 121–133.

Yamanobe, Yoshimasa, *Kōkū Gyōkai* [Civil air industry] (Tokyo: Kyōikusha, 1985).

6

KOREA

Young Whan Kihl and Mary Kihl

BACKGROUND

A modern transportation network was developed in Korea during a period of rapid industrialization since the early 1960s. Prior to this era the foundation for infrastructure building in public transportation was laid out, especially during Korea's colonial rule under Japan (1910–45), but the public investment in the transportation network was limited to a few selected sectors such as the railways and coastal shipping. The vigorous, systematic, and continuous expansion of the transportation network, however, took place only in the recent decades, (especially in highway and air transportation) as part of a series of Five-Year Economic Development Plans initiated in 1962.

Remarkably rapid developments and progress have been attained in every field of South Korea's economic activities including that of public transportation. With the rapid growth of the economy, the transportation activities have all greatly expanded, and the latter, in turn, provided an impetus for further economic growth and development.

South Korea's emergence as one of East Asia's successful newly industrializing countries (NIC) was made possible by a combination of factors including the hardworking character and highly educated labor force of the Korean peo-

The authors thank the following individuals for their assistance in obtaining the data: Dr. Myong-Chan Hwang, Dr. Tae-Il Lee, and Dr. Sung-Jick Eum of Korea Research Institute for Human Settlements; and Dr. Yong-Chool Ha, Dr. Ky-Moon Ohm, and Dr. Hoseop Yoon.

ple. The government policy of pursuing an export-led industrialization of the economy proved to be the most successful in an era of expanding world trade and production during the 1960s and 1970s. This policy made it imperative for South Korea to invest heavily in infrastructure building in highways and port facilities. The rapidly growing volume of international cargo to and from Korea, for instance, required expansion of port facilities and an increase in national flag vessels. New air routes were also opened to accommodate the increasing volume of air cargos and international travelers to and from Korea.

Over time, transportation infrastructure development in Korea was stimulated by a series of dramatic challenges with the impetus coming, first, from the requirements of the Japanese colonial rules for access to raw materials and ports; second, from the devastation caused by the Korean War; third, from intermodal competition as the republic raced to modernize and industrialize in the early 1970s; and fourth from the international marketplace as the country responded to international competition with carefully orchestrated economic plans calculated to distribute industrialization, expand resource development, and accent port and harbor construction. In terms of modal development and funding allocation, emphasis moved from rail, to highway, to air, and then to harbors.

The base of Korea's modern transportation network was introduced by Japan at the turn of the century and expanded during the thirty-five years of Japan's colonial rule in Korea. The first major rail lines, the Seoul-Pusan and Seoul-Sinuiju line, were completed by 1896. Between 1910 and 1919 a rudimentary network was completed linking all major cities and locations of raw materials and production. The colonial government also made considerable effort to construct a highway network. The Chosen Postal Shipping Company was established to assure a monopoly on both overseas and coastal shipping in Korea (Kim & Roemer: 4). By the time Korea was liberated from Japan at the end of World War II, railway links in Korea extended 6,362 kilometers with 3,738 kilometers in what became the Republic of Korea (*A Handbook of Korea,* 1979: 621).

Unfortunately the Republic of Korea had little time to expand these transportation facilities before the Korean War broke out in 1950. The war dealt a major blow to the fledgling transportation network. The railroads alone sustained damage of over 333 million won or about $25 million (the 1953 estimate) (Kim & Roemer: 32) with destruction of 61 percent of its locomotives, 68 percent of its passenger coaches, and 57 percent of the freight cars. Nearly half the stations, signals, and workshops were destroyed (*A Handbook of Korea,* 1979: 621). Highways sustained over 570 million won ($425 million) damage, while damage to ports was assessed at 100 million won (or about $74 million) (Kim & Roemer: 32).

Postwar reconstruction restored the railway system with considerable rapidity while replacement locomotives and coaches were purchased through foreign aid. Passenger coaches began to be produced locally in 1959, and, as diesel engines replaced steam engines, a diesel locomotive maintenance depot was established in Pusan (*A Handbook of Korea,* 1983). Nevertheless expansion and improvement of rail services remained insignificant until the development of the first Five-Year Development Plan in the early 1960s (*A Handbook of Korea,* 1983). Then with the launching of the five-year plans, substantial investments were made in the railroad, and in 1963 the Korean National Railroad was separated from the Ministry of Transportation to provide more effective management of the railways. By 1965 the rail lines extended 2,980 kilometers with expansion to 3,193 kilometers in 1970 (Neuner: 306).

Transportation facilities were concentrated along the Seoul-Pusan axis linking the capital city in the northwestern part of the country to the second largest city, a port in the southeast. Another corridor connected the northeast quadrant with its coal deposit and cement plants and the ports of Pusan and Inchon. An intervening corridor included Taegu, third most important industrial center (Neuner: 306).

By the late 1960s the rise of expressways threatened the continued dominance of the railroads. The 29.5 kilometer Seoul-Inchon Expressway, the first modern highway in Korea, was completed in 1968 at a cost of about $9 million. Travel time between Seoul and the coastal city was reduced from one hour to twenty minutes. In July 1970 the 428 kilometer Seoul-Pusan Expressway cut diagonally across the whole country with a 79.5 kilometer branch linking Taejŏn and Chŏngju completed in December 1970. In 1973 a two-lane highway along the southern coast linked Chŏnju with Pusan while the industrial city of Ulsan was linked to the expressway network in 1974. The Suwon-Kangneung Expressway cut through the mountains of Kangwon province in 1975 linking the east coast mineral deposits to the rest of the country while at the same time making that area accessible to tourists. The Korea Highway Corporation was established in 1969 to manage and maintain expressways, collect tolls, and open new routes.

Along with the expressway expansion came an increased proportion of paved roads in both the national and local systems. While only 17 percent of the national system was paved in 1965, the proportion increased to 50 percent in 1975. Only 2 percent of local roads were paved in 1965 with over 14 percent paved in 1975.

The number of motor vehicles also increased dramatically from 41,500 in 1965 to 200,500 in 1975. Trucks accounted for 41 percent of the 1975 fleet with passenger cars contributing 52 percent and the buses and motorcycles the rest (Neuman: 307, citing the Ministry of Construction).

Meanwhile the Korean National Railroad (KNR) began a series of dramatic innovative measures to maintain its level of passengers and cargo. Modern safety systems were introduced, all tracks replaced, and a costly project of railroad electrification begun. The Chung'ang (Central) Seoul-Chechon line was completely electrified in 1973 followed by the Taeback and Yogdong lines the next year. Part of the suburban railways around Seoul were also electrified in 1974 so as to interface with the Seoul subway, the first link of which was opened in that year. A centralized traffic control system covered all stations on the Chung'ang line with expansion planned for the Taeback line.

A microwave communication system was installed on the Seoul-Pusan line in 1977 with additional track being laid section by section along the Honam arterial line starting in 1969. The result of all this effort was to increase the railway system from 2,980 kilometers in 1965 to 5,860 in 1980—a 190 percent increase. The number of rail passengers also increased dramatically from 88 million in 1961 to 444 million in 1982, with cargo increasing from 15 million tons in 1961 to 48 million in 1982 (*A Handbook of Korea,* 1983).

With this intermodal competition Korea moved toward the 1980s with a hastily constructed but nonetheless effective land-based infrastructure. The problems associated with this rapid expansion and costly improvements to the rail facilities were, however, that large deficits developed. By 1978 the KNR had run up deficits of over $42 million, and the government determined to intervene by gradually increasing the artificially low fares and investing about $810 million in the railroads over the period of the fourth Five-Year Plan. The money including over $230 million in foreign loans was also used for further expansion of the tracks to 6,064 kilometers with an additional 100 kilometers electrified.

Simultaneous with this mass expansion was the introduction of subway lines in Seoul to address the problems of increasing congestion on the city streets. In August 1974 the first 9.54 kilometer segment of Seoul subway along Chongno Street opened. It ran with deficit for the first two years, but as the passenger volume increased from 31.7 million in the first four months of operation, it had already moved into the black by the latter half of 1976, and construction began on a second line.

With the 1980s came dramatic changes both in type and level of transport facilities and the orientation of transport activity. Within Seoul the initial subway line was expanded into a full network reaching well beyond the confines of the center city to the areas of new development across the Han River. By 1985 the city boasted a system encompassing 116.5 kilometers with a capacity for carrying 5.20 million passengers a day. This made the Seoul subway the seventh longest system in the world (*Korea Herald:* Oct. 18, 1985). The investment in the system was more than a staggering 2 trillion won (about $3 billion at the 1985 exchange rate of 800 won to 1 dollar). A 26.1 kilometer subway link was also completed in Pusan in 1987 at a cost of almost 900 billion won or about $1 billion in 1985 dollars (*Transportation in Korea, 1985:* 17).

Expressways also continued to expand with the 175.3 kilometer Olympic Expressway between Tamyon and Okp'o completed in June 1984 and the 20.6 kilometer expressway between Pusan and the new industrial town, Masan, completed in 1981. More impressive, however, was the rapid increase in the ratio of paved to unpaved roads. By 1985 up to 46.4 percent of all roads were paved. Over 68 percent of the general national roads were paved as were 26 percent of local roads (*Transportation in Korea, 1985:* 19). With the increase in paved roads the vehicle fleet grew dramatically. In 1961, for example, the total number of vehicles in the republic was 30,000; twenty years later that number had grown to 572,000. By 1984 there was a total of 948,000 vehicles including 465,000 passenger cars (49 percent of the fleet), 108,000 buses (11 percent of the fleet) and 375,000 trucks (40 percent of the fleet) (*Transportation in Korea, 1985:* 20). Four years later in 1988 the number of passenger cars alone had increased to 1,118,000 representing 55 percent of the total number of vehicles in Korea (2,035,000). (Korea Overseas Information Service, Oct., 1989). Although the proportion of private cars was rapidly increasing, public transportation was also expanding into rural as well as urban areas. Of the 5,070 intercity bus routes, 1,260 served rural areas, providing services for 3,755,000 passengers. In 1985, 86 rural routes were added and were expected to serve an additional 85,000 rural residents (*Transportation in Korea, 1985:* 22).

If the increase in subways and paved roads reflects internal development, the rise in air travel and shipping reflect increased linkage with the greater world. In 1969 the whole KAL fleet consisted of one jet aircraft, two DC-3s, one DC-4, and four turbo-props (*A Korea Handbook,* 1983: 525; *Transportation in Korea, 1985*). This had grown to forty-two aircraft by 1984. Since 1970 international aircraft have increased on the average of 18 percent a year except during the worldwide oil crisis in 1974 (*A Handbook of Korea,* 1983). Although only 11,000 international visitors arrived in Korea in 1961, the figure had jumped to 1,207,000 in 1984. Of these visitors, 44 percent came from Japan, 17 percent from the United States, and the rest from a variety of other countries. Twelve percent came for business purposes, 64 percent for pleasure, and the rest for other reasons (*Transportation in Korea, 1985:* 11, 30). The increased volume of passengers necessitated a major expansion of Kimpo Airport in Seoul as well as expansion at Cheju and Ch'ongju airports (*Transportation in Korea, 1985:* 41). Suyong International Airport near Pusan was relocated to the new Kimhae Airport west of the city, and that in turn was enlarged from 1985–87.

The merchant marine has similarly experienced steady growth. The establishment of the Korean Maritime and Port Administration in March 1976 represented a thrust at moving Korea into the ranks of major world maritime powers. This agency combined direction of both shipping and port facilities. In 1961 the Korean merchant fleet had a total tonnage capacity of only 240,000 while capacity in 1984 was over 7,707,000 tons (*Transportation in Korea, 1985:* 23). Korean flag carriers transported well over 47 percent of all Korean exports and imports by 1985 (*A Handbook of Korea,* 1987). Foreign exchange income earned by these ships was over twenty times greater than the amount earned ten years earlier.

Parallel to the increases in shipping were vigorous efforts at port expansion in almost all the fifteen trading ports in the country. This was accomplished with the aid of World Bank and Asian Development Bank loans as well as government and private investment. Construction began on ambitious plans to prepare the ports for the late 1980s when exports were expected to top $25 billion. The construction included creating tidal docks and inner harbors as well as doubling dock sizes and improving loading and unloading equipment. As a result of these efforts the annual cargo handling capacity in 1984 had topped 112 million tons, almost double the capacity of 65 million tons available in 1978. After initial concentration in Inchon, Pohang, and Pusan, the construction focus moved to the Samil area in south central Korea in the mid-1980s. This was indicative of national plans to decentralize investment and production.

When reviewing the history of the development of Korea's transportation system since the Korean War, one is keenly impressed by the rapidity of development. In a determination not only to recover from the devastation caused by the war but also to move into a position as a world-class competitor, development proceeded almost as if the country was placed in a time machine and hurled forward. Furthermore this development was in keeping with an overall comprehensive plan. The problems that ensued have been in large part spawned by the determination to create a modern transportation system almost overnight. Coordination among modes proved difficult, and at times intermodal competition drove the development process. Even more difficult was interface with other sectors of society which were similarly experiencing accelerated growth. The need for coordination between urban and regional development, a point to be explored later in this chapter, was at times overlooked. Concerns about preventative maintenance were brushed aside with the rush to new construction. The 1980s, therefore, became the time for reassessment and fine tuning.

SOCIOECONOMIC DIMENSIONS OF THE TRANSPORTATION SYSTEM AND POLICY

The comprehensive National Development Planning Act of 1963 set forth three basic national objectives: first, to secure sufficient industrial land necessary to accommodate a rapid rise in industrial activity and thereby to achieve a more rational allocation of industrial activities throughout the country; second, to disperse population from large urban centers; and third, to create employment opportunities in provincial regions and faster development of backward areas (*National Land Development Planning in Korea:* 8, 17). These objectives have continued to guide development in Korea for the past twenty-six years and have in turn provided both the stimulus and backdrop for transportation improvements and policy.

Rapid industrialization was clearly a hallmark of Korean development in the years following the Korean War. Plans were launched to establish three different types of industrial estates: (1) export-based industrial estates; (2) coastal industrial estates with heavy and chemical industries, including petrochemicals, fertilizers, and oil refineries; and (3) inland industrial estates featuring small and medium industries and light manufacturing industries.

The configuration of the industrial estates, when widely distributed throughout Korea, in large part provided the impetus for the layout of the rail, highway corridors, and the generation of port facilities. Figure 6.1 indicates this industrial distribution while Figure 6.2 and Figure 6.3 indicate the response from the rail and highway transportation sectors. Clearly the transportation corridors link major population centers such as the capital city, Seoul, with major industrial centers. The location of port facilities and the more recent expansion of these facilities similarly was stimulated by the location of coastal industrial estates. For example, the development of a major steel plant at Pohang, petrochemicals and an oil refinery at Ulsan, and a major automobile plant at Onsan stimulated heavy port construction on the southeast coast. Current port development in the Kwangyang Bay between Yŏch'ŏn and Suncheon has been necessitated by the construction of a new steel plant there and the existing petrochemical complex at Yŏch'ŏn. Figure 6.4 shows both current port facilities and future plans for expansion. When viewed with Figure 6.1, the relationship is quickly apparent.

The population of Korea in 1984 was 40,430,000. With an expected growth rate of 1.4 percent the figure will reach approximately 49,793,000 by the year 2001. In 1984, 72.6 percent of the total population lived in urban areas, a figure projected to reach 80 percent by 2001 (*Highway Network Master Plan Study:* 30). The population density of 378 persons per square kilometer in 1984 was among the most intense in the world. By way of comparison, the population density in Japan in 1984 was 314 while that in the Netherlands, another densely populated country, was 346. The comparative density figure for the United States was 24 persons per square kilometer (*National Land Development Planning in Korea:* 3).

Nevertheless, despite the overall density of the population, a steadily increasing proportion continued to migrate especially to Seoul, the capital. Reasons given for this migration included the job search, the search for better education, convenience in business transactions, and access to good public facilities (Kwon: 18). Consequently by 1980 the proportion of the population in Seoul rose to 22.3 percent of the total.

Yet by 1980 the population of Seoul had declined slightly relative to other urban centers. Among urban centers, 39 percent lived in Seoul, down 2 percent from 1975. Meanwhile the proportion of the urban population in cities over 1 million continued to rise from 22.4 percent to 27.3 percent as did that in cities from 100,000 to 500,000. These changes in the distribution of the urban population reflected a concerted policy of growth management in Seoul. The policy included (1) dispersal of nonessential functions from Seoul; (2) the creation of a multi-nuclei spatial structure (encouraging the development of multiple urban centers in contrast to one downtown center); (3) promotion of office parks and commodity distribution centers in the outlying areas of Seoul; (4) movement of governmental and educational campuses outside the city limits; and (5) relocat-

Figure 6.1
Industrial Complexes and Local Industry Promotion Areas

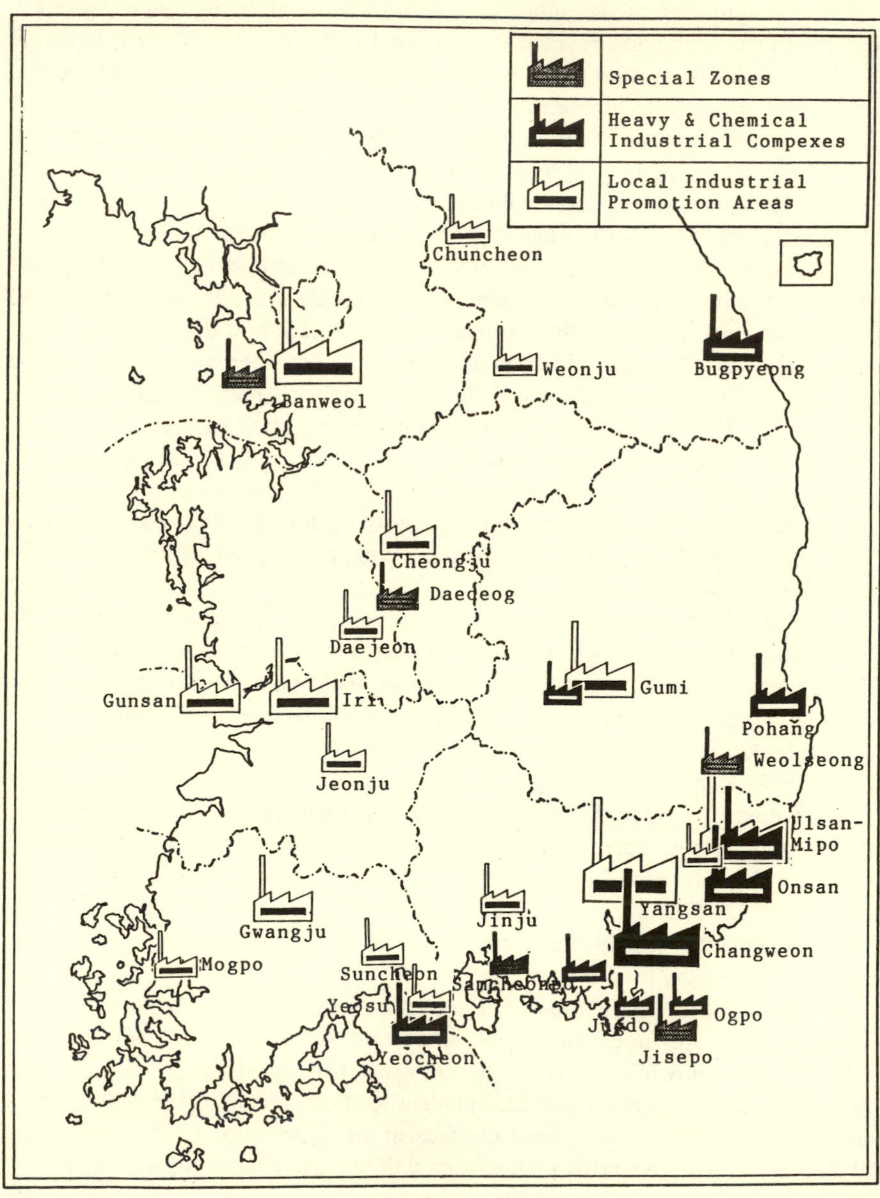

See the appendix to this chapter for a listing of the new transliteration system (McCune-Reischauer) introduced by the Republic of Korea in 1988.

Source: National Land Development Planning in Korea, 1984, p. 32.

Figure 6.2
Railway System

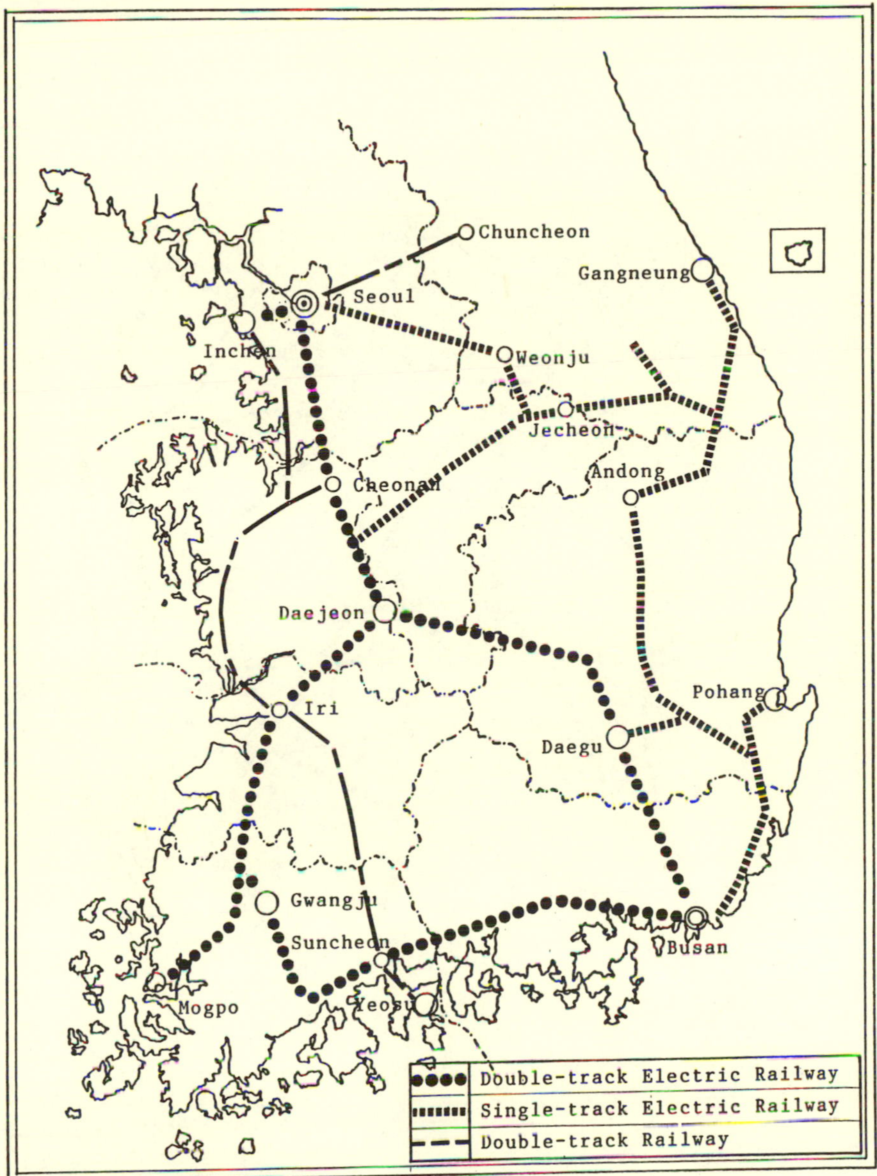

See the appendix to this chapter for a listing of the new transliteration system (McCune-Reischauer) introduced by the Republic of Korea in 1988.

Source: National Land Development Planning in Korea, 1984, p. 54.

Figure 6.3
Road System

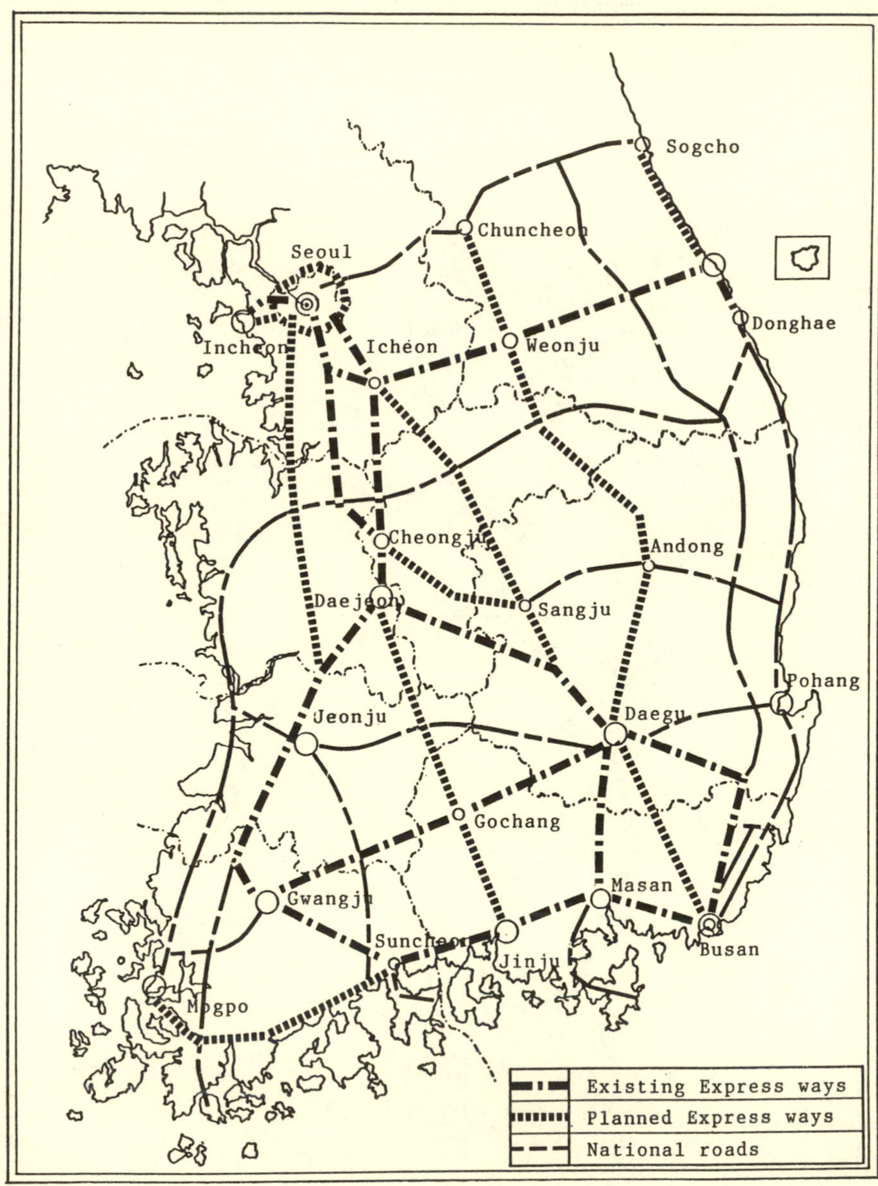

See the appendix to this chapter for a listing of the new transliteration system (McCune-Reischauer) introduced by the Republic of Korea in 1988.

Source: National Land Development Planning in Korea, 1984, p. 55.

Figure 6.4
Seaports

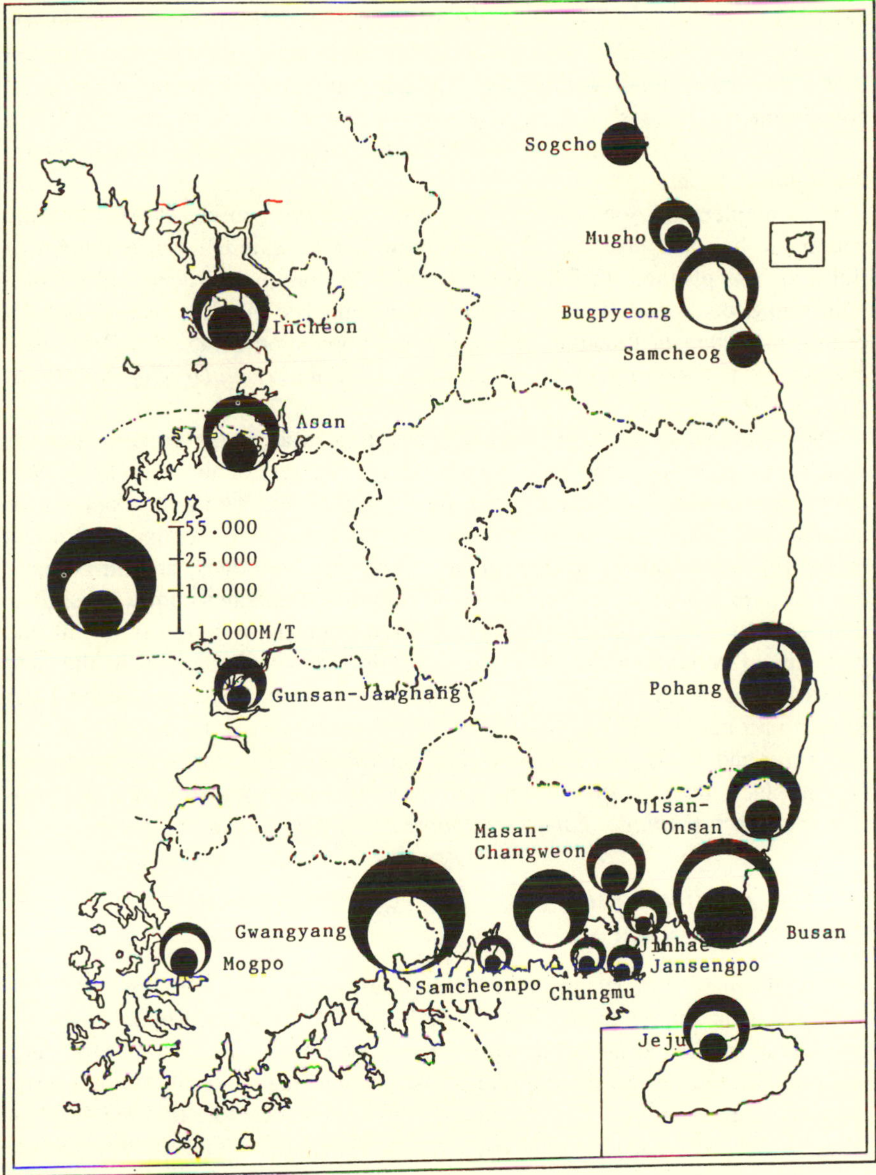

See the appendix to this chapter for a listing of the new transliteration system (McCune-Reischauer) introduced by the Republic of Korea in 1988.

Source: National Land Development Planning in Korea, 1984, p. 56.

ing agro-industries in the fringe area around Seoul (*National Land Development Plan in Korea:* 71–73).

The effective dispersion of the urban population outside the original boundaries of Seoul was only possible with the development of highways and electric railways which extended into the new suburban areas allowing for efficient travel into the capital. Within the city itself the overwhelming problem of congestion was addressed through a subway system which by the mid-1980s linked with the electric railway and extended well beyond the Han River on the south of Seoul.

In a complementary national policy, new towns were to be set up across the country to help disperse the urban population. For example, the new town of Banweol was planned for 240,000 and was to accommodate dispersed population from Seoul, while Gwacheon was to accommodate the dispersion of Seoul's central management function with a planned population of 45,000. Other new towns were to support the industrial estates. (*National Land Development Planning in Korea:* 37).

The mountainous areas in the northeastern section of the country and the agricultural southwest had long lagged behind the rest of the country in economic development. In keeping with the policy of integrating development of all areas and stimulating the economy of lagging areas, considerable investment in the 1980s was placed in these areas. Highways, railroads, and air connections were to bring tourists from the capital to the mountainous north for skiing, golf, and relaxation. Meanwhile an improved highway system was to link the port city of Mokpo in the agricultural southwest with Suncheon in the new industrial sector. A double track electric train system already extended from Seoul to Mokpo and linked Kwangju, the provincial city in the southwest with Suncheon and Pusan. In fact, with the extensive transportation infrastructure now in place, the goal of an integrated national economy involving all regions is within reach (*National Land Development Planning in Korea:* 54–55).

POLITICAL DIMENSIONS OF THE TRANSPORTATION SYSTEM AND POLICY

Centralized sectoral management and governmental direction, characteristic of the Korean public policy system, effectively minimize private-sector involvement in transportation activities in Korea. In fact, to further efficiency and effectiveness in developing and implementing modal specific policy, governmental agencies were designated to focus on each sector. In 1963 the Korean National Railroad Administration was designated to manage both construction and operation of the railroads. Similarly, the Maritime and Port Administration was established in 1976. Both continued titular coordination of activities through the Ministry of Transportation. In fact the maritime attachés in the Korean embassies in London, Washington, D.C., and Tokyo were responsible to the maritime administration's bureau rather than the Ministry of Transportation. The Korea International Airport Authority and the Korean Shipway Corporation established in 1967, on the other hand, maintained an even looser association with the Ministry of Transportation.

None of these transportation sectoral agencies maintained any formal link with the Ministry of Construction. They developed sector-specific objectives, lobbied for governmental funding, and then oversaw the implementation of these policies. The government continues to fix all prices in the transport industry. Prices for publicly owned transport enterprises such as the railways were proposed by the sectoral administration to the Ministry of Transportation, turned over to the Price Bureau of the Economic Planning Board, and then presented to a government committee on utility prices which makes recommendations to the cabinet. Prices of privately owned transport (trucks) were subject to the same reviews, but recommendations originated in the respective Ministry of Transportation divisions. In addition to price regulation, the government also indirectly affects prices through tax policies, subsidies, and user fees. Numerous special prices may also be added by the modal transport agencies.

The extent of regulation varies among modes. For example, the regulated rate for buses and railways is inflexible, while for other modes, such as highway freight, the regulated rate is regarded as a maximum and may be negotiated down by as much as 40 percent. The regulatory process not only lacks coordination among modes but also does not take into account the operation of the nonregulated sector including cars, some buses, trucks, and ships operated by nontransport companies. These operation clearly impact the regulated sector (Neuner: 307–309).

The funds flowing through Korea's public-sector transport are substantial but do not appear to generate surpluses for other parts of the economy. In addition, the degree of self-sufficiency varies considerably among the publicly owned transport sector. For example, the revenue generated by the rail sector in 1984 was 560.6 million won while costs ran 588.3 million won; the difference was to be made up by government subsidy. Most of these excess costs were attributed to the new urban railways which generated 46.6 million won against costs of 82.5 million won. The same year regularly scheduled motor vehicle transport generated 1.4 million won while costs were only 1.3 million won.

Overall water transport and air transport also generated considerably more income than expenses in 1984: 2.2 billion won income for water transport against costs of 2 million, and 940 million won for income of air transport against costs of only 839 million won (*Report on Transportation Survey: 1984:* 81–83).

Government involvement is not, however, limited to the public sector. The investment program for the fourth Five-Year Plan, for example, moved into the private sector as well, especially in the areas of road transport and ports and shipping. For road transport 460.8 billion won were invested in the public sector with 764.8 billion won invested in the private sector. In the publicly owned ports, 239.8 billion won were invested, complementing a 733.3 billion won investment in private shipping (Neuner: 317).

The government also indirectly impacts private-sector transportation through a licensing system. Those firms operating services for hire on roads or coastal areas, the two non-nationalized sectors, purchase licenses. Through the licensing procedure the government has attempted indirectly to raise the minimum requirements for size of ships and the numbers of buses or taxis in fleets. For example, a relatively stable number of licenses is maintained—a number initially tied to demand. The number of bus passengers is divided by a fixed number of passengers per bus to determine the number of bus licenses to be distributed. Similarly a factor of a fixed number of tons per truck is associated with the tons of cargo to be transported to determine the number of truck licenses to be issued. These capacity standards are unrealistic given variation in vehicle size, but they have helped to reinforce the development of larger companies (Neuner: 311–312).

Hence the public sector dominates transportation in Korea through nationalized facilities, policy statements, and investment distribution. It even directs the private sector in the two modes which are not publicly controlled through established licensure practices.

RECENT TRENDS AND FUTURE PROSPECTS

The major goal of Korean transport policy has been to develop a system that can promote as well as accommodate economic growth (*Long-Term Prospect for Economic and Social Development 1977–91,* Chapter 4: 12). Since the capacity of the transport system in the 1960s was clearly insufficient to meet the demand generated by industrial expansion and regional development let alone foreign trade, the first five economic development plans placed considerable emphasis on developing the transportation infrastructure. What was envisioned was a multi-modal transportation system first, linking the country along the Seoul-Pusan corridor; second, stimulating development in the other cities and regions; and third, facilitating foreign trade and investments. The determination was to present Korea as a world-class economic competitor. These objectives, highlighted specifically in the sequential Five-Year Economic Development Plans and the ten-year comprehensive land development plans, guided national investments, stimulated requests for international loans and investment, and required highly centralized, government-directed strategies for implementation.

An associated set of objectives were meeting increased demand for passenger and freight traffic, stimulating balanced regional growth, promoting continuous industrialization and economic growth, and reducing adverse impacts on the environment (*Long-Term Prospect for Economic and Social Development:* 121).

In outlining the first steps toward meeting these objectives, the first Five-

Year Economic Plan (1962–66) emphasized the need for high volume transportation improvements. The railroad was singled out for special emphasis; 48.4 percent of the government transportation investments in this period were to go toward railroad expansion and modernization. A double track line was constructed between Seoul and Inchon; diesel locomotives were imported along with other diesel cars and 236 box cars. Public roads were to be repaired to operate at maximum capacity. Harbors were to be repaired and loading capacity increased.

With the second Five-Year Economic Plan (1967–71), the emphasis moved from railroad to road improvement. Over 62 percent of the national transportation budget was allocated to highways. At the same time, however, passenger and cargo railroad operations were to be strengthened and basic harbor improvements at Pusan, Inchon, Ulsan, and Pohang were to be initiated. Sixteen new airplanes were to be acquired while work was to begin on four new airports: Ulsan, Yosu, Mokp'o, and Sokch'o.

The third Five-Year Plan initiated in 1972 was directed at both public roads and maritime improvements. Of the funds budgeted for transportation, 46.9 percent were for roads with 17.7 percent for maritime improvements. Expressway construction was to continue as were harbor improvements. In addition, the plan also called for electrifying the railroad and increasing its efficiency. Fifteen new airplanes were to be acquired. With the third plan also came the recognition of transportation problems associated with rapid urbanization. Traffic jams and congestion were making travel difficult, especially in Seoul, but in other cities as well.

With the fourth Five-Year Plan from 1977 to 1981 this focus on metropolitan transportation continued. Subways were to be constructed in Seoul as a means of reducing surface-level congestion, and the suburban railroad electrification project was to continue. The imbalance between modes was noted along with the need to increase efficiency in the transportation sector (*Annual Yearbook of Korean Transportation:* 94–99).

The fifth Five-Year Plan from 1982 to 1986 then focused on the need for institutional reform and structural change rather than construction. The basic transportation infrastructure was in place by 1981, and the watchwords became ''economic stability,'' ''efficiency,'' and ''balance'' rather than growth and development. Coming right after the first year of negative economic growth in 1980, the plan provided the opportunity for reassessment. The plan therefore laid the foundation for self-growth, a growth which would be well grounded at home and therefore somewhat insulated from the pressure of international oil crises and runaway inflation. The aim was to reduce the technology gap with other countries and at the same time use a system of indirect investments to raise the standard of living at home.

Specifically, in regard to transportation, the plan called for (1) improving capacity to meet domestic demand; (2) better management of railroad finance; (3) further efforts to ease metropolitan congestion; (4) ''nurturing'' air and marine transportation to allow them to respond to expected increases in international trade; (5) consolidating the transportation system with a view to establishing greater efficiency; (6) rationalizing energy use; (7) encouraging tourism; (8) increasing emphasis on transportation safety; and (9) establishing a broader transportation planning function which would provide for administrative coordination across modes, and between cities and provinces, and a review of sectoral investment policies (*Annual Yearbook of Korean Transportation:* 100).

As initially developed, the plan nevertheless called for several ambitious projects needed "to meet domestic demand." New double track railroads were to be completed between Seoul and Pusan and along the Honam line linking Taejon and the southwest port city of Mokpo. The aim was to balance development of the southeastern and the less-developed southwestern regions of the country. Plans also called for complete electrification of Seoul's railroads to expedite population dispersion to satellite cities. An ambitious highway expansion which would link industrial and population centers was also planned. Facilities at Kimpo Airport in Seoul and Kimhae Airport outside Pusan were to be expanded and improved while extensive development of the cargo facilities at Kwanyang Bay in the vicinity of the Yŏch'ŏn industrial complex and the planned second consolidated steel mills nearby were also to be provided. Unlike the previous plans which were easily met, the fifth Five-Year Plan proved to be too ambitious for an overtaxed economy. Hence the plan was modified in 1984, cutting back considerably on earlier plans for costly rail and highway improvements, leaving only the double tracking of the Honam route and reiterating the need for qualitative rather than quantitative changes (*Annual Yearbook of Korean Transportation:* 100–111).

The following charts developed by the Ministry of Transportation demonstrate the impressive record of increases in performance by the various modes within the Korean transportation system. As Tables 6.1 and 6.2 will demonstrate, among the modes, roads have been consistently dominant in passenger travel and tons of freight carried. While the railroad's share of freight transport has declined significantly in the last decade from 30 percent to 24.5 percent, the proportion of goods carried by truck has varied but is now stabilized at about 61 percent. The proportion of freight transported by ship, however, has increased steadily from 8.4 percent to 14.1 percent. In terms of long-distance transport the increase in maritime transport is even more apparent, up from 26 percent to 33 percent in the last decade. In contrast the proportion of ton-kilometers carried by rail has decreased from 52.9 percent to 45 percent. Only about 21 percent of the ton-kilometers are consistently carried by truck.

Table 6.3 summarizes rail transportation performance indicators from 1965 to 1986. Table 6.4 focuses on rail freight shipment. Table 6.5 presents the number and tonnage of ships, and Table 6.6 shows distinctions in foreign and domestic cargo ships handled at Korean ports over time. Over the period 1974–83 civil aviation increased considerably in both international and domestic mar-

Table 6.1
Tonnage Transported

			Vessel				Aircraft	
	Railway		Coastal	Ocean-going	Motor Vehicle		Domestic Line	International Line
1965	22,377	9,427	2,676	6,751	24,014	5.8	0.8	5.0
1966	24,064	11,121	2,686	8,435	24,528	8.4	1.0	7.4
1967	27,440	15,695	4,172	11,523	28,616	11.0	1.4	9.6
1968	28,857	21,397	5,602	15,795	46,093	15.6	1.7	13.9
1969	30,643	28,114	8,114	20,000	56,575	21.6	2.8	18.8
1970	31,551	33,172	10,888	22,284	61,775	26.2	0.5	25.7
1971	31,955	40,036	11,587	28,449	73,934	29.3	0.7	28.6
1972	31,547	39,994	9,286	30,708	58,673	38.8	0.8	38.0
1973	37,762	49,914	10,152	39,762	71,977	58.8	0.9	57.9
1974	39,708	53,254	11,166	42,088	81,697	70.4	0.6	69.8
1975	42,758	56,940	11.812	45,128	84,527	98.4	0.6	97.8
1976	43,629	69,586	13,829	55,757	93,751	105.7	0.5	105.2
1977	47,631	84,428	16,116	68,312	106,792	124.4	0.8	123.6
1978	49,654	95,057	17,175	77,882	144,599	153.0	11.0	142.0
1979	50,879	110,042	19,222	90,820	141,513	181.5	14.0	167.5
1980	49,008	113,265	19,230	94,035	104,526	204.4	13.0	191.4
1981	48,761	127,532	22,206	105,326	104,256	227.0	18.0	209.0
1982	47,437	134,961	26,454	108,507	108,576	265.0	30.0	235.0
1983	50,478	147,271	29,086	118,185	126,403	309.0	43.0	266.0
1984	53,661	157,402	31,731	125,671	143,629	360.0	58.0	302.0
1985	55,346	167,189	34,179	133,010	148,699	401.0	68.0	333.0
1986	58,238	191,449	37,626	153,823	168,779	469.5	78.0	391.5

Source: Ministry of Transportation, *Major Statistics of Korean Economy 1987* (Seoul: Economic Planning Board, 1987), p. 134.

Table 6.2
Passengers Transported

				Vessel				Aircraft	
	Railway	Subway		Coastal	Ocean-going	Motor Vehicle		Domestic Line	International Line
1965	107,177	--	5,512	5,504	8	1,195,471	285	208	77
1966	138,299	--	5,921	5,909	12	1,511,558	323	192	131
1967	151,972	--	6,713	6,700	13	1,674,784	391	215	176
1968	150,969	--	6,561	6,540	12	2,018,880	537	312	225
1969	154,696	--	6,080	6,076	13	2,418,612	889	619	270
1970	131,251	--	5,893	5,869	24	2,743,769	1,315	917	398
1971	128,159	--	6,409	6,371	38	3,024,229	1,620	1,105	515
1972	137,139	--	6,309	6,261	48	3,308,473	1,905	1,121	784
1973	143,009	--	7,306	7,235	71	3,855,794	2,702	1,269	1,433
1974	168,469	16,082	6,669	6,618	61	4,115,929	2,235	991	1,244
1975	220,952	34,288	5,956	5,908	48	4,542,739	2,472	906	1,566
1976	248,699	33,914	6,057	5,994	63	5,050,983	2,809	795	2,014
1977	301,592	46,574	6,791	6,737	54	5,931,452	3,413	1,097	2,316
1978	371,022	58,238	7,791	7,728	63	6,807,990	4,169	1,461	2,708
1979	423,657	66,454	7,972	7,929	43	7,609,677	4,801	1,812	2,989
1980	430,773	65,075	8,621	8,580	41	8,039,806	4,403	1,401	2,922
1981	441,129	88,326	9,281	9,230	51	8,633,130	4,784	1,555	3,229
1982	443,570	89,298	9,658	9,602	56	9,259,252	5,345	1,844	3,501
1983	469,425	115,624	9,035	8,978	66	9,901,324	6,066	2,363	3,703
1984	489,061	212,637	9,438	9,371	67	10,200,619	6,811	2,889	3,942
1985	503,123	325,238	8,599	8,534	65	10,601,047	7,849	3,467	4,382
1986	518,956	580,492	8,800	8,727	73	10,932,607	9,031	4,092	4,939

Source: Ministry of Transportation, *Major Statistics of Korean Economy 1987* (Seoul: Economic Planning Board, 1987), p. 133.

Table 6.3
Railway Transport[1,2]

	Length of Railways in Operation	Passengers			Freight		
		Passengers Carried	Daily Average Persons	Total Passenger	Tonnage Carried	Daily Average	Total Ton
1965	2,980.0	107,177	293.6	6,916.8	20,982.0	57.5	4,814.6
1966	3,062.7	138,299	378.9	8,664.8	22,351.0	61.2	5,158.1
1967	3,104.6	151,972	416.4	9,577.0	26,101.6	71.5	5,960.4
1968	3,161.2	150,969	413.6	10,590.1	27,580.3	75.6	6,672.2
1969	3,192.4	154,696	423.8	11,076.6	29,153.3	79.9	7,116.5
1970	3,193.2	131,251	359.6	9,819.1	30,298.4	83.0	7,487.5
1971	3,198.7	128,159	351.1	8,750.2	30,696.4	84.1	7,642.8
1972	3,120.6	137,139	375.7	10,062.3	30,502.3	83.6	7,084.7
1973	3,133,0	143,009	391.8	10,720.1	36,421.7	99.8	8,394.0
1974	3,143.4	168,469	461.6	10,970.1	38,325.2	105.0	8,795.6
1975	3,144.3	220,952	605.4	12,924.9	41,314.2	113.2	9,085.6
1976	3,144.3	248,699	681.4	14,305.3	42,091.3	115.3	9,501.1
1977	3,141.9	301,592	826.3	17,099.0	48,998.7	126.0	10,293.9
1978	3,152.9	371,022	1,016.5	20,059.7	48,015.5	131.5	10,697.7
1979	3,158.1	423,657	1,160.7	21,385.8	48,865.0	133.9	10,824.7
1980	3,134.6	430,773	1,180.2	21,639.9	46,775.0	127.8	10,548.9
1981	3,121.3	441,129	1,208.6	21,528.5	47,182.0	129.3	10,638.0
1982	3,121.3	443,570	1,215.3	21,033.6	45,938.5	125.9	10,720.5
1983	3,120,7	469,423	1,286.1	21,688.1	48,909.8	134.0	11,456.0
1984	3,116.4	489,061	1,339.9	21,884.3	51,928.9	142.3	11,845.2
1985	3,120.6	503,122	1,378.4	22,595.2	55,345.5	151.6	12,296.2
1986	3,113.4	518,956	1,421.8	23,562.8	58,237.8	159.6	12,813.0

[1] As of the end of year.
[2] Excludes service traffic of Office of National Railroad.

Source: Office of National Railroad, *Major Statistics of Korean Economy 1987* (Seoul: Economic Planning Board, 1987), p. 135.

kets as Table 6.7 will indicate. Increases are impressive in cargo and mail as well as passengers transported.

Table 6.8 presents the dramatic rise in motor vehicles from 1965 to 1986. The increase in private cars registered increased from 5,507 in 1965 to 364,742 in 1984. This trend will obviously continue, strongly impacting transportation planning. Table 6.9 presents available information on workers and income derived by them from various aspects of the transportation industry in 1983. Clearly this is another major impact the transportation sector has on the Korean economy. Opportunities abound for the transportation sector to continue to play a major role in shaping the direction of Korea's economic development.

Table 6.4
Freight Transportation of Railway

	Tonnage Carried			Ton-km		
	Total	Services	Self-Supplies	Total	Services	Self-Supplies
1975	42,758	41,314	1,444	9,292,821	9,085,643	207,179
1976	43,630	42,091	1,538	9,728,234	9,501,098	227,135
1977	47,631	45,999	1,632	10,508,620	10,293,935	214,685
1978	49,654	48,015	1,639	10,926,154	10,697,715	228,438
1979	50,879	48,865	2,014	11,080,816	10,824,732	256,084
1980	48,008	46,775	2,234	10,797,616	10,548,958	248,658
1981	48,761	47,182	1,579	10,814,862	10,637,936	176,866
1982	47,431	45,038	1,699	10,891,567	10,720,474	171,093
1983	50,471	48,910	1,568	11,629,221	11,456,933	173,188

Source: Office of National Railroad, *Economic Statistics Yearbook 1984* (Seoul: The Bank of Korea, 1984).

Table 6.5
Number of Vessels and Tonnage[1]

	Total		Passenger Steamship		Cargo Ship		Fishing Vessel		Other Ships	
	No.	G/T	No.	G/T	No.	G/T	No.	G/T	No.	G/T
1965	11,826	370,465	238	15,800	1,356	198,180	51,052	203,164	456	17,384
1966	12,562	440,145	234	16,561	1,377	243,713	53,294	245,962	489	18,347
1967	13,465	708,317	211	16,169	1,380	469,378	57,255	262,079	559	21,771
1968	15,753	918,603	229	17,973	1,599	639,615	62,002	292,962	646	23,447
1969	16,898	1,122,140	231	18,142	1,778	813,360	66,115	342,280	726	26,315
1970	16,770	1,206,468	230	18,630	1,779	876,730	68,355	358,366	784	28,816
1971	17,736	1,204,015	211	18,176	1,948	929,124	68,269	392,649	861	29,269
1972	16,706	1,464,357	196	18,355	1,840	1,056,582	67,679	451,767	910	33,695
1973	16,890	1,454,871	199	19,641	1,840	1,816,651	68,597	511,112	962	34,905
1974	17,104	1,897,239	183	19,263	1,834	1,381,896	68,031	602,371	1,066	37,274
1975	17,211	2,077,167	176	18,042	1,849	1,506,622	67,655	647,700	1,122	41,554
1976	18,140	2,667,755	155	17,497	1,787	2,060946	65,822	661,991	1,220	45,774
1977	19,210	2,962,218	141	20,064	1,644	2,305,103	66,506	682,591	1,337	53,931
1978	20,963	4,000,515	155	23,702	1,819	3,262,552	70,310	756,087	1,478	54,024
1979	66,528	4,666,335	143	25,386	1,793	3,844,949	74,556	752,781	1,773	60,277
1980	81,467	4,044,441	148	26,987	1,778	4,071,488	77,574	770,688	1,972	75,966
1981	84,415	5,740,395	163	28,529	1,747	4,856,162	80,500	781,582	2,005	74,122
1982	90,520	6,457,090	156	32,919	1,707	5,531,316	86,515	807,570	2,142	85,294
1983	92,740	6,967,671	162	45,227	1,744	5,994,289	88,594	828,348	2,249	99,807
1984	--	--	160	45,143	1,770	6,319,132	--	--	2,324	136,931
1985	95,144	7,538,711	156	44,690	1,680	6,478,736	90,970	858,471	2,338	138,951
1986	97,273	7,538,711	156	54,804	1,596	6,455,263	93,037	883,851	2,484	144,793

[1]Based on registered vessels.

Source: Ministry of Transportation Office of Fisheries, *Major Statistics of Korean Economy 1987* (Seoul: Economic Planning Board, 1987), p. 138.

Table 6.6
Oceangoing Vessels

	Total	Non-coastal Total	Korean Flag	Foreign Flag	Coastal
1974	44,657	33,820	5,964	27,866	10,827
1975	46,683	35,142	7,784	27,359	11,540
1976	54,979	41,447	12,222	29,225	13,532
1977	67,213	51,408	19,104	32,304	15,815
1978	78,671	61,844	30,518	31,326	16,827
1979	91,751	72,992	34,604	38,388	18,759
1980	90,204	71,353	30,673	40,680	18,851
1981	100,861	79,024	29,582	49,442	21,837
1982	106,919	80,938	38,178	42,760	25,981
1983	117,506	88,906	42,201	46,705	28,600

Source: Office of National Railroad, *Economic Statistics Yearbook 1984* (Seoul: The Bank of Korea, 1984), p. 278.

Table 6.7
Civil Aviation Traffics

	International Operation						Domestic Operation		
	In			Out					
	Passenger (person)	Cargo (ton)	Mail (kg)	Passenger (person)	Cargo (ton)	Mail (kg)	Passenger (person)	Cargo (ton)	Mail (kg)
1974	572,403	23,262	2,841,338	616,145	38,567	1,910,031	990,826	5,743	95,131
1975	704,574	29,518	1,853,955	771,137	57,189	1,838,787	887,683	5,380	239,829
1976	924,146	39,450	1,923,383	986,437	57,215	2,520,790	773,904	5,312	118,253
1977	1,055,719	43,894	2,452,979	1,139,750	65,132	2,866,093	1,081,322	5,377	173,033
1978	1,257,133	56,839	2,171,573	1,348,271	74,070	2,289,725	1,417,378	10,375	268,882
1979	1,400,302	75,776	3,663,775	1,473,046	81,725	3,458,273	1,755,585	13,198	263,973
1980	1,380,472	84,023	3,889,583	1,466,976	97,615	4,186,972	1,411,546	11,832	268,391
1981	1,516,174	90,549	3,907,451	1,614,134	106,710	4,265,092	1,456,633	16,227	329,076
1982	1,672,971	108,095	3,892,708	1,739,995	114,903	4,997,746	1,757,714	27,840	244,733
1983	1,793,420	116,498	4,247,340	1,853,403	134,866	5,593,348	2,240,824	40,819	214,282

Source: Office of National Railroad, *Economic Statistics Yearbook 1984* (Seoul: The Bank of Korea, 1984), p. 281.

Table 6.8
Number of Motor Vehicles[1]

		Passenger Cars			Trucks			Buses				
	Total	Gov't.	Private	Commercial	Gov't.	Private	Commercial	Gov't.	Private	Commercial	Motorcycle[2]	Special Model
1965	39,126	1,619	5,507	5,875	1,659	3,874	10,482	108	312	8,896	2,385	794
1966	48,838	1,845	7,481	8,176	2,020	4,773	12,639	134	403	10,351	1,322	1,016
1967	58,975	2,247	9,871	11,117	2,181	5,627	15,147	154	541	10,804	1,722	1,286
1968	78,763	2,787	14,397	15,928	2,701	7,630	21,251	204	750	11,832	2,188	1,283
1969	106,138	3,128	23,696	23,475	2,816	11,020	26,298	236	989	13,012	2,531	1,468
1970	126,506	3,547	28,687	28,443	2,983	15,258	30,060	247	1,262	14,322	2,865	1,097
1971	140,269	3,961	33,994	29,627	3,253	18,552	31,600	349	1,416	15,646	4,068	1,871
1972	145,637	4,507	36,412	29,325	3,577	21,542	29,997	389	1,541	15,620	4,297	2,727
1973	165,307	5,046	43,400	29,888	4,941	26,791	32,852	422	2,143	16,306	5,407	3,518
1974	177,505	4,837	44,618	27,007	4,927	35,330	36,576	418	2,479	17,163	6,039	4,150
1975	193,927	5,028	50,093	29,096	4,056	39,929	37,977	484	3,061	18,273	6,594	5,035
1976	218,978	5,191	61,589	29,319	5,915	49,362	38,608	538	3,876	19,229	7,342	5,351
1977	275,312	5,741	85,074	34,798	7,308	69,475	41,367	711	5,089	20,910	7,440	4,839
1978	384,536	6,128	128,804	49,954	7,586	105,402	48,898	794	7,374	22,429	12,020	7,167
1979	494,378	6,830	172,907	61,685	8,298	146,229	52,295	943	10,018	26,736	181,976	8,437
1980	527,729	7,773	178,513	62,816	8,873	165,396	52,671	1,244	13,005	28,214	216,498	9,224
1981	571,754	7,869	193,512	66,224	9,259	180,584	53,985	1,613	18,316	30,666	276,335	9,726
1982	646,996	7,839	225,631	72,341	9,070	199,215	55,654	1,855	32,111	32,360	410,286	10,920
1983	785,316	7,981	293,141	79,371	9,380	235,576	59,202	2,116	50.881	34,285	528,803	12,883
1984	948,319	8,251	364,742	92,156	9,586	288,249	62,529	2,383	69,632	36,014	640,297	14,777
1985	1,113,430	8,479	449,062	99,118	10,309	338,555	63,875	2,679	88,500	37,130	711,439	15,723
1986	1,309,434	8,928	545,269	110,029	11,364	390,625	70,612	2,997	113,083	38,547	812,349	17,980

[1]Military and diplomatic vehicles are not included. Micro-buses were included in passenger cars until 1965 and in buses since 1966.
[2]Excluding motorcycle from total.

Source: Ministry of Transportation, *Major Statistics of Korean Economy 1987* (Seoul: Economic Planning Board, 1987), p. 136.

Table 6.9
Summary of Transportation Business

	Establishment	Workers	Employees Renumeration	Transportation Income	Transportation Expense	Value Added	Tangible Fixed Asset
				By Industry			
Land Transport	4,888	410,590	1,276,805	4,469,821	4,002,642	2,277,153	3,980,347
Railway	1	34,066	202,215	469,463	476,032	251,961	2,113,111
Subway	1	3,075	10,679	27,737	31,091	16,261	538,100
Highway Express Bus	10	8,540	39,650	169,668	146,744	90,429	74,211
Inter-urban Highway Bus	148	36,140	111,717	426,679	403,276	194,730	148,830
Urban Bus	311	74,348	253,203	722,879	698,060	372,191	225,400
Sight-Seeing Bus	174	9,183	25,773	92,140	88,448	49,670	65,421
Taxicab	2,004	132,246	277,732	1,197,785	964,131	605,759	278,531
Scheduled Freight Local Freight	817	76,871	244,360	949,426	865,996	441,073	294,421
Special Freight Transport	127	6,783	30,774	130,042	121,420	72,723	80,634
Cargo Delivery	806	20,540	51,309	142,333	123,019	84,409	66,660
Hearse Transport	233	1,088	2,404	7,386	6,357	4,494	6,941
Operation of Toll Road	1	3,630	17,117	102,463	53,905	74,887	5,111
Cars Rent	8	338	1,036	3,740	3,384	2,300	2,261
Passenger Terminal	244	3,620	8,374	20,660	19,410	14,426	76,431
Freight Terminal	3	118	460	1,421	1,369	1,001	3,266
Water Transport	321	25,264	154,731	2,046,182	1,904,382	672,081	2,030,036
Coastal Passenger	51	1,643	5,180	26,228	27,718	9,406	32,767
Coastal Freight	201	5,025	20,123	107,840	95,509	69,480	129,805
Foreign Passenger	1	114	689	3,961	3,483	2,070	4,463
Foreign Freight	63	18,482	128,739	1,910,154	1,777,677	601,075	1,863,033
Air Transport	4	11,237	75,785	898,094	804,866	289,922	531,939
Carriers	1	8,095	61,587	859,650	775,879	260,323	526,941
Supporting Services	3	3,142	14,193	38,444	28,989	29,593	4,991

Source: Office of National Railroad, *Economic Statistics Yearbook 1984* (Seoul: The Bank of Korea, 1984), p. 284.

At the end of the 1980s Korea was able to boast a well-developed transportation infrastructure. A few additions were made with the initiation of the new sixth Five-Year Plan in 1987, but basically the physical structure is complete. What remains is the need for an overall transportation strategy which would favor the continuous growth of the economy by meeting traffic demands generated by other sectors of the economy, promote land development, and guide further industrial location. At the same time, the transportation system is intended to serve social justice by distributing the benefits of a higher quality of life. Such efforts cannot be accomplished without an integrated, coordinated system which can strive for balanced growth in all modes.

Each mode has three elements which determine the quality of service: vehicles, the right of way, and facilities such as terminals and control equipment. Thus far with the emphasis on right of way and basic infrastructure, there has been a lack of systematic planning among the modes and among the elements of the mode. What is needed is a total systems approach to transportation—one considering traffic demand in terms of regions, commodities, and corridors not just city by city. Other long-term policy goals should include meeting increasing demand for passenger and freight traffic, stimulating balanced regional growth, and reducing adverse impacts on the environment (*Long-Term Prospect for Economic and Social Development 1977–91:* 120–121).

With the modification of the fifth Five-Year Plan, Korea has indeed begun to move into the second phase of transportation planning—moving away from a preoccupation with facility expansion to an assessment of the quality of service provided by each mode. Bottlenecks inhibiting efficient service have begun to be addressed on a systems basis. For example, in air services, congested terminal facilities were limiting expansion of international service. These needs are now being addressed at Kimpo and Kimhae airports.

Similarly inadequate ports in the south were inhibiting the expansion of heavy industrial facilities in that area. Hence new port construction was initiated. Along with the new port development, careful consideration was given to minimizing environmental impact caused by industrial expansion. New plants are therefore being located on filled land off the coast and integrated into the harbor facility. With improved rail lines and highways linking the newly industrialized area with the less-developed region in the southwest, the potential exists for spillover of economic benefits and balanced growth.

More such integrative efforts will be needed in the future. Of particular concern will be the need to coordinate the transportation improvements in Seoul with those in the surrounding region. Otherwise plans to reduce congestion in Seoul will only export the problem to the surrounding area. Bottlenecks are already developing at the points where the city transportation system meets the national system (i.e., entrance to the expressways, bridges over the Han River, and the rail terminals).

Some effort has obviously been made at linking land development plans with transportation plans, but far more is needed if bottlenecks and congestion are to be avoided and the benefits of economic growth are to be widely shared. A major opportunity to enhance interjurisdictional linkage was presented by plans for the 1988 Olympics. New sports arenas are now in place along with appropriate support infrastructure. Transportation specific to the sports arenas has been well developed with a new widened highway and new bridges over the Han River. However, the impacts of linkage between these new facilities and the Seoul city system and the broader regional systems were not fully addressed.

The future transportation policy in Korea will have to be viewed in terms of multi-modal linkage and jurisdictional interface. Communication between the Seoul city government and the ministries of construction and transportation is single directional. The central government agencies regularly transmit information and policy pronouncement to the city, while the opposite flow rarely exists. New, more broadly based administrative units and plans with broad regional perspectives are essential if opportunities for continued balanced economic growth are to be grasped.

TRANSPORTATION POLICY ORGANIZATION AND PROCESS

Government and government-authorized organizations and institutions are participating in transportation policy formulation. With the race toward economic development, Korea's emphasis, as suggested, has been on efficient construction of infrastructure rather than on development of an effectively integrated transportation system. This emphasis is clearly reflected in the configuration of governmental bodies charged with delineating and implementing transportation policy. In the presidential system of government, policies originate from the top—that is, from the president and his staff in the Blue House. The prime minister, appointed by the president and acting as head of the administration, presides over the cabinet which decides on the matters of public policy including those related to transportation. Under President Roh Tae Woo's government of the Sixth Republic, inaugurated on Feb. 25, 1988, a series of democratic reforms were announced. These included a pledge to local autonomy and decentralization of governmental functions by 1989. The impact of these policy changes on transportation issues have yet to be seen. However, if carried out, they will present new challenges to system coordination.

The Ministry of Transportation, under the leadership of the cabinet-ranking transportation minister, has titular responsibility for ensuring a coordinated transportation system. In actuality, however, the powerful mode-specific administrations and authorities make that role difficult.

This point is underscored through observation of the following three organization charts for the Ministry of Transportation, the Korean National Railroad, and the Maritime and Port Administration. One is quickly impressed by the rather lean chart of the Ministry shown as Figure 6.5. Appropriately it includes

Figure 6.5
Ministry of Transportation

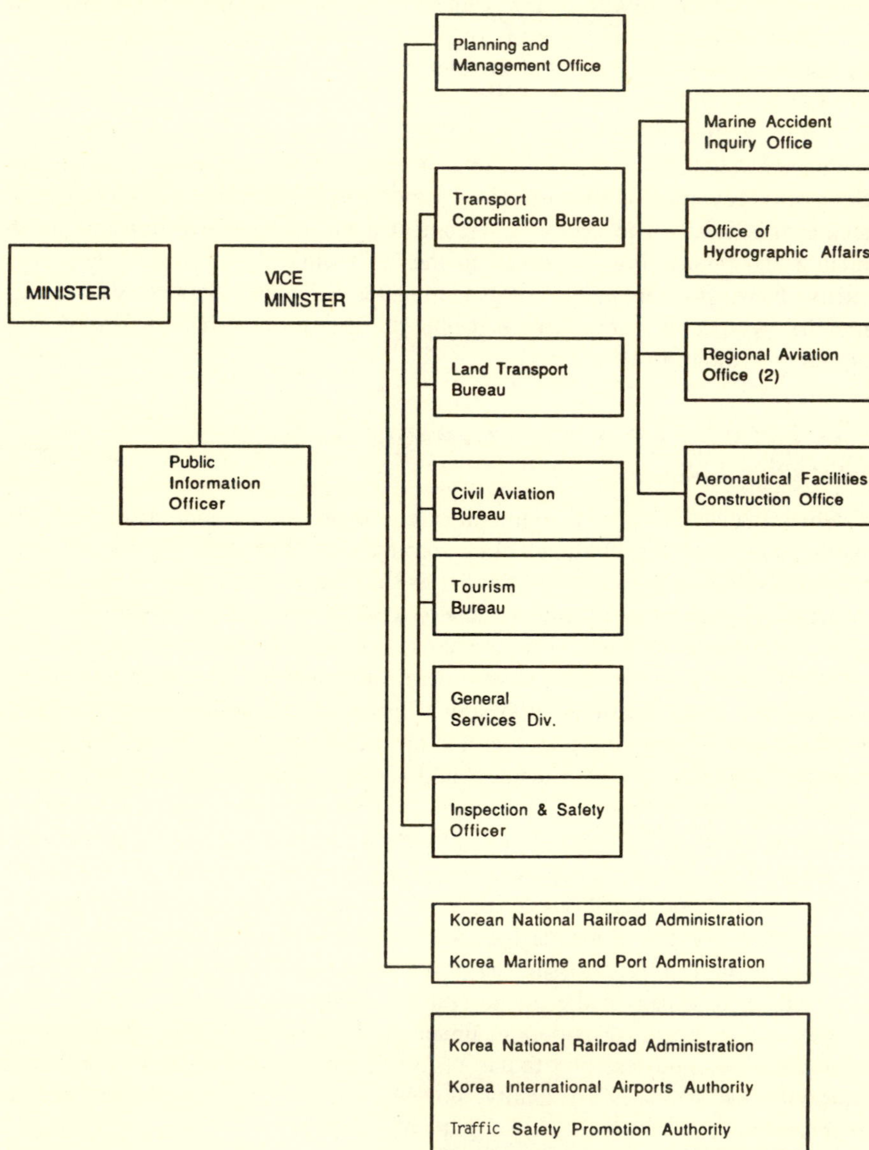

Source: Transportation in Korea, 1985 (Seoul: The ROK Ministry of Transportation, 1985), p. 4.

an Office of Planning and Management and a Transport Coordination Bureau. The planning office does prepare broad-based studies and reports and is a major source for intermodal perspectives on transportation planning. To date, however, as previously indicated, the coordination bureau has not proven to be very assertive in pursuing its mission. In actuality the modal administrations and authorities indicate mode-specific policy, and coordination has consequently proven most difficult. If adequately strengthened and supported, however, the bureau could become an important vehicle for furthering intermodal linkages. The other offices within the ministry appear to represent an array of functions not lodged elsewhere. Land transport and domestic civil aviation, two modes of transportation not directed by modal agencies, are included within the ministry, as are the broader functions of inspection and safety and general services. Then there are also offices associated with mode-specific specialized functions such as marine accident inquiry and hydrographic affairs.

The potential for overlapping functions also exists. For example, with the emphasis on tourism as a means of furthering economic development, a national corporation was set up to direct that area. There is, however, also a Tourism Bureau within the Ministry of Transportation which focuses specifically on transportation requirements. Although the ministry houses a division of Aeronautical Facilities Construction, there is a separate Ministry of Construction which focuses on construction associated with highways and other modes. Traffic safety promotion is the responsibility of still another separate authority which is only loosely linked to the Ministry of Transportation. Again this organizational arrangement makes coordinated multi-modal planning complex. Similarly, responding to problems of traffic congestion is made somewhat complex because of the sharp delineation in function between the Ministry of Construction and the Ministry of Transportation. While the Ministry of Transportation can document the level of congestion at specific locations and make recommendations, the nature and prioritization of responses is the responsibility of the larger and more powerful Ministry of Construction.

In contrast to the lean organization chart of the Ministry of Transportation, the chart of the Korean National Railroad Administration (Figure 6.6) is indicative of an all-encompassing, efficient organization. It has its own planning and management office and an array of offices associated with research and engineering, finance, construction, service operation, and service monitoring. It even has regional offices at five key locations across the country. All functional bureaus are responsible to the administrator and the deputy administrator. These administrations are directly responsible to the Ministry of Transportation, but in practice are all but autonomous. A similar but somewhat less elaborate chart is associated with the Korean Maritime and Port Administration (KMPA). As Figure 6.7 will point out, this administration has a full array of functional offices for integrative planning, construction, and management of port facilities. In addition, separate maritime and port authorities focus on each port, but these are all clearly under the KMPA. As indicated, the KMPA also dispatches

Figure 6.6
Korean National Railroad Administration

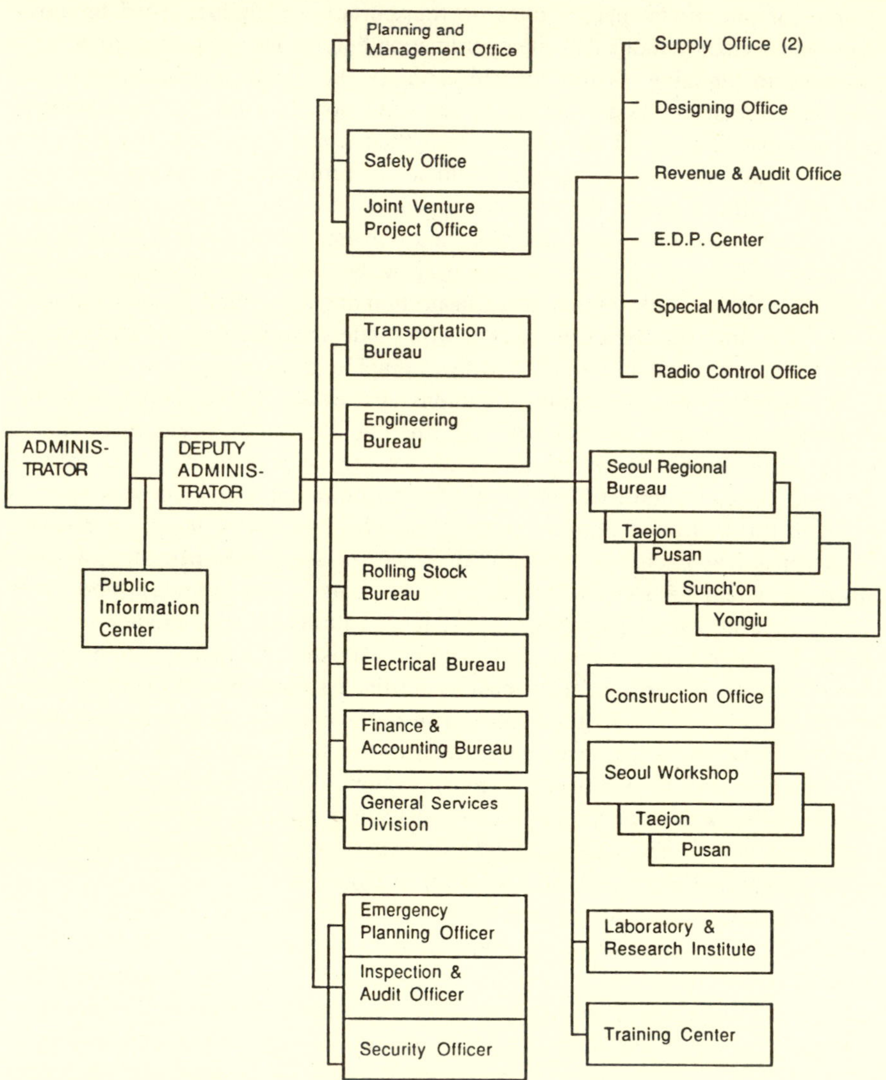

Source: Transportation in Korea, 1985 (Seoul: The ROK Ministry of Transportation, 1985), p. 5.

a maritime attaché to the embassies of major trading partners. The attaché is directly responsible to the administration and its administrator.

The contrasts apparent in the organization charts are also in the numbers and types of employees associated with each administration. The Ministry of Transportation had a total of 1,082 employees in 1985, including 2 political ap-

Figure 6.7
Korean Maritime and Port Administration

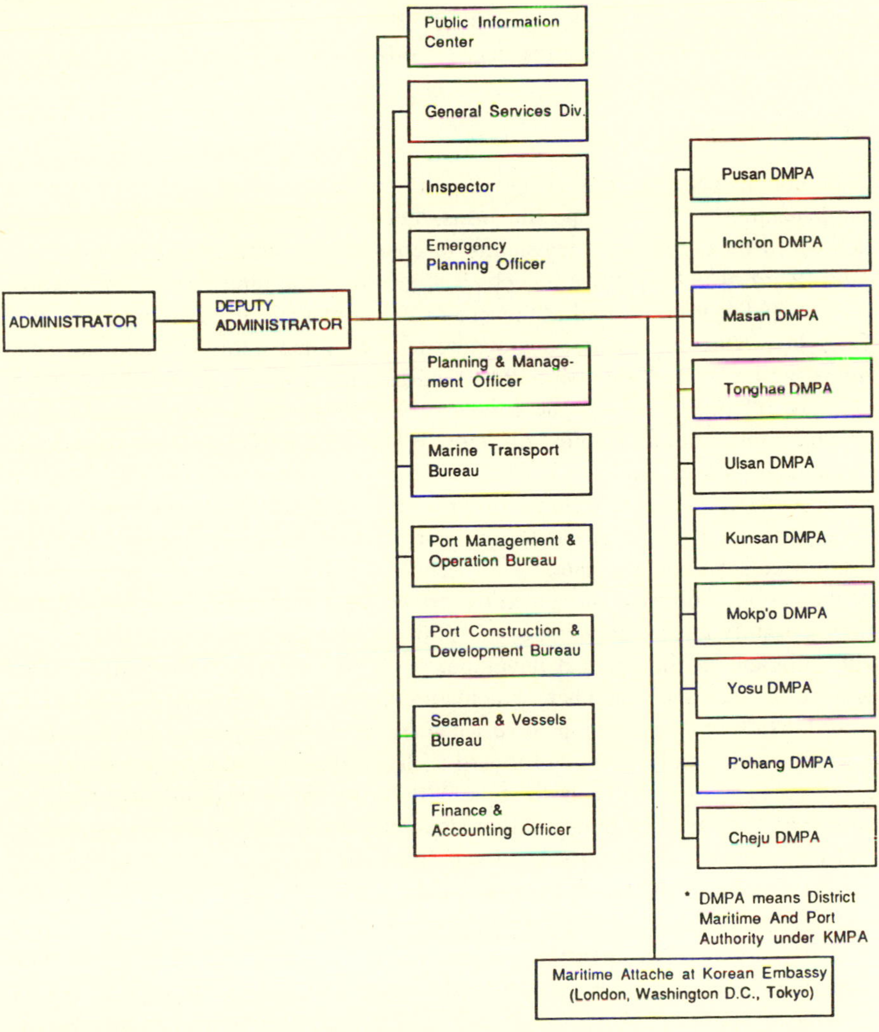

Source: Transportation in Korea, 1985 (Seoul: The ROK Ministry of Transportation, 1985), p. 6.

pointees, 22 in civil service, 118 in technical service, and 201 others. The largest number were in general service, 739. The Korean National Railroad Administration, on the other hand, had 25,805 in technical service associated with train operation, 1 political appointee, and 6,841 in general service out of a total of 39,255 employees. The more streamlined Port Authority had a total of 1,989 employees including, among others, 1,030 in general service, 1 in political service, and only 521 in technical service. The International Airport Authority had a total of 1,059 employees including, among others, 8 executives, 398 in general service, and 285 in technical services. These organizations are clearly large and complex enough to direct all aspects of policy making and implementation within these respective modes.

CONCLUSION

In Korea, therefore, transportation policy is for the most part developed and implemented on a mode-specific basis. Only the most general directives are developed by the national legislature in consultation with the Economic Planning Board of the executive branch. It is left to the administrations and authorities to spell out policy and at the same time implement it and monitor results. Only in modes not otherwise assigned to a separate administration does the ministry play an authoritative policy-making role. Even in some of these areas, like ground transportation, the Ministry of Transportation makes coordinated ground transportation planning difficult. When dealing with responses to traffic bottlenecks, for example, it is most difficult to separate out the policies associated with traffic flow (Transportation) and road design (Construction).

As discussed, these problems of interjurisdictional coordination are made even more severe when planning for Seoul, which is outside the responsibility of the national ministry but is also the primary national traffic generator. Questions certainly arise as to whether this policy-making system which was reasonably efficient in the original development of infrastructure can address what will be an increasing number of demands associated with systems operation. Coordination is difficult to achieve when issues of "turf" arise. Nevertheless, for Korea to continue to move forward with a responsive transportation system, a far greater degree of coordination will be essential: coordination between economic planning and transportation development, coordination across modes, and coordination across jurisdicational lines. In the years following the successful hosting of the Seoul Olympic Games in 1988, South Korea has continued to expand its international trade, diversifying trading partners away from a reliance on the United States and Japan and toward new trading relations with Eastern Europe, the Soviet Union, and China. The national transportation requirements, in terms of highways, rail, and ports, will continue to increase. If Korea is to continue to support an annual GNP growth rate of over 12 percent (the level registered in 1986 and 1987), the transportation infrastructure will need to be upgraded with parallel speed and efficiency, underscoring the need for continued focusing on transportation as a coordinated national system.

REFERENCES

Ahn, Moon-Suk, and Chong Bum Lee, "A Network Analysis of International Relations: A Case Study of the Transportation System in Korea," in Bun Woong Kim,

David S. Bell, and Chong Bum Lee, eds., *Administrative Dynamics and Development: The Korean Experience* (Seoul: Kyobo Publishing, 1985).

Annual Yearbook of Korean Transportation (Seoul: Kyotong Sinposa, 1984).

Che o ch'a Kyongje Sahoe Paljon o gyenyon Kyehoek Kyoto'ongbu Sokwan Sujong Kyehoek, 1982–1986 [The fifth economic and social development Five-Year Plan and the revised plan for the Ministry of Transportation, 1982–1986] (Seoul: The ROK Ministry of Transportation, 1983).

A Handbook of Korea, 3rd, 5th, and 6th editions (Seoul: Korean Overseas Information Service, 1979, 1983, and 1987).

Highway Network Master Plan Study (I): Summary Seoul: The ROK Ministry of Construction and Korea Research Institute for Human Settlements, 1985).

Hwang, Myong-chan, *Growth and Management of Seoul Metropolitan Region* (Seoul: Korea Research Institute for Human Settlements, 1982).

Im, Ho-kyu, *Hangukui Chonghap Susong Ch'egye* [Korean integrated transportation system] (Seoul: Korea Development Institute, 1979).

Kim, Kwang Suk, and Michael Roemer, *Growth and Structural Transportation,* Studies in the Modernization of the Republic of Korea, 1945–1975 (Cambridge, Mass.: Harvard University Council on East Asian Studies, 1979).

Korea Herald, October 18, 1985.

Korean Economic Yearbook 1984 (Seoul: The Federation of Korean Industries, 1984).

Korean Statistical Yearbook 1984 (Seoul: The ROK Economic Planning Board, 1984).

Korea Overseas Information Service, "Korea Overseas Information Service, Series" (mimeo), Oct., 1989.

Kukt'o Kyepal Kibanui Hwakch'ung [National land development basis and its expansion], The Second National Integrated Development Plan (Seoul: Korea Research Institute for Human Settlements, 1982) (especially pp. 87–199).

Kwon, Won-Yong, *Metropolitan Growth and Management: The Case of Seoul* (Seoul: Korea Research Institute for Human Settlements, 1980).

Long-Term Prospect for Economic and Social Development 1977–91 (Seoul: Korea Development Institute, 1978) (especially Chapter 9: Development of Transportation and Communication, pp. 120–131).

Major Statistics of Korean Economy (Seoul: The ROK Economic Planning Board, 1985).

Mills, Edwin S., and Byung-Nak Song. *Urbanization and Urban Problems,* Studies in the Modernization of the Republic of Korea, 1945–1975 (Cambridge, Mass.: Harvard University Council on East Asian Studies, 1979).

National Land Development Planning in Korea (Seoul: Korea Research Institute for Human Settlements, 1984).

Neuner, Tallman, "Transport," in Parvez Hasan and D. C. Rao, eds., *Korea: Policy Issues for Long-Term Development,* published for the World Bank (Baltimore: The Johns Hopkins University Press, 1979.

Office of National Railroad, *Economic Statistics Yearbook 1984* (Seoul: The Bank of Korea, 1984).

Repetto, Robert, et al., *Economic Development, Population Policy, and Demographic Transition in the Republic of Korea,* Studies in the Modernization of the Republic of Korea, 1945–1975 (Cambridge, Mass.: Harvard University Council on East Asian Studies, 1981).

Report on Transportation Survey: 1984 (Seoul: The ROK Economic Planning Board, 1985).

Rho, Yung-Hee, and Myong-Chan Hwang, eds., *Metropolitan Planning: Issues and Policies* (Seoul: Korea Research Institute for Human Settlements, 1979).

Study of Road User Charges: Final Report (Seoul: The ROK Ministry of Construction and Korea Research Institute for Human Settlements, 1986).

Transportation in Korea, 1985 (Seoul: The ROK Ministry of Transportation, 1985).

APPENDIX

The Republic of Korea now uses a new system of transliteration called McCune-Reischauer. Place names in Figures 6.1 through 6.4 are currently spelled as follows:

	Old	New (McCune-Reischauer)
Figure 6.1		
	Chuncheon	Ch'unchŏn
	Banweol	Panwol
	Weonju	Wonju
	Bugpyeong	Pukp'yŏng
	Cheongju	Ch'ŏngju
	Daedeog	Taedŏk
	Gunsan	Kunsan
	Gumi	Kumi
	Iri	Iri
	Jeonju	Chŏnju
	Gwangju	Kwangju
	Mogpo	Mokp'o
	Suncheon	Sunch'ŏn
	Yeocheon	Yŏch'ŏn
	Jinju	Chinju
	Samcheonpo	Samch'ŏnp'o
	Jindo	Jindo
	Jisepo	Jisep'o
	Ogpo	Okp'o
	Changweon	Ch'angwŏn
	Yangsan	Yangsan
	Onsan	Onsan
	Ulsan-Mipo	Ulsan-Mip'o
	Weolseong	Wolsŏng
	Pohand	P'ohang
Figure 6.2		
	Chuncheon	Ch'unch'ŏn
	Gangneung	Kangnung
	Inchon	Inch'ŏn
	Weonju	Wonju
	Jecheon	Jech'ŏn
	Cheonan	Ch'ŏnan
	Andong	Andong
	Daejeon	Taejon
	Iri	Iri
	Gwangju	Kwangju

	Old	**New (McCune-Reischauer)**
	Mogpo	Mokp'o
	Yeosu	Yŏsu
	Busan	Pusan
	Daegu	Taegu
	Pohang	P'ohang
Figure 6.3		
	Sogcho	Sokch'o
	Chuncheon	Ch'unch'ŏn
	Icheon	Ich'ŏn
	Weonju	Wonju
	Donghae	Tonghae
	Cheongju	Ch'ŏngju
	Daejeon	Taejŏn
	Jeonju	Chŏnju
	Gwangju	Kwangju
	Mogpo	Mokp'o
	Suncheon	Sunch'ŏn
	Jinju	Jinju
	Gochang	Koch'ang
	Masan	Masan
	Busan	Pusan
	Daegu	Taegu
	Pohang	P'ohang
Figure 6.4		
	Incheon	Inch'ŏn
	Asan	Asan
	Gunsan-Janghang	Kunsan-Janghang
	Mogpo	Mokp'o
	Gwangyang	Kwangyang
	Samcheonpo	Samch'ŏnp'o
	Chungmu	Ch'ungmu
	Masan-OChangweon	Masan-Ch'angwon
	Jinhae	Chinhae
	Jansengpo	Jansengp'o
	Busan	Pusan
	Ulsan-Onsan	Ulsan-Onsan
	Pohang	P'ohang
	Sogcho	Sokch'o
	Mugho	Mukho
	Bugpyeong	Pukp'yŏng
	Samcheog	Samch'ok

7

MEXICO

George M. Guess

BACKGROUND

The case of Mexico illustrates the dilemmas of an "upper middle income" country ($2,407 per capita gross domestic product in 1986) trying to achieve an integrated political and economic system. Since 67 percent of Mexican foreign trade has traditionally been conducted overland with the United States (Street: 389), it may be useful to focus on evolution of the land transport network as a vehicle for national development. Transportation networks can evolve through four stages—colonial establishment of coastal settlements; linkage of settlements with natural resource and inland population for export purposes; growth of feeder routes and links from inland centers; and interconnection of all population and economic centers (Taaffe, Morrill, & Gould: 182–183). Evolutionary tendencies depend on resource availability and capacity to use it properly. In Mexico transport policy evolved through the first three stages before the 1910 revolution, and rigidities in political and administrative structures inhibited evolution to the fourth stage of national integration from the end of the revolutionary civil war in 1916 to the present (1990). Mexican capability to remove the developmental bottleneck *(cuello de botella)* created by inadequate and poorly sited transportation facilities now founders on the absence of domestic investment capital and foreign exchange made unavailable largely by inappropriate past policies.

The most notable feature of the historical evolution of transportation policy in Mexico has been the failure to integrate population centers and economic resources in the most advanced stage of development and the resulting inability to plan policies that would effectively generate foreign exchange that could be applied to diversification and expansion of the transport sector (see Figure 7.1). This argument is made with the understanding that the sector has provided substantial stimuli for economic growth and some socioeconomic development (see Table 7.1).

Consistent with the first stage of the model, the Spanish conquerers under Hernando Cortes arrived at the coastal area of Vera Cruz in 1519. From this beachhead, Cortes proceeded to conquer the Aztec empire under Montezuma by manipulating the resentment of the many (already) conquered Indian tribes toward the Aztecs (Riding: 37). The initial path of the conquistadores led from Vera Cruz to Tenochtitlan (now Mexico City) inland. Cortes set the stage for modern Mexico by imposing the "values of a profoundly Catholic and intellectually repressed Spain on the ruins of a long line of theocratic and militaristic empires" (Riding: 4–5). The conquerers ruled from Mexico City, placing the Indians under landowner guardianship *(encomiendas)* which permitted exploitation of Indian labor and natural resources for the benefit of the Crown. The enormous wealth being extracted from Mexico led local *criollos* (local Spanish settlers) to seek a larger share of the pie from the *penisulares* (Spanish sent over to govern the colony), and by 1821, locals successfully replaced Spanish rule.

However, "independence" from Spain only meant less social reform and greater exploitation of Indian and *mestizo* (mixed blood, neither Indian nor Spanish) peasants, whose communal lands were replaced with *latifundios* (large landholdings or plantations). Centralized power was replaced by provincial warlords *(caciques)* sustained by *latifundistas* (the landowners). As warlords vied for the position of national *cacique* (head warlord or *caudillo*), fifty governments were established in the first thirty years of independence (eleven headed by General Santa Anna).

In short, the system that forges transport policy in Mexico must be understood in its pre-Hispanic *mestizo* context. Consistent with the authoritarian heritage of Aztec, Spanish, and *caudillo* institutions, transport policy favors the urban areas of Mexico. Elites view urban areas as the repositories of civilization and culture as well as bases of power. Roughly 14 percent (10 million out of 71 million population in 1984) of Mexico consists of Indians divided into fifty-six ethnic groups that speak over 100 different dialects (Riding: 287). While many are bilingual (Spanish-Indian), 2 percent are monolingual, speaking only an Indian language (Stevens: 403). While elites have a paternalistic fascination for Mexico's Indian roots, Indians have been excluded from the benefits of policy. Even Benito Juarez, Mexico's only Indian leader, intensified the exploitation of Indians by dismantling communal lands (Riding: 289). Transport routes have consistently excluded them, favoring such predictable lines as Mexico City–Vera Cruz and Mexico City–Texas border. Not surprisingly, from the

Figure 7.1
Mexico

Table 7.1
Relationship between Economic Development and Transportation in Latin America, 1986 (in millions of 1986 dollars)

	Country	GDP Per Capita	Value Added by Transportation & Communications	Value Added by Wholesale & Retail Trade	Value Added by Financial Services	Percent GDP/Capita on Transport
	Argentina	2361.0	7441.0	9423.0	5073.0	10.2
	Brazil	2525.0	17,504.0	47,132.0	56,563.0	5.0
High GDP Countries	Costa Rica	1971.0	368.0	836.0	658.0	7.4
	Mexico	2407.0	14,844.0	44,716.0	17,878.0	7.8
	Uruguay	2738.0	472.0	1018.0	484.0	5.9
	Venezuela	2762.0	6352.0	4588.0	6796.0	12.9
	Haiti	342.0	42.0	328.0	103.03	2.3
Low GDP Countries	Honduras	780.0	245.0	372.0	389.0	7.0
	Peru	1250.0	1631.0	3512.0	2352.0	6.5
	Paraguay	1829.0	319.0	1907.0	201.0	4.6

Note: GDP stands for Gross Domestic Product.

Source: Inter-American Development Bank, *Progreso Economico Y Social en America Latina, Informe 1987* (IADB, Washington, D.C., 1988), pp. 257, 450, 456; Organization of American States, *Boletin Estadistico de la OEA* [Statistical Bulletin of the OAS], vol. 7: January–December 1985, p. 27.

days of the conquistadores to the present, most poor Mexicans are in rural areas and are ill-served by regular transportation or communications networks.

In the second stage of the transport evolution, the original settlements are linked to important population centers and natural resource areas. The pattern of raw materials export along principal access routes should stimulate development of intermediate centers (Gilbert: 183). This is precisely what happened in Mexico. But rail transport development also stimulated institutional capacities that competed for political control with existing authoritarianism. The contradictions of the system that evolved after independence from Spain were brought into relief by rail development, and this contributed to the 1910 revolution.

During the thirty-year reign of Porfirio Díaz (1877–80, 1884–1911), Mexican railways expanded by the simple formula of "ironhanded maintenance of order and persistent wooing of foreign capital'' (Stevens: 408). Reliance on foreign capital and expertise for these projects was dictated by the fact that the state lacked income, and Mexican capitalists would not invest in low-return railroad ventures (6 percent as opposed to 12 percent in other ventures). Since the Mexicans already had reached their limit of indebtedness to Europeans (Goldfrank: 9), they had to rely on U.S. capital and, ostensibly, control of their railroads. In 1876, the major Mexican line was between Mexico City and Vera Cruz (British-owned). In an effort to interest local capital in rail ventures, Díaz made concessions available to individual states. Though the constructed lines were narrow gauge and did not connect with each other, an unintended positive benefit was that the lines served areas that otherwise would not have been (Goldfrank: 6).

Díaz then changed from a nationalistic stance to one that welcomed U.S. capital in 1880. He granted four concessions to U.S. firms: (1) a line across the Isthmus of Tehuantepec (Salina Cruz to Coatzacoalcos); (2) lines from Mexico City to Laredo and El Paso; (3) a line from Nogales through Sonora to Guaymas on the Pacific coast; and (4) additional trunk lines to emerging regional cities such as Morelos, Puebla, Oaxaca, Cuernavaca. Monterrey, and Tampico (see Figure 7.1). Unfortunately, the concessions policy which attracted foreign capital largely served the needs of the railroads themselves (tax advantages, consumption of heavy goods, cheap raw materials exports) and their cronies in the Mexican political bureaucracy.

By the early 1900s, the Díaz administration tried to rationalize transport policy by directing concessions to the most economically useful lines for Mexico. This led to the ironic solution of a government-arranged merger of the two lines (National and Central) with a purely Mexican charter, the government as major stockholder, and the United States and Britain as major bondholders and wielders of influence (Goldfrank: 14). The merger was an economic success but political failure for the regime. The new firm (National Railways of Mexico or FNM) provided service more efficiently and employed a higher proportion of Mexicans in skilled and administrative capacities (Goldfrank: 15). By its success and U.S.-British control, the new firm also served to consolidate the regime by promoting the export sector and ''containing'' the proximate threat of U.S. direct intervention (the United States had intervened militarily in eleven Latin nations between 1885 and 1910 but not in Mexico).

However, the regional differentiation and specialization provided by transport policy in this era contributed to a greater consciousness of socioeconomic difference which led to greater tension between the regime and society. Goldfrank (1976: 16) suggests that the growth of railways helped cause the revolution in five related ways. First, extension of rail line made it more profitable for *latifundistas* to extend their landholdings. Over 90 percent of reported Indian protests took place within 40 kilometers of actual or projected rail lines during the 1870s. The 1890s extension of rail lines into the Yucatán led to the final stages of the Caste war against Mayan groups, to landgrabbing, and to new uprisings. Many displaced workers and former landowners turned to armed struggle against the regime.

Second, the auction-type railway concession policy during this period fueled the perception that the regime was selling the country to foreigners. Between 1877–1910, the Díaz regime granted concessions to individuals or firms that amounted to 20 percent of the Mexican land area! Railroad concessions were only a small portion of this land, but widespread speculation involved both railroad and adjacent lands. "At best such land concessions to the rail companies were necessary to attract capital into railway development in the first place and to pay off potential political opponents. A structure in which such activity occurs can hardly be accused of looking out primarily for popular needs" (Goldfrank: 17).

Third, the rate structure favored goods in transit to and from the Untied States and retarded the growth of Mexican industry. Transportation costs for rail exceeded those for shipment by sea, and intranational fares were higher than for U.S.-Mexican trade. The Central Railroad lowered rates for U.S. cotton growers but not for north Mexican planters! Discriminatory rates also discouraged the production of necessary Mexican foodstuffs. "The price of commodities fell, when the new means of transportation could have stimulated increased production and lower food costs" (Goldfrank: 18). By refusing to focus transport policy beyond the needs of U.S. capital goods and Mexican raw materials exporters, the policy prevented the growth of a nationally diversified market that later inhibited official attempts to substitute imports with domestic products.

Fourth, railroads stimulated the growth of labor organization and political consciousness among the Mexican labor force. Disputes about wages and working conditions led first to consciousness of differences in relative privilege, then to strikes. "Although Mexican workers were responsible for most of the strikes, those from the United States went out from time to time, setting an early example of militance" (Goldfrank: 19). In short, the transfer of capital and technology brought with it ideological lessons of use to Mexican labor, effectively creating a proletariat. According to Goldfrank, "The rail workers emerged in a strong position at the end of the revolution. Foreign personnel were almost all replaced by Mexican nationals and the right to strike constitutionally protected."

Finally, rail lines had the dual effect of lulling the authoritarian regime into complacency and stimulating successful revolts. Before construction, regional *caciques* and *caudillos* defied central authority with impunity. After construction, the Díaz regime "made its authority and force felt all the way to the furthest corners of Mexican territory and repressed any indication of disturbance or revolt in fewer days than the number of months necessary earlier to achieve the same result" (Macedo, cited in Goldfrank: 20). But during the revolution, guerrillas destroyed the rails and remained relatively safe from pursuit; Mexican troops had become dependent on the railroads.

The end of the revolution in 1916 produced a new party-dominated political structure and policies that rhetorically favored economic and political justice for all Mexicans. This began the third phase of transport development, in which foreign exchange from exports stimulated growth of feeder networks in the interior (Gilbert: 1983). The rails were nationalized in 1937 and operated as a state enterprise. Though new socially oriented development policies were dependent on existing rail and road networks that favored Mexican industrial dependency (U.S. exports of capital, Mexican exports of raw materials), subsequent presidential administrations changed this situation only marginally. For example, Miguel Aleman is often referred to as the ''architect of modern Mexico.'' As president 1946–52) he assured investors with fiscal conservatism and a policy of ''growth first and justice later'' (Riding: 81). Control of the regime passed from those who fought the revolution to younger technocrats in the political bureaucracy. However, he vastly expanded public spending for transportation infrastructure, and the economy boomed. But, in a familiar pattern, ''agrarian reform was quietly shelved and labor unions were exhorted to forgo wage increases in order to underwrite national economic growth'' (Stevens: 414).

In the late 1940s, the increasingly popular doctrine of ECLA (United Nations Economic Commission for Latin America) propounded by Raul Prebisch urged breaking the shackles of dependent industrialization by diversification of production for a larger domestic market. In this fashion, foreign exchange would be saved at home rather than exported. Whether ''import substitution industrialization'' (ISI) focused on export-propelled growth (mid-nineteenth century to Great Depression) or growth via the domestic market (Depression and World War II) (Hirschman: 88), or some combination of the two, Mexico was inhibited from realizing its potential by failure to expand the transport sector around the country during the third stage with the same vigor it pursued favored lines and roads (such as Vera Cruz to Mexico City). The expanding infrastructure stimulated growth but also complementary undervelopment in rural areas.

SOCIOECONOMIC DIMENSIONS OF THE TRANSPORTATION SYSTEM AND POLICY

Public policy, in Mexico as elsewhere, is the product of competing interests, the results of which benefit some and harm others. Industrialists, for example, have had significant influence over Mexican transport policies. Early twentieth-century entrepreneurs (U.S. and Mexican) lobbied for rail lines to export raw materials to the United States (through Texas) and Britain (through port of Vera Cruz), meaning that factories and raw material sources were located far apart. As Mexican output of steel, cement, textiles, automobiles, and trucks increased, transport connections were used increasingly for export manufactures and for food imports. Factories from Mexico City to Monterrey (see Figure 7.1) rely on rails and roads to the U.S. border and to the ports of Tampico and Vera Cruz on the Gulf Coast (see Figure 7.2). *Maquiladoras* or U.S.-owned border industries are now the second highest contributor to foreign exchange behind oil and tourism (Garreau). Because of their proximity to U.S. markets, the 700 firms in northern Mexican states such as Chihuahua rely for exports on roads and rails across the U.S. border. In that only about 20 percent of Mexico's 760,373 square miles is cultivable and only 15 percent is good quality farmland (Stevens: 402), agro-industry has been less profitable in Mexico than in, for instance, Central America. Consequently, Mexican transport policies favor industries around urban areas to the detriment of rural industries and agricultural and forestry sector productivity and profitability.

The importance of Mexican industrialists to the determination of transport policy is demonstrated by the fact that manufacturing as a percentage of exports grew from 21 percent to 41 percent between 1965–72 (Kaufman: 236). Nevertheless, rural transport capacity remains marginal, and this has inhibited national integrated development efforts. For example, in 1980 the Mexican government leased 29,000 boxcars from U.S. railroads to deliver grain within Mexico.

> Because the transport system was unaccustomed to handling large tonnages of grain, much of the imported corn, wheat and soybeans was offloaded by hand into sacks and stored on the ground. Moreover, when the rail cars were emptied, many poor people converted the weather-proof cars into trailer camps for use in the winter. By the end of the year, it was estimated that 45,000 boxcars, belonging to the railroads of both Mexico and the U.S., had been tied up in the interior zones of the country (Street: 390).

Mexican intellectuals tend to view transport policy as a vehicle for maintenance of the existing order and denial of economic and political justice to the majority of Mexicans. Though the 1910 revolution was in part stimulated by the contradictions of Mexican transport policy (Goldfrank)—most notably concessions to foreigners to build lines inconsistent with national needs—the rhetoric contained in the constitution and revolutionary authoritarian party (PRM, changed to PRI in 1946) that embodied the ideals of the revolution has not substantively been put into practice (Cotler: 270). For over fifty years, the elite roles established by the revolution have channeled activities of the major groups into vertically structured hierarchical organizations controlled by a powerful central authority. In this context of "populist corporatism," the government serves the elite and maintains itself by mobilizing efforts of the official PRI party (Stevens: 422). Intellectuals would note that this authoritarian structure, designed to solidify the nation and inhibit imperialist penetration, borrowed over $100 billion from foreigners, so that 54 percent of the foreign exchange value of each export must now be applied to debt service (Rowe). Much of the foreign debt was contracted for public works such as highways, ports, airports, and rail projects.

Intellectuals would also argue that transport policies should have linked population centers and economic resources, such as arable lands, to serve the interests of the poor majority. For instance, Edmundo Flores argued in 1959 that Mexico's "agrarian revolution" (under President Lázaro Cárdenas, the government broke up 20 million hectares in large *latifundias* and redistributed them to 776,000 members of *ejidos* or collective landholdings) distinguished Mexico from countries such as Venezeula, Peru, or Colombia. The land reform stimulated the construction of many rural farm-to-market roads and contributed to the integration of rural Mexico with itself and then to urban Mexico. The latter countries continued to emphasize the traditional conquistador pattern of good roads from ports to mines, oil wells and plantations, to enable easy extraction of national wealth. That is "industry and farming would show development along a few specific lines" (Flores, cited in Hirschman: 301). Intellectuals such as Flores believed that Mexican state capitalism would control the unequal distribution of productivity gains from trade with the United States and between Mexican urban and rural sectors on behalf of the "periphery" or marginal members of society.

To a large extent, transportation policy concerns of Mexican intellectuals have been realized in practice. While the transport sector was one of the most dynamic sectors of the economy (11 percent of gross fixed capital formation, 1970–78), concentration of infrastructural development in the Central Valley (Secretária de Programación y Presupuesto, hereafter SPP, 1983: 339) distorted the process of Mexican development. Because the transport sector is a fundamental determinant of cargo costs (such as sawtimber and steel products whose transport costs are a high proportion of final prices, and whose industries are hampered by inability to ship raw materials rapidly) and time in transit (a basic efficiency issue for filling orders), it can stimulate fast national economic recovery and prevent economic disaster if market penetration routes are properly located and managed.

However, much of Mexican transport infrastructure is located in the Central Valley (see Figure 7.2). This can magnify regional development inequities by encouraging greater development of marketing and distribution centers in the Mexico City area, which absorbs capital needed elsewhere. Hence, the effects of the recession of the early 1980s was multiplied by absence of a balanced transport system throughout the country. The 1983–88 Plan (SPP, 1983: 340) notes, for example, the inadequate configuration of rail lines, antiquated signaling devices, terminals, and freight yards. It also suggests that poor wages, lack of employee development, and absence of management interest in productivity has weakened the 20,000-mile railway system and practically eliminated its contribution to development. Similarly, unequal income distribution, for example, between the urban middle classes and rural farmers, has been magnified by the dependence of the entire economy on roads and motor vehicles. Eighty

Figure 7.2
Mexican Transportation Facilities

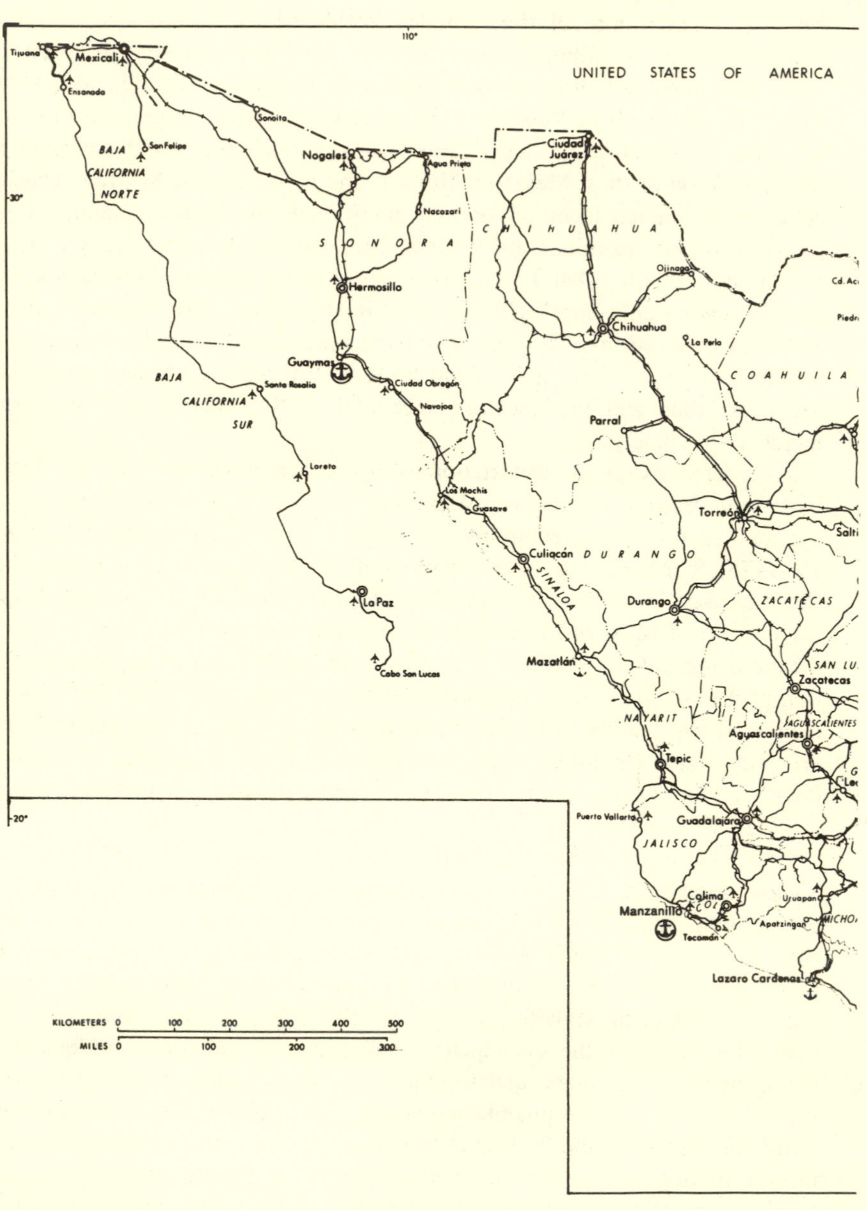

Project ports
Major industrial and commercial ports
National capital
State capitals
Principal cities or towns
Divided highways
Selected main roads
Railroads
Rivers
Principal airports
State boundaries
International boundaries
Nueva Rosita
Nuevo Laredo
Monclova
NUEVO LEON
Reynosa
Matamoros
Monterrey
TAMAULIPAS
Ciudad Victoria
Matehuala
Altamira
Tampico
San Luis Potosi
Cd. Valles
VERACRUZ
Tuxpan
Poza Rica
Guanajuato
Queretaro
HIDALGO
Pachuca
PUEBLA
TLAXCALA
Tlaxcala
Jalapa
Veracruz
Morelia
MEXICO
Toluca
Cuernavaca
MORELOS
Puebla
Orizaba
Taxco
San Andrés Tuxtla
Laguna de Ostion
TABASCO
Minatitlan
Villahermosa
Cd. del Carmen
CAMPECHE
Campeche
Progreso
Merida
YUCATAN
Tizimin
Valladolid
Peto
Pto. Juárez
COZUMEL
QUINTANA ROO
Chetumal
BELIZE
GUERRERO
Chilpancingo
Acapulco
OAXACA
Oaxaca
Pinotepa Nacional
Puerto Escondido
Tehuantepec
Juchitan
Salina Cruz
CHIAPAS
Tuxtla Gutierrez
GUATEMALA
Tapachula
HONDURAS
100°
90°
30°
20°

percent of the 400,000 tons of cargo that moved within Mexico in 1982 was shipped by road (SPP, 1983: 338). While 85 percent of the population has access to road transport via a fleet of 26,300 buses, in fact absence of road maintenance expenditures has contributed to severe problems in this core mode of transport.

In short, road transport seems to be following the legacy of years of deteriorating railroads and this will affect groups beyond Mexico to a greater extent than in the Central Valley. At some point, failure to invest in railroads and nonpetroleum-powered road vehicles (the Brazilian gasohol program succeeded in doing this years ago) may produce a serious bottleneck to additional Mexican national development. For, to a large extent, oil production and export determines the course of development in conjunction with the transport sector (SPP, 1983:325). In spite of the 1982–84 recession caused by falling oil prices, nothing in the 1983–88 Plan indicates movement away from internal dependence on oil production (52.6 percent of total exports 1984–86 versus only 2.0 percent 1970–72; Inter-American Development Bank, hereafter, IADB, 1988A: 129) for road transport. In this sense, failure to plan ahead for energy weakens the economy and the positive role that transport can play in both substituting costly oil dependence (in this case on consumption subsidies by export) and transmission of national production benefits to all regions of society. Mexico's transportation share of total energy should continue to decline as greater reliance is shifted from rail and roads to air transportation. While Mexico has the third largest road network in Latin America, a relative high rate of per capita car ownership and the highest level of energy consumption in road transport (IADB, 1982: 135), in fact industry currently consumes more energy than the transport sector. For the future, much of the cargo and medium-range trips for the middle classes will shift to air transport which is accessible through 50 major airports and 1,300 minor ones. The 1983–88 Plan (SPP, 1983: 341) suggests that 80 percent of the Mexican population has access to air transport. Given low rural incomes, however, one might challenge this assertion as a description of present behavior.

RECENT TRENDS AND FUTURE PROSPECTS

A significant step to reverse the contradictions of past transport policies was made by former president López Portillo in 1980. López Portillo (1976–82) faced several "crisis management" issues immediately. First, import substitution was focusing on consumer goods while raw materials continued to be exported without domestic processing. Second, industry was concentrated in Mexico City, Guadalajara, and Monterrey. Third, as before, Mexico was dependent on other countries for capital goods, finance, and technology (Street: 376). Fourth, Mexico was unable to absorb the rapid inflow of foreign exchange earnings from its oil exports which were tragically contributing to inflation (66 percent in 1985) and wasted resources (evident in overbureaucratization of the public sector throughout the country) that might have substituted for further foreign borrowing. A fundamental objective of the "1980–82 Global Plan" has been to reduce delays in exporting Mexican goods and importing equipment and merchandise (SPP, 1980–81: 60). The plan called for construction of rural market roads and rehabilitation of many others, In 1982, 320 million tons of goods were transported by road (SPP, 1983: 338); the remaining 80 million tons traveled by rail. As early as 1980, roads generated 70 percent of the ton-kilometers while railroads generated only 30 percent. Further, roads carry 97 percent of the passengers and rails only 3 percent. Even though the network consists of 213,000 kilometers, the Mexican road system excludes 45 percent of the rural population or 14 million (SPP, 1980:42). The 1980–82 plan stressed expansion of both rail and roads with ultimate emphasis on roads. As noted by Malone (1981: 22), the National Railways of Mexico planned to pump in $3–4 billion for electrification of high-density traffic lines and modernization of other rail lines all over the country to reduce the continuing paralysis of freight traffic both within Mexico and between the United States and Mexico. Under the plan, roads would be routed to serve potentially or currently productive areas for dairy, forestry, mining, tourism, and beef-cattle (SPP, 1970: 45). However, owing largely to the recession, the investments did not take place; contribution of the transport sector to GNP dropped accordingly from 10.7 percent (1981) to −2.0 percent (SPP, 1983: 159). Figure 7.3 shows the nation's railroad network.

As envisioned in the fourth stage of development, the transport sector would link agriculture, fishing, and industrial subsectors that require efficient movement of produce, with centers of consumption (SPP, 1980:45). Unfortunately, the plan also predicted an 18 percent growth in public sector investment *(asignación programada)* and an increase in budgetary resources for the transport and communications sector of 9.5 percent to accomplish its global development objectives (SPP, 1980:45). Instead, public expenditures fell from 27 percent of GDP (Gross Domestic Product) in 1983 to 25.3 percent of GDP in 1986 (IADB, 1988B:461). Further, total GDP per capita fell from $2,523 in 1980 to $2,496 in 1985 (IADB, 1988A:119). Value added by the transport sector fell from $15,165 (1985) to $14,844 (1986) (IADB, 1988B:457). By the inauguration of former SPP Director Miguel de la Madrid as president in 1982, Mexico was in the grips of its worst economic crisis in decades, in part because of surplus petroleum and falling world prices. Despite responsibility for an excellent plan to turn Mexico around, "the outgoing administration was considered extremely dishonest, as López Portillo reportedly enriched himself during his term by hundreds of millions, and possibly billions, of dollars" (McCartney). (This behavior is not unusual: Aleman bought up much of Acapulco during his term before building an airport and oceanfront boulevard [Riding: 81].) The present government is criticized for focusing too much on technical economic solutions and for neglecting to do the grass-roots political work necessary to preserve popular support (McCartney). For example, raising transport fares for Aero-

Figure 7.3
Railroad Network in Mexico

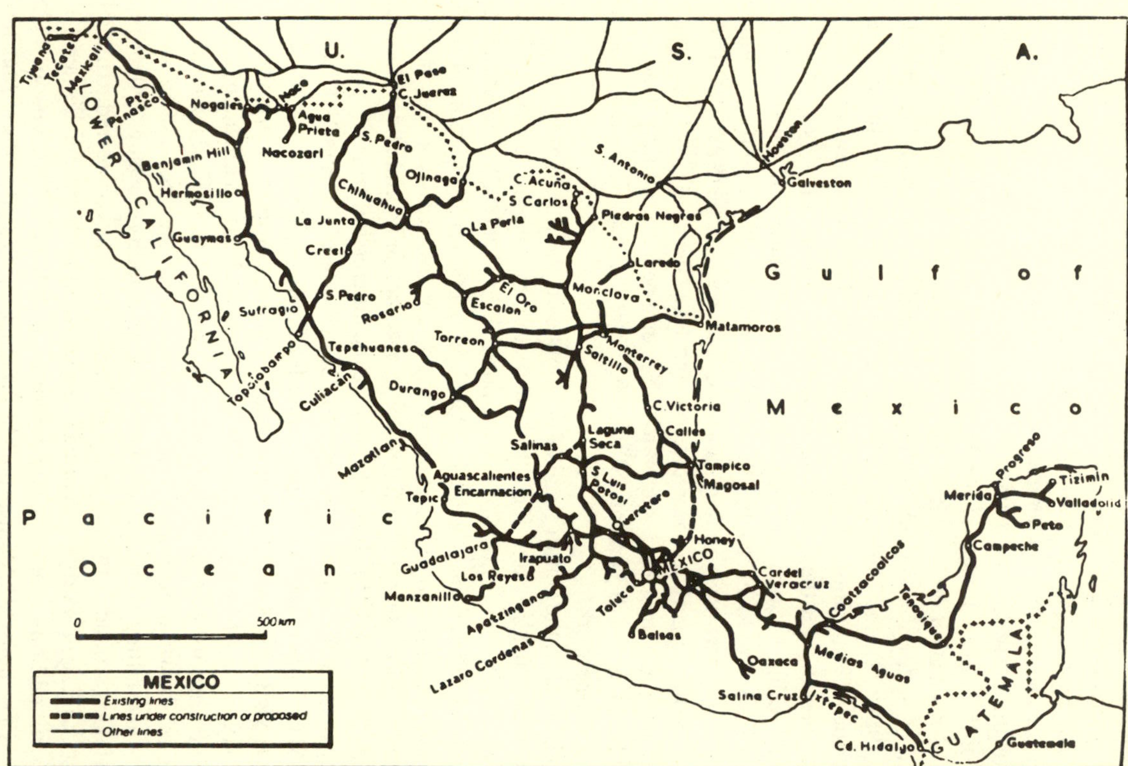

Source: Chris Bushell, *Railway Directory & Year Book 1989* (Surrey, England: Reed Business Publishing, 1989), p. 158. Courtesy Reed Business Publishing, Ltd.

mexico, FNM, and toll roads ''to strengthen the revenue base and reduce subsidies'' (International Monetary Fund, hereafter, IMF: 36, 73–77) may increase cost coverage but reduce producer usage, damaging the capability of the economy further to generate foreign exchange to pay off its debts.

The de la Madrid administration received acclaim from the IMF in 1983–84 as an example of how to bring down inflation (from 100 percent to only 66 percent), curb public spending, and negotiate postponements in repaying the principal of its then $96 billion dollar debt. But to get the economy moving before the 1985 legislative and state elections, the Mexican government went on a public spending binge (McCartney). The economy is now growing at −3.8 percent (IADB, 1988B: 358), and the peso at an incredible low of 611.4 to the dollar from 122.5 in 1976. Despite its technocratic reputation, the administration is cutting budgets politically to please its more influential constituents. With a debt service export ratio of 54 percent, little capital is available for investment at home. The results of the latest response to the IMF austerity program for long-term recovery have been staggering. Across the region, governments have been reluctant to handle political hot potatoes. Instead of firing government workers or closing money-losing state enterprises, they have cut capital spending for development projects to the bone and trimmed outlays for maintenance as well (Witcher & Walsh).

In short, the debt crisis wiped out Mexico's opportunity to reverse irrational past transport policies that have contributed to its dependence on a few exports and the control of the economy by a party-dominated bureaucracy of marginal decision capacity. According to Witcher and Walsh (1986), roads are decaying and rail lines can no longer efficiently handle their load. In the central Mexican desert, thirty-nine electric locomotives sit unused in sheds. The government bought them for use on a new electrified rail line it was building out of Mexico City, but when the debt crisis struck, the electrification money evaporated. So wheezing old diesels carry freight at 18 mph, and shippers complain because the engines can't make it up the hills surrounding the city (Witcher & Walsh).

TRANSPORTATION POLICY ORGANIZATION AND PROCESS

Through the constitution of 1917, Mexicans endowed their party-controlled state apparatus to dominate economic activity. If Mexican economic backwardness was caused by imperialist exploitation, the Mexican state would preempt control of the economy from foreign capitalists. In practice, however, the Mexican state has followed capitalist imperatives in the development of Mexico's essentially interurban transport network. It has simply taken its cut of the profits and slowed project completions. In 1980, the López Portillo administration described the transport network as ''obsolete and insufficient.'' It noted that 55 percent of the Mexican rural population (14 million people) lacked adequate surface transportation (SPP, 1980: 42). Exclusion of the majority of rural Mexico from transport access also eliminates alternative productive opportunities to generate foreign exchange in agriculture, dairy farming, and forestry. By 1986, the Mexican transport system deteriorated rapidly from lack of capital for maintenance and expansion of routes and service. Even the cities are not served properly by present policies. Mexico City Metro moves 2.5 million riders per day over only 32 miles (the New York City subway system handles 3.5 million but over 210 miles) (''Mexico's Amazing Metro'': 30). Traffic congestion is becoming a ''factor of contention between government and population'' and consumes on average 15 percent of income and 30 percent of hours awake (Riding: 379).

As noted, the Mexican political structure is unique in redefining the concept of both political and economic participation. The governmental structure is similar to most Latin countries: executive-dominated through various ministeries and subministries with window dressing from a judiciary and a legislature. The unique element is that the revolutionary party (PRI) organizes or co-opts functional groups, such as labor and industry, to control their participation and mobilize it for governmental support. Since the only branch of government with any discretionary power is the executive (Stevens: 417), and the scope and purpose of transport policies are determined from Mexico City (like most Latin countries the structure is unitary rather than federal in practice), the question is which ministries determine policy and on what basis?

Despite the urban-industrial emphasis of Mexican public transport policies, it can be argued that they have substantively contributed to urban (if not national) development. Consistent with the noted economic-transport development relationship, greater investment in Mexican transportation facilities has increased per capita gross fixed capital formation. Table 7.1 suggests that where government fails to invest in such facilities, not only will GDP per capita be lower, but also value added by wholesale, retail trade, and financial services. This is partially consistent with the Inter-American Development Bank (IADB) (1982:125) which found that while investments in transportation are critical in all stages of development, beyond a certain point investments in transportation have little effect on infrastructure or capital formation. Additionally the countries with high transport investment levels also have high levels of energy consumption occupying this, for example, in petroleum to run road vehicles. This may result in increased dependence on imported oil and actually weaken development efforts. Thus, transportation investment, if not managed carefully, can be a two-way street, leading toward and away from development objectives (IADB, 1982:111). The Mexican government substantially increased its value added, in part by high transport investments (7.8 percent of GDP), which can be linked to the improved flow of trade and financial services, the nerves of any development effort. Those countries that have not invested in transport (Haiti, Paraguay, and Peru) rank low in all the previous variables. High GDP/low transport or low GDP/high transport investment patterns would be exceptional. For instance, the low Uruguayan value added by transport, trade, and financial services may be attributed to the 1981 recession which required adjustments in public expenditure policies. Tight credit, high interest rates, and a substantial increase in the peso cost of private-sector debt contracted in dollars reduced further the already low rate of investment in the Uruguayan economy (IADB, 1984: 397). Public works such as rail modernization, airports, and roads were the biggest losers.

The relatively low Brazilian value added by transport is explicable by its high GDP ($3.4 billion in 1986 which is the highest in Latin America; Mexico is second with $1.9 billion). Conversely, the low GDP, relatively high transport level of Honduras (7 percent) is largely explicable by U.S. foreign-aid-funded roads related infrastructure as part of its strategy of surrounding the Sandinistas in Nicaragua. Obviously, this kind of investment has only indirect and long-term potential for contribution to economic development.

Hence, aggregate Mexican transportation policies are impressive in both absolute and relative economic terms. Transportation policy is determined by the PRI acting through the executive ministries of the Mexican federal government. The two most significant ministries involved in transport policies are the Ministry of Public Works (Secretaría de Obras Públicas) and Ministry of Communications and Transportation (Secretaría de Comunicaciones y Transportes or SCT). The Mexican SCT, with power over infrastructure and operations of transport systems, was given status as a dependency of the federal executive on Jan. 1, 1983 (SPP, 1983–88:341). This indicates increasing awareness by the Mexican government of the leading role which transportation policy plays in maximizing development opportunities or serving as a serious obstacle. In earlier periods of transport history, railways dominated investments. Under the dictatorial regime of "honest tyrant" Porfirio Díaz (1877–80; 1884–1911), the Mexican rail system expanded from 287 to 12,000 miles. The benefits of this expansion went almost entirely to the middle and upper classes (Stevens: 408). Policy was made largely by official concessions granted to high U.S. and British bidders to the Mexican government.

Following the revolution, transportation functions were organized into several ministries that controlled overall policy direction. In the late 1930s such subsectors as railways, now called the National Railways of Mexico, FNM or NdeM, were made independent public enterprises for purposes of obtaining financing and executing capital projects more efficiently than if controlled through their general fund parent ministries. Nevertheless, power with PRI began to shift toward Public Works and away from Transport and Communications because of the strong belief that Mexico should develop by roads, trucks, and automobiles instead of antiquated and costly rail service. For the last seventy years, highways have been the cornerstone of Mexican transport policy, and Public Works has enjoyed a favorable position within government. This sentiment was reaffirmed in 1980, when the 1980–82 Global Plan suggested that highway transport will be most important to the future of Mexican surface transport (SPP, 1980: 42). But the deteriorating railroads still carried 200 million tons of cargo annually (Malone: 22) and accounted for two-thirds of Mexican international trade (Street: 389). Hence, it should be no surprise that the $3–4 billion rail renovation project planned in 1981 was to be under the auspices of Transport and Communications. Malone (1981: 25) noted that efforts to double-track NdeM's major line from Mexico City to the Texas border (Nuevo Laredo and Ciudad Juarez) was stalled by the "highway-oriented" Ministry of Public Works. Progress improved when SCT took over in 1976 (Malone: 25).

Despite the revolutionary social goals of the PRI, the major determinant of transport policy beyond Mexico City seems to be short-term profit. Riding (1984: 173) distinguishes lower level officials in the Mexican bureaucracy who provide a service and more senior officials with authority to assign multi-billion-dollar contracts.

> The truly impressive fortunes, however, are made at the top of the government, where the major contractual decisions are made. A contract for public works or for goods made in Mexico will often be granted to a company owned by the official with responsibility for making the decision. If he has no such company, one will often be formed merely to act as intermediary. In either case, price or quality competition is overlooked: conflict of interest has long been considered one of the prerequisites of power (Riding: 174).

In the context of concessions and contracts for roads and rail lines, this familiar situation suggests that policy will favor the already well-endowed sections of the country or tourist meccas such as Acapulco. Income concentration in Mexico is partly a problem of the inefficiency of financial institutions which fail to channel savings to product investment. The current orientation of financial institutions is toward short-term investment which favors the rich with higher returns (SPP, 1983–88:305). This strategy, as noted, is not problematic until a crisis occurs (drought requiring food imports, decreased oil revenues to PEMEX, Petroleos Mexicanas, the nationally-owned oil company) in which new sources of foreign exchange are needed. At this point, the transport system that functioned so well in times of favorable world prices and local growth conditions, becomes a *cuello de botella* (bottleneck).

CONCLUSION

Despite significant improvements in transport facilities over the last three decades, Latin American countries remain geographically isolated, culturally divided, and socioeconomically dispersed from each other. Indeed, represented by persistent poverty and regional disequilibria in welfare, the isolation, division, and dispersion may be greater within countries than between them. By permitting the imbalanced concentration of economic activities, linked often by insufficient and obsolete transport networks, national policies have worked against development (defined as industrial growth with an appropriate distribution of benefits) both regionally and nationally. Much has been written on the immense gaps in income, power, and land ownership between the wealthy few and poor majority in this region. These gaps are a product of inappropriate national policies that facilitate unequal growth and development. According to Farley (1972: 45) Latin American countries are "largely enclave economies, peripherally dependent on the highly industrialized countries to which their economic activity is linked. Enclave economic activity, necessarily externally oriented, has a low level of linkage with the rest of the economy."

The transport sector affects both growth and development and involves the location and maintenance of transportation infrastructure (land, sea, and air). But, programmed to serve primarily the interests of foreign investors and already well-endowed urban areas, transport policy can be a vehicle for the intensification of underdevelopment by misallocating scarce resources. Owen (1985: 366) notes that "in low income countries farm lands remain inaccessible, industrial development is constrained by excessive transport costs, resources remain untapped and the basis for mutually beneficial trade does not exist. Developing countries have seventy-five percent of the world's people but account for only thirteen percent of the world's railway freight, ten percent of its paved highways, and nine percent of its motor vehicles." Conversely, where financing can be obtained and effectively programmed for national development needs, the transport sector can serve as the leading edge of public policy by linking economic and population centers for integrated national development. Studies by Kansky (1963) and Gould (1960) have demonstrated that for countries and regions of countries at different stages of development, there is a close statistical relationship between various measures of economic and transport development. In cases such as Mexico, transportation policy may induce both development (growth, sociocultural communication, and political integration) and underdevelopment (removal of raw materials, penetration of alien ideologies) simultaneously (Goldfrank: 3). Thus, planning and programming of transportation resources is extremely important for creation of a national market and overcoming regional disparities in wealth.

Despite the rich and diverse cultural and political history of Mexico, its transport policies have been remarkably consistent. Roads and rails have been designed to serve military and industrial conquerers, financed mostly by foreign investors. All this has occurred in the context of revolutionary rhetoric designed to generate support for a vast party-dominated bureaucracy that, with few exceptions, has been unable to promote genuine integrated national development. Transport policies have evolved through three basic stages but have been stalled at the threshold of integrating and diversifying the economy by lack of capital. As indicated, this is partly ironic in that resources from raw materials exports and, later, petroleum could not be absorbed properly by the public sector and invested efficiently in a transport network that would have profited the majority of Mexicans. It is hoped that as future administrations find foreign exchange, they can apply it toward the objectives of the now dormant 1980–82 Global Development Plan and its 1983–88 replacement.

REFERENCES

Collier, David, ed., *The New Authoritarianism in Latin America* (Princeton: N.J.: Princeton University Press, 1979).

Cotler, Julio, "State and Regime: Comparative Notes on Southern Cone and the Enclave Societies" in David Collier, ed., *The New Authoritarianism in Latin America* (Princeton, N.J.: Princeton University Press, 1979), pp. 255–285.

Farley, Rawle, *The Economics of Latin America, Development Problems in Perspective* (New York: Harper & Row, 1972).

Flores, Edmundo, "The Significance of Land-Use Changes in the Economic Development of Mexico," *Land Economics,* vol. 35 (1959), pp. 115–120.

Garreau, Joel, "Mexican Counter-Revolt, The Americanization of the North Threatens the System," *The Washington Post,* May 25, 1986, p. D1.

Gilbert, Alan, *Latin American Development: A Geographical Perspective* (Baltimore, Md.: Penguin, 1974).

Goldfrank, Frank, "The Ambiguity of Infrastructure: Railroads in Prerevolutionary Mexico," *Studies in Comparative International Development,* vol. 11, no. 3 (Fall 1976), pp. 3–24.

Gould, P. R., *The Development of the Transportation Pattern in Ghana,* Northwestern University Studies in Geography 5 (Evanston, Ill.: Northwestern University, 1960).

Hirschman, Albert O., *A Bias for Hope: Essays on Development and Latin America* (New Haven, Conn.: Yale University Press, 1971).

Inter-American Development Bank, *Economic and Social Progress in Latin America, Economic Integration* (Washington, D.C.: Inter-American Development Bank, 1984).

———, *The Impact of Energy Costs on Transportation in Latin America* (Bogota: IADB, 1982).

———, *Informe Anual, 1987* [Annual information, 1987] (Washington, D.C.: IADB, 1988A).

———, *Progreso Economico y Social en America Latina, Informe 1987* [Economic and social progress in Latin America, Information 1987] (Bogota: IADA, 1988B).

International Monetary Fund, "Mexico—Recent Economic Developments" (Washington, D.C.: International Monetary Fund, July 1, 1982).

Kansky, K. J., *Structure of Transportation Networks,* University of Chicago, Department of Geography Research Paper 84 (Chicago: University of Chicago, 1963).

Kaufman, Robert R., "Industrial Change and Authoritarian Rule in Latin America: A Concrete Review of the Bureaucratic-Authoritarian Model" in David Collier, ed., *The New Authoritarianism in Latin America* (Princeton, N.J.: Princeton University Press, 1979).

Macedo, Pablo, "Communicaciones y Obras Públicas" [Communications and public works], in J. Ballesca, *Mexico: Su Evolucion Social* [Mexico: Its social evolution] (Mexico City; Prensa Latino Americano, 1901).

McCartney, Robert J., "Mexican Leader Seen Weakening Politically, Economic Policies Criticized" *The Washington Post,* Dec. 1, 1985, p. A29.

Malone, Frank, "Rail Renaissance in Mexico," *Railway Age,* no. 182 (April 13, 1981), pp. 22–26, 75–77.

"Mexico's Amazing Metro: Mover of Millions—And Growing," *Railway Age,* no. 182 (April 13, 1981), pp. 30–31.

Organization of American States, *Boletin Estadistico de la OEA* [Statistical bulletin of the OAS], vol. 7, nos. 1–4 (January–December 1985), pp. 27–149.

Owen, Wilfred, "Transportation and World Development," *Transportation Quarterly,* vol. 39, no. 2 (July 1985), pp. 365–374.

Riding, Alan, *Distant Neighbors, A Portrait of the Mexicans* (New York: Random House, 1984).

Rowe, James L., "Mexico Again on the Brink in Debt Crisis," *The Washington Post,* June 8, 1986, p. D6.

Secretária de Programación y Presupuesto [Ministry for Programs and Budget], "Información Fundamental de la Cuenta Pública 1979" [Information fundamental to the public accounts 1979], *Programa* no. 4 (November 1980–February 1981) (Mexico City, 1981), pp. 37–73.

———, "Plan Global de Desarrollo 1980–1982" [Global development plan 1980–1982], Mexico City, 1980.

———, "Plan Global de Desarrollo 1983–1988" [Global development plan 1983–1988], Mexico City, 1983.

Stevens, Evelyn P., "Mexico's One-Party State: Revolutionary Myth and Authoritarian Reality" in Howard J. Wiarda and Harvey F. Kline, eds., *Latin American Politics and Development* (Boston: Houghton Mifflin, 1979), pp. 399–434.

Street, James H., "Mexico's Economic Development Plan," *Current History,* vol. 80, no. 469 (November 1981), pp. 374–391.

Taaffe, E. J., R. L., Morrill, and P. R., Gould, "Transport Expansion in Underdeveloped Countries: A Comparative Analysis," *Geographical Review,* vol. 53 (October 1963), pp. 503–529.

Wiarda, Howard J., and Harvey F. Kline, eds., *Latin American Politics and Development* (Boston: Houghton Mifflin, 1979).

Witcher, S. Karene, and Mary Williams Walsh, "With Mexico Focusing on Debt Repayments, Ports and Roads Suffer," *The Wall Street Journal,* June 11, 1986, p. 1.

World Bank, *Economic Memorandum on Mexico,* Appendix A (Washington, D.C.: World Bank, 1985).

8

SOVIET UNION

John P. Willerton, Jr.

BACKGROUND

Political priorities and geographical realities have guided and constrained the development of the Russian and Soviet public transportation sector. This sector has been critical to the country's modernization but has not been a top investment priority for either the Soviet, or predecessor Tsarist, regime. Public transportation policy has been influenced by the economic needs of a large, diverse, resource-rich, but less developed, country striving for industrialization and self-sufficiency in a perceived hostile international environment. Unification and integration of the various regions, peoples, and economies which comprise the USSR have been a first priority for the transportation, as well as other, sectors. The central state has assumed the leading role in the realization of this goal, with Stalinist central planning presupposing that transportation policy be dictated by Soviet federal authorities and interests. The central state supervised the development and financing of the transportation systems in the pre-1917 period. By the late nineteenth century, central governmental bureaucracies (e.g., the Ministry of Ways and Communications, the Ministry of Finance) were already in place to direct the expansion of the country's rail system. The emergence of Soviet power only resulted in a further centralization of this system.

Climatic and geographical constraints have predetermined the basic conditions for the transportation sector's evolution. Long and severe winters have limited the utility of water and long-distance road transport through much of the country. The permafrost which covers nearly half of the Soviet Union has made the development of the rail and road systems difficult, especially given the high cost of putting the necessary supply and support facilities in place. The post–World War II development of technologies to help cope with these problems has moderated, but not eliminated, these difficulties. The northward flow of many Russian and Siberian rivers has further limited reliance upon internal waterway transport, since most trade entailed the east-west transfer of goods. Most regions, including the arid south and Central Asia, relied on limited cart roads and highways until the advent of the railroad in the nineteenth century.

Full diversification of the Russian transportation system only came in the late nineteenth and early twentieth centuries. As a predominantly agrarian society, Russia had minimal transport needs beyond those met by barges, packhorses, and horse-drawn carts. The bulk of the country's population was concentrated in central European Russia, having settled in the areas with arable land. Most population centers were located along waterways or at intersections of rivers. With more internal waterways than any other country, in Russia, horse and human-drawn barges were a natural means of interregional traffic. River transport was a relatively cost-efficient means for handling bulky and more long-distance loads. Construction of waterways and canals in the eighteenth and nineteenth centuries extended the internal waterways system. Until the late nineteenth century, the population's agricultural and resource needs were met, by and large, by river transportation from the grain-producing areas to the south. Yet, the vagaries of internal waterway transport in northern and European Russia made this a less reliable means of goods conveyance, even after the arrival of the steamship in the early nineteenth century. These geographical and climatic difficulties were compounded by organizational problems within the river transport sector. Schedules of runs were open to change, with the sector often subject to unfair trading practices which stemmed from the monopolistic control exercised by European Russian trading houses (North: 47).

Reliance on highways was a recent phenomenon (e.g., the St. Petersburg-Moscow highway was built between 1817 and 1834). Dirt roads handled intraregional goods conveyance, with the system of interregional highways a small one. Indeed, the highway system extended a total length of only 24,000 kilometers at the beginning of World War I. As for Russian trade with the outside, it was limited and in the preindustrial era was more than handled by cart and foreign-owned maritime fleets.

Industrialization, with its need for various mineral and energy resources and the necessity of linking resource, production, trading, and consumption centers, led to the growth and diversification of the country's transportation system. It necessitated the development of railways, which quickly assumed an economic, political, and military significance for the further unification of the large and regionally diverse Russian empire. The flatness of the Russian plains proved conducive to railway development. The first railways, appearing in the first half of the nineteenth century, were short-distance commercial mine ventures and railways linking the Tsar's residences at Tsarkoye Selo and Pavlovsk with St. Petersburg. By the 1850s, lines connected a number of major cities in the European part of the empire (e.g., Warsaw-Vienna, St. Petersburg-Moscow). Soon major grain-producing, grain-trading, and industrial centers were linked. By 1900, over 50,000 kilometers of railroad track had been laid (Westwood: 58). The year-round reliability, better areal coverage, greater speed and capacity, and cost efficiency of the railways made them the leading element in the country's rapidly expanding transportation system.

The rail network rapidly expanded into Central Asia and Siberia in the second half of the nineteenth century. Growth of the system culminated with the construction of the Trans-Siberian Railroad, built between 1891 and 1913. A major regime investment, the Trans-Siberian Railroad linked Europe and the Far East and further enhanced European Russian control over Siberia and the Russian Far East. It concomitantly served to expand those regions' markets in the West. While insufficient product and passenger traffic made it a less profitable venture, the Trans-Siberian Railroad did facilitate the emigration of Russians eastward and did provide more direct access to the increasingly exploited, resource rich western Siberia.

The divergent histories and levels of development of the regions comprising the USSR and the old Russian empire make generalization about the country's transportation system in the twentieth century difficult. The more Westernized Baltic and Ukrainian regions, along with western Russia, have more concentrated and extensive transportation systems. Industry in the pre-Soviet period was concentrated in the historical Russian and European cities and the new and old capitals, St. Petersburg and Moscow. Railway systems had developed which linked such resource bases as those in the Ukraine (Donets Basin coal) and western Siberia (Tyumen region) to production centers. They linked urban European portions of the empire with central and western Europe, as most lines moved traffic east-west. During the pre-Soviet period, foreign investors helped to develop iron, steel, manufacturing, machine-building, and petroleum centers, while Russian entrepreneurs and the Russian state provided most of the capital for developing the necessary transport facilities. Rail lines formed the basis for the national transportation network, with rivers and highways increasingly serving as feeders. The development of railway transport resulted in a relative decline in river traffic, though the two transportation modes tended to form a more integrated system. Exploitation of Trans-Caucasus and Caspian petroleum, for instance, required transport up the Volga River and then by rail to the European consumption centers. There were problems of planning and coordination in the transportation sector. Both private companies and the state provided transport services, with state regulation carried out by a number of different (and often competitive) bureaucracies. The regulation of railroads, for instance, involved not only the Ministry of Rails and Communications (broad supervision of rail development and operation), but the Ministry of State Control (overseeing rail accounts), and the Ministry of Finances (setting of tariffs, fares, and the state purchases of private rail lines (Westwood: 82). The pre-1917 organization and functioning of transportation anticipated norms of the Soviet period.

The political and economic program of the fledgling Bolshevik regime which came to power in 1917 had important implications for the further development of the transportation system. The sole Marxist-Leninist state in a capitalist world, the Soviet regime pursued an autarkic program which necessitated the rapid integration of the country. The prerequisites for industrialization guided the expansion of the Soviet transportation network. The historical Russian cites were not conveniently located from the standpoint of modern industrial development. These cities had assumed prominence given their advantageous location for trade routes, given their location vis-à-vis food sources, and given defensive considerations. Most of the industrial plant of the country was located in these older urban settings, with three-quarters of Soviet Russia's entire industrial base located in just a half dozen cities. Yet by the early twentieth century, necessary mineral and energy resources were located elsewhere, often far removed from these labor and market centers. A goal of the Soviet regime during its first decade and the First Five-Year Plan was to construct production facilities in these and other new regions (Hunter: Chapter 2).

Transport services were key to efforts to alter the high degree of industrial concentration in the European area. The Soviet regime attempted to more equitably distribute production facilities and economic activities across regions, with the railways assuming an important role in typing them together. World War II only further encouraged the locating of industry to the east, especially in western Siberia. Less reliance was placed upon highway, river, aviation, and pipeline transportation in the pre–World War II period. These transportation modes were less cost-efficient requiring major infusions of resources if they were to be effective in conveying goods across a widely dispersed population and industrial base. Highways linking major cities (e.g., Moscow-Minsk) and traffic routes (e.g., Amur-Yakutsk) were developed, but the total system was small in comparison with the country's size (only 143,000 kilometers of hard surface roads in 1940). River transportation was relied upon in the conveyance of certain goods (e.g., timber), but the expansion of the internal waterways network only came after World War II.

SOCIOECONOMIC DIMENSIONS OF THE TRANSPORTATION SYSTEM AND POLICY

The development of transportation in the Soviet period has been closely tied to that of the top priority heavy industrial sector.[1] Transportation, however, has clearly been secondary. Investments have been limited (approximately 5 percent of total investments).[2] A constant concern has been to minimize transportation costs, especially in connecting the distant resource and production centers of Siberia and the Soviet Far East. While the rail system has constantly grown throughout the Soviet period, the regime's preference has been to intensively use facilities and equipment already in place. Taut planning has characterized this sector.

As a consequence of the regime's attention to industrialization, freight conveyance has enjoyed a much higher priority than passenger conveyance in the development of the transportation system. This enhanced the importance of the railways as they were a cost-efficient and reliable means for mass freight traffic. Costs of system expansion and provision of necessary infrastructures limited the level of investments for other transportation modes. In addition to geographical hindrances, the lack of equipment, port facilities, and vessels diminished the utility of the internal waterway and maritime sectors. The continual low priority of agriculture discouraged large-scale resource commitment to the highway system, especially in the nonindustrialized periphery. Indeed, until recently, the highways linking major urban and production centers (e.g., Moscow to Leningrad, Siberia, and the south) were among the few roadways meriting significant investment.

A major expansion and diversification of the transportation system only came in the 1950s. This expansion was related to the development of the Soviet periphery and the further exploitation of its resources. The opening of the Volga-Don Canal in 1952 facilitated more east-west freight conveyance, as the Caspian and Black seas were linked. The need for feeder roads and for the expanding rail and waterway networks encouraged the extension of the very limited Soviet highway system. Major efforts to develop the neglected agricultural sector in the post-Stalin period led to a major infusion of resources into the motor and highway sector. The cost efficiency of pipeline transport of southern and Siberian energy resources, combined with technological advances, encouraged the major investment in pipelines in the postwar period. All of these developments in the Khrushchev and Brezhnev periods signified a diversification of the country's transportation network fully consonant with the economic programs set out by political elites. Increased investments in the underfunded transport sector during this period were consistent with the resource support flowing to industry.

Today, all forms of transportation of general usage in the Soviet Union are said to comprise the country's "unified transportation system" (*edinaya transportnaya sistema,* or ETS). The ETS is a large sector, accounting for nearly 10.8 million workers (or 9 percent of the total work force) and approximately 58 billion rubles (or 4.5 percent) of the country's gross national product (Khrushchev & Nikol'skii: 241–242). Freight transport is highly concentrated and takes place along major routes which join the important European production centers, as well as extends east to Khabarovsk in the Soviet Far East (see Figure 8.1). The already intensively used European transportation network continues to grow. However, transportation network growth has been especially pronounced in the east and north, with the expansion of rail lines and with the

Figure 8.1
Major Freight Cargo Routes of the Soviet Union

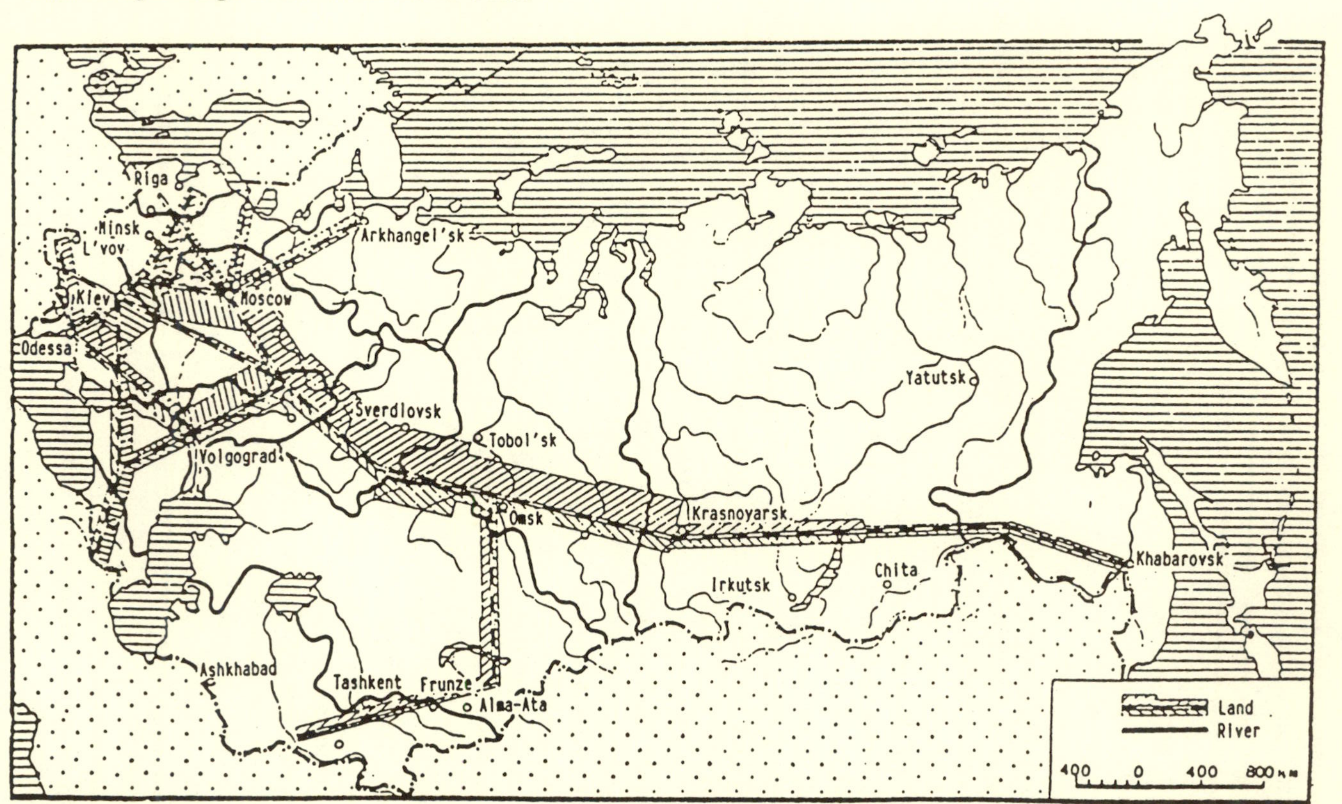

Source: A. T. Khrushchev and I. V. Nikol'skii, eds., *Ekonomicheskaya geografiya SSSR*, part 1, 2nd ed., Moscow: Moscow State University Press, 1985, p. 243.

further development of river and air connections. Rail, road, water, and air transportation services to the top priority ''territorial production complexes'' in Siberia and the Soviet Far East (e.g., the Tyumen and northwest Siberian energy complexes) continue to merit special attention.

From an administrative and planning standpoint, the Soviets differentiate among six major forms of transportation: rail, motor, maritime, internal waterway, aviation, and pipeline. Each of these transportation modes is organized separately and overseen by different ministries, though in principle the activities of all are coordinated by the central Party apparatus. The railways have assumed the dominant position throughout the Soviet period, even though their share of total freight and passenger turnover has shrunk during the past decades (Table 8.1). They are favored not only in the political clout their ministerial heads possess within the broader transportation bureaucracy, but in the relative investment advantages they enjoy within this sector. The railways have remained a productive sector, largely because their rate of increase of freight turnover has remained higher than the rate of increase of capital and labor inputs. Compared to other developed countries, Soviet railroads are labor intensive, but the long-term tendency has been to utilize fewer personnel. Generally, the system has exhibited a remarkable ability to accommodate increasing traffic on a much-overused track network. However, decline in railroad freight traffic rates in the late 1970s and early 1980s revealed that there are limits to the intensive use of existing facilities. Delays in car loading and unloading compounded system inefficiency. Such bottlenecks and system breakdowns necessitated policy changes. For instance, a January 1987 newspaper article reported a backup of over 800 east Siberian railroad cars in just one Irkutsk province river port city (*Ekonomicheskaya gazeta,* no. 1, January 1987: 4). Such loading and unloading problems derive from a host of causes. Harsh winter conditions often delay schedules. Ore trains have arrived in southern stations with contents which cannot be broken apart and unloaded. Special facilities must be created to deal with such items (*Ekonomicheskaya gazeta,* no. 5, January 1987: 4).

Approaches to upgrade and expand rail services and make them more efficient are illustrative of those adopted for other modes of transportation. Divergent organizational imperatives and perspectives have characterized the continued development of the rail system. Central planning organs have stressed technological innovation, without pressing for heightened funding. The Railroad Ministry,[3] however, has predictably pulled for more investment and an expansion of the railway infrastructure. Longer-term efforts to make the railways more cost-effective have centered on its electrification and dieselization. A 1955 decree by the Communist Party of the Soviet Union (CPSU) Central Committee initiated an extensive program of electrification, and by 1983 nearly one-third of all lines had been electrified (46,800 kilometers of track, as compared to 97,000 kilometers of track still using steam engines). The electrification program has concentrated on the major conveyance routes, with those routes handling over half of all freight cargo. In addition, research efforts have fo-

Table 8.1
Percentage of Total Freight Turnover by Types of Transportation

	1950	1960	1970	1980	1981
Railroad	86.8	82.9	67.9	58.5	58.2
River	6.7	5.5	4.7	4.2	4.2
Maritime	5.7	7.3	17.9	14.4	14.2
Road	0.1	0.5	1.7	2.2	2.3
Airline	0.0	0.0	0.1	0.1	0.1
Oil and Oil Products Pipelines	0.7	2.8	7.7	20.6	21.0

	1982	1983	1984	1985	1986
Railroad	57.6	57.4	57.3	58.6	58.0
River	4.4	4.4	4.2	4.1	3.9
Maritime	13.9	14.2	14.6	14.3	14.7
Road	2.4	2.3	2.2	2.2	2.1
Airline	0.1	0.1	0.1	0.1	0.1
Oil and Oil Products Pipelines	21.6	21.6	21.6	20.7	21.2

Source: *Statisticheskii yezhegodnik stran-chlenov Soveta Ekonomicheskoi Vzaimopomoshchi* [Statistical yearbook of the member states of the Council for Mutual Economic Assistance], Moscow: Finansy i statistika [Finance and statistics], 1985, pp. 261–262; 1986, pp. 243–244; 1987, pp. 251–252.

cused on developing better locomotives and freight cars, increasing not only their weight and volume capacity, but also heightening their speed. New locomotives and freight cars are designed not only to increase the amount that can be pulled[4] but to enhance their ability to transport goods in severe climates.[5] The cumulative effect of these efforts can be considerable. For example, the USSR railways minister contended that systemwide plans to increase the average carload (e.g., by an average of 2 tons in the second quarter of 1985) can result in significant increases in total freight conveyed (estimated at 30 million tons for that quarter over the comparable quarter in 1984) (*Sotsialisticheskaya industriya*, Aug. 4, 1985). Comparable efforts to raise the speed of trains would increase freight conveyance (e.g., 1985 plans to increase train speed by 1 kilometer per hour were projected to increase freight conveyance by 30 million tons). However, beyond raising actual performance targets in the plan, the development of new vehicles and equipment is long term. According to a March 1981 *Ekonomicheskaya gazeta* report, between ten and fifteen years are necessary to develop and fully produce a new locomotive. The slow dissemination of new technologies across bureaucracies has retarded innovations. Not surprisingly, late 1980s plan fulfillment results reveal only modest increases in freight shipments (e.g., a railroad shipment growth rate of only 1.2 percent in 1988) (*Pravda*, January 22, 1989).

A major obstacle to the full exploitation of the railroad network is its high level of concentration in the European part of the USSR (70 percent of total track). In a country averaging 6.4 kilometers of track per 1,000 square kilometers, the Ukraine and Baltic average over 36 kilometers of track per 1,000 square kilometers, with the rest of European USSR averaging between 25 and 30 kilometers of track per 1,000 total square kilometers (1983). As a result, most of the post–World War II railroad growth occurred in non-European regions (Table 8.2). The 1986-2000 Comprehensive Program states that a top priority for the railways is to further link southern regions with the central and northwestern sections of the European USSR (*Pravda*, Oct. 9, 1985). The rationale behind recent decisions to add lines connecting existing systems with northern cities—for instance, a 730 kilometer line connecting the Baikal-Amur Railroad with Yakutsk—has been to increase the exploitation of precious metals and resources (e.g., gold, diamonds, oil, gas, iron ore, and timber) in the periphery. The construction of an additional 500 kilometer railroad in the Kara Sea region will allow not only for the hauling in of equipment necessary for the production of oil, but also for the transport out of those tapped energy resources. In all, over 5 billion rubles were designated for railroad expansion and renovation in 1985, with these moneys set to construct over 1,300 kilometers of new tracks and to continue the program of electrifying existing lines (in this case, 1,480 kilometers of track) (*Pravda*, Feb. 19, 1985). Figure 8.2 shows the Soviet railroad network.

Soviet regimes have traditionally exhibited a proclivity to undertaking massive prestige projects, not only for economics of scale, but for ideological-

Table 8.2
Length of Soviet Railroads, by Republic (1,000 km)

	1940	1950	1960	1970	1975	1980
Armenia	0.40	0.46	0.52	0.56	0.59	0.71
Azerbaidzhan	1.21	1.69	1.65	1.81	1.85	1.90
Belorussia	6.44	5.36	5.38	5.43	5.46	5.51
Estonia	1.39	1.39	1.42	1.20	1.00	0.99
Georgia	1.13	1.29	1.33	1.41	1.42	1.42
Kazakhstan	6.58	8.41	11.47	13.77	14.12	14.24
Kirgizia	0.22	0.37	0.37	0.37	0.37	0.37
Latvia	3.21	3.05	3.12	2.61	2.43	2.38
Lithuania	2.01	2.15	2.09	2.02	2.00	2.01
Moldavia	0.82	1.02	0.99	1.07	1.11	1.11
RSFSR	58.68	66.82	71.70	77.55	79.75	82.63
Tadzhikistan	0.25	0.26	0.26	0.26	0.43	0.47
Turkmenistan	1.75	1.74	2.10	2.11	2.12	2.12
Ukraine	20.10	20.19	21.09	22.06	22.27	22.55
Uzbekistan	1.91	2.07	2.33	2.95	3.38	3.42
USSR	106.10	116.90	125.80	135.20	138.30	141.80

	1981	1982	1983	1984	1985	1986
Armenia	0.75	0.76	0.76	0.76	0.76	0.87
Azerbaidzhan	1.90	1.90	1.90	1.90	2.07	2.07
Belorussia	5.51	5.51	5.53	5.52	5.54	5.54
Estonia	1.01	1.01	1.01	1.01	1.01	1.01
Georgia	1.42	1.45	1.47	1.47	1.47	1.54
Kazakhstan	14.27	14.28	14.31	14.31	14.49	14.53
Kirgizia	0.37	0.37	0.37	0.37	0.37	0.37
Latvia	2.38	2.38	2.38	2.38	2.38	2.38
Lithuania	2.03	2.04	2.01	2.01	2.01	2.01
Moldavia	1.15	1.15	1.15	1.15	1.15	1.15
RSFSR	83.31	83.70	84.04	84.47	84.92	83.31
Tadzhikistan	0.47	0.47	0.47	0.47	0.47	0.47
Turkmenistan	2.12	2.12	2.12	2.12	2.12	2.12
Ukraine	22.65	22.65	22.63	22.70	22.70	22.72
Uzbekistan	3.46	3.48	3.48	3.48	3.48	3.48
USSR	142.8	143.3	143.6	144.10	144.90	145.60

Sources: Narodnoye khoziaistvo SSSR [National economy USSR], 1960 (1961), 1970 (1971), 1976 (1977), 1980 (1981), 1984 (1985), 1985 (1986), and 1986 (1987).

Figure 8.2
Railroad Network in the Soviet Union

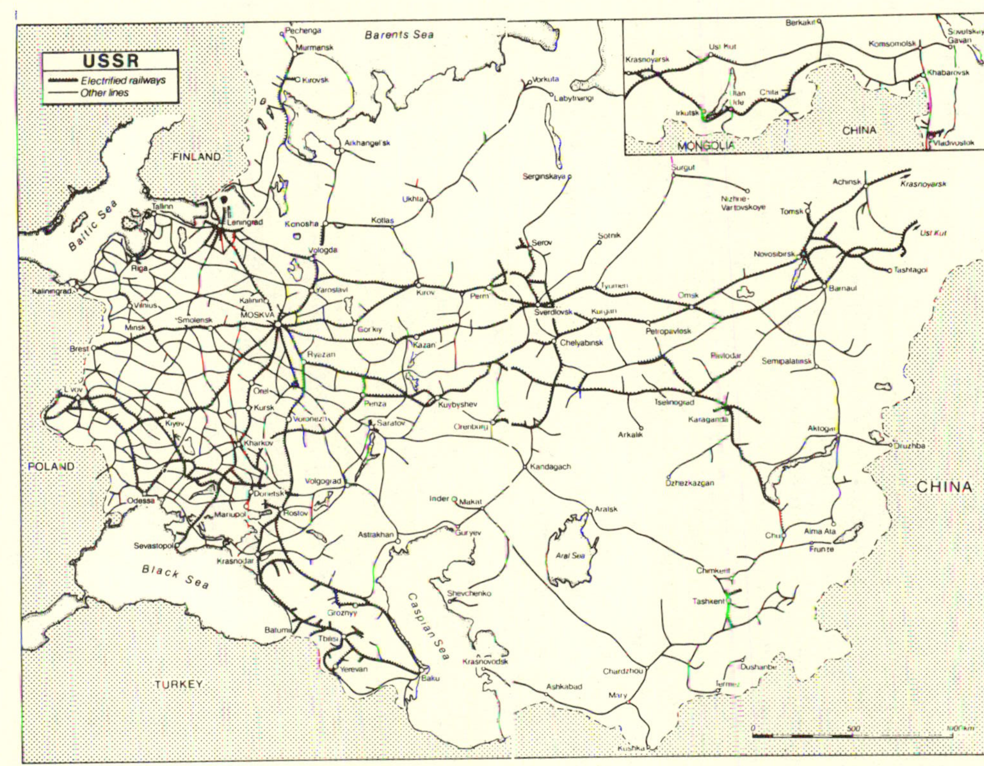

Source: Chris Bushell, *Railway Directory & Year Book 1989* (Surrey, England: Reed Business Publishing, 1989), pp. 342–343. Courtesy Reed Business Publishing, Ltd.

propaganda purposes. The Baikal-Amur Railroad (BAM) has been such a major, decade-long project, designed to link the European USSR and its production centers with the resource-rich Soviet East. Planned to transport timber, building materials, precious minerals, and energy resources, the railroad was to include 3,100 kilometers of track linking Ust'-Kut, north of Lake Baikal, with the city of Komsomol'sk on the Amur River. BAM paralleled the older Siberian railway, with plans to double track along much of the way. The lines were joined in October 1984, but the project has fallen several years behind schedule and likely will not be ready to operate regularly until the end of the Twelfth Five-Year Plan, in the late 1980s, or more probably in the 1990s. Obstacles to the construction of BAM are illustrative of those for such grandiose projects, even when they are high priorities of the national political elite. Logistical difficulties with terrain slowed the project, but fragmented planning and organizational disputes among various construction and regulatory agencies, even at lower levels, undercut plan fulfillment.

Soviet approaches to improving production or services often include efforts to perfect the planning mechanism, especially to enhance coordination of activities across organizations and bureaucracies. In this regard, activities to upgrade the existent railway system have entailed expanding the application of computer technology to the planning and development of new railroad projects. This includes the setting and fulfillment of plans for the thirty-two rail lines that comprise the national network (*Gudok,* July 19, 1985). Some railroad lines already have automated traffic control centers (e.g., the busy Donets line), while others are moving toward the development of computer-based freight-processing operations. Many planners hope these developments will lead to the creation of a centralized railroad traffic control system with regional processing centers.

Efforts in the post-Brezhnev period to increase the productivity of the railroads have focused not on increased spending but on a discipline campaign to motivate managers and workers. A late 1982 Central Committee decision to use total-output-tonnage-hauled as the chief measure of railroad output served to pressure railroad managers to increase rail efficiency. The replacement of the railways minister and the heads of several railroad administrations set the stage for a broader campaign extending down to the lowest levels. The hierarchical structure of Soviet bureaucracies heightens the pressure that can be brought to bear on subordinate personnel. Increased railroad freight traffic figures for 1984 and 1985 indicate this campaign has had economic payoffs (Kontorovich: 26–28). The expanded scale of the *glasnost* (openness) and the *perestroika* (restructuring) initiative are only strengthening these tendencies.

The high traffic density of Soviet railroads has encouraged the further development of alternative transportation systems. The expansion of the pipelines systems since the 1950s has helped to relieve the railroads of their responsibility in transporting fuels. This is no insignificant matter as fuels now account for over 50 percent of all freight conveyed in the USSR. The intensive construction of oil pipelines began in the second half of the 1950s, with the total length of pipelines growing from only 5,400 kilometers in 1950 to over 76,000 kilometers in 1983. As a result, while only 17.8 percent of crude oil and refined products were transported by pipeline in 1950, by 1960 this figure had jumped to 39.2 percent, and by 1978 was over 50 percent; in 1974, the system moved past the railroad in the total volume of oil products transported. As a result, the rapidly expanded pipeline network now accounts for 20 percent of the USSR's total freight turnover (see Table 8.1). Gas line construction has also expanded in the last several decades. The first line had been constructed in 1940–41, with resumption after World War II. In the period between 1960 and 1983, the system grew sevenfold, from 21,000 to 155,000 kilometers. The increasing reliance of the Soviet Union on these energy sources, as opposed to coal, has necessitated the construction of lines and supporting infrastructures not only in western Siberia and Central Asia, but in the consuming European regions. The hard currency earned from the country's rich oil and gas reserves further encouraged pipeline construction westward to central Europe.

Unburdening the railroads has recently proven conducive to the further expansion of internal waterways and the Soviet maritime fleet. In the past, Soviet industrial plans had relegated these transport forms to a secondary status. The percentage share of traffic moved by river transport has dropped precipitously during the Soviet period, falling from 25 percent in 1913, to 13 percent in 1928, 5.5 percent in 1960, to a little over 4 percent in 1984. While granting the slowness of river transport, Soviet specialists now view the 138,000 kilometer internal waterways network as an underused system with growth potential. The 1986–2000 Comprehensive Program calls for the fuller use of existent river and seagoing routes, as well as the development of new waterways in the north and east. Increased construction of Siberian river port and wharf facilities during the Eleventh Five-Year Plan (1981–86) facilitated the transportation of oil from the Tyumen region by a combined river-rail system. In some cases, freight transport has been shifted from the rail system to ships (e.g., between 6 and 7 million tons of Karaganda and Kuznetsk coal have been shifted from railroad to river transport in the early 1980s) (*Rechnoi transport,* Sept. 2, 1983). The use of waterways in the north has proven to be a cost-efficient alternative to highway construction, since the cost of road construction in the far north territories can run to 1 million rubles per kilometer.

The Soviet maritime fleet has grown in commercial significance during the past two decades, expanding in size to over 1,800 vessels and ranking fifth worldwide in the volume of goods transported. It currently transports 16 million tons of cargo at any given moment and accounts for a significant portion of the cargo moved between Europe and Africa, Central America, and the Far East. The growth in the maritime fleet has come with an expansion in Soviet foreign trade, with the fleet transporting 46 percent of the country's exports and nearly 70 percent of its imports. The easy conversion of maritime fleet vessels for military purposes cannot be discounted in explaining the buildup of the sector. However, Soviet desires to be more self-reliant in their foreign trade and to earn more hard currency have been important incentives. This fleet buildup has facilitated the growth of the Soviet shipbuilding industry, as well as the expansion of sea cargo facilities. The underutilized northern sea route has become increasingly important for Soviet commerce. The development of ice-breakers (including several nuclear-powered) and freighters with greater ice-breaking capabilities have helped to keep the northern waters open to nearly year-round transport.

The motor and highway transportation sector has also grown as the transportation network has diversified. Generally, expansion of the motor vehicle sector has proven costly, not only because it is labor intensive, but given the long distances entailed for much freight conveyance. Soviet plans have been predicated upon short-distance, large tonnage motor conveyance, with the average distance of transport for one ton of freight around 21 kilometers (1983). The sector has accounted for only a small percentage of the total freight turnover (2.2 percent in 1984).

A major obstacle to this sector has been the lack of usable roads. At the time of World War II, there were fewer than 150,000 kilometers of highways in the country. Those in existence generally linked the important urban and production centers in the European portion of the country. Since the end of the war, the Soviets have expanded the highway system, with over three-quarters of a million kilometers of hard surface roads in use by 1984 (Table 8.3).[6] This growth has been especially pronounced in the Russian periphery as well as in non-European republics. The primary task continues to be expansion of the network to fully connect agricultural and industrial production sites. The 1985 goals of constructing 10,000 kilometers of new hard-surfaced roads were designed to provide access to ninety-four regional *(raion)* centers and to over 2,800 collective and state farms (*Avtomobil'nyye dorogi,* Feb. 1985). Generally, when investments in light industry and agriculture rise (as during the Khrushchev and Brezhnev periods), attention to road transportation increases. This is predictable given that vehicle transport has been the major means of conveying consumer goods and foodstuffs. Roads constructed during the Eleventh Five-Year Plan (1981–86) connected a number of important production and urban centers (e.g., Khabarovsk-Komsomol'sk-na-Amure, Chita-Irkutsk, and Saratov-Penza). These road expansion efforts are necessary, but, considering the size of the country and the degree of the road system's underdevelopment, they may not be sufficient, especially if the regime desires to fully tie the agricultural sector to processing and consumer centers. Soviet planners acknowledge that the country's road system is composed primarily of low-category roads, many of which are dirt and impassable during parts of the year. This includes portions of roads which link important industrial regions (e.g., the Rostov-Ivanovo-Gorkii road). In the more developed regions, with dense road systems, attention is focused on road reconstruction and repair. In the Baltic republic of Latvia, for instance, only 100 kilometers were added to the

Table 8.3
Length of Soviet General Usage Hard Surface Roads, by Republic (1,000 km)

	1940	1950	1960	1970	1980
Armenia	2.6	3.3	3.8	5.2	6.4
Azerbaidzhan	3.0	3.2	7.9	13.4	18.3
Belorussia	11.2	12.1	11.2	22.7	34.5
Estonia	7.1	7.8	10.0	14.0	14.7
Georgia	8.1	11.1	13.2	16.4	18.9
Kazakhstan	1.1	1.9	11.2	41.1	70.8
Kirgizia	1.2	1.7	4.9	11.4	15.8
Latvia	2.6	2.9	5.1	11.1	15.8
Lithuania	2.2	7.2	9.5	12.6	16.8
Moldavia	1.1	2.1	3.5	7.1	9.0
RSFSR	67.8	82.9	116.0	209.8	322.0
Tadzhikistan	0.9	1.1	2.9	8.0	10.8
Turkmenistan	0.5	0.5	1.5	4.7	8.5
Ukraine	29.3	33.5	47.4	90.8	133.7
Uzbekistan	4.7	6.0	9.5	20.7	27.5
USSR	143.4	177.3	258.4	489.0	723.5

	1981	1982	1983	1984	1985	1986	All roads 1986
Armenia	6.6	6.7	6.9	7.0	7.2	7.3	7.6
Azerbaidzhan	19.6	20.4	21.2	21.8	22.4	22.8	24.4
Belorussia	35.3	36.1	36.5	37.5	38.4	40.8	44.4
Estonia	14.7	14.7	14.7	14.8	14.7	14.7	14.7
Georgia	19.1	19.0	19.2	19.4	19.7	19.9	21.5
Kazakhstan	72.5	73.9	75.7	76.5	78.0	80.0	95.8
Kirgizia	16.0	16.3	16.5	18.9	19.0	17.0	19.3
Latvia	16.1	16.4	16.7	16.9	17.3	17.7	20.5
Lithuania	17.4	17.9	18.7	19.3	19.9	20.4	20.9
Moldavia	9.0	9.1	9.2	9.2	9.3	9.4	10.1
RSFSR	331.2	340.5	345.5	354.5	363.8	370.9	461.8
Tadzhikistan	10.9	10.9	11.2	11.3	11.4	11.6	13.2
Turkmenistan	8.8	9.2	9.4	10.0	10.3	10.8	13.0
Ukraine	136.1	138.6	141.6	143.1	142.2	147.3	162.7
Uzbekistan	30.8	31.5	32.0	32.7	35.7	36.4	38.8
USSR	744.1	761.2	773.0	793.2	812.3	827.0	968.4

Sources: Narodnoye khoziaistvo SSSR [National economy USSR], 1970 (1971), 1984 (1985), 1985 (1986), and 1986 (1987).

Table 8.4
Passenger Conveyance in Moscow by Service (millions of passengers)

	1965	1970	1975	1980	1985	1986
Metro	1329	1628	1966	2318	2492	2552
Trolleys	801	785	910	806	864	949
Trams	701	630	637	525	500	508
Buses	1254	1519	1781	1787	2147	2295

Source: Moskva v tsifrakh, 1985 [Moscow in numbers, 1985], Moscow: Finansy i statistika [Finance and statistics], 1985, p. 83; 1987, p. 93.

road system during the 1981–85 period (*Sovetskaya Latvia,* May 21, 1986). And a significant portion of that entailed the construction of bypasses around major urban centers. Efforts at road repair, however, have been constrained by the low supply of materials, especially asphalt concrete.

A major weakness in the motor and other transport sectors is the constant shortage of equipment and the overuse of those operating. In the motor vehicle area, shortage of vehicles results in a preference for large truck fleets which operate on a common-carrier basis. This lowers costs and has proven more productive. Such fleets have come to include a significant percentage of all trucks in large urban settings (e.g., Moscow) as well as in the rural periphery. The common-carrier approach has helped in coordinating trucking with rail, ship, and aviation freight transfer.

Motor transportation assumes special importance in short-distance passenger transfer. It is difficult to generalize across cities and republics because the extent and quality of services varies significantly. For instance, the advanced Baltic republics have many more kilometers of bus routes per 1,000 residents than do the republics of Central Asia (33 to 53 kilometers compared with 5 to 7 kilometers) (*Planovoye khoziaistvo,* no. 6, 1978: 17). There is no unified organization of passenger services supervising bus, tram, and trolley systems nationally or in the various republics. While trams and commuter railways have traditionally been relied on for passenger transport, buses continue to account for an increasing percentage of total conveyance. Urban transportation statistics for 1983 reveal that buses and trams/trolleys account for 58 percent and 34 percent of all conveyance, with subways handling 8 percent of the total. In large cities, metros account for a higher percentage (e.g., see the trends for Moscow in Table 8.4). The cost efficiency of tramways, the speed of metros, and the high passenger capacity of both, have made these favored mass transit systems.[7] Suburban passenger transport is also handled overwhelmingly by motor transport (80 percent), with the railways accounting for the remainder. Average distance figures of 12 kilometers for bus and 30 kilometers for train predictably reveal the importance of the railway system for linking more outlying areas to the urban centers (Khrushchev & Nikol'skii: 250).

Urban growth has placed added pressures on the transportation system. While there have been efforts to limit the expansion of production facilities in large cities, the further building of service enterprises and housing (including "microregions" around the big cities) have contributed to serious problems of overcrowding on all urban mass transit forms. Overuse of these systems, in the context of Soviet taut planning and insufficient resource investment, result in equipment breakdowns, the absence of proper repair and maintenance facilities, frequent noncompliance with bus schedules, and the altering and cancellation of services with little or no warning. According to one report, 25 percent of all buses operating in the Russian Socialist Federal Soviet Republic (RSFSR) are under repair at any one time (*Sovetskaya Rossiya,* Sept. 20, 1984). Problems in hiring and retaining a sufficient number of operators and drivers exacerbate the effective functioning of urban mass transit services. Recent changes in Soviet law may alleviate these problems to some extent, as essentially self-employed individuals are permitted to provide repair and other types of services.

A major role in the public transport of major urban centers has been assumed by metro systems. While expensive and serving as political showcases, these systems account for an increasing percentage of all passenger conveyance in urban setting (e.g., 4 billion passengers conveyed in 1980). The Moscow metro system, first opened in May 1935, is the nation's most extensive, now moving nearly 2.5 billion passengers per year. The continual expansion of this metro system since World War II has proven to be an effective, albeit costly, way to deal with the high overcrowding that characterizes Moscow public transport. It is not at all clear, however, that the development of comparable showcase metros in other cities is also economically justified. The already operational metro systems in Leningrad (first opened in 1955), Kiev (1960), Tbilisi (1966), Baku (1967), Kharkov (1975), and Tashkent (1977), combined, transport fewer passengers than the Moscow system alone. However, a largely political rationale has encouraged the planning or construction of metros in at least one dozen other metropolitan areas, including several non-European cities.

The urban growth and pressures that have increasingly become a part of modern Soviet metropolitan life have encouraged a major expansion of the country's motor vehicle industry. Increases in automobile production in the past several decades, however, have not resulted in the automobile helping to solve problems of urban and passenger transport. The private automobile has had an uncomfortable fit with the Marxist-Leninist ideology, representing a materialism and individualism that run counter to the governing egalitarian ethos. Its slow development reflected, in part, the traditional priority of freight transport over that for passengers. Until recently, truck and bus production traditionally far out-paced that for cars. The capital-intensive costs of the automobile industry also precluded its fuller development. Automobiles have been available to the elite and the bureaucracy, but they only became available to the broader population in the past couple of decades. Khrushchev's proposal of municipal car rental fleets was one approach to making cars more available to the mass population, but this proved limited in the face of demand. Problems of vehicle maintenance and convenient accessibility obviated the full development of such fleets. Rising domestic needs and an ability to export Soviet-produced vehicles facilitated the growth of the auto industry. The Brezhnev regime exhibited an interest in the motor vehicle industry, with over 85 billion rubles invested between 1966 and 1975. Several of the most massive construction projects ever undertaken in Soviet history were car and truck plants.[8] A whole infrastructure had to be put in place, including the building of two new cities of over 300,000 inhabitants each, the creation of twenty other auto and supply plants, and the fuller development of the Volga-Kama river system for transporting the vehicles (Parker: 515–541). Car production has grown from only 4,400 in 1940 to over 1.3 million in 1982. This production, in turn, has enhanced pressures to further develop the country's highway system, as well as to expand the necessary service facilities (see Tables 8.5 and 8.6).

The motor vehicle and highway sector diverges from others in that it is relatively decentralized. The lack of an all-union (national) ministry has accentuated the influence of regional and local bodies in setting plans. Enterprises and institutions often have their own vehicle fleets, observing their own norms and usage rules. The lack of coordination across branches and regions is consequently high. Calls for the creation of a national motor transportation ministry have been forthcoming in prominent places, but such a superministry has yet to be formed (Velikanov: 70–79) (see Tables 8.7 and 8.8).

The aviation sector has only recently begun to assume some importance in overall transportation planning. From a modest total airway length of 146,000 kilometers in 1940, the system has grown to nearly 1 million kilometers in 1980. Its percentage of total cargo transported has been minimal, but its role in more rapid passenger conveyance across great distances has made it increasingly important. The development of the Siberian north and Soviet Far East has resulted in a significant increase in cargo carried (from 23.2 million ton-kilometers in 1940 to over 3,094 million ton-kilometers in 1980). The 1986–2000 Comprehensive Plan calls for more Aeroflot flights linking Siberia and the Soviet Far East with the USSR's industrial regions. Funds have been allocated to the system of landing fields and refueling stations, especially in these regions. The development of new, larger-capacity, aircraft (e.g., the Ruslan, which is designed to handle up to 150 tons) and faster, fuel efficient aircraft (e.g., the TU-204, which is designed to carry over 200 passengers) is also designed to strengthen the economic linkages across distant production, processing, and consumption centers. A problem of the aviation sector has been the underutilization of plane cargo capacity. This underuse results from the lack of equipment for transporting cargo onto and out of planes, as well as from the lack of storage facilities. Often, the equipment and facilities in place are old and out of date. A shortage of manpower has further exacerbated this under-

Table 8.5
Passenger Conveyance by Different Means of Transportation
(millions of passengers)

	1940	1960	1970	1975	1980
Railroad	1377	2231	3354	3972	4072
Maritime	10	27	39	52	52
Inland Waterways	73	119	145	161	138
Road (by bus)	590	11316	27344	36469	42176
Air	0.4	16	71	98	104

	1981	1982	1983	1984	1985	1986
Railroad	4095	4098	4149	4155	4166	4345
Maritime	55	53	52	51	50	51
Inland Waterways	146	139	142	136	132	136
Road (by bus)	42951	43691	44548	45755	47006	48810
Air	109	108	110	112	113	116

Sources: Narodnoye khoziaistvo SSSR [National economy USSR], 1975 (1976), 1983 (1984), 1984 (1985), 1985 (1986), and 1986 (1987).

Table 8.6
Passenger Conveyance by Different Means of Transportation (billion passenger-kilometers)

	1940	1960	1970	1975	1980
Railroad	100.4	176.0	273.5	322.1	342.2
Maritime	0.9	1.3	1.6	2.1	2.5
Inland Waterways	3.8	4.3	5.4	6.3	6.1
Road (by bus)	3.4	61.0	202.5	303.6	389.8
Air	0.2	12.1	78.2	122.6	160.6
Total	108.7	254.7	561.2	756.7	901.2

	1981	1982	1983	1984	1985	1986
Railroad	354.3	357.6	361.5	364.0	374.0	390.2
Maritime	2.5	2.4	2.5	2.5	2.6	2.5
Inland Waterways	6.2	6.0	6.1	5.9	5.9	6.0
Road (by bus)	401.7	412.6	423.4	434.0	446.6	462.8
Air	171.7	172.5	176.8	184.0	188.4	195.8
Total	936.4	951.1	970.3	990.4	1017.5	1057.3

Sources: Narodnoye khoziaistvo SSSR [National economy USSR], 1984 (1985), 1985 (1986), and 1986 (1987).

Table 8.7
Individual Freight Conveyance by Means of Transportation (million tons)

	1940	1960	1970	1975	1980
Railroad	605	1885	2896	3621	3728
Maritime	33	76	162	200	228
Inland Waterways	74	210	358	476	568
Road	859	8493	14623	20956	24149
Air (incl. mail)*	58	697	1844	2472	2989

	1981	1982	1983	1984	1985	1986
Railroad	3762	3725	3851	2910	3951	4078
Maritime	223	224	238	235	240	250
Inland Waterways	595	605	607	619	633	649
Road	25016	26481	26425	25631	25873	26985
Air (incl. mail)*	3130	3105	3067	3113	3183	3157

*Thousand tons.

Sources: Narodnoye khoziaistvo SSSR [National economy USSR], 1975 (1976), 1983 (1984), 1984 (1985), 1985 (1986), and 1986 (1987).

Table 8.8
Freight Turnover by Means of Transportation (billion ton-kilometers)

	1940	1960	1970	1975	1980
Railroad	420.7	1504.3	2494.7	3236.5	3439.9
Maritime	24.9	131.5	656.1	736.3	848.2
Inland Waterways	36.1	99.6	174.0	221.7	244.9
Road	8.9	98.5	220.8	337.9	432.1
Air (incl. mail)	0.02	0.6	1.9	2.6	3.1
Pipeline (oil)	3.8	51.2	281.7	665.9	1216.0
Pipeline (gas)	-	12.6	131.4	280.4	596.9
Total	494.4	1898.3	3960.6	5481.3	6781.1

	1981	1982	1983	1984	1985	1986
Railroad	3503.2	3464.5	3600.1	3638.8	3718.4	3834.5
Maritime	853.5	834.5	891.7	933.0	905.0	969.7
Inland Waterways	255.6	262.4	273.2	264.3	261.5	255.6
Road	459.9	485.3	485.8	475.2	476.2	488.5
Air (incl. mail)	3.08	3.03	3.19	3.28	3.35	3.38
Pipeline (oil)	1263.2	1306.8	1353.1	1370.3	1312.5	1401.3
Pipeline (gas)	680.9	771.5	863.4	997.3	1130.6	1240.0
Total	7019.4	7128.0	7470.5	7682.1	7807.6	8193.0

Sources: Narodnoye khoziaistvo SSSR [National economy USSR], 1975 (1976), 1984 (1985), 1985 (1986), and 1986 (1987).

utilization problem. As with other transportation systems, moneys have not been forthcoming in providing the necessary support facilities and personnel.

The critical concern for all sectors of the transportation network is to make efficient use of the limited resources available to them. Even the favored railways have been subject to severe central planning constraints. This is especially true as energy and other necessary materials have become more costly. The approach to increasing the cost-effectiveness of the sector has been the much more intensive use of existing routes and facilities. Expansion of routes has continued throughout the past several decades, but this does not automatically translate into expanded services. As the Soviet economy has become relatively more consumer oriented, the concomitant high costs of expanding and upgrading a heavy industry-oriented transport system have only increased. In the context of limited investment increases, transportation service improvements are dependent on improved planning and coordination of activities across disparate agencies.

In the centrally planned economy, effective planning and coordination of activities across bureaucracies is paramount. This has proven difficult to achieve in a complicated and compartmentalized transportation sector. The influence of the centrally planned economy on transportation policy has been to emphasize quantitative rather than qualitative measures of services (e.g., measures of weight or volume transferred, rather than speed or effective utilization of facilities) and to see demand rise much more rapidly than investment. There has been discussion of perfecting a unified transportation system, but, in reality, the system continues to be subject to the competing interests of various ministries and the state planning committee, Gosplan. Difficulties inherent in the centrally planned economy make coordination and sector efficiency difficult. As a consequence, Soviet transportation problems reflect not only geographical and logistical challenges, but also organizational complexities.

TRANSPORTATION POLICY ORGANIZATION AND PROCESS

Transportation is administered in the Soviet Union through both branch and territorial Communist Party and governmental organizations. All-union (national) and, in some cases, republic Party organs oversee and guide policy, with specific all-union or republic governmental bureaucracies responsible for the functioning of the six major types of public transportation: (1) railroad, (2) civil aviation, (3) maritime, (4) motor, (5) river, and (6) pipeline (both gas and petroleum). Defined jurisdictional boundaries separate the six forms of transportation service. These sectors and their governing bureaucracies have been characterized by autarkic development. Organizational linkages tend to be vertical, within each transportation area, rather than horizontal, across those sectors and their bureaucracies. While the Communist Party of the Soviet Union (CPSU) Central Committee oversees the work of most of these governmental organizations, there is no unified central administrative bureaucracy ultimately responsible for all transportation systems. Indeed, there is no single set of laws and regulations governing transportation. Rather, there are different railroad, maritime, aviation, motor, and river shipping rules and norms of operation, with none fully coordinated by a single political actor.

Within the dual, Party and state, hierarchical system of the USSR, basic transportation policies are set by top officials of the CPSU Central Committee's (CC) Department of Transportation and Communications and the various USSR transportation ministries (i.e., the Ministries of Railways, Maritime Fleet, Civil Aviation, Gas Industry, Petroleum Industry, Automotive Industry, Aviation Industry, and Transport Construction). Certain republic ministries, in the relatively more decentralized transportation branches (i.e., motor and river transport), also influence operations. The activities of these branch organizations are, in part, contingent upon the plans and guidance offered by the central state planning, material, and research institutions: the USSR State Planning Committee (Gosplan), the USSR Committee for Materials Supply (Gosnab), and the USSR State Committee for Science and Technology. These organizations—all part of the all-union Council of Ministers—set national economic plans, determine financing, and help with the development and provisions of new technologies. Transportation agencies are also affected by the activities of producer and other sectoral ministries. Ministries in the area of transport machinery, for instance, provide vehicles and basic equipment. Electricity and other forms of energy must be purchased from their producers. Scheduling arrangements must be set with dozens of ministries and enterprises which produce the goods shipped. Problems of coordinating production and shipping schedules across these bureaucracies are manifold.

Our knowledge of the specific policy-making responsibilities and norms for the numerous organizations at the Central Committee–Council of Ministers level is limited for the transportation as well as other sectors. However, broad decision-making characteristics can be noted. Generally, it is appropriate to differentiate basic policy-making and supervisory roles for the Party apparatus from policy-implementing roles for the state apparatus (see Figures 8.3 and 8.4). The latter assume the high public profile in the running of the transportation services, but the former are determinative in setting out policy directives and then following up on their implementation.

The CPSU Central Committee Department of Transportation and Communications is the top Party body specifically directed to oversee policy in the transportation area. The department head, deputy head, section heads, instructors, and inspectors who comprise this Party organ are all career Party professionals, with training and experience in the transportation area prior to joining the central Party apparatus. Their responsibilities include the recruitment and evaluation of higher-level personnel in the various transportation-related state organizations, the supervision of those organizations' plan fulfillment, the collection and processing of information relevant to current and future transporta-

Figure 8.3
Scheme of Communist Party Apparatus, National to Regional Levels

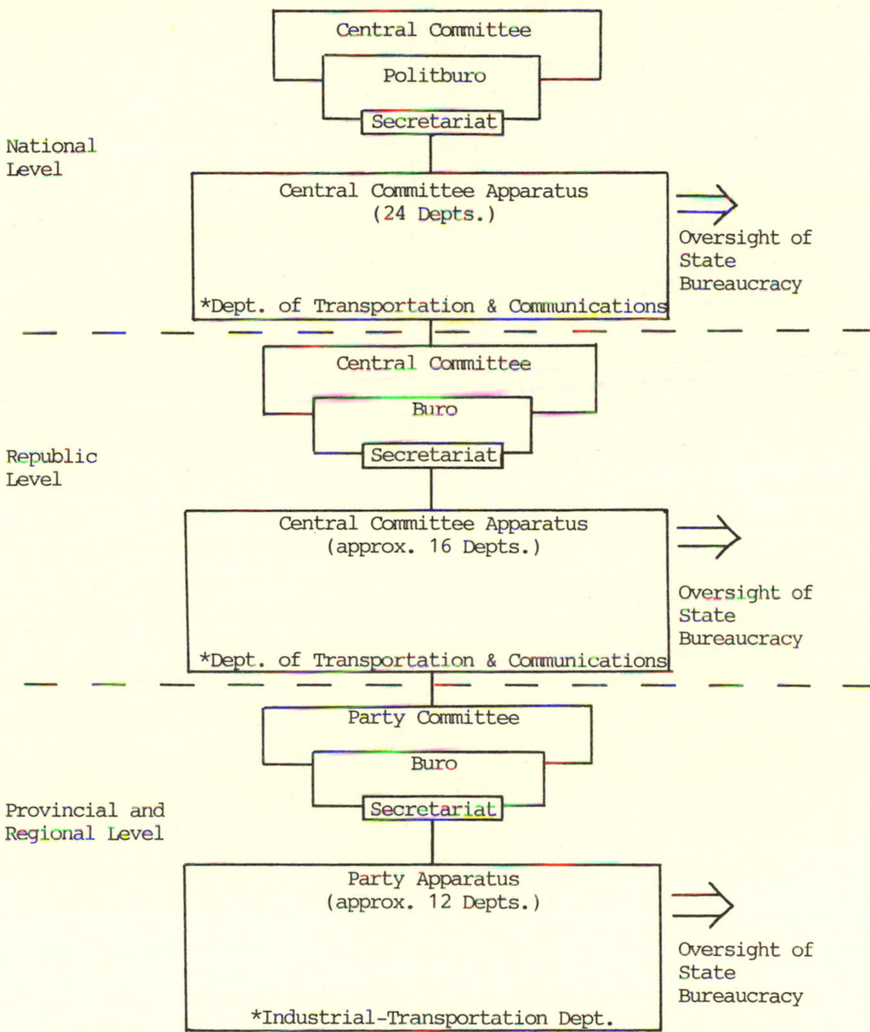

tion sector developments, and the instruction of those subordinate organs on matters within their competence. The limited number of *apparatchiki* (Party professionals) working in a CC department means that fairly extensive supervisory authority can reside with one department official (Hough & Fainsod: 423–424). A CC Transportation Department instructor, for instance, could be assigned to supervise several of the USSR's thirty-two regional railroad administrations. In this capacity, he would determine whether top-level Party and state decisions are being implemented, while instructing subordinates on means

Figure 8.4
Scheme of Soviet State Apparatus, National to Regional Levels

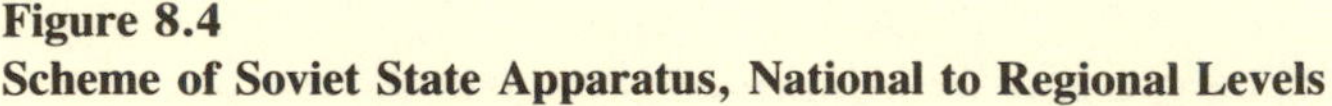

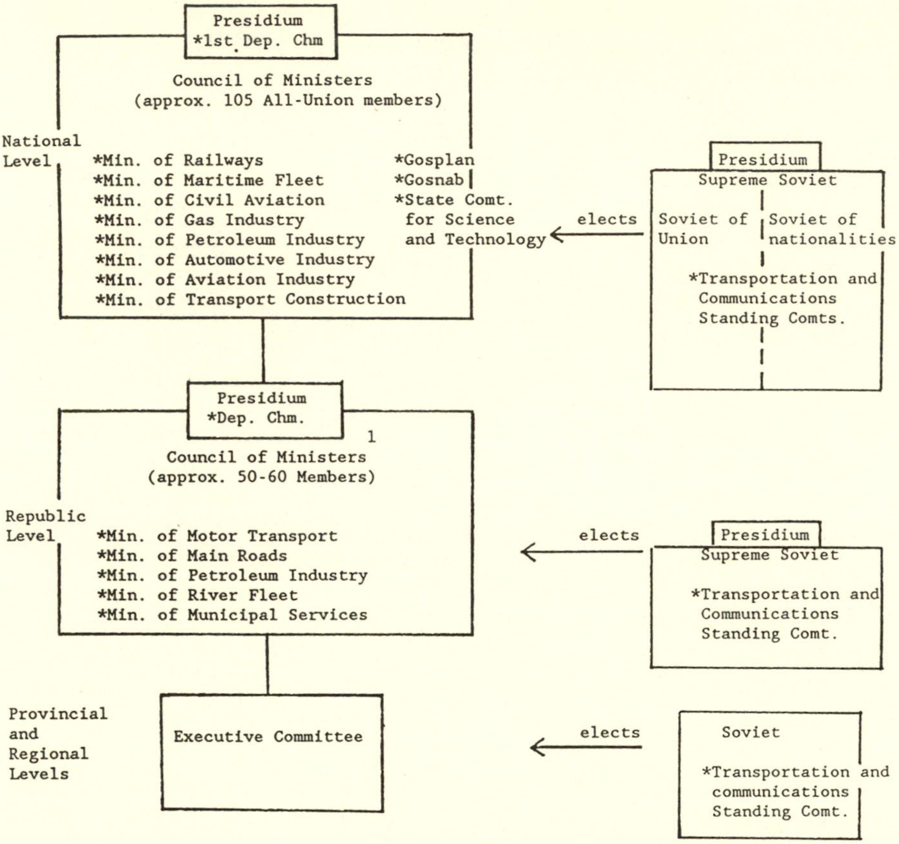

[1] The composition of republic councils of ministers varies across the fifteen republics. Different ministries and state committees are found in each republic, dependent upon the economies and resources of the republics.

of improving performance. He would be simultaneously gathering information and preparing materials for superiors which would be used to evaluate sector policy. While the supervisory functions of this CC department are extensive, they are constrained by the degree to which they oversee the work of many more governmental officials.

The CC Transportation Department deals with a wide range of state bureaucracies spanning all-union, republic, and regional levels of authority. The relationship between these Party and state officials is not necessarily an adversarial or strictly supervisory one. CC department *apparatchiki,* together with government officials, can assume an advocacy role for the transportation sector, articulating its interests within the decision-making establishment. The notion of a "sectoral complex" or "whirlpool" is useful in characterizing the relationships among sector Party and state officials (Hough: 14). Yet the degree of interrelationship among the Party and state officials dealing with transport issues is imprecise because there has been such a proliferation of transportation bureaucracies. The CC Transportation Department works with certain ministries, but other state bureaucracies dealing with transportation-related matters (e.g., Ministry of Gas Industry and Ministry of Petroleum Industry) are supervised by other Central Committee departments (e.g., Heavy Industry Department). Coordination of policies across these different complexes is difficult. For instance, the movement of agricultural products from the farm to the urban consumer can entail several transportation services, not to mention other agricultural and distribution agencies. The responsible agencies operate under different schedules, are obligated to fulfill their separate plans, and in this case may use different containerization processes in the storing and transporting of perishable agricultural produce. Shortages of parts and assemblies for vehicles and transportation facilities can result in lowered transport sector plan fulfillment as can the failure of non-transport ministries and their enterprises to adhere to strict delivery schedules. Soviet transportation specialists suggest the need to enhance "horizontal linkages" across these numerous Party and state organizations to reduce vestiges of what they describe as "departmentalism and parochialism" (Butin, Kalinin & Mokrov: 54–57). However, the incentives for branch and territorial bureaucracies to do so have been largely absent.

While routine policy making and implementing activities take place at the CPSU CC departmental and USSR ministerial level and below, majority policy initiatives entail the approval of the CPSU Politburo, the USSR's top policy-making body, and the Presidium of the Council of Ministers, the USSR's top state policy-implementing body. These initiatives are sanctioned through resolutions of the CPSU Central Committee and USSR Council of Ministers. Problems in the transportation area in the early 1980s, for example, necessitated not only publicized resolutions on improving the planning and organization of transportation (Oct. 28, 1982), but the publicized discussion of this issue at a CC Plenum held shortly after Brezhnev's death (Nov. 22, 1982). The initiation of a "discipline campaign" began with the publicly stated concerns of Party General Secretary Yuri Andropov and was followed by major pronouncements in the authoritative central press (*Pravda,* Aug. 29–30, 1985).

Traditionally, a top member of the Soviet political elite has assumed decisive oversight responsibilities for the transportation area and, in particular, for the all-important railways. That politician is usually a member of both the Party Politburo and the Council of Ministers Presidium. Leon Trotsky was appointed Commissar (Minister) for Railways and Communications in March 1920. Lazar Kaganovich, a top lieutenant of Stalin, played such a role during the period of the mid-1930s into the 1950s (he was appointed Commissar of Railways in 1935).[9] He had succeeded another powerful politician, A. A. Andreyev, and directed the transportation area in his role as a deputy chairman of the Council of Ministers. This pattern continued during the Brezhnev regime, as Kirill Mazurov, a former Belorussian Party leader and an ally of Prime Minister Aleksei Kosygin, oversaw the transportation area. The late 1982 criticisms of the transportation sectors provided the opportunity for another prominent politician (and former republic KGB head), Geidar Aliev, to be promoted into Politburo full membership and into the Council of Ministers Presidium to oversee the tightening of the railroad and transportation sectors. His unexpected retirement in October 1987 may have stemmed in part from his ineffectiveness in adequately addressing the transportation problems that most see as a major obstacle to *perestroika* (restructuring).

The historical evolution and contemporary needs of each transportation service have influenced the form of administration which characterizes each branch. The USSR Ministry of Railways had originally served as the single governmental agency managing all forms of Soviet transportation, and it continues to assume a powerful position as the central political actor administering railroads throughout the country. The railway administration continues to be a much more unified and centralized system, with its relatively close institutional ties to other industrial and construction ministries and its high share of all freight conveyance assuring it a continuing critical role in Soviet goods transport. Republics and provinces do not have independent railway bureaucracies. In administering the country's rails, the USSR Ministry of Railways governs the setting, reworking, and fulfillment of freight and passenger conveyance, is responsible for increasing the traffic and conveyance capacity of the national rail system, and directs the further expansion of the rail system. Its top personnel are trained specialists in the area, having worked their way up the all-union rail administration. The three ministers who have served since 1948, Boris P. Beshchev (1948–77), Ivan G. Pavlovskii (1977–82), and Nikolai S. Konarev (1982–present), have spent nearly their entire careers in the Ministry of Railways bureaucracy. The weight of their influence and that of their ministry as the favored transportation service is revealed by their inclusion within the membership of the CPSU Central Committee.

The USSR Ministry of Civil Aviation and USSR Ministry of the Maritime Fleet have assumed comparably strong positions as centralized bureaucracies within their respective transport sectors. This is not surprising, given the decisive role the Soviet federal government has played in the development of these branches. The foreign trade and international connections of these branches also necessitated unified central control and all-union ministerial status. The USSR Civil Aviation Ministry is responsible for air passenger and freight conveyance and for both domestic and international flights. The ministry is composed of a number of administrations *(upravleniye)*—for instance, the administration of civil aviation, which regulates more specific tasks set before the ministry (e.g., supervising local aviation authorities and airports). Aeroflot, the USSR airline, falls under the direct supervision of this ministry. Each of Aeroflot's thirty, mostly regional, directorates has its own operational targets and is responsible for its own plan fulfillment. The division of responsibilities on a territorial basis has contributed to a certain overlap of responsibilities and organizational conflicts.

The maritime fleet, petroleum industry, and gas industry ministries exhibit similar organizational structures to those of the railway and civil aviation ministries. Constant reorganizations of these bureaucracies make generalization difficult. Decision making is centralized, with regional administrations responsible for operations and plan fulfillment. The USSR Ministry of the Maritime Fleet has broad oversight responsibilities, with territorially designated administrations (e.g., the Northern Fleet and the Far Eastern Fleet) guided by their own plans. The rapid expansion of pipeline transportation merited the formation of all-union ministries, with organizational distinctions drawn between petroleum and gas. The development and operation of petroleum and gas transportation facilities necessitates extensive work with local officials, with provincial and regional executive committees and Soviet standing commissions.

Unlike other sectors, the administration of motor and river transport falls within the jurisdiction of each of the fifteen republics. Forms of organization and types of agency vary by republic. For river transport, most republics have lower-level administrations *(upravleniye),* while the Russian republic, with most of the country's internal waterways, has a Ministry of the River Fleet which falls under the direct purview of the CPSU CC Department of Transportation and Communications. All of these bureaucracies supervise the facilities, equipment, and routes which comprise their respective republics' nonoceanic transportation. However, certain functions, for instance the setting of tariffs or fares, are assumed by other, all-union actors.

Administration of motor transportation is subdivided into motor transport of general usage and departmental motor transport. The former is regulated by republic motor and road ministries, while the latter is regulated by the given organization for which the service is provided. Republic ministries are responsible not only for freight and passenger conveyance on general usage roads, but also for road development and maintenance. All told, roughly thirty republic ministries set and administer motor and road transportation policies. As a consequence, standards and operations norms are not uniform.

Republic Party Central Committee transportation departments assume supervisory functions for these republic state bureaucracies, as provincial and regional Party transport committees do in their settings. These Party organs oversee the services of the transportation agencies, though their supervisory functions are constrained by national-level Party and state officials.

The planning and coordination problems that hinder the transportation system at the national and republic level also operate at the local level. Lower-level governmental policy makers (i.e., members of soviet executive committees, *ispolkomi,* at the provincial, regional, and local levels) review the performance of the various transportation agencies. Transportation planning at these levels is complicated because the various rail, air, bus, metro, and other services are provided by separate agencies. These agencies are accountable to all-union and republic-level bureaucracies. Thus, railways and subways are guided by the USSR Ministry of Railways, trolleys and trams by the republic ministries of countryside and municipal services, and buses and taxis by republic ministries of motor transport and roads. Local needs may conflict with the targets set by these organizations' national and republic-level plans. As a consequence, lower-level administrative agencies must work with the priorities of a wide range of superior bureaucracies, but with the latter assuming the preeminent position.

CONCLUSION

Many Soviet transportation specialists have called for a more unified and efficient transportation complex through the creation of a single national state committee (or ministry) for transportation, with that organ granted broad supervisory authority over all transportation services. Under such a proposed change, provincial, regional, and local authorities and transportation agency officials together would form transportation commissions and coordinating bureaus to better balance regional and branch plans, to ensure their fulfillment, and to increase sectoral efficiency while reducing labor and energy waste (Butin et al.: 90–92). Predictably, many bureaucrats, including those at the republic and lower levels, have opposed such efforts, viewing them as threats to their own organizational prerogatives and interests. At the 1986 Twenty-Seventh CPSU Congress, even USSR Railways Minister N. S. Konarev described such a single transportation agency as "a radical solution" to contemporary sectoral problems, even though his ministry would likely assume the preeminent position in any such reorganization. Less comprehensive organizational reforms have also been promoted to further centralization efforts in individual transportation sectors. For example, there have been suggestions to further integrate the decentralized automobile and highway transportation sector through the creation of a national motor transport ministry (Velikanov: 73). The USSR Academy of Sciences' Institute of State and Law, assisted by transportation branch institutes, drew up draft principles for a single set of transportation laws in 1985. However, these have yet to be put fully in place.[10]

In principle, the Soviet planned economy presumes central state coordination of production and distribution activities across all regions and sectors. In the transportation sector, this means that the national ministries, for instance the railways, together with regional subunits, oversee the cooperation of lower-level officials in meeting the needs of the rails and other transport modes. In fact this often is not the case. Local or branch authorities may not be responsive to the needs of centrally administered services. Local representatives of different services are accountable to their branch ministries. They are not so responsive to other, higher-level ministries.

Recent consolidations of state bureaucracies in selected areas (e.g., agriculture and machine building) reveal the Gorbachev regime is adopting a new approach to streamlining the policy process. The unveiling of the USSR Aviation Code and the development of a unified air traffic control system are two important steps in the direction of a more integrated civil aviation system. Such efforts, combined with the public rhetoric of top elites, indicate a heightened possibility for a more unified transportation sector. The views of the political elite are becoming much more compatible with the views of sector specialists who have called for as much. Enhancing transportation performance is necessary to the economic revitalization that General Secretary Gorbachev and the central elite desire. Party Secretary Yegor Ligachev emphasized this at a March 1987 national conference on railway transportation (*Kazakhstanskaya Pravda,* April 24, 1987: 2). In the spirit of the *glasnost* campaign, he detailed various problems of the railways, though he especially stressed management and worker responsibility. A few months later the Politburo called for the technical modernization of the railroads, with more advanced rolling stock, equipment, and automation (*Pravda,* June 6, 1987).

Nearly all modes of transport were planned to change over to full economic accountability and self-financing in 1988. It is unclear what type of state assistance can be expected given these accounting reforms. In late 1987 the Politburo charged various state organizations, including Gosplan and the Ministry of Railways, to develop by 1989 a comprehensive program for radically modernizing the railway trunk lines in the period 1991–2000 (*Pravda,* Dec. 18, 1987). Yet political elite commitment of additional resources to this and to other transport sectors has been vague to date. The era of *glasnost* has permitted a much more open and detailed public discussion of the problems besetting the Soviet transportation system. The media, with official backing, are much more explicit in identifying the agencies responsible for inefficiencies or accidents. Increasing attention has been given to disruptions of regular freight shipments, with growing reports of the impact of strikes and violence (e.g., in Armenia and Azerbaidzhan) on regular train and other traffic. In addition, officials responsible for the transportation sector have come under increasing public fire, with USSR Railroad Minister N. S. Konarev subjected to especially intense criticism by Supreme Soviet deputies during his confirmation hearings in the summer of 1989. The long-serving Railroad Minister was subjected to a humiliating rejection of his nomination by the Supreme Soviet, with this decision reversed only a month later and in the absence of a viable alternative nominee (*Izvestia,* August 5, 1989). The Gorbachev regime appears committed to transportation reform as an important part of the restructuring effort. The full contours of the regime's strategy are not completely clear, but past experience must temper our expectations regarding major policy or investment changes.

NOTES

1. The sector is also of importance to the domestic Soviet military effort. Troops and materiel are often conveyed by rail, air, and water routes used primarily for civilian purposes. For illustrative examples of the regime's concern over assuring effective mil-

itary transportation and cooperation between civilian and military authorities, see the Ministry of Defense daily, *Krasnaya Zvezda,* August 15, 1985, p. 1, and Jan. 28, 1987, p. 2.

2. See Central Intelligence Agency, *Handbook of Economic Statistics,* 1985, p. 66, which provides figures combining transportation and communications.

3. The title Railroad Ministry is used for purposes of clarity, although the translation from Russian would be Ways (or Means) of Communication (Ministerstvo putei soobshcheniya).

4. For instance, the new, 12-axle, electric locomotive, VL-15, is said to pull up to 6,000–8,000 tons *(Zarya Vostoka,* Nov. 17, 1985).

5. The new automatic dumping car can move freight in low temperature areas (*Rabochaya gazeta,* Jan. 7, 1986).

6. These figures are increased if administrative roads are included in the totals to 1.1 million kilometers of hard surface roads and 1.5 million kilometers of total roads in 1984.

7. Crouch notes that Soviet planners are guided by volume of passenger traffic in developing transit systems. Bus lines are put in when passenger traffic per hour is approximately 5,000–6,000; trams are put in when it is 7,000–8,000; and metro lines are added to existing systems when the passenger traffic is over 15,000 per hour (Crouch: 242).

8. These are the Tol'yatti auto plant, with the first cars produced in 1970, and the Kama River truck plant, with the first trucks produced in 1976.

9. It was also during this time period and Lazar Kaganovich's tenure that the purges devastated the railroad and transportation sector. The military hierarchy was one of the few that was as decimated by the purges of the 1930s.

10. The Gosplan Institute of Complex Transport Problems has undertaken scientific studies to enhance plan fulfillment, but their work has not suggested ways of integrating the sector.

REFERENCES

Aksenov, I. Ya, *Edinaya transportnaya systema* [Unified transportation system] (Moscow: Transport, 1980).

Ambler, John, Dennis J. B. Shaw, and Leslie Symons, eds., *Soviet and East European Transport Problems* (New York: St. Martin's Press, 1985).

Atlas avtomobil'nykh dorog SSSR [Atlas of automobile roads of the USSR] (Moscow: Glavnoye upravleniye geodyezii Kartografii Ministerstva Geologii SSSR, 1966).

Avtomobil'nyye dorogi [Automobile roads], February 1985.

Balakin, V. A., S. A. Voitovich, M. Ya. Kantor, and V. M. Kopelevich, *Planovo-Ekonomicheskaya rabota v transportnom stroutel'stve* [Planning-economic work in transportation construction] (Moscow: Transport, 1984).

Biriukov, V., ''Vazhnyi etap kompleksnoi programmy razvitiya transporta'' [The highest stage of the complex program for the development of transportation], *Planovoye khoziaistvo* [Planned economy], no. 5, 1981.

Butin, I. A., N. G. Kalinin, and V. S. Mokrov, *Transportnyi kompleks sotsialisticheskoi ekonomiki,* [The transportation complex of the socialist economy] (Moscow: Moscow State University Press, 1984).

Central Intelligence Agency, *Handbook of Economic Statistics* (Washington, D.C.: USGPO, 1985).

Crouch, Martin, "Problems of Urban Transport," *Soviet Studies*, vol. 31, no. 2 (1979), pp. 231–256.

Ekonomicheskaya gazeta [Economic gazette], no. 1, March 1981, January 1987.

Gluzhenko, T. B., *Morskoi transport SSSR* [Maritime transport USSR] (Moscow: Transport, 1984).

Gudok [Whistle], July 19, 1985.

Gustafson, Thane, *Reform in Soviet Politics: Lessons of Recent Policies Land and Water* (Cambridge: Cambridge University Press, 1981).

Hardt, John P., "Maritime Developments Involving the Soviet Union," in Joint Economic Committee, Congress of the United States, *Issues in East-West Commercial Relations* (Washington, D.C.: U.S. Government Printing Office, 1979).

Haywood, Richard M. *The Beginnings of Railway Development in Russia in the Reign of Nicholas I, 1835–1842* (Durham, N.C.: Duke University Press, 1969).

Hough, Jerry, "The Man and the System," *Problems of Communism*, vol. 25, no. 2 (March–April, 1976).

Hough, Jerry F., and Merle Fainsod, *How the Soviet Union is Governed* (Cambridge, Mass.: Harvard University Press, 1979).

Hunter, Holland, *Soviet Transport Experience: Its Lessons for Other Countries* (Washington, D.C.: The Brookings Institution, 1968).

Hunter, Holland, and Deborah Kaple, "Transport in Trouble," in *Soviet Economy in the 1980s: Problems and Prospects*, part I, U.S. Congress Joint Economic Committee (Washington, D.C.: U.S. Government Printing Office, 1983).

Ivanov, V. N., *Avtomobilnyi transport: Problemy, perspektivy* [Automobile transportation: Problems, perspectives] (Moscow: Transport, 1981).

Izvestiya, August 5, 1989.

Kazakhstanskaya Pravda [Kazakh pravda], April 24, 1987.

Khrushchev, A. T., and I. V. Nikol'skii, eds., *Ekonomicheskaya geografiya SSSR* [Economic geography of the USSR], part 1, 2nd ed. (Moscow: Moscow State University Press, 1985), pp. 241–265.

Kolesov, L. I. *Mezhotraslevyye problemy razvitiya transportnoi sistemy Sibiri i Dal'nego Vostoka* [Interbranch problems in the development of the transportation system of Siberia and the Far East] (Novosibirsk: Nauka, 1982).

Kontorovich, Vladimir, "Discipline and Growth in the Soviet Economy," *Problems of Communism*, vol. 34, no. 6 (November–December 1985), pp. 18–31.

Kovrigin, A. G., *Finansy zheleznodorozhnogo transporta* [Finances of railroad transportation], 2nd ed., (Moscow: Transport, 1984).

Krasnaya Zvezda [Red star], August 15, 1985; January 28, 1987.

Markova, A. N., *Transport SSSR: Osnovnyye etapy ego razvitiya* [Transportation USSR: Basic stages of its development] (Moscow: Nauka, 1977).

Narodnoye khoziaistvo SSSR [National economy USSR] (Moscow: annual statistical yearbook for the entire nation).

Narodnoye khoziaistvo [National economy] (annual statistical yearbook for each of the fifteen Soviet republics).

Nikitenko, V. G., and Y. G. Gutsev, *Transport v narodnokhoziaistvennom komplekse BSSR* [Transportation in the national-economic complex of the BSSR (Belorussia)] (Minsk: Nauka i Tekhnika, 1978).

North, Robert, *Transport in Western Siberia* (Vancouver: University of British Columbia Press, 1979).

Orlov, Boris Pavlovich, *Razvitiye transporta SSSR, 1917–1962: Istoriko-ekonomicheskii ocherk* [The development of transportation in the USSR, 1917–1962: Historical-economic overview] (Moscow: USSR Academy of Sciences, 1963).

Parker, W. H., "The Soviet Motor Industry," *Soviet Studies,* vol. 32, no. 4 (1980), pp. 515–541.

Petrov, E. V., and I. M. Aliksieva, *Statistika avtomobil'nogo transporta* [Statistics of automobile transportation] (Moscow: Transport, 1983).

Planovoye khoziaistvo [Planned economy], no. 6, 1978.

Pravda, February 19, 1985; August 29–30, 1985; October 9, 1985; June 6, 1987; December 18, 1987; January 22, 1989.

Problemy razvitiya transporta SSSR: Kompleksnaya ekspluatatsiya [Problems in the development of transportation in the USSR: Complex exploitation] (Moscow: Transport, 1983).

Rabochaya gazeta [Worker gazette], January 7, 1986.

Rechnoi transport [River transport], September 2, 1983.

Rezer, S. M., *Upravleniye transportnymi predpriyatiyami* [Administration of transportation enterprises] (Moscow: Nauka, 1982).

Sotsialisticheskaya industriya [Socialist industry].

Sovetskaya Latvia [Soviet Latvia], May 21, 1986.

Sovetskaya Rossiya [Soviet Russia], September 20, 1984.

Symons, Leslie, and Colin White, eds., *Russian Transport* (London: Bell, 1975).

Transport i sviaz': statisticheskii sbornik [Transportation and communications: Statistical handbook] (Moscow: Central Statistical Administration of the USSR Council of Ministers, 1957 and 1972).

Velikanov, D., "Avtomobil'nyi transport: Zadachi ego dal'neishego razvitiya" [Automobile transport: Goals of its further development], *Kommunist,* no. 15 (1983), pp. 70–79.

Westwood, J. N., *A History of Russian Railways* (London: George Allen & Unwin, 1964).

Whiting, Allen S., *Siberian Development and East Asia: Threat or Promise?* (Stanford: Stanford, University Press, 1981).

Williams, Ernest W., Jr., *Freight Transportation in the Soviet Union* (Princeton, N.J.: Princeton University Press, 1962).

Zarya Vostoka [Dawn of the east], November 17, 1985.

Zhelezko, S. N. *Sotsial'no-Demograficheskiye Problemy v zonye BAMa* [Social-demographic problems in the BAM zone] (Moscow: Statistika, 1980).

Zheleznodorozhnii transport SSSR v dokumentakh [Railroad transportation of the USSR in documents] (Moscow: Transport, 1957).

9

UNITED KINGDOM

William L. Waugh, Jr., and Jane P. Sweeney

Britain has been best known for its outward orientation during its centuries as a major sea power and world trader. This orientation toward the sea and empire, described by Alfred Thayer Mahan (1890), is ingrained in the British character, and the central role of London in the British social, economic, and political systems is certainly a major factor in British transport policy. One has also to consider Britain's central role in the Industrial Revolution and the impact that the growth of manufacturing and domestic trade had on the development of the nation. As the focal point of empire and nation, London became and continues to be the center of the transportation network in Britain, the principal sea and air terminal for overseas transport, and the principal land terminal for rail and roadway.

Internally, in the past decade in particular, transport policy has been shaped by the reversal of much of the Transport Act of 1947, which nationalized inland transport, and by the tension between the current government's preference for private-sector services and the long-standing political support for public-sector intervention to preserve essential services. The resulting debate has been fueled by the reorganization of local government in Britain since 1974. The thrust of that reform was to permit greater local discretion in policy making, including transportation, and to encourage more regional planning and coordination. Government policy more recently has deemphasized that local orientation in favor of greater reliance on private-sector answers to transportation needs and more centralized planning of limited national programs. As a response to public opposition to many programs, the procedures for reviewing and planning transportation programs, as well as permitting citizen participation in decision making, were reevaluated and revised (Adams: 129). As a result, public participation in decision making has declined significantly. The relationship between local and central governments is the theme of the case to follow involving South Yorkshire and subsidies for passenger buses. The context for that case will be provided in terms of the evolution of transport policy and its present form.

While the nationalization of transport services can be most closely associated with the Labour Party, which implemented the Transport Act of 1947, there has been support for such massive public-sector interventions within all three major parties. Pressures to achieve economies of scale, coordination of services during wartime, reductions in wasteful competition, preservation of the social service aspects of transport, targeting of investments, and improved industrial relations have precipitated most nationalizations (Thompson & Hunter: 8–12). More recently the need to maintain services in areas that may not provide sufficient economic incentive for private firms to operate has also come into play.

The political debate centers on the proper role of the government in the transport system, including its role in developing the national "motorway" or expressway system; influencing the distribution of freight hauling among inland waterway, roadway, and rail systems, and among port facilities; stimulating the development of intercity passenger rail service to alleviate congestion problems on the roadways; maintaining passenger and freight transport services in rural areas; encouraging the development of more private air service among the major cities, as well as expanding existing facilities; and coordinating its own efforts with those of its European partners. The joint projects to develop the Concorde supersonic transport and expand its service and to connect Britain and the Continent via the English Channel tunnel also are major political issues at the national level.

The following discussion of the evolution of the British transport system will provide context for the analysis of current transport policy and the South Yorkshire case.

BACKGROUND

British internal transport has been characterized as having had three principal phases: the eras of inland waterways (1750–1830), railroads (1830–1920), and highways (1920 to the present) (Fullerton, 1975). While national policy favored the focusing of resources on international trade and transport, the development of internal transportation networks tended to reinforce that orientation.

A flourishing coastal trade stimulated the development of a network of navigable waterways to connect factory towns and port facilities and to avoid the more dangerous sea routes. A series of Canal Acts between 1758 and 1803 promoted the development of the system for the short distance movement of bulk commodities by barge and narrow boat. Canals were initially built to transport coal and minerals from South Lancashire and other mining areas, especially in the north and midlands, to the major manufacturing centers and port cities, such as Liverpool. Indeed, manufacturing centers grew up near the waterways, taking advantage of the relatively inexpensive transport. The waterways also provided means of transporting fish and other goods from coastal trading centers into the interior. By 1830 Britain had approximately 6,500 kilometers (km) of navigable inland waterways and had opened much of the interior, including the Scottish Highlands, to canal trade. The last canal, the Manchester Ship Canal, was built between 1889 and 1894 (Fullerton: 10–13, 21–23).

As the Industrial Revolution progressed, the need for transportation, not constrained by the available canal and river networks, stimulated the development of a rail system. Railroads also offered a quicker means of delivering raw materials and finished goods. Between 1830 and 1850 the competition between railways and inland waterways demonstrated the advantages of the former. By 1848 all the major cities in Britain were accessible by rail, with Edinburgh and Holyhead (the transportation link with Ireland) being added to the system in 1850 and Cardiff added in 1852 (Fullerton: 16).

"Railway mania" accounted for the 3,600 km of rail in 1845–46 and 10,000 km in 1851. Without effective regulation there was little coordination of the building of railways. Small companies financed short lines and, without adequate study, many failed. A Railway Board was formed in 1844 to provide some regulation, but it was abolished in 1845. The rate of growth declined after 1852. By 1920, there were 32,700 km of rail in Britain—much redundant because of parallel lines between cities being run by competing companies. The approximately 200 railway companies slowly declined as economic competition intensified. In 1920 there were still 110 companies, but the fifteen largest owned 84 percent of the track. The competition was maintained at least in part by the Railway Act of 1844 which encouraged interregional, rather than intraregional, merger to prevent monopolies within regions.

From the 1920s on, the number and length of routes began to contract, largely as redundant routes were abandoned (Fullerton: 17–27). The remaining four large railways were nationalized in 1948 under the Transport Act of 1947, and management of the rail system was accomplished after 1962 by the British Railways Board. The board has been responsible for maintaining services to most parts of Great Britain, often with government subsidies for noneconomical routes, although most recently national policies have meant reduced subsidies (*Britain 1986:* 305). The British Railways Board Reports of 1963 and 1965 indicated that the railway system had been reduced to approximately 20,000 km (Fullerton: 36). That mileage slowly declined to 16,803 km in 1985. Figure 9.1 shows the nation's railroad network.

Notwithstanding the renewed interest in rail transport, the railway system's importance to the national transportation network was eclipsed by that of the

Figure 9.1
Railroad Network in the United Kingdom

Source: Chris Bushell, *Railway Directory & Year Book 1989* (Surrey, England: Reed Business Publishing, 1989), p. 70. Courtesy Reed Business Publishing, Ltd.

growing roadway system, by automobiles and trams and buses, after 1920. In 1920 there were approximately 288,000 km of roadways, most not well maintained and very few paved. Nonetheless, the number of automobiles increased to 1 million by 1930 and over 13 million by the 1970s (Fullerton: 30–32). By 1984, the road network had expanded to approximately 370,700 km with almost 3,000 km of motorways. Also by 1984 there were 20.8 million licensed vehicles on the road, including 17.7 million private automobiles and light trucks; 600,000 heavy trucks; 1.2 million motorcycles, scooters and mopeds; and 116,000 public passenger vehicles such as taxis (*Britain 1986:* 299). Intercity bus routes proved less expensive than railways in transporting people, and trucks supplanted trains in moving bulk commodities, particularly for short distances.

Britain was slow to develop an extensive highway system to support traffic. At least in part, that slowness can be attributable to the scarcity of resources caused by world wars I and II and the Depression. The principal reason, however, was that roads have been considered largely a local responsibility throughout much of the history of the automobile in Britain. The Ministry of Transport was formed in 1920 to provide subsidies for major intercity roadways and a few secondary roads, but county councils bore much of the responsibility for building and maintaining roads.

Local property taxes provided most of the funding, and most traffic, until after World War II, was local. When the automobile was introduced in numbers in the early 1900s, motorists supported a road fund to maintain local roads. The Development and Road Improvement Fund Bill was passed by Parliament in 1909 to collect taxes for road building and maintenance, and the Road Board was created the following year to distribute the funds to local governments. There was very little real planning; the monies were principally spent for the paving of local roads. The board itself was very slow to dispense funds, and the road fund was undermined when the Transport Ministry, which was dominated by railroad people, eliminated the gas tax which provided a large part of the monies. The road fund was raided by Winston Churchill in 1926 and 1927, and the fund was collapsed into the general fund in 1937. The Miscellaneous Financial Provisions Act of 1955 abolished the fund altogether (Dunn: 100–102).

Increasing automobile, truck, and bus traffic, however, prompted the national government to provide more funding for the national trunk roads in 1936 and again in 1948. The development of controlled-access four-lane roads known as motorways began in 1957 to connect the industrial centers. The national goal was to double the capacity of the motorway network between 1970 and 1990, having motorways within 16 km of all cities of 80,000 or more inhabitants (Fullerton: 32–38). But local funding exceeded national funding for roads and highways until 1959 when congestion in the urban areas and poor intercity roadways prompted the national government to act. National funding was doubled between 1960 and 1965 as the first sections of the motorway, the intercity expressway, system was being built. By 1970, expenditures were eight times

Table 9.1
Transportation Employment, 1948 and 1978

MODES YEARS	1948	1978
Sea Transport	165,000	84,000
Ports and Inland/ River Transport	160,000	75,000
Railways	576,000	216,000
Roadways	319,000	220,000

Source: D. Maltby and H. P. White, Transport Policy in the U.K. (London: Macmillan, 1982), pp. 6-8.

those of 1955. Road building had been a major focus in the platform of the Conservative Party in 1967 and 1970. However, funding decreased after 1970, and by 1975 local spending again exceeded national spending on roadways (Dunn: 106–107).

Air service from London to Paris and Brussels was established in 1929, and passenger service, albeit limited, was established among the largest cities in Britain by 1935. By the 1970s there were thirty-three airfields with significant commercial traffic (Fullerton: 41–42) and over 100 other licenced airfields. International flights, however, have been dominated by the two London airports, Heathrow and Gatwick, and the airports at Manchester and Glasgow. Other major airports are Aberdeen, Luton, Birmingham, Belfast (Aldergrove), Edinburgh, Newcastle upon Tyne, and East Midlands.

SOCIOECONOMIC DIMENSIONS OF THE TRANSPORTATION SYSTEM AND POLICY

The importance of the transport sector to the British economy has made transport policy a volatile issue at the national, regional, and local levels. As Table 9.1 indicates, the importance of the transport sector to British employment is considerable. Drastic reductions in employment in that sector since World War II have had a tremendous impact on the British economy. Nonetheless, as a 1977 White Paper on transport policy indicated, there is no coherent or clearly defined national policy and no clear public consensus on what should be done (Adams: 129–130).

Recent national transport policy in Great Britain has reflected the Thatcher government's overriding interest in stimulating economic competition and reducing the central government's role in operating public companies and authorities. The government's efforts have generally been in the direction of reducing public subsidies and insisting on using market mechanisms to determine locations and levels of service. Those efforts have been more successful in terms

Table 9.2
Modes of Transportation of Inland Freight (in percentages)

MODES YEARS	1970	1980	1985
Railways	10.5	9.4	9.0
Roadways	87.9	86.9	87.0
Waterways	0.4	0.3	0.5
Pipelines	0.1	3.2	3.5

Source: United Nations, Annual Bulletin of Transportation Statistics for Europe (New York: UN, 1980, 1986).

of freight transport than they have been in terms of passenger transportation, but they have caused a major reevaluation of the philosophy of transportation in Great Britain. At the same time there has been considerable interest in expanding the capacities of the air, rail, and roadway systems, particularly outside of London, to facilitate commerce and industrial development.

As the data in Tables 9.2, 9.3, and 9.4 indicate, rail freight and passenger service have been declining, roadway freight hauling and passenger service have been increasing steadily, and inland waterway and pipeline freight have increased. The most pronounced gains in the past fifteen to twenty years have been in the use of private passenger vehicles and the movement of goods via pipeline.

In terms of national policy toward roadways, the ''motorway box'' or ''ringway'' controversy in the London metropolitan area exemplifies the recent debates concerning how to deal with increasing congestion in the urban areas. The Conservative Party wanted a motorway box—three rings of expressways around London—that would have required the removal of 15,000 to 20,000 homes. A Labour win in the Greater London Council in 1973 curtailed those plans. Labour proposed limiting traffic in central London, limiting parking, special buses, bus and taxi lanes, pedestrian streets, and the like. The oil crisis in early 1970s preempted the issue. Increased emphasis on passenger rail ser-

Table 9.3
Freight Traffic Trends (in billions of ton-kilometers)

MODES YEARS	1970	1980	1985
Railways	24.5	17.6	16.0
Roadways	85.0	95.9	102.6
Inland Waterways	2.0	2.3	-
Pipelines	2.7	9.4	9.7

Source: United Nations, Annual Bulletin of Transportation Statistics for Europe (New York: UN, annual).

Table 9.4
Passenger Traffic Trends (in billions of passenger-kilometers)

MODES YEARS	1970	1980	1986
Railways	30.4	30.3	30.8
Roadways- Private Vehicles	264.0	431.0	430.0
Roadways- Public Vehicles	53.0	45.0	41.0

Source: United Nations, Annual Bulletin of Transportation Statistics for Europe (New York: UN, annual).

vice by the national government is now viewed as the preferred course to reduce traffic.

Despite efforts to increase rail transport, the length of usable track has been decreasing since World War II. As Table 9.5 indicates, the decrease has been considerable, particularly for freight transport. The increases in electrification of lines to over 24 percent of the total are mostly for intercity passenger service. Railway employment is only a fraction of what it was twenty years ago.

National railway policy is supporting increased emphasis on InterCity 125s (high-speed trains) that can operate at speeds up to 125 mph (*Britain 1986:* 305). Electrification of the railways and increasing the capacities of freight-hauling trains are also priorities. The Transport Act of 1981 encouraged privatization of the non-railway activities of British Rail, selling of nonessential properties, and greater reliance on competitive bidding for services (*Britain 1986:* 307).

By the 1970s approximately two-thirds of all freight was being moved by trucks rather than rails (Fullerton, 1975: 30–32). Traffic congestion and greatly increased haulage, however, have prompted the central government to attempt to divert heavy vehicles away from residential areas and central business districts, to reduce noise and pollution levels caused by heavy vehicles, and to encourage through grants the construction or modernization of railway lines and inland waterways to carry freight (Britain 1986: 302) (see Tables 9.6 and 9.7).

Bus service has declined in the past decade, particularly in rural areas where routes have not been economically viable for traditional bus service. There has been some experimentation encouraged by the central and local governments with minibuses, postbuses (mail vehicles carrying a few passengers), and ride-sharing. The Transport Act of 1980 sought to encourage more private-sector development of passenger services, including transferring the operations of the National Bus Company, the largest public-sector bus and coach operator with over fifty subsidiaries in England and Wales and some 14,000 buses, to the private sector. The act further sought the encouragement of competing bus lines

Table 9.5
Railways

CHARACTERISTICS YEARS	1960	1970	1980	1986
Length of Railways (Km)	29,562	18,989	17,983	17,010
Electrified Lines (% of Total)	6.9	16.7	20.7	24.4
Freight Lines (% of Total)	-	22.9	18.2	13.7
Passenger Traffic (Millions of Km)	407.0[1] 4.5[2]	315	346	330
Passenger Traffic (Millions)	-	824	736 (1979)	695
Freight Traffic (Millions of Km)	197.2[1] .8[2]	101	87.8 (1979)	68.0
Employees	514,500	214,500	212,300	15,800

Source: United Nations, Annual Bulletin of Transportation Statistics for Europe (New York: UN, annual).

Notes: 1. British Rail
2. Ulster Transit Authority

along the routes previously maintained by the National Bus Company. Local authorities are free to subsidize transportation for special populations, such as the elderly and handicapped. Taxi service was also encouraged in the act. Innovation and transition grants were made available to support the change over to private-sector operations in rural areas (*Britain 1986:* 304). Significant privatization of passenger transportation has not been achieved under the act, however, because of the high start-up costs of such systems and the economic viability of such businesses, particularly in rural areas (Barrett: 201–202). The breakup of the National Bus Company into its constituent parts, moreover, promises to reduce the feasibility of maintaining "social service," economically nonviable routes that have been subsidized by the more profitable routes (Glassborow: 109–110).

In freight hauling, national policy has supported greater use of inland waterways with some success, although the percentage of freight moved is still quite small (see Table 9.8). Increases in pipeline use have been dramatic, but still only represent a small portion of the total freight haulage and are largely restricted to the movement of petroleum products. The increases in coastal ship-

Table 9.6
Roadways in Britain

CHARACTERISTICS YEARS	1960	1970	1980	1986
Total Length (in Km)				
Motorways	604	1,133	2,573	3,080
Trunk Roads		13,948	12,463	-
Principal Roads		34,208	34,247	-
All Other		307,999	290,200	371,020
Expenditures for All Roads (Millions of Pounds Sterling)	504	802	1,979	3,182

Source: United Nations, Annual Bulletin of Transportation Statistics for Europe (New York: UN, annual).

ping, too, are due to the transport of North Sea oil. In terms of national policy toward the sea trade, the Rochdale Report of 1963 suggested encouraging greater use of the North Sea and English Channel ports, at the expense of Bristol, Manchester, Glasgow, and other Irish Sea ports. In recent years, however, seaport trade has been declining (see Table 9.9), except for the movement of petroleum through the North Sea ports.

In terms of the development of a coherent transportation network, the Royal Commission on Transport in 1920 urged greater integration of Britain's transportation systems as a goal of national policy. As a response there were some efforts to increase coordination and integration of the services providing passenger transport in the London metropolitan area in the 1930s through a special

Table 9.7
Road Vehicles

VEHICLES YEARS	1970	1980	1986
Mopeds	443,033	473,000	433,400
Motorcycles	700,300	937,000	821,400
Automobiles, including Taxis	11,604,457	15,350,000	18,360,000
Coaches, Buses, Tolleys	79,267	76,000	76,300

Source: United Nations, Annual Bulletin of Transportation Statistics for Europe (New York: UN, annual).

Table 9.8
Waterways, Seaports, and Pipelines

CHARACTERISTICS YEARS	1970	1980	1986
Inland Waterway, Freight Carried (In Millions of Tons)	11.0	9.0	7.5
Inland Waterway (In Million Ton-Kilometers)	2,000.0	2,300.0	2,500.0
Seaports, In-Out Freight (In Millions of Tons)	250.2	231.6	299.0
Coastal Shipping (In Millions of Ton-Kilometers, including One-Port Traffic)	24.0	51.3	56.3 (1983)
Coastal Shipping, National Traffic (In Millions of Tons Unloaded, including One-Port Traffic)	73.0	102.8	79.2
Sea Transport (In Millions of Tons)	121.5	-	153.6
Pipelines (Km)	1,634.0	3,166.0	3,642.0
Pipelines (Ton-Kilometers)	2,665.0	9,426.0	9,730.0

Source: United Nations, Annual Bulletin of Transportation Statistics for Europe (New York: UN, annual).

authority. Integration of services again became an issue in the 1960s, and the 1968 Transport Act created similar authorities in five other metropolitan areas, including providing funding for bus-rail terminals. Concern about deteriorating transport services precipitated additional national funding for ''socially necessary'' rail services and subsidies for bus routes. By the 1970s there was increased interest in providing more funding for public transportation, particularly electrified railways, and decreasing the emphasis on road building.

Seven of the largest airports, representing the vast majority of the passengers and air cargo, are managed by the British Airports Authority (BAA). Here, too, the government has been seeking to privatize the airports under BAA management. Aldergrove Airport is managed by Northern Ireland Airports Ltd.,

Table 9.9
Traffic at Selected Seaports (millions of tons loaded and unloaded)

PORT YEAR	1970	1980	1982
Immingham/ Grimsby	23.7	22.2	27.6
Liverpool/ Garston	30.7	13.5	11.5
London	63.8	54.2	46.9
Southampton	28.2	24.0	21.0
Tees and Hartlepool	22.7	39.4	35.7

Source: United Nations, Annual Bulletin of Transportation Statistics for Europe (New York: UN, annual).

and eight airports in Scotland are controlled by the Civil Aviation Authority, but most of the other airports are owned and managed by local airport authorities (*Britain 1986:* 316).

Privatization and competition have been the foci of national policies concerning airline operations, as well as policies relative to railways. The government intends to sell its remaining shares in British Airways, a limited public company. British Airways provides service to some seventy-two nations and in 1984 carried 18.2 million passengers in contrast to the 6.8 million passengers carried by independent lines, approximately one-third by British Caledonian Airways, and 15.1 million passengers on charter flights (*Britain 1986:* 314). British Air purchased British Caledonia in 1988 after lengthy debate.

In recent years transportation policy in Britain has focused on the role of the national government in promoting and supporting transport networks. The Thatcher government has been a proponent of more private-sector initiatives. The clearest examples of that reorientation have been in the airline industry. International air service had been largely the province of the British Overseas Airways Corporation (BOAC) and British European Airways Corporation (BEA), but the growth of privately owned, but government subsidized, airlines has changed that picture considerably in the last decade.

Policy relative to transportation manufacturing has followed the same pattern. Threatened industries were initially subsidized and then nationalized, particularly those representing large defense contractors such as Rolls-Royce Ltd. and British Aerospace which were placed under the National Enterprise Board (NEB) along with British Shipbuilders. The government under Prime Minister Margaret Thatcher, however, has transferred Rolls-Royce and British Leyland from the NEB to the Department of Trade and Industry to emphasize the role of those enterprises in economic development and trade and privatized British Aerospace in 1981 (Maltby & White: 168–170).

In terms of government policy within the context of the European Community (EC), support has been given to the expansion of competitive transport services. Transport was one of the areas of cooperation and nondiscrimination specifically addressed in the Rome Treaty (Article 3) (Bayliss, 1979). However, Britain is less involved in coordinating its rail, roadway, and inland waterway networks with those of the other EC members than it is involved in the coordination of sea and air transport networks. In fact, it is argued that the strength of the British shipping capacity mitigates against other EC members' developing strong shipping industries. Britain can dominate shipping among and from the EC member states. Particularly given the history of British sea transport and the importance assigned it by the government, the encouragement of competition within the EC would tend to strengthen Britain's own industries. Increasing competition in air transport is more problematic because other EC members are seeking to protect their own national airlines. The Netherlands and Britain have been the only EC members to advocate greater cooperation (Erdmenger: 6–8). British and Dutch emphasis on road transport has also been criticized as inconsistent with the emphasis on railways in other member states which complicates the development of an integrated system (Erdmenger: 17).

The decades of economic decline in Great Britain have generally meant reduced funding for national transportation activities across the board. During the 1970s, government expenditures for transportation were reduced from 5.5 percent of total expenditures to 4.5 percent. Transport is not a major area of expenditure, in other words (Maltby & White: 31–33). Fifty percent of public funding has been transfers from the national government to local governments, most through the Rate Support Grants. Additional direct funding is provided to local authorities through the Transport Supplementary Grants (see case study to follow for an explanation of TSGs), and special funding for rail services is provided through the Public Service Obligation Grant. In 1979–80, 20 percent or £616 million of public expenditures went to British Rail, the National Freight Corporation, Scottish Bus Group, and the National Bus Company; 17 percent or £519 million of expenditures went for the construction and maintenance of the motorways and trunk roads; and fully 57 percent or £1,761 million of expenditures were spent on local transport (with 21 percent going for fare subsidies) (Maltby & White: 35).

The Thatcher government has tried to shift more of the fiscal burden for transportation to county and municipal governments and to the private sector. Reductions in services and increased fares have offset some of the costs of subsidy, but the fragmentation of the transport authorities and the separation of economically viable and nonviable services have meant increased pressure to eliminate the latter rather than permit cross-subsidy (i.e., profit-making services or routes making up for losses on other services or routes). The largest problem has been the lack of investment capital, although loans through the EEC's European Investment Bank have helped somewhat. The overriding strategy has been to eliminate government subsidies of freight service and intercity passenger service and to reduce the subsidies for other passenger services. Funding levels are generally determined by analyses of the levels of congestion or traffic (Maltby & White: 178–180).

During the spring of 1988 work began on the Eurotunnel, actually three tunnels, to span the 22 miles of the English Channel. While the Thatcher government is supportive of the joint British-French effort, the approximately $11 billion project is being privately financed with $9.2 billion in loans (with the largest portion, 23 percent, coming from Japanese banks) and $1.4 billion in stock. Completion of the project is expected in 1993. It is expected that 16.5 million rail passengers will use the tunnels during the first year, and 7 million tons of freight will be transported. Rail shuttles will be used to move automobiles and trucks through the tunnels. The project has generated some controversy in southeastern England because of the need to develop roadway and rail links to the British terminal. Environmentalists and others oppose that sort of development of the Kent countryside. There is also some fear that the Eurotunnel will mean unemployment and economic decline in the Channel ports and among the firms operating the ferries between England and the Continent. In France, the project is viewed as a boon to the economically depressed north with construction providing employment and economic development following the movement of goods and people to and from the French terminal. Europeans also see the project as a potentially positive factor in the economic and political integration of the European Community, as the English Channel becomes less of a geographic barrier to interaction (Vita: 32A).

POLITICAL DIMENSIONS OF THE TRANSPORTATION SYSTEM AND POLICY

Roadway financing was reorganized when local governments were reorganized in 1974. Prior to the reorganization, the national government assumed responsibility for providing general funding for roadways and provided categorical grants for specific kinds of roads and means of transportation. In 1974 those intergovernmental transfers were consolidated into Transport Supplementary Grants (TSGs) which were designed to permit greater discretion by the local governments. Very similar to the A-95 grant review being used in the United States during the 1970s, the block grants or TSGs required that local governments plan expenditures based on local needs. Controversies quickly arose over local priorities and the allocation of available resources. The county officials viewed public transportation as an essential service that should not have to be self-supporting (Gyford & James: 138–139; Alexander: 157).

The Labour Party had campaigned for country office on a platform that included free bus service, and, as a step toward accomplishing that, froze bus fares when they assumed local office in 1974. The county subsidized bus fares to hold them at the same level. The national policy of the Labour government, however, was that transportation services should be self-supporting to reduce public expenditure (Gyford & James: 139).

Meetings were held between officials of the government in London and the Labour government in South Yorkshire in September of 1975. The local officials pursued the matter through the party organization. The Minister of Transport, Dr. John Gilbert, went to South Yorkshire to discuss the issue in April 1976 but was not successful in resolving it. The local officials reaffirmed the importance of local autonomy and discretion as well as the principle of transportation as an essential public service (Gyford & James: 140).

Economic crisis during the summer of 1976 brought the issue to the fore. A devaluation of the pound necessitated massive loans from United States and Western European banks and from the International Monetary Fund. The conditions of the IMF loans required reductions in public spending. At the same time, the Ministry of Transport was reorganized in 1976 and the incoming U.S. Secretary of State, William Rodgers, was committed to the reductions in spending (Gyford & James: 140–141).

Meetings were held in the ensuing months as both sides tried to reconcile their differences and/or to gain sufficient political advantage to win the conflict. At issue were the county's expenditure estimates and program for 1977–78 which would determine the TSG settlement. The other counties in the region had accepted the government's ceiling on expenditures and adjusted their estimates accordingly. When the allocation of funds was made, South Yorkshire's refusal to conform cost the county over 700,000 pounds that they would have received if the council had cooperated with the government. The stand on principle was costly for South Yorkshire, and the reduction of funding as a punishment for the county was resented by the other governments and authorities in the region. South Yorkshire's officials pursued the matter of the punishment through the district's representatives in Parliament and the party's local government conference during early 1977. That support was forthcoming at the party's annual conference in the fall. The conference sided with the local councils and their pursuit of socialist objectives (Gyford & James: 141–146).

The impasse was resolved when South Yorkshire submitted its expenditure program for 1978–79. The expenditures did not include most of the subsidies being provided for bus service; rather, those expenditures were carried in the county council's general budget. The expenditure program was approved and full TSG funding was resumed (Gyford & James: 146). This case provides an interesting and telling view of British transport policy. The reorganization of local government was intended to provide greater autonomy to local authorities. The party system, too, should have suggested greater bottom-up policy making as, indeed, South Yorkshire represented a stronghold of Labour support. The success of South Yorkshire in circumventing the will of the Labour government in Parliament is one of the reasons why the current policy has had to adjust to local and regional concerns rather than simply providing national solutions to transport problems. National policy was to encourage regional development and autonomy, and the price has been the loss of national coordination and planning.

TRANSPORTATION POLICY ORGANIZATION AND PROCESS

The administration of British transport policy is illustrated in Figure 9.2.While Parliament is the ultimate determinant of transport policy, the incumbent government sets policy and is responsible for administering programs. The major structures and procedures of current British transport policy have been established by a series of transportation acts, largely originating since World War II.

The reorganization of local government in 1974 and concomitant reforms in local finance have changed the central government role in transport policy and finance by increasing the reliance on grants to local authorities to support road building and maintenance (Gyford & James: 138).

Administratively, the Secretary of State for Transport is responsible for motorways in England, the Secretary of State for Scotland is responsible for those trunk roads in Scotland, the Secretary of State for Wales does the same for Wales, and the Northern Ireland Department of the Environment is the responsible body for building and maintaining both trunk and nontrunk public roads in that jurisdiction. County councils in England and Wales and regional or islands councils in Scotland have been responsible for secondary or nontrunk roads.

Support for research on roadway construction, traffic engineering, road safety, and other transportation concerns is provided by the central government through the Transport and Road Research Laboratory of the Department of Transport (*Britain 1986:* 300).

Transportation planning and coordination is achieved on the local level by Passenger Transport Authorities (PTAs) with the support of technical and administrative staff through the Passenger Transport Executives (PTEs). The PTEs are responsible for preparing the expenditure estimates necessary to apply for annual transport supplementary grants from the central government.

Although there have been some changes in the structure of public transportation in Britain under the Thatcher government, the largest part of national rail, bus, and air transportation and much of national freight transport have been the responsibility of publicly owned agencies. Indeed, local public transportation authorities still administer many ports, airports, and other facilities. For example, underground railway services are currently maintained in London, Glasgow, and Liverpool by independent authorities, and a light transit system has recently been built in Tyneside with the electrification of two rail lines (*Britain 1986:* 307).

Figure 9.2
The Structure of Transport Administration and Policy

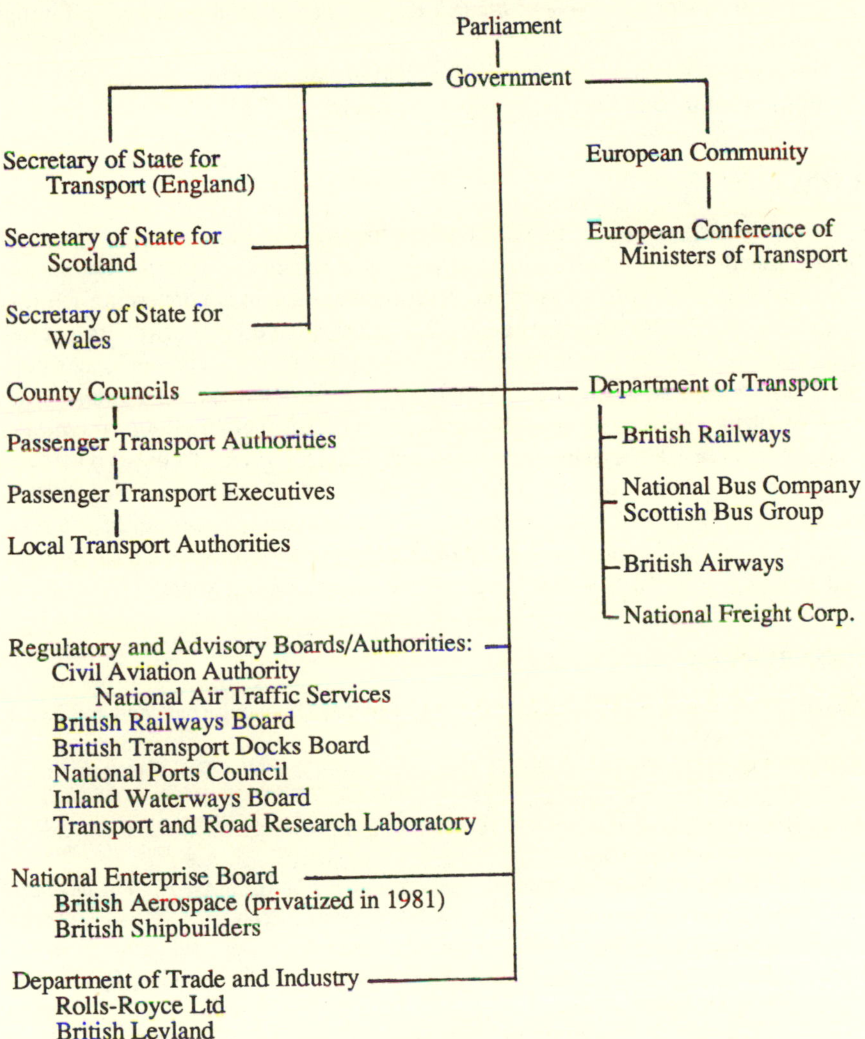

The Civil Aviation Authority is charged with maintaining air safety, including licensing and training of personnel and assuring airworthiness, and the National Air Traffic Services is responsible for traffic flow and safety (*Britain 1986:* 314–315).

Because of economic problems, transportation-related manufacturing has also been within the government province. The National Enterprise Board (NEB) has been responsible for overseeing the public corporations, including British Aerospace (until it was privatized in 1981), British Shipbuilders, and British

Leyland (until it was transferred to the Department of Trade and Industry by the Thatcher government). Rolls-Royce Ltd., a major defense contractor, was also brought under government control to prevent financial collapse or foreign ownership.

The government coordinates British transport policy within the context of the European Community and the European Conference of Ministers of Transport.

CONCLUSION

British transport policy in recent years has largely been one of decreased public spending and involvement and increased reliance on the private sector. The Thatcher government has raised fundamental questions concerning the role of government in the transport sector. While there have been efforts to coordinate and plan transportation networks, to coordinate with economic development efforts, there is no clear national policy as to what should be done. The strategy of the present government has been to either abolish public freight and passenger service altogether, transferring profitable services to the private sector, or to require that financial viability be achieved. The notions that transportation should be a social service and "essential services," particularly in rural areas and for special populations, should be subsidized have been challenged and should be central to the political debate in the coming years.

REFERENCES

Adams, John, *Transport Planning: Vision and Practice* (London: Routledge and Kegan Paul, 1981).

Aldcroft, Derek H., *Studies in British Transport History, 1870–1970* (Newton Abbot, England: David & Charles, 1974).

Alexander, Alan, *Local Government in Britain Since Reorganization* (London: George Allen & Unwin, 1982).

Barrett, B.M.M., "United Kingdom," *Public Transport in Rural Areas: Scheduled and Non-Scheduled Services,* Round Table 65 (Paris: Economic Research Center, European Conference of Ministers of Transport, 1984), pp. 197–254.

Bayliss, Brian T., *Planning and Control in the Transport Sector* (London: Gower Publishing Company, 1981).

———, "Transport in the European Communities," *Journal of Transport Economics and Policy,* vol. 23 (January 1979), pp. 25–43.

Britain 1986: An Official Handbook, "Transport and Communications" (London: Central Office of Information, Reference Services, 1986).

Buchanan, Malcolm, Nicholas Bursey, Kingsley Lewis, and Paul Mullen, *Transport Planning for Greater London* (Farnborough, England: Saxon House, 1980).

Dunn, James A., Jr., *Miles to Go: European and American Transportation Policies* (Cambridge, Mass., and London: The MIT Press, 1981).

Dyos, H. J., and D. H. Aldcroft, *British Transport: An Economic Survey from the Seventeenth Century to the Twentieth* (Leicester, England: Leicester University Press, 1969).

Erdmenger, Jurgen, *The European Community Transport Policy towards a Common Transport Policy* (London: Gower Publishing Company, 1983). Originally published as *EG unterweg-Wegezur Gemeinsamen Verkehrspolitik* (Baden-Baden: NOMOS, Verlagsgesellschaft, 1981).

European Conference of Ministers of Transport, *1982 Transport Statistical Series: Trends in Investment, Infrastructure, Rolling Stock, and Traffic* (Paris: ECMT, 1985).

Fullerton, Brian, *The Development of British Transport Networks* (London: Oxford University Press, 1975).

Glaiser, Stephen, and Coriane Mulley, *Public Control of the British Bus Industry* (London: Gower Publishing Company, 1983).

Glassborow, D. W., "The Constraints Imposed by Physical Planning on Regional Transport Organisation: Report on Some Aspects of British Experience in Recent Years," *The Regionalisation of Transport and Regional Planning in Practice Seminar,* Council of Europe, Strasbourg, December 5–6, 1983, pp. 107–130.

Gyford, John, and Mari James, *National Parties and Local Politics* (London: George Allen & Unwin, 1983).

"London Transport and Traffic," Reference Services, Central Office of Information (London), Report No. 125/83 (October 1983).

Mahan, Alfred Thayer, *The Influence of Seapower upon History* (Boston: Little, Brown, 1890).

Maltby, D., and H. P. White, *Transport Policy in the U.K.* (London: Macmillan, 1982).

Richards, Peter G., *The Local Government System* (London: George Allen & Unwin, 1983).

"Road Safety in Britain," Reference Services, Central Office of Information (London), Report No. 45/86 (July 1986).

Robson, William A., *The Development of Local Government* (Westport, Conn.: Greenwood Press, 1978).

Smith, Robert G., *Ad Hoc Governments: Special Purpose Transportation Authorities in Britain and the United States* (Beverly Hills, Calif.: Sage Publications, 1974).

Stewart, John, *Local Government: The Conditions of Local Choice* (London: George Allen & Unwin, 1983).

Thompson, A.W.J., and L. C. Hunter, *The Nationalized Transport Industries* (London: Heinemann Educational Books, 1973).

United Nations, *Annual Bulletin of Transport Statistics for Europe* (New York: UN, annual).

Vita, Mathew C., "Old Foes Channel Energies for Tunnel," *Atlanta Journal/Atlanta Constitution,* July 3, 1988.

10

UNITED STATES

Frank McKenna and David Anderson

BACKGROUND

The United States transportation system is possibly the most extensive networks of highways, railways, rivers, and air systems in any country. Indeed, the productivity, protection, and economic progress of the country depend largely on its transportation system and policy. However, national transportation policy almost defies definition. While the components are readily identifiable, the combined meaning is at best elusive. "Past, as well as contemporary, studies have reached the ineluctable conclusion that transportation policy is uncoordinated, imbalanced, inconsistent, and/or, incoherent; recommendations are often in the form of suggestions, and a call for additional research is ubiquitous" (Levine, 1978: 2). After 100 years, the concept of a national transportation policy seems to escape scholars and the public despite the existence of a statement on national transportation policy. However, because of the extensive involvement of the private sector in the development of U.S. transport systems, it is understandable that policy is less clearly defined than in other countries.

This chapter provides a historical overview of U.S. transportation system development and discusses the trends affecting U.S. national transportation policy. By providing an overview of how the main modes of water, rail, roads, and air transit developed, their impact on the formulation of this policy can be shown. The economic, ideological, political, sociocultural, and technological factors impacting U.S. transportation policy are also discussed in their historical context. The following will illustrate the extensive involvement of the private sector in system development and the corresponding fragmented development of U.S. transportation policy. This chapter will conclude by noting some of the future transportation issues that need attention by the U.S. Department of Transportation and federal policymakers.

The prolonged lack of a cohesive national transportation policy had a pronounced effect on the development of U.S. transportation systems. In the absence of clear policy directives, the politics, technology, and economics of the free market system shaped the development of America's transportation networks.

In the United States, transportation systems have traditionally been developed at the behest of the private sector. The transportation system development has necessarily been tied closely to commerce. Indeed, the evolution of the transportation network has at times dictated geographical trends in the United States. For example, ''railroad towns'' exist not only where markets once did, but also at railroad intersections. Developing modes of transportation were frequently financed by private interests, so the profit motive was inherent in transportation patterns. This involvement resulted in a transportation system that extended toward new markets and population centers in an unplanned fashion (O'Sullivan, 1980). Ideally, the concept of intermodal transportation would have been a national priority. Instead, the private sector dominated decision-making processes by effective lobbying or by taking actual financial control of the development process.

America developed as an idustrialized nation earlier than other countries, except England. With little historical perspective to utilize in planning for the massive urban growth of the eighteenth and nineteenth centuries, growth in the United States took place with little regard for the efficient, effective and equitable use of intermodal transportation. Researchers have come to a variety of conclusions on this matter that frequently ignore or deny previous studies (Schaeffer & Sclar, 1980; Michaels, 1980). The fact remains that Americans routinely deal with traffic jams and flight delays while low usage continues of the rail and water transportation systems. These are indicators of poor public transportation systems and intermodal coordination.

The advent of the internal combustion engine gave rise to additional freedoms unknown in many countries. The technology greatly affected American society. The resulting changes in urban and geographical settling trends made the existing fixed-line forms of transportation less useful if not somewhat impractical for many potential public transportation users. The flexibility and autonomy that automobiles brought to the American public greatly affected society and created vast public health, safety and welfare concerns, including air and noise pollution (Luna, 1971: 3). Settling patterns were accompanied by poor planning in the fixed-line transportation systems, which saw the systems become less popular and practical for the suburban public.

The military played an important role in the development of the interstate and defense highway system. The military and its political allies combined resources to encourage the development of better, faster, and more economical means of transporting both people and goods (Luna, 1971: 6). In 1983, the interstate highway system (43,028 miles) accounted for only 1 percent of the total U.S. roadways; however, 20 percent of all road travel occurs on this system which is scheduled for completion in 1991 (Highway Statistics Division, 1988). The military presence in national transportation policy brought about what is probably the most well-planned sector of the transportation system (see Figure 10.1). The military-industrial complex, as it is known, has also created a host of political accountability problems. It is not uncommon to hear of delays in marketing of innovative technologies, sweetheart contracts, and influence peddling attributed to this mutually beneficial relationship.

Water transportation was the first mode of public transportation that was used on a large-scale basis by industry for the movement of goods. Compared to the land travel available during colonial days, waterways provided an inexpensive and reasonably reliable method for transportation of goods and passengers. Seafaring vessels played an integral part in the development of the commerce of the United States as a developing nation. The population and commerce of the colonial United States was geographically quite limited to areas accessible by water for many years (Luna, 1971; Frankel, 1982). The colonies were dependent on England for many goods and products.

The introduction of the steam-powered engine and the steamboat proved to be the first major technological breakthrough in water transportation. Steamboats made river transportation much faster and more economical. The construction of various canal systems by the government contributed to the development of water transportation and led to the settling of certain areas of the country. The canals served as feeder routes to the rivers and created new passages for commerce among existing markets. One of the most notable was the Erie Canal system which connected New York City to the Great Lakes. From the Great Lakes, travelers could access the Ohio and Mississippi rivers by means of the Miami-Erie canal system in western Ohio. The canals made barge travel and trade between New York and New Orleans possible through the interior water routes of the country. Many other markets of the interior continent were made accessible through the canal-river network. The heyday of the canal system was between 1825 and 1850 when the canal systems provided the most economical means of transportation.

As a result of the new water transportation routes in the nineteenth century, trading markets shifted. The trade in the Northwest Territory (as the region including Ohio was called) shifted more toward these markets and away from the southern markets. This reorientation in the economy of the upper Mississippi valley and the Great Lakes region set the stage for the polarization of the economy and the polity of a country. This economic tension became a factor leading to the U.S. Civil War (O'Sullivan, 1980: 61).

During the 1830s, the railroads were just becoming popular and receiving

Figure 10.1
The National System of Interstate and Defense Highways
(status of improvement as of June 30, 1989)

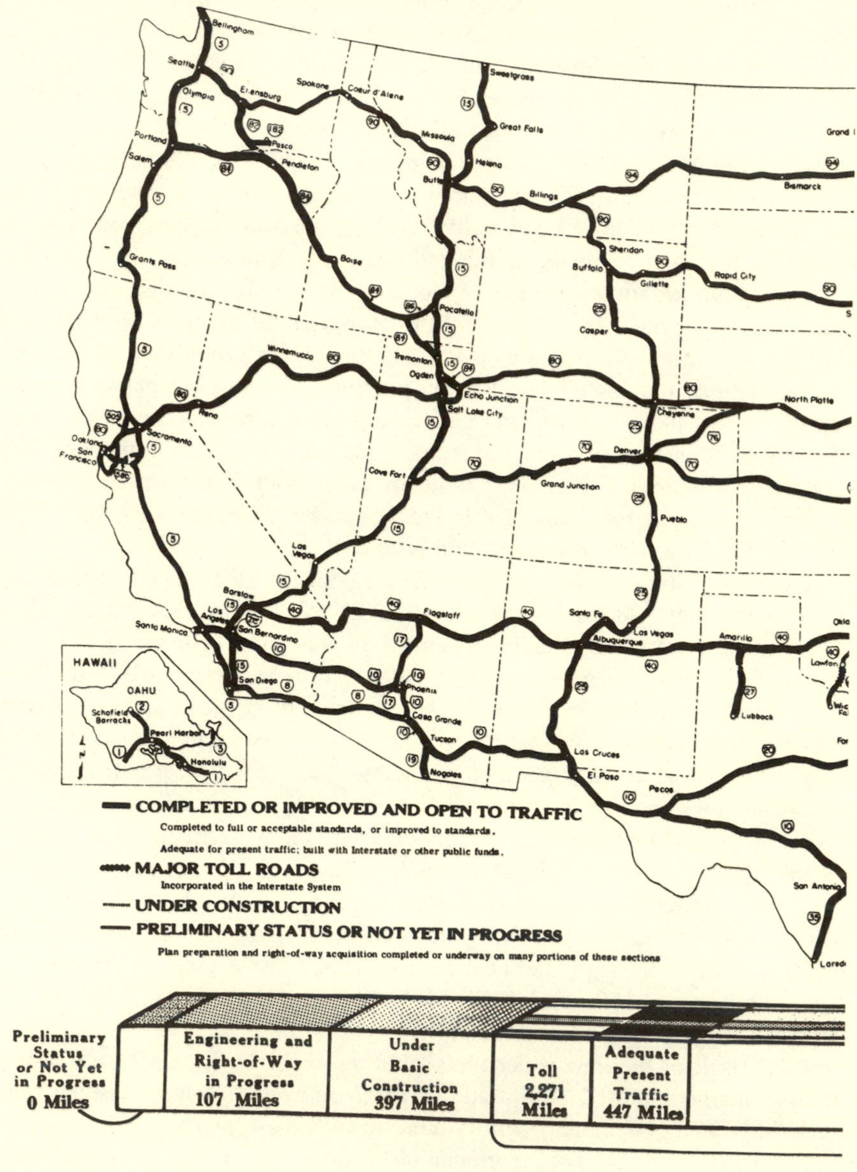

Source: U.S. Department of Transportation, Federal Highway Administration, Washington, D.C.

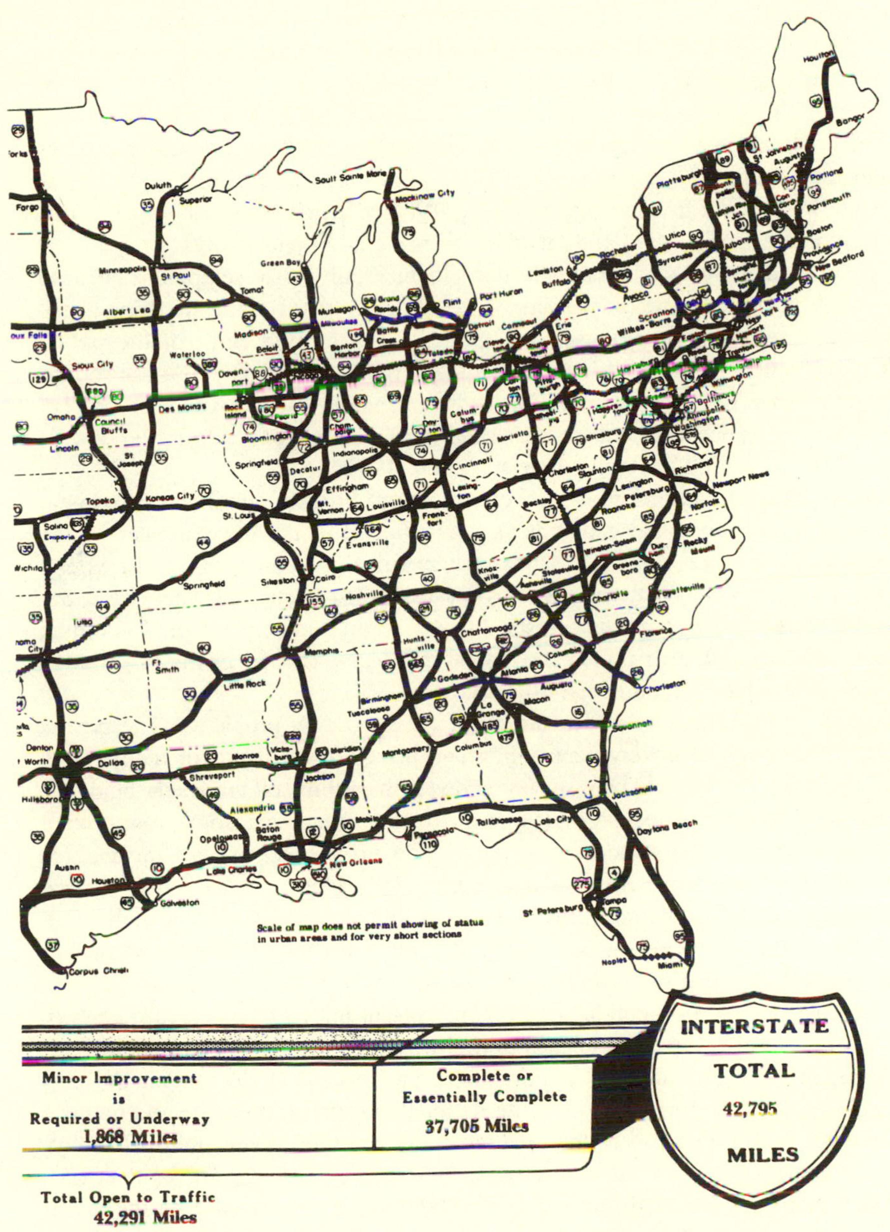
Scale of map does not permit showing of status in urban areas and for very short sections
Minor Improvement is Required or Underway 1,868 Miles
Complete or Essentially Complete 37,705 Miles
INTERSTATE
TOTAL
42,795
MILES
Total Open to Traffic 42,291 Miles

regular usage. The earliest routes served as feeders to the waterways and generally radiated from these important transportation centers. To this day these routes serve as important commercial intermodal transition points. Railroad construction grew rapidly between 1870 and 1890. The rail pattern was so complete by that time, there have been relatively few changes in the country's rail pattern since (Luna, 1971: 7). See Figure 10.2 for a map of the current system. Only about half of all the railroad investments came from state and local governments. Development was helped slightly more by the southern states than the northern states. Frequently, half of a railroad company's stock was owned by English investors (O'Sullivan, 1980: 65). These investors were primarily interested in developing markets to make additional profits.

State land grants were routinely used to lure railroad development because railroads meant economic expansion. One of the most revealing statistics of the U.S. government's intentions is the grant of 131 million acres of the public domain, with a right-of-way that extended 6 miles, to encourage a transcontinental railroad network. In return the federal government received a 20 percent reduction in the cost of mail delivery and a 50 percent reduction in the cost of all other freight and passenger service (Luna, 1971: 8).

While the railroads, along with their associated infrastructural and equipment expansion, proved to be economical and valuable in the development of the country, there were various instances when a railroad company would extend lines for purely speculative reasons. For example, many rail lines were designed to terminate at military posts, but some rail companies would continue their lines beyond such points and create company railroad towns in order to achieve speculative commercial objectives.

In 1807, Congress ordered a survey of transportation problems. The results formed the basis of government policy and private investment for many years (O'Sullivan, 1980: 65). This survey showed the utility of the roads being financed by state and local governments. It also noted that some roads were financed through the collection of tolls. The private sector had pushed for macadamized roads which were made with "macadam," a hardened surface allowing greater speeds and heavier loads with less susceptibility to inclement weather. The private sector believed that "toll roads" were worthy of investment and thus began the popularity of the turnpike.

The national preoccupation with laying rails in the latter nineteenth century set the stage for a similar emphasis in highway construction. Urban road building began to receive federal support under the Federal Highway Act of 1944 (Friedlaender & Simpson, 1978). The national system of interstate and defense highways was a response to the upsurge in automotive travel, political lobbying, and cries for the "national defense." The interstate system, as it is now called, is 40,000 miles of limited access highways that were built on the premise of being faster and safer routes for transit than the existing roadways. Proponents also argued that the interstate system would alleviate congestion in the urban areas by circumventing major cities with bypasses and beltways. This

Figure 10.2
Railroad Network in the United States

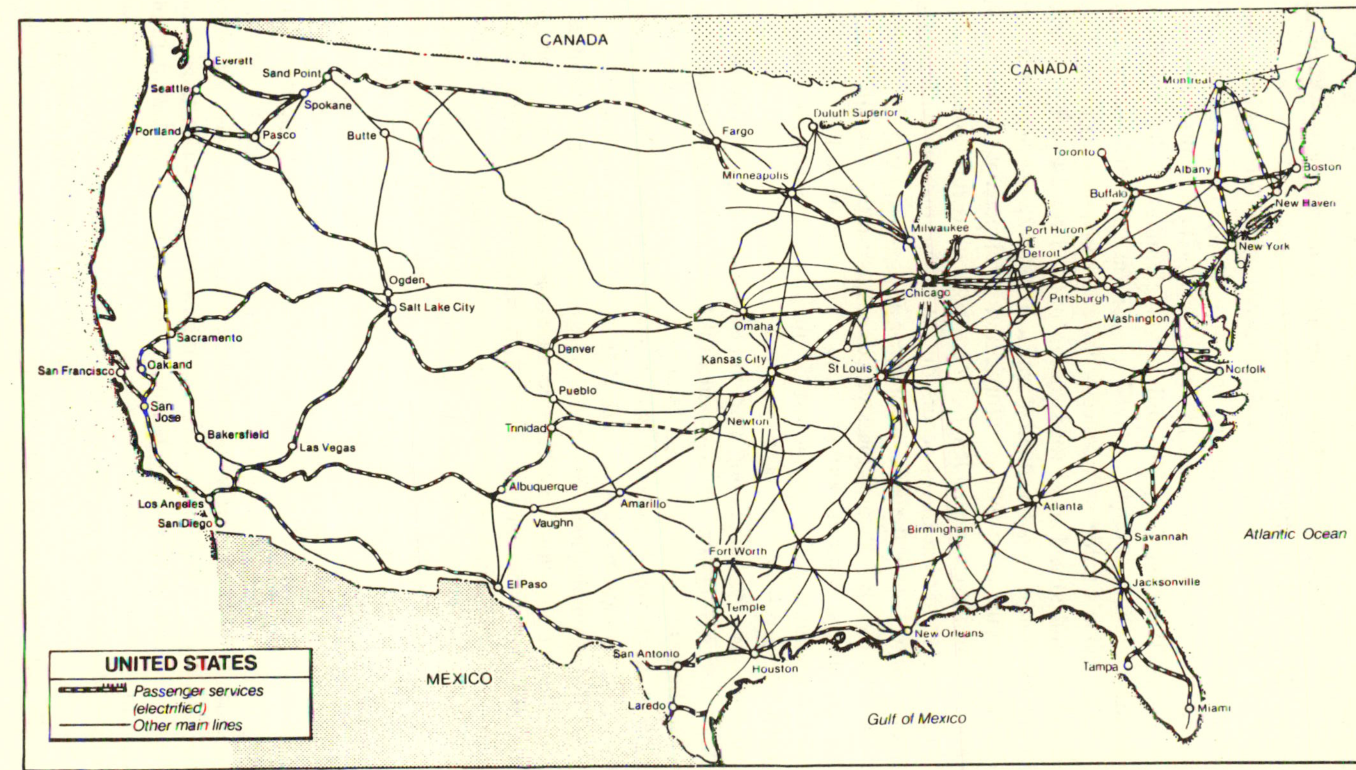

Source: Chris Bushell, *Railway Directory & Year Book 1989* (Surrey, England: Reed Business Publishing, 1989), pp. 162–163. Courtesy Reed Business Publishing, Ltd.

system serves as the primary network for commerce as well as for military transit routes.

As of 1983, the United States had 3,879,638 miles of roadways, of which 69 percent (22,677,527 miles) was considered "locals," 21 percent (806,851 miles) "collectors," and 9 percent (352,232 miles) "other arterials," with a slim 1 percent (43,028 miles) serving the interstate system (Federal Highway Administration, hereafter FHA: 2). In 1983 this 1 percent of the nation's roadways received 20 percent (335,882 million vehicle-miles) of the nation's total vehicular travel. Other arterials received 49 percent (803,967 million vehicle-miles) of this nation's traffic with collector streets receiving 17 percent (287,185 million vehicle miles) and local roads being utilized for 14 percent (222,072 million vehicle-miles) of all vehicular traffic (FHA: 2). Review of available statistics shows some other telltale information: 17.1 percent of this country's roadways are considered urban, leaving 82.9 percent as rural roadways; however, 57.5 percent of total travel occurs on the urban roadway with only 42.5 percent of all travel using the vast majority of all roadways (nearly 83 percent) (FHA: 2). This clearly indicates massive congestion in those highly urbanized areas of the country. More important, these statistics point to the major failing of U.S. transportation policy: public use of mass transit systems in urban areas is far below the levels of other post-industrial countries.

Needless to say, the burgeoning auto industry had a considerable impact on the political process, not only in the industrial Midwest but also in the nation's capital (Snell, 1978). When the Ford Motor Company introduced mass production and interchangeable parts, by way of the assembly line, it was undoubtedly the major technological breakthrough of that period. When the Model T started rolling off the assembly lines, the price of automobiles dropped significantly. The ownership of an automobile became an economic reality of the times for many families. More and more middle-class Americans could afford the newest mode of transportation thanks to mass production and the related drop in cost.

Following World War II, the demand for automobiles increased significantly. Car production tripled during that decade, and by 1960, 77 percent of all households owned at least one car and were spending over 10 percent of family income on automobile travel (O'Sullivan, 1980: 77). The increased reliance on automobiles was accompanied by the continuing call for more and better roads.

The automobile industry's lobbying efforts over the years have had an increasingly significant impact on the consumer and the political process. As reliance on the automobile grew, the industry's clientele became synonymous with the American public. Improving the highways of America thus became politically wise and economically feasible. The auto industry was extremely successful in its lobbying efforts.

However, the downside to the government's assertive road building programs was that roads promoted increasingly diffused metropolitan areas (Lisco, 1981). U.S. metropolitan areas have continued to grow to amazing proportions, yet few, if any, of the largest metropolitan areas have adequate public transportation systems.

With employment opportunities so widely distributed, the present urban mass transit systems cannot possibly satisfy the public transportation needs of the American society (Baker, 1984). This piecemeal development of transportation systems in the United States has effectively created a situation where the automobile is virtually indispensable to the average household. In short, the automotive industry has affected government activity in such a manner as to guarantee itself a market for an indefinite period (Sclar, 1978). The diffusion of urban populations, with commuting distances of up to fifty miles, insures the automobile industry future markets as it proves to be the most convenient mode of transportation for the average commuter.

The air transportation industry developed as a result of the military uses of aircraft during World War I. After the war, the developing U.S. airline industry bought surplus government planes with an eye toward using them for cargo and passenger transport. Air travel has become immensely popular since that time. The commercial airline industry again revolutionized travel by cutting transit time significantly.

The first nonmilitary use of commercial airlines was by the U.S. government. The Kelly Act of 1925 encouraged the growth of the young airline industry by providing a government contract for mail service delivery. There was a stipulation in the act, however, that the airlines would provide passenger facilities (Luna, 1971: 11). Within a year this mode of travel became so popular that there was legislation passed that authorized the Secretary of Commerce to designate and establish civil airways and navigational facilities. It was not until the passage of the Federal Airport Act of 1946, some twenty-one years after the passage of the Kelly Act, which provided $520 million for airport improvements, that the federal government became involved in the actual operations of airports (Luna, 1971: 11)).

With the start of World War II, the private sector was again involved in government-financed research and development. In particular, much of this funding went for the development of technologically advanced aircraft. The transfer of such technological advances to the private sector after the war, combined with the increased demand for air travel, helped to usher in the contemporary era of air travel. Airline transportation is now the predominant mode of intercity passenger travel (Luna, 1971: 12).

U.S. military contracts helped to finance much of the research and development conducted by several notable airline companies. This assistance had a significant impact on modern air transportation capabilities. The development of the jet engine is probably the second most notable technological breakthrough in air transportation, behind the actual advent of flight. The use of jet engines not only has cut down travel times but also has had a significant impact on the amount and quality of services provided (e.g., more flights can be flown with fewer aircraft). Regulatory and safety issues, however, still need to be addressed before this industry can be considered as a more-than-adequate mode of transportation (Morrison & Winston, 1986). The increasing number of incidents of near-mid-air collisions and mechanical failures in the 1980s attests to this statement.

SOCIOECONOMIC DIMENSIONS OF THE TRANSPORTATION SYSTEM AND POLICY

America's transportation networks developed in a unique environment. The American capitalist system fostered a strong public-private cooperative relationship. The ideological concepts that are the very tenets of this political structure had, and continue to have, strong influences on the sociocultural values of the U.S. citizenry. By the very nature of the system, the socioeconomic profit incentives found Americans leading the way in almost all instances of technological advancement which improved transportation.

Historically, the American economy has encouraged the private sector to "take the lead" in many areas. Transportation was one such area. With profits to be made or lost, based upon transportation costs, industrialists have been quick to research and develop improved methods of transportation. This large, diversified, and plentiful country needed to be linked in many ways. The transportation systems continually implemented the latest technologies for the economic benefit of business and arguably for society. For decades technological breakthroughs were being implemented as quickly as possible. Inevitably, there were economic barriers; however, there were virtually no political barriers until late in the twentieth century. Public-private relationships have characterized the development of the U.S. transportation system with the principles of the free market system in an unregulated business environment being the norm. The U.S. government has been involved in, or actively encouraging, the development of improved modes of transportation by fostering a positive or favorable business climate to induce private-sector activity.

Transportation regulation for safety concerns has become a major issue since the post–World War II era. While the regulatory climate has been near optimal, from the business perspective, the results of such mild regulation were mixed. Historically, the colonial United States prospered greatly during its period of self-imposed isolation and later as a leading international trading partner in the world economy. The price that was paid for such development was little or no governmental regulation during the development of the transportation systems and the accompanying pitfalls, usually in the areas of worker and patron health and safety. As a result of such policies, the United States is now facing a semicoordinated transportation system that continues to suffer from economic difficulties in the wake of various regulatory activities and funding competition at the federal, state, and local levels. Every mode of transportation has undergone significant stress because of the regulatory-deregulatory battle (Thompson, 1984).

The United States is a capitalist nation and as with all capitalist nations, the private sector tends to play a very significant role in the policy arena (Brosch, 1984; Steinman, 1985). As a result, government-directed transportation policies have been limited, fragmented, and looked upon with some degree of suspicion. In short, the profit motive and the inherent pressure for market efficiency has greatly affected U.S. transportation policy. President Reagan's deregulation of the airline industry serves as one example. A capitalist economy, in theory, functions best in a deregulated environment. In short, the true capitalists believe that the government that governs least, governs best.

A philosophy of limited government was still very much a part of the U.S. ideology, particularly under the Reagan Administration. This position is quite often associated with the Republican Party which operates on a platform that the more the private sector is allowed to do without governmental involvement, the more efficiently the private sector can operate. The greater the efficiency of business, the more likely a strong and growing economy will result. The influence of the Reagan Administration during the 1980s is one reason why deregulatory trends are generally popular in the United States today.

To give perspective to the importance of transportation to the U.S. economy, the following economic and employment data should be understood. Deregulation of the transportation industry under the Reagan Administration began in 1980. With the passage of the Motor Carrier Act of 1980 and the Staggers Rail Act by Congress, it is generally agreed that the trucking and rail industries experienced increased flexibility that led to reduced shipping costs for many industries. There has also been speculation as to the impact of deregulation on transportation safety. Nevertheless, in 1980 transportation-related expenditures in the public and private sectors totaled 19.8 percent of the country's gross national product (GNP), nearly one-fifth of the GNP of the world's greatest economic power! This figure dropped to 18.1 percent in 1986 for a dollar total of $766.8 billion. (Transportation Policy Associates, hereafter TPA, 1988: 1).

Of that figure 54.5 percent ($416.9 billion) was spent on private automobiles, 20.3 percent ($155.8 billion) on non–Interstate Commerce Commission authorized trucks, 17.9 percent ($137.5 billion) on federally (ICC) authorized carriers, and 7.4% ($56.6 billion) on other transportation expenses. (TPA, 1988: 1). Transportation is also a significant business expenditure, representing 13 percent of total business expenditures in 1986 at a total cost of $50.5 billion, of which, 37.2 percent ($18.8 billion) was spent on "for-hire carriers," 37.4 percent ($18.9 billion) in the area of "transport equipment manufacturers" with the remaining 25.4 percent ($12.8 billion) being spent on "petroleum and rubber for transportation" (TPA, 1988: 1). As a further illustration of the importance of transportation industries in the U.S. economy, consider that: transportation accounts for the use of the following products of other industries: 72 percent of lead, 71 percent of rubber, 64 percent of petroleum, 26 percent of zinc, 23 percent of steel, 23 percent of cement, 16 percent of aluminum, and 11 percent of copper (TPA, 1988: 1).

Employment statistics serve as one final indicator of the massive impact of transportation industries on the U.S. economy. Over 10 percent of the U.S. civilian employment is attributed to transportation-related industries as of 1986 (see Table 10.1). The 11 million employees were distributed as follows: 23.5 percent (2.6 million) were employed in the "for-hire transport services," 18 percent (2 million) by "transport equipment manufacturers," 27.4 percent (3 million) in the "automotive sales and services" industry with the remaining 31.1 percent (3.4 million) being government employees (TPA, 1988: 1).

POLITICAL DIMENSIONS OF THE TRANSPORTATION SYSTEM AND POLICY

Transportation policy in general and urban transportation policy in particular are very much linked to the prevailing political winds (Rubin, 1985; Weiner, 1983). In recent presidential administrations, transportation policy has been either promoted or bemoaned by the administration in power leaving the actual responsiveness of the system to the bureaucracy. U.S. transportation policy is so closely linked to the political arena that quite often policy decisions are made with little regard to professional recommendations (Boyle, 1983; Derthick & Quirk, 1985). The prevailing regulatory environment greatly complicates the political process and the accompanying funding activities.

The political environment, however, may not be as strong a factor as the collective economic clout of the public. The drive for self-gratification is certainly one important sociocultural characteristic of American society. Nowhere is this more apparent than in the transportation field where approximately 10 percent of the nation's GNP is attributable to the automotive industry. The single-user automobile is reflective of this individualistic attitude. This is one reason why multi-user modes of transportation are not perceived as favorably by many Americans as in other countries. In other words, most Americans prefer to use their cars for their singular transportation needs. This simple preference has basically driven transportation policy for three decades (Crandall et al., 1986; Warren, 1982). The sprawling freeways of the Los Angeles area represent the more recently developed metro areas as compared to "older" areas characterized by concentric rail systems exemplified in Chicago and some East Coast metropolitan areas.

This chapter has illustrated that technological innovations have generally propelled U.S. transportation policy, which has therefore developed in response to these innovations. The government is usually not heavily involved in developing transportation technology; instead, the private sector and markets assume the responsibility for developing and implementing new technologies (Bailey, 1970; Salomon, 1986). The transportation industry itself is basically privately owned and operated. Furthermore, the political process and funding of transportation improvements have repeatedly proven to be the stumbling blocks of technologically improved transportation systems in the United States. The tech-

Table 10.1

Employment in Transportation and Related Industries (number of persons in thousands)

	1960	1970	1980	1982	1983	1984	1985	1986
Transportation Services								
Air Transport	191	351	453	442	450	479	537	560
Bus-Intercity	41	43	38	37	32	38	36	36
Local Transport	101	77	79	84	86	81	90	96
Railroads	885	627	532	432	377	371	346	325
Oil Pipeline	23	18	21	22	22	21	19	18
Taxi	121	107	53	45	40	39r	38	37
Trucking & Trucking Terminals	770	998	1,189	1,121	1,133	1,212	1,285	1,311
Water	232	215	213	194	189	214	214	183
Totals	2,364	2,436	2,578	2,377	2,329	2,455	2,565	2,566
Transport Equipment Manufacturing								
Aircraft & Parts	646	669	652	612	580	602	647	673
Motor Vehicles, Equipment, Tires	829	914	904	792	875	968	964	931
Railroad Equipment	43	51	71	38	30	36	34	29
Ship & Boat Building & Repair	141	170	221	207	199	205	193	185
Other Transportation Equipment	33	111	149	167	190	170	130	136
Totals	1,692	1,915	1,997	1,816	1,874	1,981	1,968	1,954
Transport Related Industries								
Automotive/Accessory Retail Dealers	807	996	1,048	994	999	1,088	1,185	1,238
Automobile Wholesalers	215	320	418	413	405	417	433	428
Automotive Services & Garages	251	384	571	580	587	673	730	763
Gasoline Service Stations	461	614	561	550	531	573	611	613
Highway & Street Construction	294	331	268	218	220	251	264	280
Petroleum	311	333	533	621	579	575	568	478
Other Industries:								
Truck Drivers & Deliverymen	1,418	1,356	1,327	1,294	1,282r	1,386r	1,407	1,428
Shipping & Receiving Clerks	240	359	498	482	407	432	477	455
Totals	3,997	4,693	5,224	5,152	5,010	5,395	5,675	5,683
Government Transport Employees								
U.S. Department of Transportation	38	66	72	62	63	63	61	61
Highways - State & Local	499	568	532	509	504	519	549r	555e
Post Office	83	103	92	93	92	95	104r	110
Other	18	12	13	10	10	9	9	9
Totals	638	749	709	674	669	686	723	735
TOTAL TRANSPORTATION EMPLOYMENT	8,691	9,793	10,508	10,019	9,882	10,517	10,931	10,938
TOTAL EMPLOYED CIVILIANS	65,778	78,627	99,303	99,526	100,834	105,005	107,150	109,597
PERCENT TRANSPORTATION OF TOTAL	13.2%	12.5%	10.6%	10.1%	9.8%	10.0%	10.2%	10.0%

r = Revised   e = Estimated

Source: "Transportation in America," 6th Edition, Transportation Policy Associates, Washington, D.C. (1988).

nology exists to further improve the transportation system and has existed for many years.

RECENT TRENDS AND FUTURE PROSPECTS

The United States transportation system has been subject to a variety of trends. It has been illustrated that innovative transportation technology has repeatedly caused shifts between transportation modes as better and faster methods of travel and cargo transit developed. However, the more recent trends in ridership, average passenger and freight revenues, total miles transported, and intermodal comparisons tend to be more revealing into the current state of affairs.

Major trends of transit ridership are shown in Figure 10.3. The six major periods of the ridership growth and decline of this century are shown. Periods of growth in ridership occurred during the two world wars, during the growth of street railways, and during the 1970s and 1980s which are characterized by the intergovernmental partnership. Drops in ridership occurred during the Great Depression and during the growth of the suburbs.

Another indicator of the popularity of the various modes of cargo transport is reflected by total outlays, which are closely akin to the market share of the respective industries (see Figure 10.4). The chart illustrates the increased usage of the air and highway cargo carriers while the rail industry has lost a great deal of business it once had in the 1960s.

Passenger transport systems paralleled the experience of cargo lines except for the airlines. Clearly, the airlines are becoming increasingly popular, especially in light of the decline in relative terms of automobile usage. Figures 10.5 and 10.6 indicate the changes in intercity passenger travel by mode. (See also Appendices A, B, C, and D to this chapter for data indicating the relative popularity of the various modes of transportation.)

Many transportation policy issues will need to be addressed or continue to be addressed in the future. Three of the main areas are (1) urban mass transit; (2) regulation; and (3) rural transportation. Mass transit in metropolitan areas is an issue that will continue on the policy agenda for some time. Roughly 60 percent of all Americans live in metropolitan areas (Bailey, 1970). However, with falling ridership and the popularity of the automobile remaining stable, mass transportation systems are trying to perform more services with less income. As a consequence, one of the subissues associated with mass transit is cost containment. Many cities are reporting falling transit ridership levels; cost-containment issues are addressed along with maintaining minimum service levels for people who need services—services which may be and quite often are operating at insufficient levels. The typical dilemma concerns whether service cuts or revenue enhancement options, or both, should be pursued? The ever-present alternative of increasing user fees is complicated by the impact of such measures on the elderly and other riders on low and fixed incomes thus causing a possible decline in ridership (Alexander, 1984; Elliott, 1981).

Figure 10.3
Major Trends of Transit Ridership

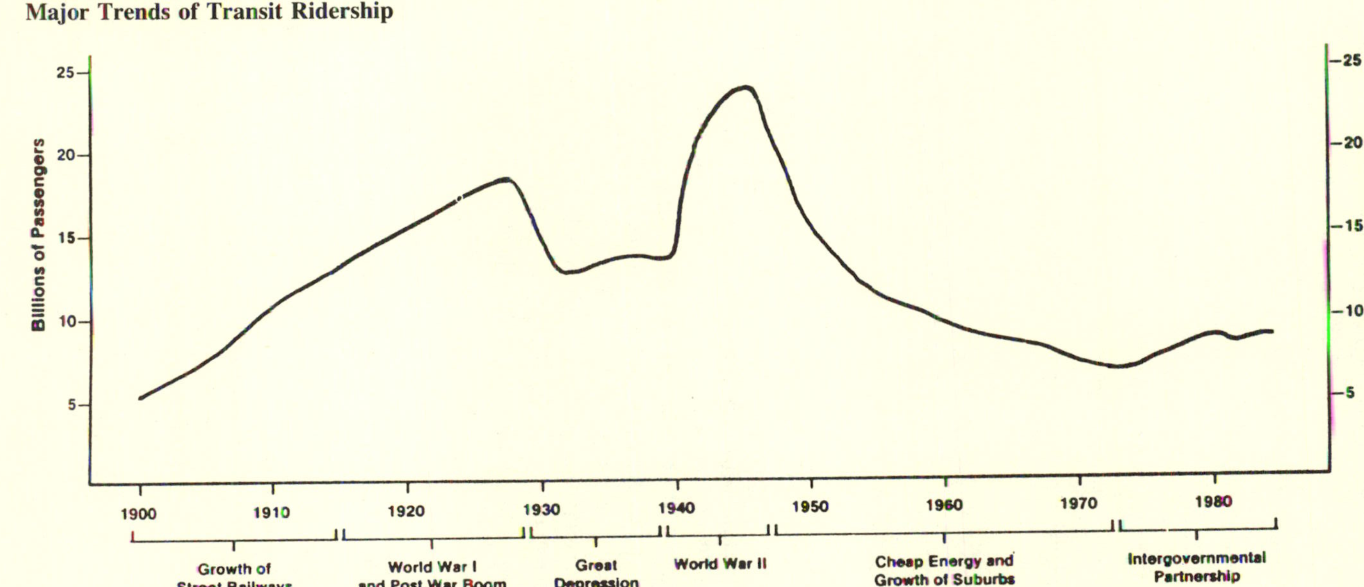

Source: APTA Statistical Department, *Transit Fact Book,* 1985 Edition, Washington, D.C.: American Public Transit Association, 1985, p. 31. Courtesy American Public Transit Association.

Figure 10.4
Relative Shares of Total Outlays for Freight Transportation by Mode[1]

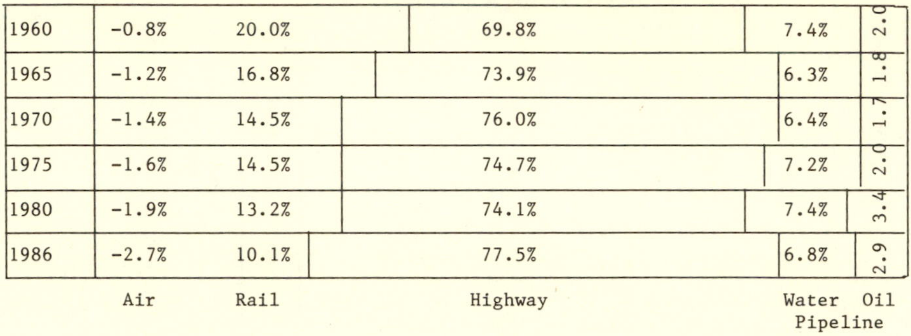

Year	Air	Rail	Highway	Water	Oil Pipeline
1960	-0.8%	20.0%	69.8%	7.4%	2.0
1965	-1.2%	16.8%	73.9%	6.3%	1.8
1970	-1.4%	14.5%	76.0%	6.4%	1.7
1975	-1.6%	14.5%	74.7%	7.2%	2.0
1980	-1.9%	13.2%	74.1%	7.4%	3.4
1986	-2.7%	10.1%	77.5%	6.8%	2.9

1 Exclusive of "Other Carriers" and "Other Shipper Costs"

Source: "Transportation in America," 6th Edition, Transportation Policy Associates, Washington, D.C. (1988).

The diffused metropolitan areas find little help from rail networks (Metzer, 1984). Cities such as Los Angeles have vastly different needs than cities such as Boston and Chicago, which developed in the more traditional radial or concentric pattern (Schaeffer & Sclar, 1980). Even with this key distinction in development patterns, those cities are not necessarily any better off, because the long-held belief that traffic would act as a deterrent to automotive travel has not materialized (Vaughan, 1985).

The trend in transportation policy is toward deregulation, particularly under the Reagan Administration as noted. Critics of such deregulatory efforts, however, have questioned the wisdom of such policies (Lazarus & Ashley, 1985).

Figure 10.5
Changing Distribution of Intercity Passenger-Miles, 1970–1986

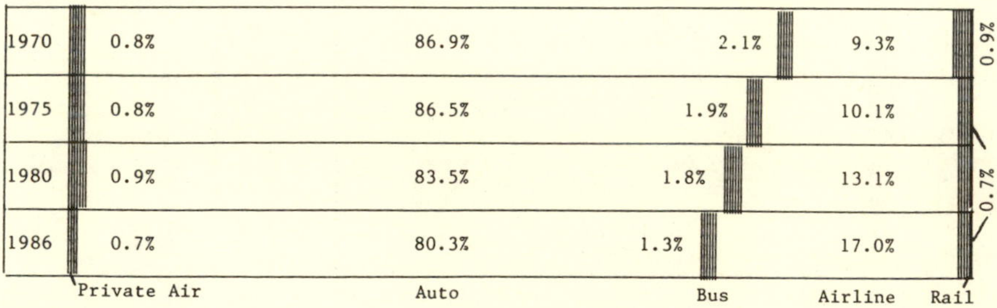

Year	Private Air	Auto	Bus	Airline	Rail
1970	0.8%	86.9%	2.1%	9.3%	0.9%
1975	0.8%	86.5%	1.9%	10.1%	
1980	0.9%	83.5%	1.8%	13.1%	0.7%
1986	0.7%	80.3%	1.3%	17.0%	

Source: "Transportation in America," 6th Edition, Transportation Policy Associates, Washington, D.C. (1988).

Figure 10.6
Changing Distribution of Intercity Passengers, 1970–1986

	Air	Bus	Rail (total)	(Amtrak)	(Commutation)
1970	18.5%	47.7%	33.8%	Non-Com. 9.3%	24.5%
1975	23.5%	43.3%	33.2%	2.1%	31.1%
1980	29.1%	39.1%	31.8%	2.2%	29.6%
1986	38.3%	32.3%	29.4%	2.0%	27.4%

Source: "Transportation in America," 6th Edition, Transportation Policy Associates, Washington, D.C. (1988).

A systematic study of transportation regulations may indeed reveal that additional areas need to be deregulated, that some areas may need regulation, and that some previously regulated areas will need to be deregulated. For years the U.S. Department of Transportation has been trying to improve the safety of transportation carriers and the effects of these systems on the environment. Regulation is central to the issue of safety as witnessed by numerous manufacturing regulations.

Compared to urban transportation, rural transportation is a much neglected area (Kaye, 1982; Saltzman & Newlin, 1981). The U.S. rural transportation infrastructure is generally in need of repair (Chicoine & Walzer, 1984). However, between 1956 and 1970 the federal government funded $16 billion of urban highway development while spending only a half billion dollars on public transit during the same period. Later, the Reagan Administration discontinued two major infrastructure funding programs. Indeed, the infrastructure needs of American cities and rural areas are spiraling upward faster than available funding levels. Rural and small local governments need additional funding programs that target their specific needs (Burkhardt, 1979). The Reagan Administration had severely cut back funding to state and local governments in the face of growing needs while not relinquishing additional funding mechanisms or processes to support transportation and other infrastructure programs (see Table 10.2). In short, urban and rural areas are in need of funding and much hands-on technical training (Coldren, 1979).

TRANSPORTATION POLICY ORGANIZATION AND PROCESS

The United States government combined all transportation agencies and authorities into the U.S. Department of Transportation in 1966. The agency has since undergone several reorganizations. In 1971 the Secretary of Transportation forwarded a statement on national transportation policy to Congress. While

Table 10.2

Federal and State/Local Government Expenditures for Transport Facilities and Services (millions of dollars)

Year		Airways	Airports	Highways	Rivers/ Harbors	Railroad#	Transit	Total
1950	Federal	115	44	503	189	-	-	851
	State/Local	-	101	3,652	136	-	-	3,889
	Total	115	145	4,155	325			4,740
1960	Federal	429	79	2,753	287	-	-	3,548
	State/Local	-	342	7,407	237	-	-	7,986
	Total	429	421	10,160	524			11,534
1970	Federal	965	111	5,181	376	40	133	6,806
	State/Local	-	969	14,321	444	-	345	16,079
	Total	965	1,080	19,502	820	40	478	22,885
1980	Federal	2,135	656	12,036	1,156	1,064	3,881	20,928
	State/Local	-	2,501	27,152	1,168	-	3,308	34,129
	Total	2,135	3,157	39,188	2,324	1,064	7,189	55,057
1982	Federal	1,622	408	10,736	1,204	1,052	3,550	18,572
	State/Local	-	2,818	30,545	1,422	-	4,218	39,003
	Total	1,622	3,226	41,281	2,626	1,052	7,768	57,575
1983	Federal	1,773	553	10,991	1,158	961	3,989	19,405
	State/Local	-	3,014	32,986	1,458	-	4,985	42,443
	Total	1,773	3,547	43,977	2,616	961	8,974	61,848
1984	Federal	2,693	780	12,762	1,190	2,198@	3,900	23,523
	State/Local	-	3,585	35,090	1,329	-	6,300	46,304
	Total	2,693	4,365	47,852	2,519	2,198	10,200	69,827
1985	Federal	2,263	879	15,092	1,189	917	3,491	23,831
	State/Local	-	3,744	40,623	1,495	-	6,890	52,752
	Total	2,263	4,623	55,715	2,684	917	10,381	76,583
1986	Federal	3,237r	939	15,166r	1,075r	777	3,472e	24,666
	State/Local	-	4,257r	45,741r	1,725r	-	7,035e	58,758
	Total	3,237	5,196	60,907	2,800	777	10,507	83,424
1987p	Federal	3,236	1,001	14,155	1,043	619	3,387e	23,441
	State/Local	-	4,538e	48,217	1,800e	-	7,226e	61,781
	Total	3,236	5,539	62,372	2,843	619	10,613	85,222

Includes Amtrak and Northeast Corridor Project   r = Revised   e = Estimated   @ Includes loan default   p = preliminary

Source: "Transportation in America," 6th Edition, Transportation Policy Associates, Washington, D.C. (1988).

policy is established by elected officials in the United States, it is equally common for broad guidelines to be provided to the professional staff in order to form actual policy statements and implement the policies consistent with the desires of the electorate. Perhaps this information combined with the decided lack of government involvement in the development of the transportation system helps to explain the 1971 statement by the Transportation Secretary which described the national transportation policy as ''an uneven fabric ill-suited to today's needs, and . . . itself a major contributor to the problems facing transportation today'' (U.S. Department of Transportation, 1973: 3).

Since the creation of the Department of Transportation numerous legislative acts have affected transportation policy. The U.S. Department of Transportation is the agency primarily responsible for policy implementation. However, each department in the federal government has a role or responsibility which causes it to influence transportation policy in some fashion (see Figure 10.7). The Department of Transportation is made up of nine subagencies directed by the Secretary of Transportation (see Figure 10.8). A few regulatory agencies also get involved in transportation policy and related matters; these include the interstate Commerce Commission, Federal Maritime Commission, Federal Energy Regulatory Commission, and the Civil Aeronautics Board. With this many entities involved in policy administration and enforcement, not its formulation, the lack of a cohesive national policy becomes readily understandable.

The 1971 statement by the Transportation Secretary on national transportation policy indicates that ''the basic infrastructure of transportation is, in fact, in place. Society's new task, as a mature industrial economy, is one of a somewhat different nature—providing service to the millions who want to use the transportation system. Questions of service, as distinguished from questions of construction, require development of a new set of outlooks and relationships.'' The evolution of transportation policy has consequently been increasingly focused on regulation of transportation modes, improving service, expanding transport capability, and limiting harmful side effects of our transportation system. These somewhat fixed goals continue to be pursued in a complex political, economic, and social environment in order to improve the existing transportation system.

For decades improving transportation systems meant sparked economic growth in the country. As the interstate highway system nears completion, and infrastructure programs are discontinued, the political practice of competition for large government contracts and dividing the federal ''pie'' into equal shares for the various regions will become less of a policy issue.

The transportation industry will remain an economic factor in this country despite the decline of brick-and-mortar activity at the federal level. At one time, transportation and related activities employed approximately one out of seven working Americans and also accounted for an estimated 20 percent of the gross national product (U.S. Department of Transportation, 1967; 1). With

Figure 10.7
Transportation Responsibilities in the Executive Branch

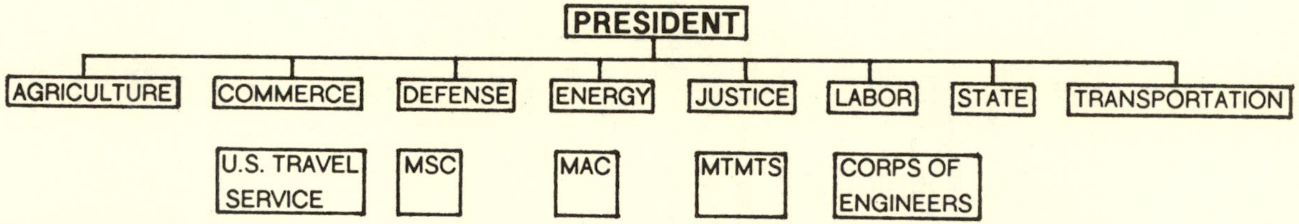

PRESIDENT

AGRICULTURE | COMMERCE | DEFENSE | ENERGY | JUSTICE | LABOR | STATE | TRANSPORTATION

U.S. TRAVEL SERVICE | MSC | MAC | MTMTS | CORPS OF ENGINEERS

DEPARTMENT	RESPONSIBILITIES
President	Rules on matters relating to international air transport by U.S. and foreign carriers. Nominates (Senate confirms) members, and appoints the chairman of the FERC, FMC, and ICC.
Agriculture	Office of Transportation is responsible for developing USDA transport policies for agriculture and rural development and for representing their interests before Federal and state regulatory agencies with respect to rates, charges, tariffs and services of transport carriers.
Commerce	U.S. Travel Service plans and carriers out a comprehensive program designed to stimulate and encourage travel to the U.S. by foreign residents. Accomplishes a quinquennial census of transportation, including "Truck Inventory and Use Survey" and "Commodity Transport Survey."
Defense	Military Sealift Command provides ocean transportation for DOD cargo and personnel and, as directed, for other U.S. agencies and departments; and operates ships in support of other U.S. agency programs. Military Airlift Command provides air transportation for DOD cargo and personnel on a worldwide basis; and furnishes weather, rescue, and audio visual services fo the U.S. Air Force.

	Military Traffic Management and Terminal Service directs military traffic management, land transportation, and common-user ocean terminal service within the U.S., and for worldwide traffic management of DOD's household goods moving and storage program. Provides for procurement of commercial freight and passenger transport services. Corps of Engineers constructs, improves, and maintains river, harbor, and port facilities; and administers laws for the protection and preservation of navigable waters and related wetlands. Compiles and publishes statistical data on domestic/foreign waterborne commerce.
Energy	Develops and implements national energy policies; administers petroleum and natural gas pricing, allocation, and import/export controls; assures energy supplies; and performs regulatory functions over oil and gas pipelines not assigned to FERC.
Justice	Performs a key role in ensuring strong competition in transportation under the U.S. free-enterprise system -- such responsibilities becoming more pronounced as a result of recent laws sharply reducing transportation regulation, especially as they related to antitrust issues.
Labor	Administers and enforces laws relating to wage earners, their working conditions, and employment opportunities, including court actions under the Longshoremen's and Harbor Workers' Compensation Act and the Employee Retirement Income Security Act (ERISA).
State	Develops policy recommendations and approves broad policy programs concerning international aviation and maritime transportation, especially as they affect U.S.-foreign relations; e.g., bi-lateral pacts.

Source: "Transportation in America," 6th Edition, Transportation Policy Associates, Washington, D.C. (1988).

Figure 10.8
U.S. Department of Transportation Organization and Responsibilities

SECRETARY

- COAST GUARD
- NATIONAL HIGHWAY TRAFFIC SAFETY ADM.
- FEDERAL AVIATION ADMINISTRATION
- RESEARCH & SPECIAL PROGRAMS ADM.
- FEDERAL HIGHWAY ADMINISTRATION
- ST. LAWRENCE SEAWAY DEVELOPMENT CORP.
- FEDERAL RAILROAD ADMINISTRATION
- URBAN MASS TRANSPORTATION ADM.
- MARITIME ADMINISTRATION

Secretary of Transportation	Principal assistant to President in all matters relating to Federal transportation programs. Major aides include a Deputy Secretary, General Counsel, and Assistant Secretaries for Policy & International Affairs, Administration, Public Affairs, Governmental Affairs, and Budget & Programs. The underlined formulates transport policy and implementation plans; coordinates U.S. interests in international transport affairs; analyzes social, economic, and energy aspects of transport; assesses performance of transport system; and coordinates environmental and safety programs within DOT. Most of CAB's residual functions were transferred to DOT and placed largely in Office of Assistant Secretary for Policy & International Affairs. They include: economic regulation of international air transport (routes and rates), determination of carrier fitness for domestic air services, protection of consumers (baggage, overbooking, etc.), ensuring adequate service to smaller communities, grant of antitrust immunity, and protecting U.S. carriers against foreign actions.
Coast Guard	Maintains network of rescue vessels, aircraft and communications facilities to protect lives and property on the high seas and navigable waters of U.S. Enforces Federal laws governing navigation, vessel inspection, port safety and security, marine environmental protection, and resource conservation. Sets ship construction and safety standards. Regulates Great Lakes' pilotage. Carries out R&D programs.
Federal Aviation Administration	Promotes civil aviation, including R&D programs; promulgates and enforces safety regulations; develops and operates nation's airways system; administers Federal-aid airport programs; and certifies and registers aircraft and commercial/private pilots.
Federal Highway Administration	Administers Federal-aid highway program of financial aid to states for highway construction and rehabilitation. Develops and administers highway safety program, including aid to states and local communities. Coordinates an helps fund R&D programs. Its Office of Motor Carrier Safety regulates safety performance of interstate commercial motor carriers, including hazardous materials movements and cargo security/noise abatement programs. Makes road checks, prosecutes violators. Develops highway data.

Federal Railroad Administration	Consolidates U.S. support and promotion of railroad transportation; administers and enforces rail safety regulations; administers rail financial-aid programs; and conducts R&D programs to improve railroad freight and passenger services and safety.
Maritime Administration	Promotes merchant marine; grants ship mortgage insurance; maintins National Defense Reserve Fleet; sponsors R&D for ship design, propulsion and operations. Its Maritime Subsidy Board awards ship operating subsidies to liner carriers (ship construction subsidies have been discontinued) and determines scope of subsidized shipping services and routes -- in line with MarAd's determination of ship requirments, services, and routes needed for the U.S. foreign waterborne commerce.
National Highway Traffic Safety Administration	Implements motor vehicle safety programs and issues standards prescribing levels of safety needed; conducts test programs to assure compliance with standards and need for them; helps fund state/local safety programs; maintains national poor-driver register; sets fuel economy standards for autos with EPA and DOE; and assesses penalties for violators of its standards.
Research & Special Programs Administration	Serves as DOT's research, analysis, and technical development arm; and to conduct special programs, with emphasis on: pipeline safety, movements of hazardous materials, cargo security, R&D, university research programs, and commercial air carrier data formerly collected, collated, and published by the CAB.
St. Lawrence Seaway Development Corp.	Administers the operation and maintenance of the U.S. portion of the St. Lawrence Seaway. Works closely with its Canadian counterpart to determine and set toll levels.
Urban Mass Transportation Administration	Develops comprehensive, coordinated mass transport systems for urban areas, including financial aid for equipment and operations; R&D and demonstration projects; aid for technical studies; planning, engineering, and designing.

Source: ''Transportation in America,'' 6th Edition, Transportation Policy Associates, Washington, D.C. (1988).

such an incredible societal impact, it is obvious that transportation issues will always be near the forefront of American politics.

The primary issues of mass transit, rural transportation, and all transportation regulatory issues will continue to be debated in the American political system. The emphasis will remain on issues such as modernization, efficiency, and equity. The airline industry, being the unrivaled king of intercity passenger transport, may eventually see greater regulation after the market has been allowed to complete the economic "survival of the fittest" test on the industry. The discontinuance of federal funding of infrastructure assistance programs will force greater reliance by state and local governments on user fees, motor fuel taxes, and similar revenue extraction techniques to maintain the current road system. The pervasive funding decisions of the Reagan Administration will greatly affect the budgeting activities of state and local governments unless the Bush Administration reenacts some of these programs. The political conflict over the enormous federal deficit, and unprecedented trade imbalances, leaves a bleak future for any attempt to reinstate these programs.

Finally, the political system of the United States is designed in such a way that transportation policy has been effectively a form of "indirect subsidy." The system of contracts, land acquisition, and regulation, purported to provide benefits for all citizens, actually assists in maintaining a high degree of entrepreneurialism which primarily benefits smaller segments of society (Albritton: 411). The concept of an indirect subsidy and the associated entrepreneurial activity should not be particularly surprising, as the most unique and distinctive characteristic of the United States transportation system is the high level of involvement of the private sector in developing policy and the operating components of the transportation system.

REFERENCES

Albritton, Robert B., "Welfare and Transportation," Virginia Grey, Herbert Jacob, and Kenneth N. Vines, eds., *Politics in the American States* (Boston: Little, Brown, 1983).

Alexander, James, "Progress in Motion," *Black Enterprise,* October 1984.

Allen, P. M., J. L. Denrubourg, and M. Sanglier, *Dynamic Urban Growth Models: Interim Report* (Washington, D.C.: Research and Special Programs Administration, U.S. Department of Transportation, 1978).

Alling, Phillip C., "Gathering Intelligence for Transportation Planning," *Management & Shipping Management,* October 1984.

Alm, Richard, "What Reagan's Budget Will Mean to You," *U.S. News & World Report,* Feb. 13, 1984.

Anderson, J. Michael, *Reference Brief FY 84 and FY 85 Budget Chronology* (Washington, D.C.: Congressional Research Service, November 1984).

Bailey, John A., *Constraints Against Introduction of New Technology or Innovative Marketing in Urban Transportation* (Chicago: The Transportation Center at Northwestern University, October 1970).

Baker, Carole, "The Uneven Impact of Washington's Metro," *Planning*, June 1984.

Ben-Akiva, Moshe, Nicholaos Litinas, and Koji Tsunokawa, "The Continuous Logit Model and Distribution of Trips and Urban Densities," *Transportation Research*, March 1985.

Boffey, Phillip M., "Outlook for Key Domestic Programs," *New York Times*, Feb. 2, 1984.

Boyle, Daniel K., *Transportation Energy Contingency Planning: Quantifying the Need for Transit Actions* (Washington, D.C.: Office of Planning Assistance, U.S. Department of Transportation, 1983).

Brosch, Gary L., "Growing Transportation Problems: The Private Sector Response," *State Government*, Winter 1984.

Burkhardt, Jon E., *Planning Rural Public Transportation Systems: A Section 147 Demonstration Program Technical Assistance Manual* (Washington D.C.: Federal Highway Administration, U.S. Department of Transportation, 1979).

Burkhardt, Robert, "Airlines Differ on Airport Problem," *Journal of Commerce and Commercial*, Jan. 17, 1985.

Chicoine, David, and Norman Walzer, *Financing Rural Roads and Bridges in the Midwest* (Washington, D.C.: Office of Transportation and Agricultural Marketing Services, U.S. Department of Agriculture, October 1984).

Coldren, Fred, ed., *Rural Rides: A Practical Handbook for Starting and Operating a Rural Public Transportation System* (Washington D.C.: Farmers Home Administration, U.S. Department of Agriculture, November 1979).

Crandall, Robert W., Howard K. Grunespecht, Theodore E. Keller, and Lester B. Lave, *Regulating the Automobile* (Washington, D.C.: The Brookings Institution, 1986).

Derthick, Martha, and Paul J. Quirk, *The Politics of Deregulation* (Washington, D.C.: The Brookings Institution, 1985).

Elliott, John M., "No Fare: Key to Transit Jam," in Robert L. Morlan and David L. Martin, eds., *Capital, Courthouse, and City Hall* (Boston: Houghton Mifflin, 1981).

Farnsworth, Clyde H., "Borrowing in 1985 Projected at $274 Billion," *New York Times*, Feb. 2, 1984.

Federal Highway Administration, "Our Nation's Highways—Selected Facts and Figures," Highway Statistics Division, Office of Highway Planning, Federal Highway Administration, 1988.

Frankel, Ernst G., *Regulation and Policies of American Shipping* (Boston: Auburn House, 1982).

Friedlaender, Ann, and Robert Simpson, *Alternative Scenarios for Federal Transportation Policy* (Washington, D.C.: Research and Special Programs Administration, U.S. Department of Transportation, 1978).

Fuerbringer, Jonathon, "President Sends Hopeful Message with 1985 Budget," *New York Times*, Feb. 2, 1984.

———, "Senate Approves G.O.P. Package For a 'Down Payment' on Deficit," *New York Times*, May 18, 1984.

Gordon, Marion, "EMME-2: A New Generation in Transportation Planning," *Mass Transit*, July 1986.

Hamilton, Martha M., "President Says 'Wait' to Those Who Press for Increase in Taxes," *Washington Post*, Feb. 2, 1984.

Harsha, Barbara, "System Essential to Viability of Urban Areas," *Nation's Cities Weekly,* March 10, 1986.

Jansson, Jan Owen, *Transportation System Optimization and Pricing* (New York: John Wiley & Sons, 1984).

Jaroslovsky, Rich, "Reagan's Record Sparkles on Inflation but Shows Failure in Fight to Cut Deficit," *Wall Street Journal,* Feb. 2, 1984.

Karmin, Monroe W., and Robert J. Morse, "Drowning in Debt," *U.S. News & World Report,* Feb. 13, 1984.

Kaye, Ira, "Transportation," in Don A. Dillman and Daryl J. Hobbs, eds., *Rural Society in the U.S.: Issues for the 1980s* (Boulder, Colo.: Westview Press, 1982).

Kemp, Michael A., *The Consequences of Short-Range Transit Improvements: An Overview of a Research Program* (Washington, D.C.: Urban Mass Transportation Administration, U.S. Department of Transportation, 1978).

Kolko, Gabriel, "Railroads and Regulations, 1877–1916," in Marilyn Gittell, ed., *State Politics and the New Federalism* (New York: Longman, 1986).

Lave, Lester B., "Conflicting Objectives in Regulating the Automobile," in Robert H. Haveman and Julius Margolis, eds., *Public Enterprise and Policy Analysis* (Boston: Houghton Mifflin, 1983).

Lazarus, Monte, and William C. Ashley, "Transportation after Deregulation," *Long Range Planning,* Fall 1985.

Levine, Harvey A., *National Transportation Policy: A Study of Studies* (Lexington, Mass.: Lexington Books, 1978).

Levinson, Herbert S., and Robert A. Weant, "Transportation Planning: An Overview," *Planning,* June 1984.

Lewis, Arnold, "Long-Range Planning: An Economic Indicator?" *Business & Commercial Aviation,* August 1985.

Lisco, Thomas E., "Mass Transportation: Cinderella in Our Cities," in Robert L. Morlan and David L. Martin, eds., *Capital, Courthouse, and City Hall* (Boston: Houghton Mifflin, 1981).

Luna, Charles, *The Handbook of Transportation in America* (New York: Popular Library, 1971).

Lundbert, Barry D., and Thomas L. Aller, "Joint Development in Cedar Rapids," *Planning,* June 1984.

Metzer, J., "Railroads and the Efficiency of Internal Market: Some Conceptual and Practical Considerations," *Economic Development & Cultural Change,* October 1984.

Michaels, Richard M., ed., *Transportation Planning and Policy Decision Making: Behavioral Science Contributions* (New York: Praeger, 1980).

Mogridge, M.J.H., "Road Pricing: The Right Solution for the Right Problem?" *Transportation Research,* March 1986.

Morrison, Steven, and Clifford Winston, *The Economic Effects of Airline Deregulation* (Washington, D.C.: The Brookings Institution, 1986).

"National Transportation Statistics: Annual Report" (August 1988), Washington, D.C.: Research and Special Programs Administration, U.S. Department of Transportation, Report #DOT-TSC-RSPA-88-2.

O'Sullivan, Patrick, *Transport Policy: Geographic, Economic and Planning Aspects* (Totowa, N.J.: Barnes & Noble Books, 1980).

Padron, Manuel, "Build Here: Transit's Rallying Cry," *Planning,* June 1984.

Phillips, Karen Borlang, and Laurence T. Phillips, "Research, Politics, and the Dynamics of Policy Development: A Case Study of Motor Carrier Regulatory Reform," *Policy Sciences,* December 1984.

Plous, F. K., Jr., "A Desire Named Streetcar," *Planning,* June 1984.

Pustay, Michael W., "A Comparison of Pre- and Post-Reform Motor Carrier Service to Small Communities," *Growth and Change,* January 1985.

Rand McNally Handy Railroad Atlas of the U.S. (Chicago: Rand McNally, 1982).

Ripley, Randall B., and Grace A. Franklin, *Policy Implementation and Bureaucracy* (Chicago: Dorsey Press, 1986).

Rubin, Irene S., *Shrinking the Federal Government: The Effect of Cutbacks on Five Federal Agencies* (New York: Longman, 1985).

Salomon, Ian, "Telecommunications and Travel Relationships: A Review," *Transportation Research,* May 1986.

Saltzman, Arthur, and Lawrence W. Newlin, "The Availability of Passenger Transportation," in Amos H. Hawley and Sara Mills Mazie, eds., *Nonmetropolitan America in Transition* (Chapel Hill: University of North Carolina Press, 1981).

Schaeffer, K. H., and Elliot Sclar, *Access for All: Transportation and Urban Growth* (New York: Columbia University Press, 1980).

Sclar, Elliot, "Land Use and Transportation," in Marcus G. Raskin, ed., *The Federal Budget and Social Reconstruction: The People and the State* (Washington, D.C.: Institute for Policy Studies, 1978).

Snell, Bradford, "The Right to Travel," in Marcus G. Raskin, ed., *The Federal Budget and Social Reconstruction: The People and the State* (Washington, D.C.: Institute for Policy Studies, 1978).

Spencer, Rich, and Howard Kurts, "Reagan Says Proposals Freeze Real Domestic Spending for '80s," *Washington Post,* Feb. 2, 1984.

Steinman, Kirk, *Public/Private Partnership in Transit* (Washington D.C.: Office of Planning Assistance, U.S. Department of Transportation, 1985).

Strakie, David, "Efficient and Politic Congestion Tolls," *Transportation Research,* March 1986.

Tevanian, Janice, "Examining the Options for Transit in Communities," *Public Management,* February 1986.

Thompson, Stephen J., *Deregulation of Transportation* (Washington D.C.: Congressional Research Service, December 1984).

Transit Fact Book, 1985 ed. Washington, D.C.: American Public Transit Association, 1985.

Transportation Policy Associates, *Transportation in America: A Statistical Analysis of Transportation in the United States,* 6th ed. (Washington, D.C.: Transportation Policy Associates, 1988).

U.S. Department of Transportation, *First Annual Report, Fiscal Year 1961 (Part 1)* (Washington, D.C.: U.S. Government Printing Office, 1967).

U.S. Department of Transportation, *Implementing Transportation Policy: The Second Annual Report on the Implementation of the Statement on National Transportation Policy* (Washington, D.C.: U.S. Government Printing Office, 1973).

U.S. Department of Transportation, "National Transportation Statistics: Annual Report," Research & Special Programs Administration, Washington, D.C., 1988.

Vaughan, Rodney J., "A Continuous Analysis of the Role of Transportation and Crowding

Costs in Determining Trip Distribution and Location in a Linear City,'' *Transportation Research,* March 1985.

Warren, William D., ''Changes in America Inter-City Rail Transportation: 1950–1980,'' *Transportation Quarterly,* January 1982.

Weiner, Edward, *Urban Transportation Planning in the United States: A Historical Overview* (Washington, D.C.: Office of the Assistant Secretary for Policy and International Affairs, U.S. Department of Transportation, 1983).

Wills, Michael J., ''A Flexible Gravity-Opportunities Model for Trip Distribution,'' *Transportation Research,* April 1986.

Winters, Phillip D., *The Federal Budget for Fiscal Year 1985* (Washington, D.C.: Congressional Research Service, October 1984).

Appendix A
Domestic Intercity Ton-Miles by Mode* (billions)

Year	Rail		Truck: ICC Truck		Truck: Non-ICC Truck		Oil Pipe Line		Rivers & & Canals		Great Lakes #		Air		Total +
	Amount	%	Amount	%	Amount	%	Amount	%	Amount	%	Amount	%	Amount	%	
1940	379	61.3	21	3.4	41	6.6	59	9.5	22	3.6	96	15.5	.02	.00	618
1950	597	56.2	66	6.2	107	10.1	129	12.1	52	4.9	112	10.5	.30	.03	1,063
1960	579	44.1	104	7.9	181	13.8	229	17.4	121e (81)	9.2	99e (70)	7.5	.89	.07	1,314
1970	771	39.7	167	8.6	245	12.7	431	22.3	205 (156)	10.7	105 (70)	5.4	3.50	.18	1,954
1980	932	37.5	242	9.7	313	12.6	588	23.6	311 (227)	12.5	96 (62)	3.9	4.84	.20	2,487
1981	924	38.1	241	9.9	286	11.8	564	23.2	312 (231)	12.8	98 (62)	4.0	5.09	.21	2,430
1982	810	36.0	218	9.7	302	13.4	566	25.1	288 (217)	12.8	63 (36)	2.8	5.14	.23	2,252
1983	841	36.0	229	9.8	346	14.8	556	23.8	291 (226)	12.5	68 (43)	2.9	5.87	.25	2,337
1984	935	37.2	252	10.0	354	14.1	568	22.6	317 (243)	12.6	82 (50)	3.3	6.50	.26	2,515
1985	895	36.4	250	10.0	360	14.4	564	22.6	306 (233)	12.5	76 (48)	3.1	6.71	.27	2,478
1986r	889	35.5	259	10.4	375	15.0	578	23.1	321 (245)	12.8	72 (46)	2.9	7.34	.29	2,501
1987p	976	36.5	277	10.4	389	14.5	587	22.0	353 (270)	13.2	82 (52)	3.1	8.70	.34	2,673

* Includes both for-hire and private carriers and also mail and express.
\# Figures in parentheses show traffic originating and terminating with each waterway segment.
e Estimated
r Revised
\+ Total excludes Coastwise Traffic, which should be added for comparability with Tonnage Total (Page 7).
p Preliminary

Source: "Transportation in America," 6th Edition, Transportation Policy Associates, Washington, D.C. (1988).

Appendix B
Passenger-Miles, 1976–1986 (millions)

	1976	1977	1978	1979	1980	1981	1982	1983	1984	1985	1986
Air carrier, domestic operations, certificated, all services	151,379	163,219	187,812	212,701	204,367	201,438	213,631	232,165	250,687	277,836	307,885
Total majors*	136,972	147,078	168,222	183,500	182,985	173,560	180,229	191,888	202,658	223,850	252,724
Total nationals**	12,666	14,304	17,503	20,634	20,467	25,149	27,368	33,709	37,504	48,553	50,026
Total large regionals***	1,741	1,837	2,087	8,567[†]	712	1,648	4,426	5,552	7,642	4,952	4,861
Total medium regionals***	-	-	-	-	251	1,352	3,888	1,476	3,262	905	569
General aviation, intercity	12,100	12,800	14,100	15,500	14,700	14,600	13,100	12,700	13,000	13,000	12,400
Highway											
Passenger car and taxi[r]	2,479,895	2,551,259	2,636,968	2,561,372	2,556,671	2,600,902	2,682,389	2,755,453	2,817,314	2,899,300	2,998,066
Intercity bus	25,100	26,000	25,600	27,700	27,400	27,100[r]	26,900	25,600	24,600[r]	23,800[r]	23,700
Class I rail	4,470	4,588	4,666	4,835	6,516[r]	6,213[r]	6,027[r]	6,097[r]	6,207[r]	6,547[r]	6,770[e]
Amtrak	4,268	4,204	4,154	4,876	4,503	4,762	4,172	4,246	4,552	4,786[r]	5,011

[r] = revised.
[e] = estimated.
- = figure included in large regionals.
* Prior to 1980, total majors were labelled trunks.
** Prior to 1980, total nationals were labelled locals.
*** Prior to 1980, large and medium regionals were labelled other; includes domestic and international operations.
† 1979 increase is caused by the entry of many small air carriers into the commercial air carrier field following deregulation of CAB entry regulation. Many of these carriers apparently did not survive long, based on the data for the following year, although some of the profitable ones may have moved up to the 'Nationals' category.

Source: Transportation Systems Center, *National Transportation Statistics Annual Report,* Washington, D.C.: U.S. Department of Transportation, 1988, p. 62.

Appendix C
Domestic Intercity Freight Federally Regulated
(percent of total ton-miles per mode)

				Water c					
Year	Rail*	Truck°	Oil + Pipeline	Domestic Coastwise	Great Lakes	Rivers & Canals	Air@	Ton-Miles#	Regulated
1940	100	37.9					100		
1950	100	38.2					100		
1960	100	36.5	84.0e	7.0	1.0	21.0	100	1,570	57.5e
1970	100	41.3	85.1	4.6	1.2	15.1	100	2,212	60.9
1980	100	43.6	90.0	2.1	0.4	9.2	0	3,118	56.0
1981	91	43.1r	90.0	2.9	0.2	8.6	0	3,065	52.9r
1982	69	39.4r	90.0	2.8	0.1	6.2	0	2,885	45.4r
1983	54	33.6r	90.0	4.3	0.0	6.9	0	2,987	40.6r
1984	50	34.5r	90.0	2.5	0.0	7.8	0	3,109	40.1r
1985	48	33.8r	90.0	2.1r	1.8r	6.0r	0	3,068r	38.8r
1986	38	33.1r	90.0	2.0r	1.5r	6.1r	0	3,104r	36.0r
1987e	32	33.0	90.0	2.0	1.2	6.2	0	3,210	33.8r

e Estimated
r Revised
* Figures based on assumption that rail contract rates are unregulated.
° Figures through 1982 assume4s ICC truckers 100% regulated, then contract carriers deregulated (removal of tariff filing, easing of entry, and removal of shipper contracts limit).
@ Small, but unknown percentage state regulated. Federal economic regulation of air freight (entry, rates, services) repealed by Act passed by Congress in 1977.
+ Percentage increased in 1977 through 1979 with entry of Trans Alaska Pipeline.
c Percentages for water modes computed on basis of traffic originating and terminating within each segment.

Note: Where no figures are shown, data were unavailable.

Source: "Transportation in America," 6th Edition, Transportation Policy Associates, Washington, D.C. (1988).

Appendix D
Number of Vehicles, 1976–1986

	1976	1977	1978	1979	1980	1981	1982	1983	1984	1985	1986
Air carrier											
domestic and international certificated, all services	2,507	2,543	2,521	2,598†	2,718	2,763	2,664	2,659	2,757	3,100	3,627
General Aviation	178,304	184,294	198,778	210,339	211,045	213,227	209,779	213,293	220,943	210,654	220,044
Motorcycle	4,933,332	4,933,256	4,867,864	5,422,132	5,693,940	5,831,132	5,753,858	5,585,112	5,479,822	5,444,404	5,262,322
Passenger car & taxi (thousand)[r]	110,189	112,288	116,573	118,429	121,601	123,098	123,702	126,444	128,158	131,864	135,431
Intercity bus	20,100	20,100	20,400	21,300	21,400	21,500	22,000	20,300	20,100	20,200	n/a
Local transit											
Motorbus††	52,382	51,968	52,866	54,490	59,41	60,393	62,114	62,093	78,864	79,237	n/a
Subway & elevated	9,662	9,587	9,515	9,470	9,641	9,749	9,815	9,891	9,841	10,116	n/a
Surface rail	963	992	944	959	1,103	1,075	1,016	1,013	1,007	993	n/a
Trolley coach	685	645	593	725	823	751	763	686	686	686	n/a
Total**	63,735	63,235	63,961	65,644	70,931	72,011	73,751	73,730	90,571	91,205	n/a
Class I Rail											
Freight cars	1,331,705	1,287,315	1,226,500	1,217,079	1,168,114	1,111,115	1,039,016	1,007,165	948,171	867,070	798,453
Locomotives	27,612	27,667	27,400	28,097	28,396	27,808	27,073	25,838	24,506	22,932	21,161
Passenger train-cars***	3,416	3,358	2,409	2,215	2,219	2,115	1,807	730	736	684	514
Total	1,362,733	1,318,340	1,256,309	1,247,391	1,198,729	1,141,038	1,067,896	1,033,733	973,413	890,686	820,128
Amtrak											
Passenger train-cars	1,974	2,154	2,084	2,026	2,128	1,830	1,929	1,880	1,844	1,818	1,793
Locomotives	374	369	441	437	448	398	396	388	387	382	369
Total	2,348	2,523	2,525	2,463	2,576	2,228	2,325	2,268	2,231	2,200	2,162
Truck											
Combination[r]	1,224,917	1,239,613	1,341,707	1,386,374	1,416,869	1,261,202	1,265,321	1,304,041	1,340,144	1,403,266	1,398,937
Single unit[r]	26,651,008	28,074,672	29,994,157	31,527,430	32,249,718	33,382,908	34,117,054	34,117,054	36,167,319	37,792,895	38,767,562
Total[r]	27,875,925	29,314,285	31,335,864	32,913,804	33,666,587	34,644,110	35,382,375	36,722,615	37,507,463	39,196,161	40,166,499
Water transport											
Total inland water vessels	31,027	33,149	32,428	33,984	36,285	*	38,872	*	38,837	38,493	37,664
Non-self-propelled vessels											
Dry cargo barges & scows	23,164	24,937	24,037	25,420	27,426	*	29,479	*	29,730	29,287	28,308
Tank barges	3,623	3,770	3,946	4,000	4,166	*	4,413	*	4,114	4,252	4,260
Total	26,787	28,70	28,048	29,492	31592	*	33,92	*	33,84	33,539	32,58
Self-propelled vessels towboats & tugs	4,240	4,379	4,30	4,92	4,693	*	4,890	*	4,993	4,94	5,096
Oceangoing steam & motor ships (1,000 gross tons & over)	842	840	879	865	864	853	832	788	744	737	720
Total	31,869	33,989	33,127	34,849	37,149	n/a	39,704	n/a	39,581	39,230	38,384

n/a = not available.
r = revised.
† Figure as of June, 1979. All other figures are as of December of their respective year.
†† Prior to 1984, excludes most rural and smaller systems funded via Sections 18 and 16(b)2, Urban Mass Transportation Act of 1964, as amended. Series not continuous between 1983 and 1984.
* Change in collection methods, see Appendix A, p. A-21.
** Excludes commuter railroad; includes cable cars, inclined plane cars, ferry boats and aerial tramway cars.
*** Figure obtained by addition/subtraction.

Source: Transportation Systems Center, *National Transportation Statistics Annual Report*, Washington, D.C.: U.S. Department of Transportation, 1988, p. 66.

11

WEST GERMANY

Herbert Baum

BACKGROUND

The historical development of the modern transportation system in Germany began with the introduction of the railroad. In 1835 the first German railroad line was opened between Nuremberg and Fürth. During the triumphant advance of the railroad, inland shipping lost much of its significance. With the expansion of waterways and economies of scale of domestic shipping firms at the end of the nineteenth century, domestic shipping again secured its position alongside the railroad. It was not until World War I that roadway transportation began to play a competitive role.

Because of the dominant position of the railways in the early years, the government saw a need to secure monopoly controls with regulatory elements. Thus the principle of public interest with social considerations was anchored in the transportation services. With the rise of competition of inland shipping and roadway freight transportation, however, the monopoly of the railways was liquidated although parts of the monopoly controls were retained and still burden the railways today (Predöhl, 1958; Voigt, 1966, 1973).

At the end of the nineteenth century, the German transportation economy was drawn into the great worldwide depression with the consequences of tre-

This chapter was originally written in German by the author and translated into English by Karen Fletcher, Alan Mitchell, and Amy Thomson, graduate assistants at Bowling Green State University, Bowling Green, Ohio.

mendous overcapacities and cutthroat competition. Transportation policymakers reacted by shutting out competition through an interventionary system of market regulation (e.g., tariffs, restrictions on market access, and compulsory cartels). In addition to the "guardian angel function" vis-à-vis the transportation industries, the National Socialists' conception of a centrally controlled economy was already evident.

After World War II, top priorities included the removal of war debris and the reconstruction of the transportation infrastructure. After the division of Germany, the west-east links lost much of their significance, and the main transportation flows were concentrated in the north-south direction. The growth of motorization and the increase in suburbanization required an expansion of the roadway network.

In its regulatory policy the Federal Republic of Germany or West Germany continued the management course of the prewar period. With governmental market regulations, the transportation sector became a publicly administered branch. A first step toward liberalization was undertaken in the "small transportation reform" of 1961, including the introduction of tariff margins. The model of "controlled competition" was predominant (Hamm, 1980a; Seidenfus, 1975).

In passenger transport in cities and congested areas, infrastructural bottlenecks and an imbalance between individual and public transport with high congestion costs were already evident in the 1960s. Transportation policymakers attempted to check these developments by expanding the roadway network and improving public transportation. These efforts were not successful, however.

In the early 1970s a priority for public transportation was instituted under the framework of the "policy of internal reforms." The investment emphases were transferred to urban public passenger transport. Subway and commuter train projects were undertaken in several cities. Financing (volume in the last fifteen years: 30 billion deutsche marks or DM) came from the petroleum tax on car drivers in accordance with the Municipal Transport Finance Law of 1971. While the quality of public transportation was thus improved, no all-encompassing change in the intermodal split was achieved. Instead, advances in transport capacity and the resulting high costs formed the basis for a growth in the deficit of public transport operators (Baum & Kentner, 1980).

After the end of the first oil crisis in 1973, exorbitant financial bottlenecks in government budgets led to a policy of financial consolidation vis-à-vis the public transportation system. This meant a turn away from expensive transport systems and a reemphasis on conventional solutions. The restrictions on individual transport were relaxed for economic and employment reasons. The transport policy became ideologically more open and in general once again more pragmatic.

Nevertheless the public transportation system retained its importance. From the mid-1970s on, the government developed a policy of environmental protec-

Table 11.1
Economic Data for Transportation Sector, 1985

Mode of Transportation	Gross invested assets (in Bill. DM)	Net Value Added (in Bill. DM)	Employees (in 1,000)	Revenues (in Bill. DM)
German Federal Railroad (DB)	194.6	13.5	297	23.4
Transport Network incl. under the DB	116.6	-	-	-
Non-federally owned Railroads	6.8	0.5	11	1.0
Inland Shipping	8.1	1.1	11	3.3
Inland Ports	8.7	0.2	14	0.3
Maritime Shipping	28.5	3.0	23	9.3
Sea Ports	18.9	1.4	24	2.6
Public Transportation System	61.1	9.0	178	11.9
Road freight transport	30.8	25.8	295	60.5
Airlines	9.9	7.6	38	13.5
Airports	10.7	1.5	15	2.4
Pipelines	4.3	0.4	1	0.7
Roads and Bridges	477.2	-	-	-
Waterways	38.3	-	-	-
Total for Transportation Sector	898.0	64.0	907	128.6
All Economic Sectors	8057.9	1791.2	25471	-
Share of Transportation (%)	11.1	3.6	3.6	-

Source: The Federal Minister of Transportation, ed., *Verkehr in Zahlen 1986* [Transportation in figures 1986] (Bonn, 1986: 36 ff).

tion—that is, reduction in noise and air pollution, energy-saving measures, and prevention of traffic accidents. Attempts to achieve this goal were made through investments as well as administrative and taxation measures (see Tables 11.1 and 11.2).

In the center of the present transportation policy is the deregulation of the transportation markets which, according to the verdict reached by the European Court in 1985 and the decision of the European Community (EC) Ministers' Council, should be completed by 1992. Because of cross-border transportation for foreign firms in West Germany, the barriers to market access will presumably be lifted and the prices liberalized. The German transportation policy does not prevent deregulation. Yet it places emphasis on a harmonization of the conditions of competition such as tax burdens of transportation firms, sizes and weights of trucks, and application of working conditions. Currently the German transportation policy is experiencing a phase of international consensus with a balance of interests between the providers and consumers of transportation services (Baum, 1984).

Table 11.2
Federal Government Expenditures for Transportation Sector (in million DM)

Mode of Transportation	1960	1970	1980	1985
Transportation Sector Total:	3600	11192	24283	25269
% of Investments in Transportation Sector	68	57	49	49
Federal Highways	1700	5108	6830	6158
Improvements in Local Transportation Networks	–	970	2373	2632
Federal Waterways	377	794	1765	1949
Railroads	1103	3358	11397	13100
Aviation	169	309	494	424
Other Transportation Expenditures	251	653	1424	1007
Total Federal Government Expenditures	41450	88207	217085	258745
% of Investments	17	17	15	13
Share of Transportation in Total Federal Government Expenditures (%)	8.7	12.7	11.2	9.8
Share of Transportation in Total Federal Government Investments (%)	–	43	38	37

Source: The Federal Minister of Transportation, ed., *Verkehr in Zahlen 1986* [Transportation in figures 1986] (Bonn, 1986: 107).

SOCIOECONOMIC DIMENSIONS OF THE TRANSPORTATION SYSTEM AND POLICY

The modal split in freight transportation in the Federal Republic of Germany has changed considerably since World War II. The market share of the roadways (presently 30 percent) has decreased drastically; the share of inland shipping (22 percent) is significantly lower; and the share of long-distance road freight transport (43 percent) has nearly doubled. The modal shares are significant to transportation policy decisions because they determine the impact on the transportation infrastructure and the necessary investments, the extent of external effects, and the economic position of the transportation firms.

The change in the modal split is induced by the effects of the commodity structure, the regional structure, and substitution. In the past it has been determined by the commodity structure effects. The modal split of the railroad and inland shipping has decreased with the decline in importance of bulk goods such as coal and steel. Road freight transport, on the other hand, has benefited from the rising share of high value goods. The modal shares were changed at the expense of railways through the displacement of a series of transport-intensive firms—for example, steel production and automobile manufacturing on the coast. In addition, roadway transportation has gained advantages in quality over the railways and inland shipping so that substitution has also resulted.

The commodity structure is a function of economic change. Transportation policy can do nothing against changes in demand. If it would attempt to manipulate the modal split through an interventionist strategy like prohibition of transport, it would produce disadvantages on the production side. Through liberal competition, policy in the transport sector can certainly contribute to the transportation firms' efforts at improved performance and quality in order to mitigate the impact of the commodity structure through substitution.

A central problem of the German transportation policy, which overshadows many branches and blocks many efficient solutions, is the deficit of the German Federal Railways (DB). The DB has shown a deficit since the beginning of the 1950s; the current losses amount to 3.5 billion DM per year. Railway revenues cover only up to 50 percent of its expenditures. The debt of the DB equals 36 billion DM. Causes of the deficit are manifold: declining market shares of the DB in freight as well as in regional passenger transportation, the railroad's strong dependency on the growth of its most important transported goods (raw materials), mistakes in marketing policy (e.g., neglect of investments and improvements in quality), neglect of economic profitability goals as a consequence of political instrumentalism, overstaffing and inadequate progress in productivity as a result of the influence exerted by the strong railway labor union, and insufficient capital (Aberle & Willeke, 1973).

The main problem in the DB's economic and financial crisis is the distribution of property rights of the public good—the Federal Railways. Decision making, responsibility, and financing in important branches of the business often go awry because of the legal framework and the actual conduct of the authorized powers. The consequence is regulation of the DB at the expense of its own economic well-being. There is a need for a redistribution of property rights which would affect the status of the firm, ownership regulations, competition, and financial relations between the DB and the government.

The managerial concept of the DB shows that the necessity for structural adjustment is recognized and corrective measures have been introduced: reduction in the number of workers, increase in productivity, closure of secondary routes, and implementation of aggressive marketing.

For lasting consolidation, the DB would have to take full commercial responsibility for revenues and investment activities. This would require that a path other than the currently favored "separate sales accounting" approach be taken (Aberle & Weber, 1987). The "separate sales accounting" attempts to distinguish among commercial, unprofitable, and public interest branches of the railroad and to delegate responsibility according to the government. Aside from the problems of cost allocation, a negative aspect would also be the fact that the DB as a unit of operation would be divided and parts of the business competency transferred to political authorities.

A primary theme of the reorganization of the railways is the reduction of social and public burdens (i.e., tariff reductions, maintenance of secondary routes, and operational duties). Some compensation payments are made, but not to the full extent and not in accordance with economic value. A specific-use reimbursement plan would entail specific reimbursement of the initiators according to economic performance, as is already agreed upon between several states and the DB. Insofar as the appointed institutions would have to examine whether or not the performance was proportionately representative of the compensatory payments, an obstacle against public waste would be erected. Figure 11.1 shows the nation's railroad network.

With economic growth and subsequent changes in the production structure, the types of goods transported and the demands for quality in transportation performance also change. Increasing competition in the industrial markets leads to competition by prices among industries and to productivity pressure in the transportation sector.

Thus natural affinities of certain shippers for certain types of transportation have been broken up. Roadway transportation, especially intracompany transportation, was able to gain enormous market shares because of its qualitative advantages. In recent years transportation shippers have increasingly expected additional logistical output such as extra efforts in transportation processing, storage, and information services. Adaptation on the supply side of the structural change is under the purview of the transportation firms. The task of transportation policy is to establish a frame of action for the transportation firms so that competition in the transport markets can develop as an innovative process and the demands of the transportation consumers can be met. This is the basis behind demands for deregulation of the transportation markets and the reduction of governmentally induced distortions and restraints in competition.

Combined transport (container and piggyback) evolved from the technological developments in transportation which came out of the U.S. shipping industry and has, since the end of the 1960s, spread to inland shipping. Combined transport offers operational as well as managerial advantages: through improved transshipment the high level of stoppages is reduced; heterogeneous small high-value goods are combined and turned into bulk goods through transportation technology; through norms in load unity the transfer between transportation modes is facilitated; the transportation infrastructure is better utilized; and the impact on roads and the environment is alleviated.

Development of combined transportation caught on most quickly in road transportation; the railroad and inland shipping reacted hesitantly. The volume of combined rail/road traffic since the beginning of the 1970s has more than doubled: 16 million tons in 1985. The transportation policy promotes combined transportation through regulation and investment policy measures (e.g., with special rules for vehicle taxes or with investment subsidies for container terminals). There is, however, conjecture that investments in the DB terminals are oversized.

The piggyback transport includes the transportation by semi-trucks or whole

Figure 11.1
Railroad Network in West Germany

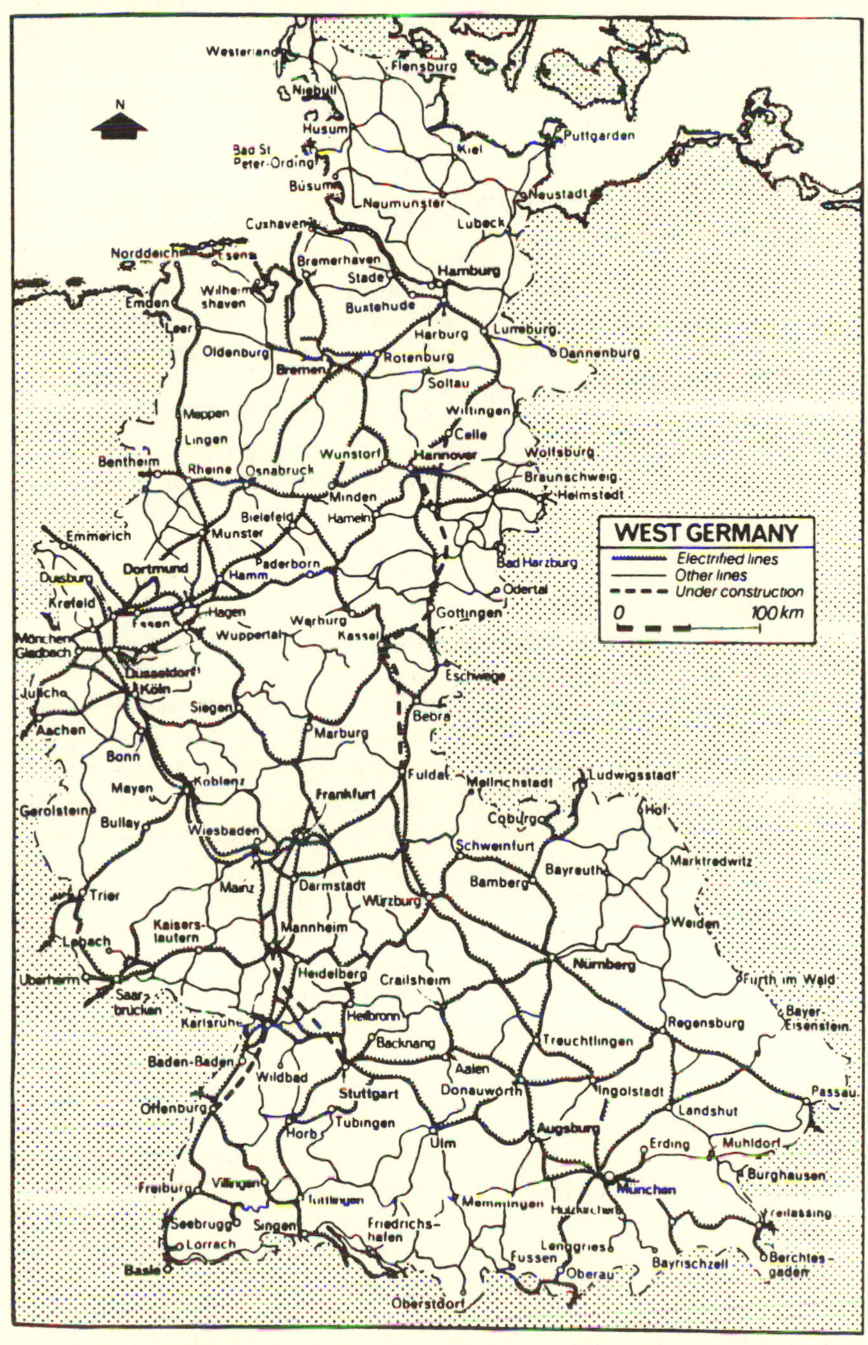

Source: Chris Bushell, *Railway Directory & Year Book 1989* (Surrey, England: Reed Business Publishing, 1989), p. 298. Courtesy Reed Business Publishing, Ltd.

trucks carried by trains on rails. Individual shipments of single roadway transportation firms are coordinated into mass transportation for partial stretches, thereby enabling them to be transported by rail. The DB offers junction transport between several stations (''rolling highway''). Despite a considerable upswing in recent years, the railroad option is not yet regarded as sufficiently attractive (see Tables 11.3, 11.4, and 11.5).

POLITICAL DIMENSIONS OF THE TRANSPORTATION SYSTEM AND POLICY

Underlying the transportation sector are strong political and ideological influences. The high degree of politicization results from the far-reaching transportation policy decisions and the instrumentalism evoked in political election goals. Furthermore, transportation policy positions are influenced to a high degree by political events and developments (van Suntum, 1986).

The differences in the basic convictions of the political parties in the Federal Republic of Germany are relatively significant. Conservative parties have more of a preference for private transportation—individual transportation and road freight transport. Socialist parties, on the other hand, place priority on public transportation, especially the railroad and urban public passenger transport. Policy inconsistencies also stem from the federalistic structure of West Germany. Above all, conflicts arise between the transportation policy of the federal government and that of the states and cities which represent certain solutions because of special interests, which include construction of economically unprofitable inland waterways and preventing the closing of unprofitable railroad routes. The potential for conflict becomes even greater if, as in the European transportation policy, there is rivalry among national interests (Jürgensen & Aldrup, 1968).

In order to guarantee a certain continuity in conception, planning, and implementation of transportation decisions, the transportation administration has been conceded a relatively powerful position. Occasionally, however, the administration exhibits its own ''dynamics'' which is not democratically legitimate and which can hinder the implementation of the political will.

As desirable as a ''de-ideologization'' of the transportation policy is, it cannot be forced. One can only trust that the forces of competition and economic growth will exert such pressure on the transportation sector for efficiency that no ideological impetus would be allowed. This trend has in fact been ascertainable in recent years.

A primary cause of the strong politicization of the transportation sector is its instrumental economic and political function. Contributions to the global goals of full employment, price level stability, economic growth, reduction of regional disparities, and social equality are required of the transport economy and of the transportation policy. The expediency of such a policy affects the sectoral and global relations. Harmonious as well as conflicting goals exist.

The greatest contribution to economic growth is afforded by the transporta-

Table 11.3
Transportation Capacity, 1985

Capacity Indicators	1960	1985
German Federal Railroad:		
Length of network (hundred km)	30.7	27.6
Seating Capacity (thousands)	1225	977
Loading Capacity (million tons)	6.9	8.8
Transported Containers (thousands)	----	926.1
Piggyback Transportation (transported trucks in thousands)	----	485.7
Automobiles Transported by Train (number of vehicles in thousands)	----	122
Inland Shipping:		
Number of Freight Ships	7611	3143
Carrying Capacity (thousand tons)	4902	3277
Number of Pusher Crafts	5	107
Maritime Shipping:		
Number of Commercial Ships	2706	1523
Tonnage (in thousand gross-register-tons)	4762	5294
Road Freight Transportation:		
Number of Trucks (thousands)	182	257
Long-Distance Transport (thousands)	43	55
Short-Distance Transport (thousands)	139	202
Loading Capacity (in thousand tons)	1040	2615
Long-Distance Transport (in thousand tons)	395	800
Short-Distance Transport (in thousand tons)	645	1815
Pipelines:		
Crude Oil Piplines (length in km)	455	1715
Airlines:		
Number of Airplanes	208	536
Urban Public Transportation System:		
Length of Commuter Train Routes (in km)	139	425
Length of Streetcar Routes (in km)	3018	1477
Seating Capacity (thousands)		
Commuter Trains	152	555
Streetcars	1045	601
Buses	670	1955

Source: The Federal Minister of Transportation, ed., *Verkehr in Zahlen 1986* [Transportation in figures 1986] (Bonn, 1986: 50ff).

Table 11.4
Volume and Modal Split of Commodity Transport

Transportation Mode	Volume Transported (in million tons)				Share of Transportation Mode (%)			
	1960	1970	1980	1985	1960	1970	1980	1985
Railroads	317.1	378.0	350.1	324.4	18.7	13.3	10.8	11.1
Inland Shipping	172.0	240.0	241.0	222.4	10.2	8.5	7.5	7.6
FRG ships	103.4	137.5	126.4	105.3	–	–	–	–
Foreign ships	68.6	102.5	114.6	117.1	–	–	–	–
Long-Distance Road Transport	99.2	164.9	298.2	335.7	5.9	5.8	9.2	11.5
Commercial Transport	71.3	104.8	140.9	146.8	4.2	3.7	4.4	5.0
Intra-company Transport	23.5	41.1	99.6	119.1	1.4	1.4	3.1	4.1
Foreign Trucks	4.4	19.0	57.7	69.8	0.3	0.7	1.8	2.4
Pipelines	13.3	89.2	84.0	69.2	0.8	3.1	2.6	2.4
Air Transport (in thousand tons)	81.0	386.9	710.3	873.0	–	–	–	–
Short-Distance Road Transport	1090.0	1972.0	2255.0	1965.0	64.4	69.3	69.9	67.4
Commercial Transport	470.0	769.0	900.0	795.0	27.8	27.0	27.9	27.3
Intra-company Transport	620.0	1203.0	1355.0	1170.0	36.6	42.3	42.0	40.1
Total Transport in the FRG	1691.7	2844.5	3229.0	2917.6	100	100	100	100
Maritime Shipping	77.2	131.9	154.0	138.9	–	–	–	–
Transportation without Short-Distance Transport	601.7	872.5	974.0	952.6	100	100	100	100
Railroads					52.7	43.4	36.0	34.1
Inland Shipping					28.6	27.5	24.8	23.4
Long-Distance Road Transport					16.5	18.9	30.6	35.2
Commercial Transport					11.9	12.0	14.5	15.4
Intra-company Transport					3.9	4.7	10.2	12.5
Foreign Trucks					0.7	2.2	5.9	7.3
Pipelines					2.2	10.2	8.6	7.3

Source: The Federal Minister of Transportation, ed., *Verkehr in Zahlen 1986* [Transportation in figures 1986] (Bonn, 1986: 194 ff).

tion sector if it is efficiently utilized and if its capacity on the basis of aggregate economic cost-benefit criteria is expanded. A thoroughly desirable side effect is the fact that infrastructural investments have a positive impact on employment (15,000–20,000 persons per billion DM investment volume) (Schmidt, 1976).

Considerations for economic growth alone, however, are not sufficient justification for investment. In contrast, attempts to lower the inflation rate by keeping transportation prices low or to promote economically disadvantaged groups are ineffective. The results are too inexact and the impact too mild. Such attempts place an unnecessary burden on the profitability and efficiency of transportation firms through price-costs-gaps and misinformation through regulated prices, for example (Baum, 1980). Nor should the regional-political effectiveness be overestimated. The transportation infrastructure is ubiquitous

Table 11.5
Volume and Modal Split of Passenger Transport

Transportation Mode	Number of People Transported (in millions)				Share of Transportation Mode (%)			
	1960	1970	1980	1985	1960	1970	1980	1985
Railroads	1400	1053	1167	1135	6.1	3.4	3.1	3.3
Short-DistanceTraffic	1270	919	1016	995	–	–	–	–
Long-Distance Traffic	130	134	152	140	–	–	–	–
Urban Public Transportation System	6156	6170	6745	5809	26.8	20.1	18.1	16.6
Air Transport	4.9	21.3	35.9	41.7	0.0	0.1	0.1	0.1
Airlines	4.4	15.9	24.8	28.9	–	–	–	–
Charter Flights	0.5	5.4	11.1	12.8	–	–	–	–
Transport via Taxis and Rented Cars	123	290	365	335	0.5	1.0	1.0	1.0
Transport via Privately Owned Cars	15300	23120	28915	27605	66.6	75.4	77.7	79.0
Total	22984	30654	37228	34926	100	100	100	100

Source: The Federal Minister of Transportation, ed., *Verkehr in Zahlen 1986* [Transportation in figures 1986] (Bonn, 1986: 172 ff).

to a large extent so the effects on specific locations are often insignificant. In some cases it can be ascertained that improvements in the transportation connections generate ''evacuation effects'' through the commuting tendencies of the population (Aberle, 1981).

In light of this experience, instrumentalism of the transportation sector for goals of the economic policy would make little sense. Insofar as sectoral and global policies are mutually reinforcing, the congruous effects should be realized. Where conflicts exist, transportation policy should ensure efficient development of the transportation sector and repress other demands.

The third political factor consists of foreign policy developments and events which produce a demand for action in transportation policy.

For the Federal Republic of Germany, the most influential integration fact was the founding of the European Communities (Willeke, 1987). The European Economic Community (EEC) Treaty of 1957 proclaimed the goal of common transportation markets. The EC Commission has worked steadily toward harmonization and liberalization. Aside from the unification of technical and social regulations and a certain degree of price liberalization, there has been little success. This was due to the predominance of the member-states with an interventionistic transportation policy, namely, West Germany, France, and Italy.

Liberal tendencies, however, have become more effective with the expansion of the EC and these have also led to deregulation steps and a far-reaching deregulation program. In the meantime, the efforts of the EC Commission at harmonization and liberalization have gone further, including infrastructure investments, maritime ports, and airline transport policies, and have affected the German transportation policy. As a result of economic integration and the subsequent increase in frontier crossing transport, the problem of transit by trucks, which places great stress on the infrastructure, through non-EC countries, especially Austria and Switzerland, has arisen.

The increased trade between Western and Eastern Europe likewise causes a growth in the number of traffic routes. This cooperation is promoted through infrastructural ties like the Rhein-Main-Donau Canal. The Federal Republic of Germany trades with the Council for Mutual Economic Assistance (COMECON) countries through bilateral agreements over market shares of the transportation service, but the results are not yet satisfactory, due in part to lack of reciprocity. The German transportation policy also takes responsibility for the protection of maritime shipping. In addition to the protectionist proclivities of developing countries, unfair competitive practices by subsidized or state-owned shipping firms are evident. In order to minimize damage to German shipping companies, the government attempts to eliminate such distortions at the bilateral level. It is also pressing for countries to accede to the United Nations Conference on Trade and Development (UNCTAD) Code of Conduct for Liners.

Finally, a need for action in transportation policy arises from political crises (Willeke, 1980). Examples would be the Suez Crisis (1956), the Yom Kippur War (1973), or the Iran Crisis (1979–80). Crises affect the transportation sector either through restrictions in supply as a consequence of energy shortages or because of increased demands, for example, in the event of threatening military conflicts. In crisis situations the transportation policy should provide for the continuation of transportation capacity, especially the railroad and urban public transport. For this purpose there would presumably exist an optimum of reserve capacity which is based on costs and benefits. Subsidies for the preservation of transportation firms are, in this respect, to interpret as insurance premium. Growing demands produced by a crisis situation must not even in the event of available reserves lead to an absolute restriction in quantity but should be accommodated by lowering the quality of performance to a certain degree. This is to ensure that subsidies used for supply in case of a crisis will not be used too extensively.

RECENT TRENDS AND FUTURE PROSPECTS

In passenger as well as in freight transport, new transportation technologies are being developed and in some cases tested. The innovations are relevant to a broad spectrum of different elements of transportation production (e.g., motors, vehicles, transportation infrastructure). Transportation policy promotes new technologies through investments or through financial assistance. Undoubtedly technological advances have been made which have then been introduced into conventional transportation systems. New technologies have not, however, gone beyond the testing stage. Technological progress made in the transportation sector has consisted of evolutionary developments rather than complete system changes. Implementation of the advances is the responsibility of industries and transportation operators. The government has no head start to better assess the marketability of innovations. It is, as experience shows, questionable whether economically useful results will develop. The subsidized (thus far with 4.2 billion DM) Airbus project is an example of a case where, even with outstanding technology and favorable market conditions, the industry could not reach the profit zone. This suggests that the government, in its promotion of technology, concentrates on basic research and globally supported projects and refrains from subventions for specific projects.

Information technologies and data transmission are of decisive importance for the economic development of industrial states. In West Germany, a system of telecommunication services of the German Postal Service has been constructed since the end of the 1970s using video-screen texts, long-distance data transmission, and facsimile systems.

The transportation sector plays both a substitutive and a complementary role for telecommunication services.

In freight transportation, shorter transport times make it necessary to develop technology for optimizing the production process. Through improvements in the informational and logistical requirements of shippers and transportation operators, the flows of traffic can be coordinated. From this, a rationalization and reduction of transportation production is to be expected. Thus, in freight transportation a complementary connection is to be expected.

In passenger transport there is competition from telecommunication services. These include picture telephones, video-conferences, banking services, teleshopping, and telecommuting. Limits to substitution arise out of advantages of personal communication such as conclusion of treaties and employment (Ewers & Fritsch, 1985). Forecasters expect that in the next ten to fifteen years telecommunications will not significantly affect passenger transportation.

The integration of the German economy with the world market allows for a rapid diffusion of new technologies. The task for transportation policy is then to build up the necessary infrastructure without hesitation so that a private network which is both complementary to and competitive with the German Postal Service can be established.

Sociocultural developments create a number of demographic and social factors which determine the mobility of the population. These include population growth, age structure, motorization, work and leisure time, living and consumer preferences, and environmental conscience.

According to available data, a further increase in individual transportation via private automobiles can be expected. Populated regions will spread increasingly; living preferences of the population will favor suburbanization. Despite declining population figures, motorization will continue to grow from 24.5 million in 1985 to 30 million automobiles in the year 2000. The overall weak economic growth has led to decreasing distances and frequencies driven. In private transportation in congested urban areas, however, reductions are lowest; substitutions and reductions in travel are taking place primarily in other transportation modes. Shorter workdays and increased part-time labor will allow private automobile transportation to increase. From this perspective there is a need for policy action to alleviate the resulting traffic jams and improve transportation flows in the urban areas.

Investments in transportation have in the past been made a priority of the public transportation system. Attempts were also made to force self-regulation of the public transportation through either a strategy of "do nothing" or through the intentional allowance of bottlenecks. The age of efficient city highway construction is to a large extent over, in part because of the limited amount of available land. Possibilities for improvements, however, still exist through the roadway network. Technical-organizational advances of traffic management are likewise not yet exhausted.

Regulatory policy in urban transport should enable the efficient utilization of the transportation infrastructure (Rothengatter, 1974). Today its emphasis is on administrative rationing—privileges and restrictions. A drawback of regulations is that their effects are crude rather than selective. Principles of the market mechanism are neglected. There should be a confrontation between demands and prices for transportation services and for public infrastructure benefits. In this sense the pricing policy in private and public passenger transport should be modified.

The desolate economic situation in urban public passenger transport has become increasingly acute in recent years. The degree of cost coverage reaches only 30 to 40 percent. The causes lie in decreasing population figures including foreigners, in the decline in school traffic, in high unemployment, in the small degree of capacity usage, and in high personnel costs. Because of the declining demands, reductions in public transportation services are unavoidable. This applies especially to the sparsely populated regions, but also to congested areas in times of weak demand. Minimal standards in transportation services are, nevertheless, to be maintained. The substitution of railway transport by bus transport also provides possibilities for savings in rural areas. In local passenger transport even in less populated regions and despite declining numbers of passengers, improvements could be made in transportation through cooperation (e.g., regional joint transport enterprises).

With increasing understanding of the dangers to the environment, the exhaustibility of resources, and the potentially dangerous side effects of technology, quality of life demands are being made. Transportation policy addresses these trends with the goals of environmental protection, increased transportation safety, and energy conservation.

Table 11.6
Energy Consumption by Economic and Transportation Sector (in Petajoules)[1]

Sector Groups	1960	1970	1980	1985
Total Energy Consumption	4269	6753	7530	7390
Industry	2072	2661	2582	2293
Households	1536	2934	3282	3386
Transportation	661	1158	1666	1711
incl: Rail Transport	250	118	74	60
Road Transport	372	936	1447	1497
Air Transport	10	67	109	124
Inland Shipping	29	37	36	30
Docking of Seagoing Ships	108	155	120	122

[1] A unit of electrical energy or work that is equivalent to the work done in raising the potential of one coulomb of electricity one volt, or in maintaining for one second a current of one ampere against a resistance of one ohm.

Source: The Federal Minister of Transportation, ed., *Verkehr in Zahlen 1986* [Transportation in figures 1986] (Bonn, 1986: 264).

Environmental problems are especially evident in highly congested areas where both motor vehicle and rail transport are affected. In the evaluation of new investments, effects on the environment are taken into consideration. Measures to protect the environment in road construction are of considerable size, accounting for 10 percent of the investment costs. Attempts are being made through the transportation policy to reduce existing environmental effects through a change in the modal split and through investment measures and emission standards for polluting components (Marburger, 1974; Willeke & Kentner, 1975) (see Tables 11.6, 11.7, and 11.8).

Thus far a tax solution for the internalization of external environmental costs has not been realized. Since environmental deterioration depends on traffic flow, polluting emissions, and health hazards, only estimates of the costs of prevention measures (i.e., costs necessary to retain certain emission standards) are considered. Even here empirical knowledge is insufficient. In addition, in view of the manifold sources of pollution and multicausal effects, in recent years the originator principle has become less relevant than the common burden principle.

To diminish the toxic emissions from automobiles in connection with *waldsterben* (dying forests), legal limits were established which could most effectively be achieved through the installation of catalytic converters. To accelerate the conversions, incentives through the vehicle tax and the fuel tax were of-

Table 11.7
Air Pollution

Emission	Carbon-monoxide		Sulfur-dioxide		Nitrous-oxide		Organic Compounds		Dust	
Emitting Source (%)	1966	1982	1966	1982	1966	1982	1966	1982	1966	1982
Power Plants, and Central Heating Plants	0.2	0.4	41.3	62.1	23.6	27.7	0.5	0.6	25.2	21.7
Industry	13.8	13.6	35.7	25.2	30.6	14.0	25.0	28.0	58.5	59.7
Households and Small Consumers	52.0	21.0	19.9	9.3	5.8	3.7	46.0	32.4	13.7	9.2
Transportation	34.0	65.0	3.1	3.4	40.0	54.6	28.5	39.0	2.6	9.4
Total (in Million Tons)	12.5	8.2	3.2	3.0	2.0	3.1	1.4	1.6	1.8	0.7

Source: The Federal Minister of Transportation, ed., *Verkehr in Zahlen 1986* [Transportation in figures 1986] (Bonn, 1986: 273).

fered for lead-free gasoline. The effect on the supply of low-pollutant vehicles, however, is still relatively small.

Again and again the discussion of a speed limit, 100 kilometers per hour (km/h) on the federal highways and 80 km/h on other roads, comes up in the Federal Republic of Germany. The argument changes: first it was over fuel conservation, then over a decrease in pollution emissions, and currently it is over decreasing the number of traffic accidents. A major test with the speed limit at 100 km/h on the expressways, in 1984–85, demonstrated through observed driving behavior that only a small reduction in pollution can be expected. Technological measures in environmental protection as well as in traffic safety and energy conservation are thought to be more efficient.

An increase in transportation safety is an important goal of transportation policy (Diekmann, 1972). The number of casualties in roadway traffic in West Germany is currently 10,000 per year; the number of injured 470,000 per year. Through multifaceted activities in the fields of transportation law, vehicle and road technology, rescue systems, and accident research and education, the number of accidents could be reduced. Especially effective measures are the compulsory seat belt requirement, special measures for beginner drivers (e.g., drivers license after testing), infrastructure measures (e.g., elimination of high accident risk sites), building of bypass roads and bike paths, and protection of residential areas (e.g., quieter traffic and restrained truck traffic).

The future tasks of transportation policy are determined by the accumulated problems of the past and the demands which are shaped by political, economic,

Table 11.8
Environmental Impact on Households in the Federal Republic of Germany, 1978

Type of Impact	Noise from Street Traffic		Railroad Noise		Air Noise		Noise from Business & Industry		Fumes, Exhaust & Dust Collection	
Intensity of Impact	1000	(%)	1000	(%)	1000	(%)	1000	(%)	1000	(%)
Continuously	7132.8	31.1	1024.1	4.5	990.8	4.3	789.4	3.4	3517.6	15.3
Strong	4740.4	20.7	429.9	1.9	575.2	2.5	319.3	1.4	1838.7	8.0
Somewhat	2392.4	10.4	594.2	2.6	415.6	1.8	470.1	2.0	1678.9	7.3
Occasionally Strong	2427.2	10.6	425.7	1.9	2994.3	13.0	462.1	2.0	1744.1	7.6
Affected Households Total:	9560.0	41.6	1449.8	6.3	3985.1	17.4	1251.5	5.5	5261.7	22.9
Unaffected Households:	6593.6	28.7	17864.4	77.8	12987.8	56.6	18575.4	80.9	12544.6	54.7
No Reply*:	6802.1	29.6	3641.5	15.9	5982.8	26.0	3128.8	13.6	5149.4	22.4
Households Total:					22955.7 Thousand					

*Including those households which replied "occasionally some impact."

Source: The Federal Minister for Transportation, ed., *Verkehr in Zahlen 1986* [Transportation in numbers 1986] (Bonn, 1986: 275).

technical, and sociocultural developments. Within this framework, transportation policy should ensure that the efficiency of the transportation infrastructure is improved and that it is not unduly burdened by other political demands. This basic principle has far-reaching consequences which can be programmatically summarized as follows: deregulation of the transportation markets, promotion of innovation through competition, efficiency-oriented investment policy, optimal utilization of the transportation infrastructure on a market-economy basis, commercialization of the managerial policy of the railroad, promotion of flexible adjustment of transportation firms to structural changes, and internalization of external costs. Such an efficiency-oriented transportation policy would have a positive influence on the reduction of transportation costs, improvements in quality of service, productivity, competitiveness, and economic growth. Financial regulations would have to be met for those groups involved with transportation which would be disadvantaged under the goal of efficiency. Income distribution and regional policy goals are easier to achieve through the well-defined measures of governmental financial policy than through transportation policy.

TRANSPORTATION POLICY ORGANIZATION AND PROCESS

Goals of the transportation policy in the Federal Republic of Germany have evolved as problems have arisen, and the significance of certain aspects has changed. The goals can be summarized as follows (The Federal Minister of Transportation, 1985):

- Economic modal split;
- Cost-efficient and guaranteed transportation for the population and the economy;
- Financial consolidation and structural adjustments of the railroad;
- Improvements in transportation infrastructures in cities, including the economic stabilization of local public passenger transport;
- Environmental protection, reduction in the number of traffic accidents, and energy conservation in the transportation sector;
- Reduction of factors restraining mobility in certain handicapped regions and population groups; and
- Contribution in promoting a single market in Europe.

This list of goals cannot be considered complete. Notably absent is coordination and weighting of the goals. Inconsistencies also appear in West Germany because different priorities are often recognized by the national, state, and local governments. At most one can speak of a "goal catalog" which structures the qualitative direction of the transportation policy efforts.

The regulation policy forms the competition and the market processes in freight and passenger transport. The main instruments are the policies for tariffs and market access. The model of "controlled competition" is still predominant in the Federal Republic, although it will become increasingly liberalized in the upcoming years under pressure from the European deregulation policy.

According to the tariff policy, the railroad has the role of price leadership; tariffs of the competing transportation modes are approved only insofar as they do not harm the status of the railroad. The tariffs on freight transport are differentiated according to the value of goods transported, distance, and weight. In passenger transport the tariffs are dependent on distance and quality of performance. The rigid tariff regulations have been relaxed over the years through tariff margins, exceptional tariffs, and special agreements (Hamm, 1980b; Seidenfus, 1988; Baum, 1983).

The market access is restricted. In roadway freight transportation a system of licensing and contingents exists (maximum number of licenses); in passenger transportation licenses are also required; and in air transportation within the Federal Republic a monopoly exists for the German Lufthansa. Access to intra-company transportation with trucks and inland shipping is not restricted. The consequences of the market access restrictions are insufficient competition and supranormal profit for the "happy few" who do possess a license. Trading of licenses is not allowed; their transfer is only permissible with the sale of an entire transportation firm. Under such conditions, licenses can fetch high prices (some 200,000 DM per license). Although the licensing system has become more flexible over the years, it still greatly restricts the competition.

The German air transport market is composed of both airline and charter transportation. In addition to strong competition among international air carriers over quality levels, competition over prices has been growing. Liberalization impulses in international airline transportation can be expected from the deregulation policy of the EC. The current system which restricts competition through bilateral air transport agreements will still be maintained in transportation with third countries. In the German air transportation market, policymakers assume that charter and airline modes perform independent tasks and any overlapping of the market fields should be avoided. Access to the regional air transportation market has become easier because its function as a feeder to large airports complements rather than competes with Lufthansa's functions.

Finally, the transportation policy influences the supply side of the market through incentives to market exits. This applies especially to domestic shipping for which a chronic overcapacity is presumed. Since 1969 high premiums have been paid for the scrapping of obsolete ships. The scrapping fund is financed through contributions from shipping firms which the government temporarily supported. Through scrapping, the number of ships was significantly reduced, and the remaining fleet exhibits a high degree of modernity. Because comparable support for market exits in other countries bordering the Rhine River did not succeed, the goal of capacity equilibrium in inland shipping was not achieved.

Investments in the transportation sector cover transportation infrastructure and rolling stock (vehicles) of transportation firms. In transportation policy, infrastructure investments are the most significant.

The goals of the investment policy are maintenance of the infrastructure substance; speedy completion of current projects; development of regional linkages; expansion of the transportation network where economically appropriate; conservation of energy, protection of the environment and nature; and urban development aspects.

Plans are developed as a special investment program (Federal Transportation Plan) for a ten-year period and regularly reassessed. The needs assessments come from the federal government, the states, and the local communities.

The process provides for an integrated transportation planning ''in one casting'': plans would not be formulated for certain individual transportation modes but rather for all transportation types jointly, with consideration for uniform goals and methods.

The planning process can be classified into the following stages: first, prognosis of transportation development and of the modal split is prepared. Second, demands are ascertained with a differentiation between indisposable needs (substitute investments and completion of projects already underway) and new projects. New projects are evaluated through cost-benefit analyses whereby a complete set of economic criteria—transportation costs, energy conservation, transportation safety, impact of noise and air pollution as well as political, ecological, and economic profitability criteria, as in the case of railroad investments—are applied. Third, there is the selection of investment programs in which varying degrees of priority are established and brought into conformity with the financial possibilities. An investment volume of 126 billion DM is distributed for 1986–95 as follows: 40 percent for federal highways, 28 percent for DB, 11 percent for local public passenger transport, 11 percent for urban roads, 6 percent for domestic waterways, 2 percent for aviation, and 2 percent for other purposes (The Federal Minister of Transportation, 1985).

The investment planning exhibits certain weaknesses: methods and results of transportation forecasting are controversial. Elements of past investment plans are always carried over in the continuation of the planning process without adequate efficiency analyses. In cost-benefit analysis different types of transportation consider different benefit effects so that a compatibility of results is not available.

The object of transportation financial policy is to increase government revenues for financing the transportation sector (Funck, 1977). The volume of the federal government's transportation budget now and in the near future amounts to 25 billion DM, about 10 percent of the total federal budget. Approximately half of the funds are reserved for investments.

The primary financial sources are the fuel tax with an income of 22.3 billion DM and the vehicle tax with 7.4 billion DM (1985). Added to these are the parking fees and canal fees from inland shipping.

A principle of non-affectation applies to taxes. Until 1973, a 50 percent compulsory allocation for road construction existed. Since then tax resources can be used for general transportation purposes. The vehicle tax is not reserved for any specific use; the states receive the tax revenues and then channel them to the cities to be used for financing the road infrastructure.

Collecting taxes for the transportation infrastructure is entirely appropriate. The impact of the fuel tax on roadway transportation is proportionate to usage intensity and to this extent reflects the principle of equivalency. The vehicle tax is a fixed tax and, considering the high share of fixed costs, justified. Whether the current 3:1 ratio of fuel taxes to vehicle taxes is correct or not is controversial. The higher the marginal social costs of transportation, the more justified a rise in the share of petroleum tax would be. There is, to be sure, discussion over a redistribution of tax burdens. Because no comprehensive cost assessment exists, however, any statement about the appropriateness of the ratio is currently not possible.

The financial system can, however, be criticized for its methods of tax collection. The road users are called upon to finance more and more of the public transportation system and the railways. This "cross-subsidization" is responsible for oversized investments and misallocation of funds.

The task of subsidization policy is to lower the level of subsidies and to achieve the greatest possible economic yield. The Federal Republic of Germany has no subsidization concept at its disposal which is intended for the medium term and includes a step-by-step reduction of subsidies. In such program subsidy occasions, types and lengths of duration would have to be examined.

Property rights regulation in the transportation sector in West Germany is dualistic. Proprietor of the transportation infrastructure (railways, roads, inland waterways, and airports) is the government. Transportation firms are partially in private hands (freight transport, inland shipping, ocean shipping, pipelines, and automobile transportation) and partially public property (DB, local public passenger transport, and Lufthansa). The market operations of the private transportation firms are in part controlled by the government and regulated by taxes.

The government's supply and administered market controls are balanced by private interest representation of the transportation industries and of the shipper. Important associations include the Federal Association of German Freight Transportation, the Federal Association of German Industry, the Association of Automobile Industries and the German Automobile Club.

Reasons behind the nationalization of certain transport firms are found in the governmental and sociopolitical functions which have been transferred to the transportation sector. Furthermore, the transportation sector is viewed as a means of achieving political goals.

The mixed transportation economy has resulted in distortions in competition at the expense of private transportation firms, inefficient allocation of transportation services, and insufficient investments as a consequence of an expanding infrastructure which prefers public transport.

Different calculation procedures have been developed to determine the infrastructure costs (wear and tear) (i.e., complete cost calculations vs. expenditure calculations). According to the existing cost calculations, roadway transport covers up to 100 percent of its costs, the railroad up to 60 percent, and inland shipping only up to 10 percent. Politically a fair pricing over the short term would be impossible; at most, cost coverage can be approximated. In the medium term, however, the goal of equal treatment must be kept in mind. Thus meeting the external costs of transportation is recommended, although no comprehensive quantitative estimation exists.

Because the transportation infrastructure is under the ownership of the government, elements which disturb competition could be eliminated through a division of rail network and railroad operation into separate firms. This solution would, however, entail considerable disadvantages. First, the financial burdens would only be transferred from one account to another. An additional "rail" infrastructure administration would presumably lead to higher costs. Furthermore, distortions in competition through the proportion of railroad user fees would be possible. Transfer of the ownership of the rail network to the federal government could endanger an optimum capacity if, under pressure from other political departments, the rail network became oversized.

The most consequential way to solve the problems resulting from mixed ownership would be privatization of the public transportation firms. In the 1970s the DB considered privatization, and a few services which did not immediately affect the central activities of the DB were made legally independent. For example, bus services of the DB were reorganized into legally private regional transportation companies. Privatization of all DB services is not a realistic alternative considering the associated legal and political problems. Certain branches, however, could become more efficient outside of the strict rules of the government budget and the public-service sector.

REFERENCES

Aberle, Gerd, *Verkehrspolitik und Regionalentwicklung: Integration und Evaluierung der Verkehrspolitik im Rahmen der Regionalpolitik und der regionalen Entwicklungsplanung* [Transportation policy and regional development: Integration and evaluation of the transportation policy under the framework of regional policy and regional development planning] (Bonn, 1981).

Aberle, Gerd, and Ulrich Weber, *Verkehrswegebenutzungsabgaben für die Eisenbahn* [Paying for using the infrastructure of railways] (Darmstadt, 1987).

Aberle, Gerd, and Rainer Willeke, *Wege zur Sanierung der Eisenbahn—Die Bundesbahn im internationalen Leistungsvergleich* [Possibilities of readjustment of the railways—An international comparison] (Frankfurt, 1973).

Baum, Herbert, *Staatlich administrierte Preise als Mittel der Wirtschaftspolitik* [Public administered prices as means of economic policy] (Baden-Baden, 1980).

———, "Possibilities and Limits of Regulation in Transport Policy," Report of the

62nd Round Table on Transport Economics of the European Conference of Ministers of Transport (Paris, 1983).

———, "Deregulation of rates for international road haulage within the European Community," *Journal of Transport Economics and Policy*, vol. 18 (1984), pp. 23–50.

Baum, Herbert, and Wolfgang Kentner, "Tariff Policies for Urban Transport," Report of the 46th Round Table on Transport Economics of the European Conference of Ministers of Transport (Paris, 1980).

Diekmann, Achim, *Wirtschaftliche Aspekte der Verkehrssicherheit* [Economic aspects of road safety] (Stuttgart, 1972).

Ewers, Han-Jürgen, and Michael Fritsch, *Telematik und Raumentwicklung* [Telematics and development of land use] (Bonn, 1985).

The Federal Minister of Transportation, ed., *Bundesverkehrswegeplan 1985* [Federal transportation infrastructure plan 1985] (Bonn, 1985).

———, ed., *Verkehr in Zahlen 1986* [Transportation in figures 1986] (Bonn, 1986).

Funck, Rolf, "Stassenverkehrsteuern" [Taxes on road traffic] in *Handwörterbuch der Wirtschaftswissenschaft* [Handbook of economics], vol. 7 (Stuttgart, 1977), pp. 468–479.

Hamm, Walter, "Regulated Industries: Transportation," *Zeitschrift für die gesamte Staatswissenschaft,* 1980a, pp. 576–592.

———, "Verkehrspolitik" [Transportation policy] in *Handwörterbuch der Wirtschaftswissenschaft* [Handbook of economics], vol. 8 (Stuttgart, 1980b), pp. 249–257.

Jürgensen, Harald, and Dieter Aldrup, *Verkehrspolitik im europäischen Integrationstraum* [Transportation policy in the European Market] (Baden-Baden, 1968).

Marburger, Ernst-Albrecht, *Die ökonomische Beurteilung der städtischen Umweltbelastung durch Automobilabgase* [An economic assessment of the environmental impact due to automobile air pollution] (Bentheim, 1974).

Predöhl, Andreas, *Verkehrspolitik* [Transportation policy] (Göttingen, 1958).

Rothengatter, Werner, *Kosten- und nachfrageorientierte Preisbildung im Verkehrssektor* [Cost- and demand-based pricing in the transportation sector] (Karlsruhe, 1974).

Schmidt, Kunibert, *Verkehrsinfrastrukturinvestitionen als Mittel einer wachstumsorientierten Konjunkturpolitik* [Transportation infrastructure investments as means of a stabilization policy] (Bentheim, 1976).

Seidenfus, Helmut St., "Sektorale Wirtschaftspolitik" [Sectoral economic policies] in *Kompendium der Volkswirtschaftslehre* [Compendium of economics], vol. 2, 4th ed. (Göttingen, 1975), pp. 206–274.

Seidenfus, Hellmut St., et al., *Ordnungspolitische Szenarien zur Verwirklichung eines Gemeinsamen Europäischen Verkehrsmarkets, Teil A: Szenarien und ökonomische Wirkungszusammenhänge* [Regulatory scenarios on the implementation of a common European transport market, part A: Scenarios and economic issues] (Münster, 1988).

van Suntum, Ulrich, *Verkehrspolitik* [Transport policy] (München, 1986).

Voigt, Fritz, *Verkehr* [Transportation], vol. 2, Die Entwicklung des Verkehrssystems [The development of the transportation systems] (Berlin, 1966).

———, *Verkehr* [Transportation], vol. 1, *Die Theorie der Verkehrswirtschaft* [The theory of transportation economics] (Berlin, 1973).

Willeke, Rainer, ed., *Bedingungen nachhaltiger Energiesicherung für den Verkehr*

[Conditions for long-term energy conservation for transportation] (Düsseldorf, 1980).

———, "Liberalisierung und Harmonisierung als Aufgabe einer gemeinsamen Verkehrpolitik im EG-Raum" [Liberalization and harmonization as task and chance of a common transport policy in the EC], *Zeitschrift für Verkehrswissenschaft* [Journal of transportation policy], vol. 58 (1987), pp. 71–99.

Willeke, Rainer, and Wolfgang Kentner, *Die Kosten der Umweltbelastung durch den Verkehrslärm in Stadtgebieten* [The costs to the environment of traffic noise in urban areas] (Bentheim, 1975).

12

ZAIRE

Kendall Stiles

BACKGROUND

Transportation in Zaire is lacking in almost every respect: structurally, institutionally, financially, and technically. Two problems that have their roots deep in Zaire's history seem to be the principal causes of these shortcomings: external penetration in the form of foreign investment and management, and internal corruption and mismanagement. The two, as will be seen, are mutually reinforcing.

Beginning in the fifteenth century, at roughly the same time Columbus was traversing the Atlantic, Portuguese explorers were mapping the region now known as ''Bas'' Zaire at the mouth of the Congo River. These explorers quickly discovered the limits of access to the Congo hinterland via this river route. A series of sixty-six waterfalls and rapids makes the river utterly unusable from the port of Matadi to the ''Stanley Pool'' near the present capital of Kinshasa—a distance of some 400 kilometers (see Figure 12.1). The river drops roughly 250 metres over this short space, traversing on its way some of the most inhospitable jungle and mountains in Africa. This obstacle effectively barred European penetration of the hinterland for 400 years, until the renowned British explorer Sir Henry Morton Stanley arrived at the mouth of the Congo in 1871, coming from the east, from Zanzibar, on the Indian Ocean in a 999-day journey.

The discovery of the Congo River's extensive inland network by Stanley immediately changed the significance of the entire Congo territory for the King

Figure 12.1
Zaire's Transportation System

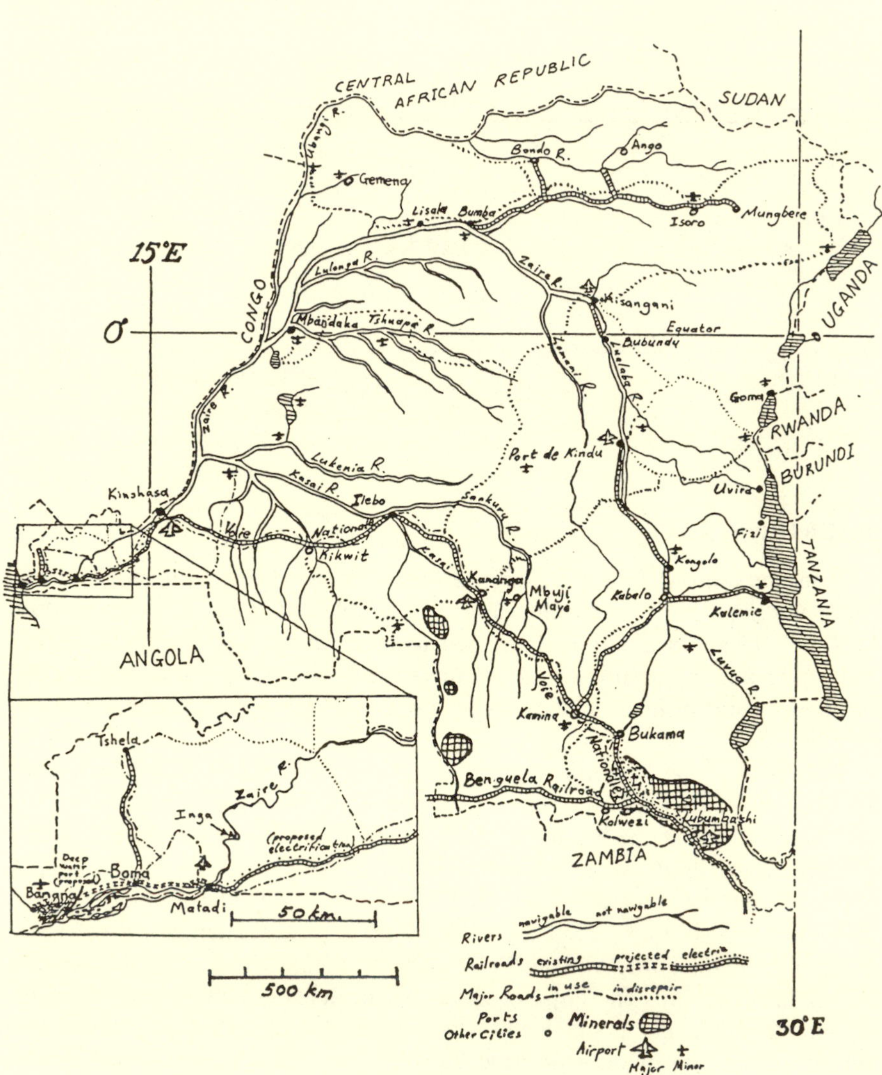

of Belgium, Leopold II, who held "title" to the land. After an unsuccessful British attempt at traveling up the Congo, Leopold commissioned a consortium of European investors to investigate the possibility of building a railway to connect Stanley Pool to Matadi. As put by Stanley, "The Congo River without a railway to connect it to the sea, is not worth a penny." With the advice of Stanley, under the direction of Albert Thys, the project was finally financed largely from the coffers of the king himself in the late-1880s.

Starting in 1890, this all-important railway was constructed. The effort lasted eight years and cost thousands of lives. The essential modus operandi was the use of native Congolese and "imported" Senegalese and Chinese porters, who died in large numbers in the process (estimated at 1,800). The first locomotive made the trip on the finished railway in 1898 and represented the first major railway in Black Africa. At the turn of the century, until the 1920s, Zaire's transportation network was unequaled.

In the early years, the best developed transportation systems in the colony were those linking major agricultural centers in the north, which produced rubber for export, to the ports of Matadi and Boma. When copper and gold mining began in the beginning of the century in the far southeastern region of the country, near the source of the Congo, efforts began to build railways linking the mines to the navigable sections of the river.

The colonial administration significantly expanded the rail network during the next thirty years, building a line in 1931 from the mining sectors in the southwest (Lubumbashi) to the lower Congo tributaries in order to shorten the distance to Kinshasa. Likewise, international rail connections south to the Indian Ocean via South Africa as well as due west to the Atlantic via Angola, both from the Shaba region were completed by World War II, both with the intent of increasing the flow of copper from Shaba to the wealthy nations. From this point, the essential transportation system of the Congo was merely "fine-tuned." The railway from Kamina to Kabalo in 1956 represented the last major infrastructural investment of the Belgian administration.

Throughout Zaire's history, roadways have always been second-rate, both in terms of their extent and quality as well as their social and political significance. To illustrate, the *voie nationale,* the original mixed rail/river route going through the southern sections of the country, was used in order to earn money from user fees which would go to pay the Belgian government for its construction. This discouraged the construction of alternate roads in the northern regions that might compete with the *voie nationale*. In spite of their low priority, the Belgians did manage to lay some 145,000 kilometers of dirt roads before independence.

Since independence, with few exceptions, each year has seen decline in the conditions and use of Zaire's transportation network. It is difficult to understand this collapse without some notion of Zaire's contemporaneous political experiences. Independence came to Zaire much more quickly than either the Belgians or the local Congolese had anticipated. As a result, neither had prepared adequately for an orderly transfer of power, let alone proper professional training of government officials. In addition, the problems that were to beset the relatively inexperienced transportation officials were extreme by any measure. When the difficulty of the circumstances and the inexperience of the staff are compounded by instability in the highest levels of government, the catastrophic outcomes can be appreciated more easily.

After the declaration of independence on June 30, 1960, martial law was imposed by President Patrice Lumumba to quell mutinies among the police forces. Within three days, Moise Tshombe declared independence in the southern Shaba region, and Belgium deployed troops. Copper output came to a halt, and the southern railways were taken out of state control. By September, United Nations forces occupied the southeastern region, replacing Belgian forces. However, a new rebellion erupted in the northeast under the leadership of Mobutu Sese Seko. For a period of roughly thirteen months, three separate governments ruled Zaire. Even after the two irredentist regimes were subdued in 1963, major violent outbursts continued. At one point in 1964, 1,000 Belgian paratroopers were airlifted to the northeast to rescue European nationals. Only in 1965 was central government established with reasonable success by Mobutu who quickly eliminated many civil rights and representative bodies to rule by decree and promote a personality cult. Regional tensions erupted yet again on two occasions in the late-1970s when the government required foreign support to put down two invasions into the Shaba region.

Transportation routes during the first five years of the republic were jeopardized by this political upheaval. Directly, war in the Shaba region cut off copper exports with the severing of railway links. Likewise, communication to the northeastern region was severely disrupted during the secession. As portrayed vividly in André Lederer's thorough description of Zaire's waterways, port traffic declined significantly during the 1958–65 period, by over 50 percent, from 1,400,000 tons to 625,000 tons, at Matadi. Because the conflicts were of a fairly low intensity, damage to infrastructure was slight, thus allowing for the quick increase in use immediately after the wars.

Indirectly, the lack of unified government and stable government revenues completely disrupted investment plans in infrastructure. In addition, as we shall see in the section dealing with administration of transportation, an investment strategy aimed at the personal enrichment of government officials and those individuals brought into government to shore up its political foundation began to dominate fiscal programs in Zaire. Political survival of the regime itself was naturally the first priority of the government, and the system of patronage that developed to insure this survival inhibited long-term transportation projects.

Finally, the eventual structure of Zaire's transportation system, like that of many states, became the victim of "pork-barrel" politics which disproportionately benefitted those regions on the southern Kinshasa-Lubumbashi axis. The income from copper and the instability of local government in the Shaba region prompted the central government to concentrate on ways of insuring a continuous flow of, and control over, copper. Unlike that of many developed, industrialized countries, Zaire's transportation is not the result of a continuous, incremental accrual of investments; it is a vehicle for economic and political survival of a beleaguered regime.

Zaire's export earnings swelled dramatically when, following a 300 percent devaluation of its currency in 1968 which made its exports more attractive, the world price of copper rose from roughly fifty cents to $1.40 per pound by 1974. The volume of copper production increased by 171 percent from 1965 to 1973, with an increase in value from roughly $3 million to $15 million. This swelling of Zaire's export earnings naturally precipitated a period of intense investment in nearly all sectors of the economy, including especially energy and transportation. Much of the investment was done with borrowed funds. Zaire's foreign debt by 1975 was already at $3 billion (half of Zaire's GNP).

In the mid-1970s, major infrastructural projects were begun, including the erection of rail bridges over the Zaire River at Matadi, the extension of a railway from Lubumbashi to Kinshasa, the expansion of Air Zaire with the addition of a 747 jumbo jet, and the electrification of the Matadi-Kinshasa railway. Each of these projects had some merit. In particular, the recently finished Kinshasa-Lubumbashi railway will allow the evacuation of copper directly through Matadi, which will greatly increase the financial viability of this major port. Likewise, although unneeded, the electrification of the Matadi-Kinshasa railway will make use of the massive increase in electrical capacity of the country since the partial start-up of the Inga by hydroelectric power plant. However, given the accelerating collapse of more traditional means of transportation, such as roads and rivers, these investments seem very ill-advised.

To illustrate the lack of maintenance of the conventional transportation network, it should be pointed out that of 160,000 km of road in 1985, only 2,000 km are asphalted, and only 22,000 km of the rest are now in service. "Since the troubled times of 1960–1964, parts of the country have been literally isolated. Due to lack of maintenance, the majority of dirt roads have deteriorated . . . Except for the Matadi-Kinshasa road, it is almost impossible to travel from any one regional capital to another with anything but an off-road vehicle" (Ngandu, 1984: 71).

Likewise, river transport during the 1970s deteriorated significantly, even as new earnings from copper flowed into the country. It is reported, for example, that in 1971 alone, 279 ships saw either accidents, loss of anchor, or damage to goods on board, of which six sank. The same figures for 1976 were 186 accidents and fifteen sinkings. Six passengers drowned on Zaire's rivers in 1971 and nineteen drowned in 1976. The vast majority of river ports, especially along the underutilized Zaire River in the north, are in disrepair, if not completely destroyed by wear. The total length of navigable rivers declined from 2,986 km in 1970 to 1,713 km in 1980. For most of the traditional transportation, by road and river, conditions in 1985 were far worse than they were at independence.

By 1979, due to the coincidence of massive borrowing to finance "showcase" projects and declining copper earnings, the country had fallen into severe debt with foreign private bankers and foreign governments. It therefore was required to receive assistance from the International Monetary Fund, including the introduction of a large number of primarily European technocrats into the senior levels of Zaire's public and semi-private administration. Their task was to correct the country's severe financial problems with efficient and professional management. In addition, it was hoped that the corruption in the public sector could be somewhat mitigated with the direct involvement of foreign supervisors. However, after three years, most of these IMF-sponsored officials had returned, discouraged and frustrated.

In at least one case, the electrification of the Matadi-Kinshasa river, even though their task was to increase fiscal responsibility and reduce indebtedness, the foreign supervisors actually exacerbated the problem. The rationale for electrification is difficult to find, although some connection to the billion-dollar Inga hydroelectric plant is plausible. In spite of World Bank, European Economic Community (EEC), and Western countries' disapproval, Belgian administrators in 1979 decided to approve the electrification of the Kinshasa-Matadi railway. This has been explained in terms of Belgian construction interests, although it also appears that the new officials in the newly created Inga Free zone (ZOFI) would benefit from the project, since it assured a massive infusion of fresh capital ($360 million over five years from 1979–83 inclusive, of which $90 million would be devoted to electrification of the Matadi-Kinshasa Railways [CFMK]—the railway of the lower Zaire—alone).

The following sections focus on the economic, social, and political demands on Zaire's transportation system as well as on its administrative structure to describe the problems of international penetration and official corruption.

SOCIOECONOMIC DIMENSIONS OF THE TRANSPORTATION SYSTEM AND POLICY

As already indicated, the principal economic demand on Zaire's transport system prior to and since independence has been the linkage of Zaire's natural resources with their foreign markets. The railway links from Kinshasa to Matadi, and those paralleling the nonnavigable portions of the Zaire River, were built with the intent of providing access to the country's mineral and rubber wealth. The early years have been described as "pillage" and a "vicious system of exploitation," in that private companies, most of which were Belgian, operating with a franchise from the King, forced local inhabitants to assist, often at the peril of their lives, in harvesting rubber and mining copper. "These private interests created Congo's transportation system. The development and expansion of means of communication paralleled economic expansion and, in turn, stimulated it. . . . The [transportation system] of today [1969] was conceived and built around the need for export" (Said, 1969: 135, 138).

As early as the 1930s, due to financial pressure on private corporations involved in extending the railway lines to Lubumbashi and converting to 1.067 meter gauge, the Belgian Ministry for the Colonies bought back the franchise and created the National Office of Colonial Transportation (OTRACO). This government agency controlled, first and foremost, the railway from Kinshasa to Matadi. This public enterprise, headquartered in Brussels, was expected to operate on a commercial basis, thus blurring the distinction between ''political'' and ''economic'' actors. By independence, the role of OTRACO had expanded to include all river transport as well as port authorities. Only the railways of the eastern regions operated independently, and they were unified in 1973 under the National Corporation of Zairian Railways (SNCZ).

During the first decades of the twentieth century, the rather clumsy rail-waterway routes along the Zaire and Kasai, which required frequent transfer of materials from train cars to ships and back again, were financially viable only because no alternatives existed. A major threat to Zaire's transportation link to the copper mines was the completion of the Benguela railway through Angola. When completed in 1929, it provided a cheaper and faster route to the ocean for Zaire's copper. Because it was built and administered by British concerns, this took away potential revenues for OTRACO. In addition, eastern railway routes, although requiring greater ocean travel, were a cheaper means of shipping exports to the European markets. This foreign competition to transport Zairian ore supplemented the western and southern linkage routes to the Indian Ocean and would continue to limit transport earnings in Zaire until 1975.

During the period of 1960 to 1965, following independence, imports declined first due to business concerns over the Zairian situation, then to the civil war in the east. The civil war was naturally accompanied by bridge demolition and rebel occupation of railway terminals. In addition, government policy prohibited the cutting down of tropical forests in the lower Zaire region, which had made up close to 90 percent of the exported tonnage going through Boma, in order to prevent serious deforestation. Finally, the regular supply of imports from the United States was cut off due to longshoremen strikes which interrupted traffic for months at a time. Given these dramatic changes in government policy, combined with the uncertainty and disruption of normal economic activities, it is indeed rather difficult to determine, from 1960 to 1965, what the total economic demand on the transportation system actually was. We will see that, once political conditions returned to normal, the transportation system was ill-equipped to cope with the much greater demand of the period after 1974.

Although demand on the Matadi port increased dramatically after 1965, actual use of the Matadi port zone increased only slightly, primarily because of the lack of maintenance of the port's facilities. In addition, customs processing was remarkably slow and unprofessional due to the lack of training of customs officials; the port area was typically clogged by a proliferation of empty railway cars (up to 300 at a time); and the generally awkward process of boat-to-train transfer delayed the movement of goods. In fact, the port functioned so poorly that many importers of high-cost goods (such as appliances) unloaded at Boma and used either the normally much slower roads or much more expensive air transport to Kinshasa.

Foreign investors were eager to participate in the show-case projects of the late-1960s and early-1970s, and financiers would later provide loans to the copper-rich nation. Plans for an all-rail *voie nationale* to replace the rail/river *voie nationale* were formulated during this period and provided both a logical extension of the Belgian strategy before independence to link Lubumbashi to Kinshasa, as well as to provide increased revenues for the state by bringing Benguela railway traffic back to Zaire. A plan to construct a railway/roadway bridge over the lower Zaire emerged as early as 1968 and was taken up again in 1971 when Mobutu negotiated with the Japanese government for a loan of $150 million to finance the project. This was done despite feasibility studies which indicated that the bridge would not be profitable without a railway link to Banana, which would itself have been technically infeasible. More will be said regarding the outcome of these and other foreign investments.

Although the Benguela railway had always been a competitor to OTRACO (later renamed the National Office of Transportation [ONATRA], its interruption in the mid-1970s due to the Angolan civil war was a mixed blessing. The burden on Zaire's own transportation network to and from the Shaba mines was taxed nearly beyond capacity. The southern *voie nationale* of river and rail was used to supply Shaba with essential provisions. For the first time, the volume of imports at Matadi exceeded preindependence levels in 1974. However, this increased volume required major restructuring of port procedures. This problem was exacerbated by the oil crisis which sent transportation costs soaring. Uncertainty also existed in the eastern and southern routes out of Shaba, since violence between Mozambique and Zimbabwe and among South Africans have threatened or cut off railway links since 1977. General disrepair of Matadi's port and rail facilities left it unprepared for the increase in demand after 1974. The result of these pressures was the general congestion of Matadi port. At the end of 1974, 80,000 tons of imported merchandise sat cluttering the docks, unable to move. Out of thirty-six locomotives at the time, only eighteen were in service, and these only marginally. In 1975, in order to cover the rising costs of energy and other imported provisions, ONATRA was permitted to raise its charge by 30 percent, which in turn discouraged its use. By 1977, in spite of reduced competition, the Matadi port and the Matadi-Kinshasa railway were being used only at 1970 levels. Clearly, Zaire was not able to take advantage of the increased economic demands on its transportation system.

By 1975, Zaire's external debt was at $3 billion, or roughly half the GNP. Policies of promoting local (meaning political insiders and bureaucrats) control of foreign investment had resulted in rampant cost overruns, corruption, and inefficiency during the early-1970s. However, with high indebtedness, the need for foreign exchange became primary. Beginning in 1976, Zaire entered into a series of arrangements with the International Monetary Fund and a variety of ad hoc international groups to manage its debt. In addition to periodic rescheduling to postpone payment of interest, Zaire was required to increase its export earnings. Hence the emphasis on transportation from Shaba to Matadi seen since this time. Although other national transport systems are important, getting the copper and cobalt and diamonds to Europe and America is urgent and will affect the survival of the regime.

Because of the need for external capital to rebuild and expand transportation and other infrastructure facilities, this liberalization of exports was accompanied by liberalization of foreign investment rules. Culminating in 1979, a series of investment codes (temporarily overruled from 1970 to 1975) provided for guaranteed profit repatriation, partial or total tax exemptions, a waiving of social security contributions by foreign mining firms, loans to defray start-up costs, and additional advantages for firms that reinvest profits. At least one Kinshasa intellectual described the advantages to foreign firms as ''exorbitant.'' During the period 1970 to 1978, roughly $135 billion was invested in Zaire, of which 20 percent, or $27 billion, went into transport-related projects. These projects were typically large-scale, show-case investments involving several firms from several countries whose activities were coordinated by the state. Large-scale projects, such as the bridge at Matadi or the deep-water port at Banana, diverted attention from basic improvements and maintenance, but were perhaps inevitable, given the economic demands of foreign investors. Foreign firms operating in Zaire were typically attracted to show-case projects because of their high price, high profit potential, high visibility, and state endorsement. The state received the capital and, in some cases, the useful facilities they needed, but in addition obtained personal benefits and privileges. (An illustration follows: In 1979, it was discovered that state officials sold 200 tons of cobalt to a Swiss shadow firm, owned by the head of Zaire's state marketing agency, at $25 per pound, which then resold it at $442 per pound for an $8 million profit, which stayed tucked away in Swiss banks.)

A major foreign investment project in transportation was the proposal, first presented in 1978, to electrify the Matadi-Kinshasa railway. At this particular time, foreign officials directly controlled (as much as possible) key Zairian bureaucracies to remedy Zaire's corruption and debt. Two Belgians administered ONATRA. Considering 80 percent of ONATRA's external funding came from German investments, Belgian firms looked forward to increased access to Zairian investment opportunities with the arrival of their compatriots in Kinshasa. In 1978, a $50 million investment project for railway electrification was included in ONATRA's five-year plan. Other proposed improvements in the railroad were to cost $37 million. These proposals were discouraged by World Bank analysts, who considered the priority of electrification to be very low and the project premature. The Belgian authorities, with the endorsement of the state, signed a tentative contract and commissioned feasibility studies in 1980. Behind-the-scenes pressure by Belgian investors and contractors finally led to a meeting between Belgian and Zairian officials in 1984 and the signing of an agreement. Surprisingly, even the Belgian development loan agency waived its policy of withholding loans to Zaire and provided a $10 million credit. It might be added that this Belgian loan came at a time when Zaire was threatening to nationalize Belgian copper processors in Zaire, and therefore served to ease tensions. The total loans, however, covered only the first two years of construction. The future of the project was quite uncertain, but the short-term earnings of the Belgian firms involved were guaranteed.

The Banana deep-water project likewise was concocted primarily by foreigners (in this case the EEC had a major role) for the short-term benefit of foreign investors (in this case a Swiss construction firm). Although the project will undoubtedly have some benefit in Zaire by allowing the arrival of tankers and other deep-water ships, the priority of such a project at this point in time is questionable. The World Bank is skeptical of the Banana project, pointing out the adequacy of Matadi for Zaire's needs, as well as the impracticality of building a rail link to Boma and Matadi—a necessary parallel project to make the deep-water port viable.

Finally, the rail/road bridge at Matadi was in fact completed in 1983 in record time with Japanese investment and technical assistance. However, because of the near impossibility of building a railway from Matadi to Boma, only half the bridge is in use. In the bitter words of a Belgian analyst: "A luxurious bridge that didn't work was far preferable to simple maintenance with no prestige." Meanwhile, road conditions in the north deteriorated. The supply of corn and other staples from the hinterland to the capital city fell by 50 percent in eight years (1971–79). During that period, the population of Kinshasa rose by roughly 120 percent. The principal victims were the urban poor. The completion of the *voie nationale* represents a rare case of a major new investment reducing pressure for maintenance, in that the rail/river port of Ilebo, which is in serious disrepair, is no longer nearly so essential.

POLITICAL DIMENSIONS OF THE TRANSPORTATION SYSTEM AND POLICY

It is not the place here to discuss whether the Belgian subjugation of the Congo was politically or economically motivated. Suffice it to say that political dimensions quickly emerged. In colonial times, the transportation system served more than an economic and social function. Given the fairly high level of African militancy in the central and northern regions of the country, the transportation system served to bring in colonial troops to suppress uprisings. The transportation system also served to perpetuate itself, in that the taxes required from the local populations required to construct the railroads and ports were collected most easily from townspeople living near those very transportation lines. Note that these tax collections are not user fees in the sense of a toll, but merely income taxes which disproportionally went to the expansion of the colonial transportation network. Also note that many rebellions occurred over the issue of unjust taxation, hence making the transportation even more indispensible for the deployment of the troops mentioned earlier! To this extent, the transportation network was self-perpetuating within the purely politico-administrative colonial framework.

Since colonial times, the colonial administration has been replaced with a local administration of a very peculiar nature. The transportation system is one of the crucial political plums for the Mobutu Administration. Both Mobutu Sese Seko, as a presidential monarch, and his political aristocracy, it has been observed, have an insatiable desire for more revenue. However, they are nearly incapable of managing the nation's finances in order to increase their wealth. The result is a conflict between the goals of short-term and long-term accumulation of wealth. While the ruling class would certainly have much more to gain from a transportation system that is both up-to-date and in good repair, they prefer to seek out much higher short-term gains to be obtained by cooperating with multilateral public and private agencies in the construction of massive infrastructural showcases. While the transportation projects might seem unwarranted from both a technical and an economic standpoint, even allowing for the kleptocratic nature of the Mobutu regime, they become intelligible in the context of short-sighted bureaucratic greed.

One cannot understand the massive infrastructural projects in Zaire since 1970 without being aware of the diplomacy of Zaire with the major lending agencies of the world: the World Bank, the IMF, and the EEC. For example, the construction of a deep-water port at Banana was urged by European consultants who based their optimistic assessment on unrealistic assumptions of industrial growth in lower Zaire. The port idea was identified in 1979 by EEC development administrator Claude Cheysson as a way of placating Zaire's demands for new assistance, in spite of a general EEC policy statement urging maintenance and rehabilitation of transportation facilities, rather than new construction. As of 1985, three feasibility studies, costing roughly $800,000, concluded that the project was viable and urged final EEC approval for implementation. The result of endorsing the Banana project was to inhibit efforts at improving the Matadi, Boma, and Ilebo ports, all of which were suffering from inadequate quays and antiquated machinery and equipment.

Zaire's debt crisis has been all the more impressive because of the willingness of Western powers to sustain its survival. Zaire's position in central Africa and its significant mineral resources make it a strategic prize worth the price—especially to the United States, which has shipped hundreds of millions of dollars in aid since 1965 when it assisted in the accession of Mobutu's forces. Because Zaire is surrounded by relatively unstable countries such as Angola, Sudan, and Uganda, Western powers are eager to maintain Zaire's stability in spite of the costs in personal freedoms for the Zairian people. The United States also cannot afford to allow Zaire to default on its foreign debt, since much of it is held by American banks. This financial vulnerability is even greater where the Europeans are concerned, and since the late-1970s, several European governments have assisted in the rescheduling of Zaire's debt. Likewise, Europeans see political benefits (as noted in the EEC loan case) in extending investment funds to Zaire's transportation system. West German firms have by far invested more than any other country (roughly 80 percent in the 1970s) with Belgium and Japan close behind. This global presence has allowed Zaire to extract significant concessions from the West, including sizable loans for transportation.

Domestically, transportation has been the object of contention for both anti-Mobutu and pro-Mobutu forces. As mentioned, during the repeated invasion of the Shaba region since 1977, the railway lines have been an obvious and frequent target. Although the present situation is not as precarious as the 1960–65 period, it is known that rebels harbored in Tanzania and Zambia could strike at any moment against major mines and transportation routes.

As will be discussed in more detail later, the distribution of power and wealth in Zaire is far from fair and equal. Although large foreign investments are sought, they are not distributed evenly throughout the country. There exists, at the national level, a southern bias for foreign investment. Consider the distribution of foreign direct investment in infrastructure and raw materials in the period 1969–75: southern region (Kinshasa, Kasai, and Shaba provinces): 79 percent; northern region (Upper-Zaire, Bandundu, Kivu, and Equateur provinces): 21 percent. The southern bias is supplemented by a distinct urban bias in central government expenditures. Although precise figures are not available, there exists a widespread belief among each level of public administration that the rural regions, including their populations, are worth very little to the country. This attitude is not limited to the capital, but the notion of urban hierarchy is perpetuated at all levels of administration. Thus, a town administrator feels far superior to a village official, while a village official feels those in the hinterland are nearly worthless. These attitudes are often translated into policy, especially with regard to road construction.

The widespread use of patronage and the emergence of a politico-commercial class has been discussed in detail by several scholars. Because the graft and corruption are difficult to document, it is difficult to say to what extent these problems exist in the case of transportation in Zaire. It is plausible to conjecture that a great many former politicians of the Popular Revolutionary Movement (MPR) and political allies of Mobutu have obtained positions in ONATRA and the SNCZ in order to preserve their support for the regime. In addition, given the pattern of behavior of such types of individuals in other ministries, it is plausible to imagine that billions of zaires (the country's monetary unit) in state and foreign investment have been secreted into private and foreign accounts. While the scale of magnitude is not precisely known, it can be again conjectured plausibly that the corruption of political appointees has made a significant impact on Zaire's transportation system in the form of reduced revenues for the state, reduced investment in infrastructure, diminished public confidence, misdirected funds, and inefficiency. The important question is not whether there is corruption, but only how much and in what ways it has affected the system.

RECENT TRENDS AND FUTURE PROSPECTS

General observations regarding the present and future state of Zairan transportation must emphasize the lack of basic day-to-day maintenance in favor of new infusions of foreign capital and loans. The state of Zaire engages in "grandiose and unproductive development schemes . . . [T]he almost total neglect of agriculture and the transportation and productive infrastructures have further aggravated the rapidly deteriorating situation" (Callaghy, 1984). An additional example of questionable foreign investment is the construction of a trans-African superhighway cutting across the northeastern region of the country, linking Uganda to the Central African Republic. While not in itself objectionable, it is the priority granted to this and to the other projects listed that concerns observers. The aims of the trans-African highway, for example, could be served by extending the existing Bondo-Mungbere railway in northern Zaire. In fact, such an extended railway would likely be more practical, considering the relative abundance of railway vehicles and the relatively small fleets of trucks and commercial vehicles in the region. Also, the money to be invested in the improvement of Matadi-Banana railway links mentioned earlier would show an even greater return if efforts were made to better link the northern regions to the south by completing the north-south rail line with a Kindu-Bubundu railway. Overall, investments in rehabilitation would doubtless return larger dividends than the relatively useless bridge at Matadi (a bridge which will connect nothing until the Banana-Matadi railway is completed).

Today, Zaire's transportation facilities and equipment are in general disrepair and are shrinking in both size and effectiveness. Although precise data on the subject are extremely rare (requests by the author for current data from Kinshasa, the Zairian embassy, and the World Bank have been rejected), it is possible to reconstruct an image of the current situation (see Figure 12.2 and Table 12.1). To begin, Zaire's maritime fleet of 85,000 registered gross tons (six vessels) is 23 percent smaller than it was in 1978. This fleet is controlled by a subsidiary of UK/West Africa Lines and is therefore considered by some to be non-Zairian. The length of Zaire's navigable river network has declined from nearly 3,000 km in 1970 to roughly 1,700 km, primarily because of sedimentation in portions of the rivers that are paralleled by railways. Use of river transport has continued its fifteen-year decline since the early 1970s. With a base figure of 100 for 1968, river use was at a high of 116 in 1971 and has declined to roughly 80 in 1984 (the figure is based on "traffic units": 2 passenger/km = 1 ton/km = 1 traffic unit). This situation cannot be helped by the fact that such rudimentary processes as nighttime navigation are not practiced due to poor facilities and conditions (in this case, lack of replacement headlights for most ships). The major ports are in serious disrepair, even as

Figure 12.2
Volume of Maritime Transportation

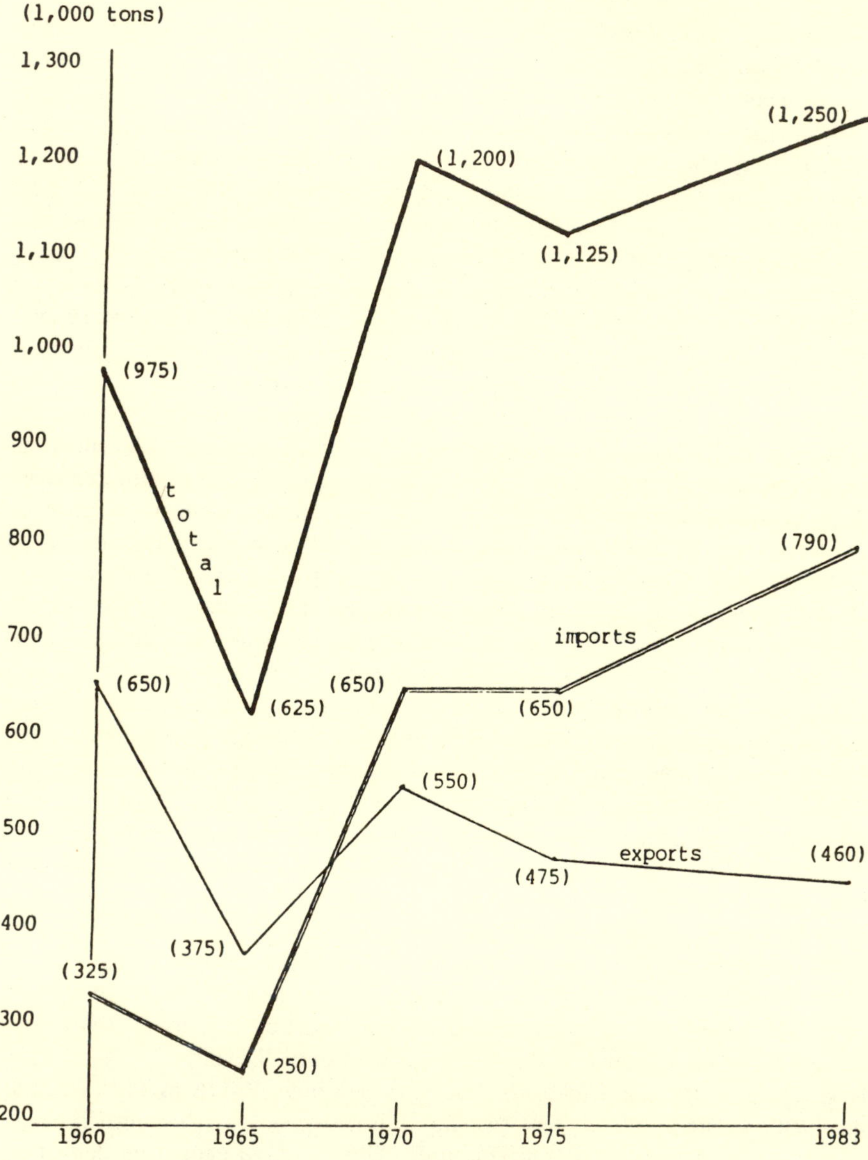

Source: A. Lederer, *L'Evolution des Transports à l'ONATRA durant les années 1960 à 1977; L'Année Politique et Economique Africaine*, 1984.

Table 12.1
River Transportation

	1970	1980	1981	1982	1983
LENGTH OF NAVIGABLE RIVERS (km)	2,986	1,713	1,713	1,713	1,600
CARGO TRANSPORTED (1,000 tons)	1,128	--	821	766	775

Sources: George Thomas Kurian, Encyclopedia of the Third World, 3rd ed. (New York: Facts on File, 1987); L'Année Politique et Économique Africaine, 1985 [Political and economic yearbook of Africa, 1985] (Dakar: Société Africaine d'Edition, 1985); Mashida Ngoy-Munokowa Ngandu, Zaire: Structures politico-administratives et productivité de l'économie nationale (Ph.D. dissertation, Munich, 1984); République du Zaire, Département de l'Économie Nationale et de l'Industrie, Conjoncture Économique [Economic report] (Kinshasa: République du Zaire, Departement de l'Économie Nationale et de l'Industrie, 1983); André Lederer, L'Évolution des Transports a l'ONATRA durant les années 1960 à 1977 (Brussels: Académie Royale des Sciences d'Outre-Mer, 1978).

plans are being made to construct a deep-water port at Boma. The port of Kisangani is vulnerable to dramatic fluctuations in the water level of the Zaire, experiencing both debilitating low water levels as well as periodic flooding.

In land traffic, the shining hope remains the railway network (see Table 12.2). In Zaire's annual economic report, railways always come first in the section on transportation. Zaire has by far the largest extent of railways in Africa (South Africa excluded). Until 1987, however, its expansion was slow.

Table 12.2
Railway Transportation

	1960	1970	1980	1982	1983	1984	1985	1986
TOTAL PASSENGERS (millions)	2.0	5.1	--	--	--	--	--	--
(million passenger-km)	344	901	544	389	372	346	292	330
TOTAL FREIGHT (million ton-km)	1,725	2,610	--	1,772	1,860	1,863	1,955	1,785
LENGTH OF LINES (km)	5,024	5,024	5,088	5,088	5,088	5,100	5,252	5,269

Sources: F. Scott Bobb, Historical Dictionary of Zaire (Metuchen, N.J.: Scarecrow Press, 1988); Europa World Year Book (London: Europa Publishers, 1989); United Nations Economic Commission for Africa, Economic Conditions in Africa (Addis Ababa: UN, 1973, 1983, 1984); B. R. Mitchell, International Historical Statistics--Africa and Asia (New York: New York University Press, 1982); André Lederer, L'Évolution des Transports a l'ONATRA durant les années 1960 à 1977 (Brussels: Académie Royale des Sciences d'Outre-Mer, 1978).

Table 12.3
Road Transportation

	1960	1970	1975	1980	1981	1984	1985
TOTAL ROADWAYS IN GOOD REPAIR (1,000 km)	142	68	69	24	--	58	43
TOTAL PRIVATE VEHICLES (1,000)	45	65	85	75	78	102	--
TOTAL COMMERCIAL VEHICLES (1,000)	32	49	76	27	28	30	--

Source: Europa World Year Book (London: Europa Publishers, 1989); F. Scott Bobb, Historical Dictionary of Zaire (Metuchen, N.J.: Scarecrow Press, 1988); UN Statistical Yearbook, 1985-86 (New York: United Nations, 1986); Ngoy-Munokowa Ngandu, Zaire: Politico-administrative structures et productivité de l'économie nationale [Zaire: Politico-administrative structures and national economic productivity], Ph.D. dissertation (Munich, 1984); J.D. Gould, Bureaucratic Corruption in Zaire New York: Pergamon Press, 1980); B.R. Mitchell, International Historical Statistics--Africa and Asia (New York: New York University Press, 1982); and L'Année Politique et Économique Africaine [Political and economic yearbook of Africa] (Dakar: Société Africaine, 1985).

Even with the completion of the all-rail *voie nationale,* Zaire's railways are still in poor repair, especially in the north, where the narrow-gauge line serves purely local needs, rather than providing for more expeditious transport of foodstuffs from the hinterland to the capital. Financially, the railways are suffering from a ''lack of means.'' The state places preeminent priority on the transportation of minerals from Shaba to Matadi and believes sacrifices must be made in achieving this goal. ONATRA, which controls the lower Zaire railway and waterway systems, has become more self-sufficient overall, but at the cost of allowing less profitable connections (such as the Ilebo port) to collapse. As of 1983, the SNCZ controlled 131 diesel and electric locomotives, to which could be added ONATRA's 53, giving a total of 184 locomotives in Zaire. These locomotives operate a system of over 8,000 cars of various types, including nearly 400 passenger cars. Out of a total of roughly 6,000 km of railways, of which roughly 4,700 km is standard 1.067 meter gauge, Zaire has 853 km of electrified railways.

With respect to roads, although the EEC has made major investments in repair of major routes, the road system is still deplorable (see Table 12.3). Only those major roads in the lower-Zaire region linking southern capitals to Kinshasa are somewhat reliable. In recent years, road use has fluctuated dramatically, between 1 billion and 600 million passenger/km. The change in fuel prices seems to be the most reliable factor in predicting road use: total passenger road use declined by 32 percent from 1979 to 1980. The country has roughly one passenger car per 200 inhabitants, one bus per 6,000 inhabitants, and one

Table 12.4
Civil Aviation

	1970	1975	1980	1982	1983	1984	1985
TOTAL DISTANCE FLOWN (million km)	--	15	10	8	8	7	5
TOTAL PASSENGERS (1,000)	--	445	439	378	331	338	131
(million passenger-km)	465	632	834	683	582	602	355
TOTAL CARGO (million ton-km)	14	45	34	31	32	32	30

Source: Europa World Year Book (London: Europa Publishers, 1989); UNECA, Economic Conditions in Africa (Addis Ababa: UN, 1973, 1983, 1984); B. R. Mitchell, International Historical Statistics--Africa and Asia (New York: New York University Press, 1982); George Kurian, Encyclopedia of the Third World, 3rd ed. (New York: Facts on File, 1987); UN Statistical Yearbook, 1985-86 (New York: United Nations, 1986); ICAO Yearbook (Geneva: International Civil Aviation Organization, 1986); UN Survey of Economic and Social Conditions in Africa, 1986-87 (New York: United Nations, 1988).

goods vehicle per 300 inhabitants. It has been pointed out that the problem of road maintenance in the north and northeast, which inhibits the arrival of goods into ports and train depots, reduces the financial viability of these river and rail services. This, in turn, lowers their significance to national policymakers. The national significance will tend to decline further with administrative decentralization. It should be noted that many other African countries suffer from poor road conditions, but in the case of Zaire, where dense vegetation and difficult terrain make land communication nearly impossible without good roads, this condition is especially problematic.

Finally, Zaire's air transport system is among the best in Africa, with Air Zaire, a state-dominated enterprise, carrying nearly the entire passenger load (see Table 12.4). Five smaller firms also carry unscheduled cargo transportation, but Air Zaire is also dominant in this area. With a high of 45 million ton/km of cargo carried in 1980, levels of cargo transport declined to roughly 30 million ton/km in 1985. Air Zaire has recently upgraded its fleet to include one 747, two 737s, one DC 10, and two DC 8s.

The current five-year plan provides for a 57.7 billion zaire (roughly $18 billion) investment in transportation. This represents over one-third (34.8%) of the total planned public investment. One can scarcely imagine a higher proportion of public investment in transportation infrastructure (see Table 12.5). This clearly bodes well for Zaire's future development. However, this and other similar figures must be put in the context of past trends. With increased decentralization of administration, increased indebtedness and the maintenance of authoritarian rule, the future trend will certainly be in the direction of increased urban- and export-bias at the expense of rural and provincial transportation.

Table 12.5
Budgets of Selected National Transportation Agencies (in US$ millions; local currency, in millions of zaires, in brackets)

	1980	1981	1982	1983	1984
TOTAL TRANSPORT AND COMMUNICATION	8.3 [25]	8.4 [18]	1.9 [6]	0.3 [12]	--
TOTAL PUBLIC WORKS	42.3 [127]	72.0 [240]	7.3 [107]	1.9 [70]	--
ONATRA TOTAL (1980-84 period)			28.6 [1,030]		
of which:					
Ports			5.9 [212]		
Rivers			9.9 [358]		
Railways			11.5 [414]		

Sources: République du Zaire, Departement de l'Économie Nationale et de l'Industrie, Conjoncture Economique [Economic report] (Kinshasa: République du Zaire, Département de l'Économie Nationale et de l'Industrie, 1983); Annual Report, 1984 (Washington, D.C.: International Monetary Fund, 1984).

The completion of the *voie nationale* will provide significant savings in foreign reserves which have previously been spent on shipping ore through southern routes and will increase SNCZ and ONATRA earnings, which will in turn release public funds for other activities. However, if the current trend of corrupt management continues, these increased SNCZ and ONATRA earnings will simply be expatriated.

Overall, Zaire's transportation system is very fragile. Each mode is almost entirely dependent on one or more other modes. There exists little in the way of back-up systems that can be used in the event of the failure of one or another mode. If, for example, an accident occurs in the mouth of the Zaire River downriver of the major port of Matadi, the vast majority of the country's international trade comes to a grinding halt. Even more serious is the fact that if, for whatever reason, the few alternative outlets for the nation's goods are eliminated (war in Angola has made the relatively short Benguela railway linking the copper mines of Shaba to the Atlantic unusable since 1975), the entire transportation system may become clogged. The transportation network in Zaire suffers from systemic as well as discrete dysfunctions which require both explanation and remedy.

These structural problems are exacerbated by a national administration that is more interested in short-term private financial gains (most of which are achieved through graft) rather than long-term public benefits. The result is a preference for large-scale projects built with borrowed funds rather than domestically financed rehabilitation or maintenance programs. Existing transportation systems, especially in the areas of road and river transport, are rapidly declining in utility due to their worsening state of repair.

TRANSPORTATION POLICY ORGANIZATION AND PROCESS

Almost the entire Zairian transportation system is controlled by either ONATRA or the SNCZ by virtue of the fact that both of these ostensibly "uni-modal" institutions (ONATRA over waterways, SNCZ over railways) are in fact multimodal. Transportation is generally administered by the State Commissioner of Transports and Communications (see Figure 12.3). The National Office of Transports (ONATRA) comes under his jurisdiction and, since its creation as a result of the reorganization of the colonial OTRACO in 1972, is responsible for a variety of transportation systems. Specifically, the entire national river transportation network and the combined river-rail network in lower Zaire are under its special tutelage, along with national railways, ports and naval yards. The SNCZ has clear authority over the bulk of the nation's railway network, including the relatively small narrow-gauge regional networks of the far eastern regions of the country in 1973. In addition, just as ONATRA administers a multi-modal system, SNCZ administers several major river ports along the *voie nationale* and in the northeast, as well as lake and river transport on the eastern frontier. ONATRA and SNCZ have essentially split the nation's land and water transportation geographically, with a north-south dividing line just east of Kinshasa.

The retention of this primarily regional transportation administration in independent Zaire has served several purposes, including (1) satisfying the interests of administration officials by retaining old patterns and positions; (2) insulating the strategic lower Zaire from penetration by various private and "modal" interests; (3) increasing the coherence and reducing the cost of transportation administration; and (4) increasing opportunities for graft by consolidating state control in highly dynamic regions. The most interesting administrative development has been the creation, in 1981, of ZOFI which places all of the various transportation systems related to the Inga power station (including electrification of the Matadi-Kinshasa railway, in particular) under the direct authority of the president. While this ostensibly highlights the salience of the region for national policy making and permits the development of special foreign investment codes in the area, EEC officials considered the move a way of consolidating public graft and limiting accountability.

Air Zaire, Zaire's only airline with regularly scheduled passenger and cargo flights, seems to be a special case. Rather than being a completely privatized corporation, the airline, which is one of the largest in sub-Saharan Africa, is managed by senior public officials who received their appointments through the

Figure 12.3
Structure of Transportation Administration

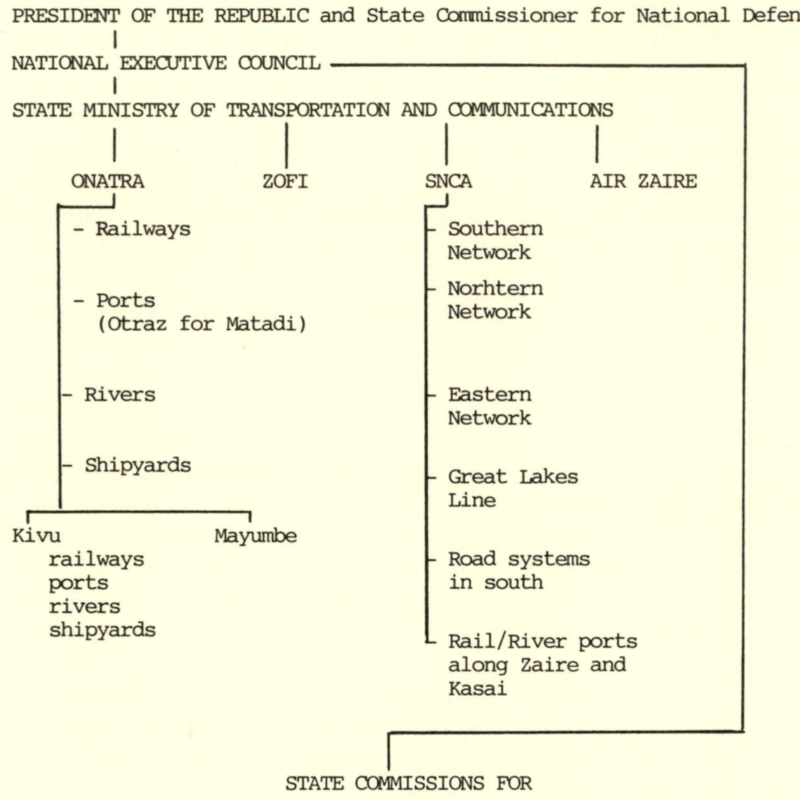

STATE COMMISSIONS FOR

- Economiy and industry
- Planning
- Finance and Budget
- Public Works and Territorial Development
- Rural Development
- Territorial Administration and Decentralization (supervising eight provincial governments responsible for roads and various minor facilities)

Source: Mashida Ngoy-Munokowa Ngandu, Zaire: Structures politico-administratives et productivité de l'économie nationale [Zaire: Politico-administrative structures and national economic productivity], Ph.D. Dissertation (Munich, 1984) and André Lederer, L'Évolution des Transports a l'ONATRA durant les années 1960 a 1977 [The evolution of transportation at ONATRA from 1960 to 1977] (Brussels: Académie Royale des Sciences d'Outre-Mer, 1978).

good graces of the president. However, it has been difficult for them to make a profit, and many European consultants have been brought in to essentially take over management. As a parastatal (state-dominated) corporation, Air Zaire benefits from both loose supervision and generous subsidies. In 1975, Air Zaire borrowed public funds to buy the only 747 in sub-Saharan Africa, along with several passenger jets, none of which were essential. In spite of these investments, passenger kilometers of Air Zaire increased by a mere 0.1 percent from 1972 to 1982 and shows no signs of positive growth in the future. The same can be said for cargo transportation.

Road transportation does not merit a national administrative office but is managed at the provincial level. It is interesting to note that any program administered at the local level tends to stagnate. It is well known that local administrators tend to keep a certain portion of publicly allocated funds. When asked what the most important problem in rural development was, local agricultural technicians in Zaire ranked inadequate roads as the second most important problem. The most important problem was apathy on the part of the central government. In what is an unusual pattern for a Western institution, most recent EEC lending projects have often focused on road rehabilitation. Four of five transportation projects in 1985 involved road repair with a total commitment of roughly $80 million and a total of over 600 km of roads involved. It should be noted that the most important project, involving rehabilitation of part of the Kinshasa-Lubumbashi road, was under severe financial stress and of questionable viability.

The process of staffing transportation agencies in the early years after independence was done rather precipitously with a large number of generally undertrained local Zairian clerks and mid-level officials. As described in detail by Young and Turner (1985), a powerful class of bureaucrats emerged in Zaire as the dominant political group. When Mobutu came to power in 1965, he felt it necessary, for political purposes, to increase the benefits going to this bureaucratic class by allowing them control of most of the major industries and businesses. Thus developed a ''bureaucratic-commercial'' class which remains to this day and plays an important role in maintaining government control over the economy, including the transportation system (Young & Turner, 1985: 115). Young and Turner also call the political system a ''kleptocracy'' based on corruption and graft, which helps to explain the ''bleeding'' of foreign assistance in infrastructure.

There exists also an important class of Belgian and European technocrats who have participated in Zairian administration since independence. A large number of original colonial administrators were retained in the early years, although their numbers are declining. Many new foreign advisers and administrators have arrived since the mid-1970s in conjunction with major development projects and IMF readjustment. There exist tensions between the ''old Congo hands'' who remain and these new advisers. Ironically, the generational rivalry exists also among Zairian nationals and has promoted an alliance between the more experienced Belgians and Zairians and their less experienced, college-educated counterparts. In general terms, the rivalry focuses on the issues of control and tenure, as well as the goals of development. The pre-colonial generation sees the colonial administration as the ideal, including its emphasis on large-scale infracstructural development, and seeks to perpetuate the old colonial system. The new generation, historically, has been more sensitive to intellectual currents in the West concerning development.

Important changes in public administration took place after the consolidation of Mobutu's regime in the late 1960s. In the colonial and early-independence phase of development, Zaire's bureaucracy was expected to maintain strict nonpolitical status. Civil servants were not permitted to associate with a political party. After 1967, however, Mobutu not only encouraged political mobilization of the civil service, he required it. This attempt at politicization of the bureaucracy was carried out with changes in hiring and promotion policies, although it met with limited success. Only those younger public officials of a purely Zairian background responded significantly, since they carried with them neither an apolitical tradition nor a Western education. Most important, however, many former politicians have found themselves in the civil service at the end of their career, typically involved in one parastatal or another. The extent of patronage is significant in Zaire and represents one of the most serious flaws of the administrative system. As indicated earlier, corruption is rampant and national finances are in disarray. Corruption is so pervasive that some analysts have concluded that all national financial statistics are useless as indicators of actual activity.

For transportation planning, the official process is quite simple, in that each division proposes five-year spending and revenue plans (1986–90 is the current plan) to the central administration. There exists a single-party national assembly, which approves routinely the budgetary decisions made in the State Commission for Planning and the State Commission for Finance and Budget. The past several plans have listed transportation as second or third in order of importance behind agriculture. Among transportation agencies, the most prominent institutions, ZOFI and ONATRA, come out quite well, with such parastatals as SNCZ and Air Zaire receiving significant support in the form of subsidies and concessional loans. Since the early 1970s, each division is responsible for its own financial management. This presumably promotes better management. However, in the case of ONATRA, throughout the 1970s and into the 1980s, the vast majority of its funding came from outside sources. For example, in 1975, ONATRA provided for only 3 percent of its own funding. This fraction had increased to 22 percent by 1981 and continues to increase in small increments. Air Zaire's financial condition has been lamented in national economic reports. In 1985, SNCZ was listed as the fourth largest corporation in Zaire, with a turnover of roughly $1 billion. ONATRA, Air Zaire, and the shipping firm Compagnie Maritime Zairoise (CMZ) ranked fifth, eleventh, and fifteenth, respectively.

As mentioned, roads receive little national attention and are administered at the local level. Road building costs are taken out of provincial and territorial budgets. There exists a marked bias in favor of urban centers in Zaire; therefore, roads located in more remote areas receive less attention. This is epitomized by the nearly complete lack of usable roads in the central regions of the country, between the Zaire and Kasai rivers. In response to IMF liberalization demands, Zaire has introduced increased administrative decentralization to allow savings in central government expenditures. Much like the U.S. ''New Federalism,'' the plan proposes to shift responsibility for certain public programs from the federal to the local jurisdictions. It is expected, however, that, given the regions' low level of technical competence in the areas of planning and development, this process will simply result in intensified urban bias. Even worse, it could result in a cessation of investment in the more impoverished regions of the country. Considering the importance of transportation to economic growth, there exists in decentralization a clear risk that certain regions of the country will become perpetually impoverished. It is interesting that it is primarily in the area of road rehabilitation that the EEC donors have operated. Clearly this fills an important lacuna of administration and effort.

REFERENCES

L'Anné Politique et Economique Africaine, 1985 [Political and economic yearbook of Africa] (Dakar: Société Africaine d'Edition, 1985).

Annual Report, 1984 (Washington, D.C.: International Monetary Fund, 1984).

Bobb, F. Scott, *Historical Dictionary of Zaire* (Metuchen, N.J.: Scarecrow Press, 1988).

Callaghy, Thomas, ''Africa's Debt Crisis,'' *Journal of International Affairs* (Summer 1984), pp. 61–79.

——, ''External Actors and the Relative Autonomy of the Political Aristocracy in Zaire,'' *Journal of Commonwealth and Comparative Politics,* vol. 21, no. 3 (1983), pp. 70–71.

Cornet, Rene, *La Bataille du Rail—La Construction du Chemin de fer de Matadi au Stanley Pool* [The rail war—the construction of the railway from Matadi to Stanley Pool] (Brussels: Cuypers, 1958).

Curtin, Philip, S. Feierman, L. Thompson, and Jan Vansina, *African History* (Boston: Little, Brown, 1978).

Day, John R., *Railways of Southern Africa* (London: Barker Limited, 1963).

Europa World Year Book (London: Europa Publishers, 1989).

European Economic Communities, *EEC Zaire Assistance Report, 1985* (Brussels: European Economic Communities, 1986).

Fetter, Bruce, *Colonial Rule and Regional Imbalance in Central Africa* (Boulder, Colo.: Westview Press, 1983).

Gould, J. David, *Bureaucratic Corruption in Zaire* (New York: Pergamon Press, 1980).

ICAO Yearbook (Geneva-International Civil Aviation Organization, 1986).

Katzenellenbogen, S. E., *Railways and the Copper Mines of Katanga* (New York: Clarendon Press, 1973).

Kurian, George Thomas, *Encylopedia of the Third World,* 3rd ed. (New York: Facts on File, 1981).

Lederer, André, *L'Evolution des Transports à l'ONATRA durant les années 1960 à 1977* [The evolution of transportation at ONATRA from 1960 to 1977] (Brussels: Académie Royale des Sciences d'Outre-Mer, 1978).

Mitchell, B. R., *International Historical Statistics—Africa and Asia* (New York: New York University Press, 1982).

Muepu, Tshimuanga, "Investissement Externe et Integration Economique au Zaire" [Foreign investment and economic integration in Zaire], *Geneva-Afrique* (1982), pp. 105–132.

Ngandu, Mashida Ngoy-Munokowa, *Zaire: Structures politico-administratives et productivité de l'économie national* [Zaire: Politico-administrative structures and national economic productivity], Ph.D. dissertation (Munich, 1984).

République du Zaire, Department de l'Economie, Nationale de l'Industrie, *Conjoncture Economique* [Economic report], annual.

Said, Shafik-G, *De Leopoldville a Kinshasa: La Situation économique et financière au Congo ex-Belge au jour de l'indépendance* [From Leopoldville to Kinshasa: The financial and economic condition of the former Belgian Congo at independence] (Brussels, 1969).

Stiles, Kendall, *Structure and Process of I.M.F. Decision-making,* PhD. dissertation (Baltimore, 1987).

United Nations, *UN Statistical Yearbook, 1985–86* (New York: United Nations, 1986).

United Nations, *UN Survey of Economic Conditions in Africa, 1986–87* (New York: United Nations, 1988).

United Nations Economic Commission for Africa, *Economic Conditions in Africa* (Addis Ababa: UN, 1973, 1983, 1984).

Willame, Jean-Claude, *L'épopée d'Inga* [The Inga saga], (Paris: L'Harmattan, 1986).

———, *Patrimonialism and Political Change in the Congo* (Stanford: Stanford University Press, 1972).

Young, Crawford, and Thomas Turner, *The Rise and Decline of the Zairian State* (Madison: Wisconsin University Press, 1985).

CONCLUSION

Tsuneo Akaha

The experience of the five advanced market economies (France, Japan, the United Kingdom, the United States, and West Germany) surveyed in this book shows many cross-national parallels in terms of the following patterns: (1) the changing balance between public- and private-sector involvement in the development of public transportation infrastructure and services; (2) the sequence of modal development (i.e., from railway and inland waterway to automobile, roadway, and air transportation); (3) the difficult job of ensuring a balanced intermodal development amid changing modal demands; (4) the formidable goal of providing sufficient and reliable transportation capacity to meet the growing demands of the dynamic economies; and (5) the equally challenging task of interagency policy coordination.

The initial impetus for government involvement in the provision of public means of transportation in the advanced market economies had come from the nationally acknowledged need to rebuild the transportation infrastructure severely damaged in World War II and the equally widespread recognition of the lack of private capital to take on that massive task. During this period, the public sector was best equipped to construct and operate a national rail transportation given its better areal coverage, greater speed and capacity, and cost efficiency, in comparison with its contemporary competition—namely, waterway and roadway transportation.

As the private sector expanded (thanks in important measure to the publicly financed development of transportation services), however, the ideological appeal and the economic rationale of market-driven transportation services gained in popular support, to the detriment of government-sponsored and financed counterparts, particularly the railroad. Where this transition has come relatively gradually or over an extended period of time, such as in the United States, political battle between the ''winners'' and ''losers'' has been comparatively subdued and limited. Whereas in other countries, such as Japan and the United Kingdom, where this transition has come either over a fairly short time or unevenly, intense political debate has resulted. The volume and velocity of the political debate notwithstanding, the dynamic growth of the private sector in the market economies has placed automotive and air transportation in the ''winners' '' category and rail and inland waterway transportation, where it had previously been strong, in the ''losers' '' category. The latter category has also included rural populations who continue to be heavily dependent on publicly provided modes of transportation, most notably the railroad. When urbanization has meant, as it most certainly has, expansion of the tax base in heavily populated areas of private transport supporters and the reverse in the sparsely populated areas, public funding for the railroad has naturally lost its political support.

In short, the balance between public- and private-sector involvement and intermodal balance are two sides of the same coin representing public transportation development.

The degree of difficulty in ensuring optimal intermodal balance is to a large extent a function of the speed of private-sector development and the evenness thereof in terms of both geographical and sectoral distribution. As the demand for the various modes of transportation changes in accordance with the socioeconomic needs of the market, the slower such a change, the easier the public and/or private transport economy's task of responding to it. The most difficult is the operation of a transport economy within a market economy in which the demand for one mode of transportation such as roadways expands significantly faster than the ability of that sector to satisfy the demand or the decline in the demand for another mode such as railways. These declines come faster than the losses in its revenue can be absorbed by the transport sector, public or private. The ascending curve of the growing mode demand and the descending curve of the declining mode demand often do not meet at an optimal point in terms of the transport economy's ability to generate a sufficient surplus from the first mode to absorb the growing deficit in the latter mode. In a centrally planned economy, the national government may be able to shift gains and losses among transportation modes as well as from one area of the country to another. In a capitalist country with a clear distinction between the public side of the transport economy and the private side (the former most typically managing the rail mode and the latter the other modes), such a transfer cannot easily be justified except in times of widespread political support for heavy government involvement, as was the case in the immediate postwar period.

As far as interagency coordination is concerned, the market economies have been no better nor less well equipped for the task. On the one hand, the central authorities in the market economies theoretically have the advantage over their counterparts in the centrally planned economies of being more open to the feedback from the private sector and presumably being able to respond to the growing need of intermodal coordination. On the other hand, however, intermodal coordination is much more difficult in the market economies than in the centrally planned economies because shifts in intermodal balance are faster and more drastic in the former.

All in all, however, the record of public transport development and management in the five advanced market economies has been quite impressive.

The experience in the centrally planned economies (China, East Germany, and the Soviet Union) surveyed in this book has been less spectacular. The record of their moderate achievements has been counterbalanced by an either excessively rigid or erratic management of public transportation. "Winners" and "losers" have been determined not by market-driven changes in the socioeconomic structure of the countries but by state-initiated policies. More often than not, supply has been determined not by the consumer of the given service, such as the public, but by its producer, namely, the state. Criteria used in determining demand have often included noneconomic factors. Serious inadequacy in supply has often resulted from absolute shortfalls in domestically available capital and technological input or outright miscalculation of demand.

In the centrally planned economies, a shift from railway and inland waterway to other modes of public transportation is a much more recent and much less pronounced phenomenon than in the advanced market economies. However, there is no question that the demand for automobiles will grow in the centrally planned economies and will put mounting strains on their transport economy which is predominantly geared toward rail transportation. Until very recently intermodal balance was not a major concern in the centrally planned economies, and interagency competition for scarce resources rendered policy coordination next to impossible.

Decentralization processes in the centrally planned economies are much more recent and more controlled than in the advanced capitalist economies as well. Moreover, the impetus for reduced central control over the transportation sector of these economies comes not from dynamic growth of the private sector (because there is no such sector in the centrally planned economies) but from the general failure of their national economies to generate sufficient financial resources and technological innovations to meet the changing socioeconomic demands in the countries. And the latter, such as the demand for private automobiles, are increasingly affected by developments in the market economies.

Market economies, which are more or less integrated with the other market economies, can and have overcome shortages in capital investment or deficiency in technological rigor in the transport sector by incorporating the needed resources from other open economies into their transport development programs. Centrally planned economies, on the other hand, have had to rely mostly on internally generated resources for investment and technological advancement. The paucity of indigenous factors of transportation development in these economies is evident in the fact that the recently initiated decentralization process, which is explained by domestic needs and priorities, at least theoretically, is accompanied by increasing reliance on foreign sources of capital and technology.

This association of domestic decentralization and external liberalization, carefully controlled as the latter may be at this point, poses a serious political challenge to the central authorities. First, it accelerates the growth in domestic demand for domestically unavailable modes of transportation, particularly automobiles and aircraft for passenger travel because it is those items that the central governments want most to develop with financial and technological input from overseas and for which unmet domestic needs are the greatest. If the central governments fail to meet that demand, that will further expose their inability to satisfy the society's growing needs. Second, to take the example of automobiles, their private ownership has at least two political consequences: (1) it is anathema to the Marxist-Leninist ideology which has long rejected privately owned and privately operated modes of transportation, resulting in an almost exclusive reliance on railways for public transportation; and (2) the high cost of automobiles, domestically produced or imported, will certainly prevent the vast majority of the population from owning one, thus exposing car ownership by a few as a symbol of social privilege and an indication of wealth disparity, which in turn are difficult to justify within the framework of socialism.

In contrast to the relatively robust development of public transportation in the advanced market economies and centrally planned economies and the rather autonomous, self-contained development in the centrally planned economies, the evolution of public transportation systems and policies in the developing countries (Brazil, South Korea, Mexico, and Zaire) surveyed in this volume has been characterized by extensive and often disruptive penetration by external agents and factors. In fact, with the exception of postwar South Korea, "dependent development" most accurately describes the history of public transportation development in these countries. Quite often externally oriented development has, at best, distorted and, at worst, disrupted overall economic development.

Developing countries often lack the basic socioeconomic, political, and technological necessities for a healthy and balanced development of public transportation. Those requirements include (1) a national consensus in support of political and resource commitment to the long-term development of public transportation; (2) stable economic growth that both generates transport demand and provides financial resources to meet the demand; (3) technically competent and appropriately placed bureaucratic talents; (4) a close and mutually supportive relationship between central, regional, and local governments; (5) careful policy planning based on a sound economic analysis and a clear, comprehensive understanding of the long-term socioeconomic implications of current policy and with a view to developing an appropriate mix of transportation modes to meet the constantly changing demand structure; (6) an administrative structure that allows for continual intermodal policy coordination; and, finally, (7) access to transportation technology that is both affordable and appropriate for the changing needs of the public transport sector.

Today, there is the additional requirement that national policymakers fully understand and respond to the consequences of growing global interdependence. Transnational forces of market, technology, capital, and labor no longer allow a strictly autonomous and independent development of national transport systems. Even countries with well-developed market economies have only recently realized this requirement. Ironically, the developing countries, which may have realized this need earlier than their developed counterparts, given their pre- and postwar experience with foreign political and economic interjection, do not have the wherewithal to translate that recognition into practical public policy.

Developed or not, all contemporary societies must have policymakers in the transportation sector who clearly understand the global trends being shaped by the dynamic changes underway in other countries, particularly in the advanced market economies, where public-private and intermodal transformations are the fastest and the most drastic. What follows, then, is a brief look at the global trends in public transportation since the 1970s.

Intermodal distribution has shown marked changes due to differential impacts on the various modes of public transportation, first, of the slowdown of the world economy caused by the two oil crises and, second, of the structural change in the developed market economies and, to a lesser degree, in developing market economies and even centrally planned economies, from raw-material-based industries to high-value-added manufacturing industries. The rail sector has declined and continues to decline, particularly in the advanced market economies, due to the competition from fast-growing automotive and air transportation. This pattern is particularly strong in freight transport. With the exception of high-speed trains, the decline of rail transportation is likely to continue in the advanced market economies. A future decline is likely in the centrally planned economies as well although it will be much slower. Among the developing market economies, there is great potential for growth in rail transportation except in the newly industrialized countries where the pattern will increasingly resemble that in the more advanced countries.

The automotive sector enjoys a strong, steady growth in both passenger and freight transport thanks to its accessibility and convenience. Between 1970 and 1985 automobile ownership increased by an average of 3.1 percent a year in the United States, 2.4 percent in the United Kingdom, 3.9 percent in West Germany, 6.6 percent in Japan, and 3.5 percent in France. Numbers are expected to grow further in these and other advanced market economies. There is also a tremendous growth potential in developing countries as their standard of living improves and the demand for fast and convenient transportation grows.

Maritime transport has suffered a major decline since the 1970s due to the slowdown of the world economy. The world's total seaborne freight declined by 14.6 percent (or 1.3 percent annually) between 1973 and 1985. Particularly affected was the seaborne transportation of crude oil. It dropped by a whopping 53.1 percent (or 6.1 percent annually) during the same period. The resulting surplus tanker capacity, currently estimated at about 60 million dead-weight tons, continues to be a serious problem.

Air carriers, particularly long-distance carriers, have greatly benefited from the internationalization of national economies, rising living standards, and the increasing demand for high-speed travel in all contemporary societies. The volume of civilian air transport in the world jumped from about 461 billion passengers in 1970 to more than 1,360 billion passengers in 1985, a 300 percent increase. Air freight recorded a similarly phenomenal growth, from 20.5 billion ton-kilometers in 1970 to 39.3 billion ton-kilometers in 1985, or by 370 percent.

These trends are most likely to continue through the 1990s and beyond. The survey presented in this volume will have served its purpose if it enhances the awareness among transportation policymakers in the countries selected for the study and elsewhere of the developments beyond their national jurisdiction. The collective effort of the chapter authors will also have served its function if their work additionally stimulates cross-national comparative studies of public transportation. (See the Appendix for cross-national comparisons of transport data.) Such studies are badly needed in the increasingly similar world economy where many, if not most, policy problems and opportunities in this sector have been and continue to be experienced much more widely than realized. Only careful analyses of the rich experiences of the advanced market economies, the developing market economies, and the centrally planned economies can generate such an awareness.

APPENDIX: COMPARATIVE NATIONAL TRANSPORT STATISTICS

Appendix A
Gross Domestic Product and Net Material Product, 1985 (current prices)

Country	In millions of national currency units		In million U.S. dollars
Brazil	1406077	cruzados	226787
China (NMP)(a)(b)	467300	yuan renminbi	-
East Germany (NMP)	233620	marks der DDR	-
France	4585340	francs	510333
Japan	316114000	yen	1325203
Korea	74978000	won	86180
Mexico	45588000	pesos	177475
UK	350450	pounds	454540
USA	3959610	dollars	3959610
USSR (NMP)	577500	rubles	-
West Germany	1839910	deutsche marks	624969
Zaire (c)	1926	zaire	3851

Notes:
(a) NMP stands for net material product.
(b) 1983
(c) 1975

Source: United Nations, *National Accounts Statistics: Main Aggregates and Detailed Tables, 1985* (New York: United Nations, 1987).

Appendix B

Gross Domestic Product and Net Material Product in Transport, Storage, and Communications, 1985 (in millions of national currencies, current prices)

Country		
Brail	18761	cruzados
China (NMP)	16500	yuan renminbi(**a**)
East Germany (NMP)	9760	marks der DDR
France	222704	francs(**b**)
Japan	19652	yen
Korea	6194	won
Mexico	2003	pesos
UK	20957	pounds
USA	254578	dollars
USSR (NMP)	35100	rubles
West Germany	106210	deutsche marks
Zaire	84	zaires(**c**)

Notes:
(a) 1983
(b) 1984
(c) 1977

Source: United Nations, *National Accounts Statistics: Main Aggregates and Detailed Tables, 1985* (New York: United Nations, 1987).

Appendix C
Motor Vehicles in Use and Production of Passenger Cars, 1985 (in thousands)

Country	Units in Use(a)	Units produced
Brazil	9293.3	754
	1796.4	
China	3211.1(b)	9(f)
	284.8(c)	
France	20940.0	2631
	3224.0	
East Germany	3306.2	210
	656.8	
Japan	27844.0	7647
	17377.0	
Korea	556.7	262
	541.0	
Mexico	4853.9(d)	285
	2030.2(d)	
UK	17272.3	1048
	2424.7	
USA	132108.0	8002
	39583.0	
USSR	9630.9(e)	1332
	8303.5(e)	
West Germany	25844.5	4165
	1629.0	
Zaire	102.9(d)	-
	30.3(d)	

Notes:
(a) First row is passenger vehicles; second row, commercial vehicles.
(b) civil motor vehicles
(c) private motor vehicles
(d) 1983
(e) 1981
(f) motor vehicles including 269,000 trucks

Source: Data for China come from State Statistical Bureau, People's Republic of China, *Statistical Yearbook of China, 1986* (Oxford: Oxford University Press; Hong Kong: Economic Information & Agency; Beijing: China Statistical Information & Consultancy, 1986). All other data come from United Nations, *Statistical Yearbook, 1985/86,* 35th issue (New York: United Nations, 1988).

Appendix D
Railway Passenger and Freight Traffic, 1985 (in millions)

Country	Passenger-kilometers	Net Ton-kilometers
Brazil(a)	15578	92167
China	241600	812600
France	60890	58486
East Germany	22451	69216
Japan	328450	22099
Korea	22595	12086
Mexico(a)	5887	44592
UK(a)	30084	12720
USA(a)	17864	1377264
USSR	374000	3718400
West Germany	41202	63881
Zaire	Not available	Not available

Note:
(a) 1984

Source: United Nations, *Statistical Yearbook, 1985/86*, 35th issue (New York: United Nations, 1988).

Appendix E
Merchant Shipping Fleets, 1985 (in thousands of gross registered tons)

Country	
Brazil	6057
China	Not available
France	8237
East Germany	1434
Japan	39940
Korea	7169
Mexico	1467
UK	14344
USA	19518
USSR	24745
West Germany	6177
Zaire	85

Source: United Nations, *Statistical Yearbook, 1985/86*, 35th issue (New York: United Nations, 1988).

Appendix F
Goods Loaded and Unloaded in International Maritime Transport, 1985 (in thousands of metric tons)

Country	Loaded	Unloaded
Brazil	146364	48864
China	59580	70680
France	57713	153232
East Germany	11982	13141
Japan	93821	603277
Korea	31899	101111
Mexico	69540	10956
UK	147940	141959
USA	319217	362481
USSR	154047	77149
West Germany	44475	91870
Zaire	2057	779

Source: United Nations, *Statistical Yearbook, 1985/86,* 35th issue (New York: United Nations, 1988).

Appendix G
Civil Aviation, 1985 (in thousands)[a]

Country	Kilometers flown(b)	Passengers carried	Passenger-kilometers	Freight ton-kilometers
Brazil	57.7	1297.0	7370.0	513.1
China	24.2	1300.0	3761.0	217.1
France	195.7	10982.0	28238.0	2722.9
East Germany	Not available		Not available	
Japan	168.1	6311.0	31181.0	2650.0
Korea	66.3	2925.0	11100.0	1311.6
Mexico	77.6	3328.0	7853.0	92.9
UK	347.6	19558.0	60382.0	2286.2
USA	628.6	29435.0	107197.0	4137.2
USSR	113.0	3215.0	11742.0	205.0
West Germany	192.9	8536.0	22058.0	2356.9
Zaire	4.9	131.0	355.0	30.5

Note:
(a) Statistics for other than passengers are in millions.
(b) passenger flights only

Source: United Nations, *Statistical Yearbook, 1985/86,* 35th issue (New York: United Nations, 1988).

Appendix H
Employment in Transport, Storage, and Communications, 1986 (in thousands)

Country	
Brazil	1916(a)
China	12220(b)
France	1369(a)
East Germany	645
Japan	3530
Korea	733
Mexico	Not available
UK	1454
USA	6195
USSR	12513
West Germany	1527
Zaire	Not available

Notes:
(a) 1985
(b) transport, post, and telecommunications

Source: The figure for China comes from State Statistical Bureau, People's Republic of China, *Statistical Yearbook of China, 1986* (Oxford: Oxford University Press; Hong Kong: Economic Information & Agency; Beijing: China Statistical Information & Consultancy, 1986). All other data come from International Labour Office, Geneva, *Yearbook of Labour Statistics,* 1987, 47th issue (Geneva: ILO, 1987).

SELECTED BIBLIOGRAPHY

Tsuneo Akaha and Troy Lyons

This is a select listing of published works of current relevance to both public transportation policymakers and analysts. The editor has attempted to achieve current relevance by including mostly, if not exclusively, publications from the 1970s and 1980s. The inclusion of earlier publications is limited to those that provide an essential historical background to the contemporary public transportation system and policy of the twelve countries surveyed in this volume. Moreover, except for foreign language entries the chapter authors provided the editor, only English language publications are included in this bibliography.

The first section includes general English-language works that are not country-specific, including major periodicals, sources of statistical data, energy and environmental implications of transportation (particularly of automotive transportation), urban transportation, international maritime transportation, transportation policy issues common to European countries, and those directly relevant to economic development in developing countries. The section is followed by a country-by-country listing of recent works.

GENERAL

Good bibliographical sources in English on transportation include Bob J. Davis, ed., *Information Sources in Transportation, Material Management, and Physical Distribution: An Annotated Bibliography and Guide* (Westport, Conn.: Greenwood Press, 1976); Kenneth U. Flood, *Research in Transportation: Legal/Legislative and Economic Sources and Procedure* (Detroit: Gale Research Company, 1970); and Kenneth N. Metcalf, *Transportation: Information Sources* (Detroit: Gale Research Company, 1965).

English language periodicals of direct relevance to public transportation policymakers and analysts include *Journal of Maritime Law and Commerce; Marine Policy; Journal of Maritime Policy and Management; Maritime Policy Reports; Ocean Development and*

International Law; Ocean Management; Seatrade; Transportation; Transportation in America; Transportation Journal; Transportation Law Journal; Transportation Quarterly; Transportation Research; and *Transportation Science. Transportation Research* has carried special issues on the following topics of direct policy relevance: air transportation (vol. 8, no. 3, August 1974); effects of energy shortage on transportation balance (vol. 8, nos. 4–5, October 1974); automobile choice and its energy implications (vol. 14A, nos. 5–6, October–December 1980); public policy (vol. 18A, no. 2, March 1984); technology development (vol. 18A, no. 4, July 1984); transportation research (vol. 19A, no. 5/6, September–November 1985); managing transportation (vol. 21A, no. 2, March 1987); telecommunications and travel interactions (vol. 22A, no. 4, July 1988); and transportation research in Japan (vol. 23A, no. 1, January 1989).

Statistics on various modes of transportation in European and North American countries are available in United Nations, *Annual Bulletin of Transport Statistics for Europe* (New York: United Nations, annual). Similar data for Asia-Pacific nations are found in United Nations Economic and Social Commission for Asia and the Pacific, *Transport and Communications Bulletin for Asia and the Pacific* (New York: United Nations, irregular).

Statistics related to automobiles and roadway transportation are found in Motor Vehicle Manufacturers Association, *Facts and Figures* (Detroit: Motor Vehicle Manufacturers Association, various editions); Motor Vehicle Manufacturers Association, *World Motor Vehicle Data Book* (Detroit: Motor Vehicle Manufacturers Association, various editions); International Road Federation, *World Road Statistics 1978–1982* (Washington, D.C.: International Road Federation, 1983); International Road Federation, *World Road Statistics 1981–1985* (Washington, D.C.: International Road Federation, 1986); and *Ward's Automotive Reports.*

Representative works on public policy covering different modes of transportation include Alan Altshuler, ed., *Current Issues in Transportation Policy* (Lexington, Mass., and Toronto: D. C. Heath, 1979); David Banister and Peter Hall, eds., *Transport and Public Policy Planning* (London and New York: H. W. Wilson, 1981); G. J. Bell, D. A. Blackledge, and P. J. Bowen, *The Economics and Planning of Transport* (London: Heinemann, 1983); Ken J. Button and David Gillingwater, *Future Transport Policy* (London, Sydney, and Dover, N.H.: Croom Helm, 1986); Gayton E. Germane, *Transportation Policy Issues for the 1980s* (Reading, Mass., and Menlo Park, Calif.: Addison-Wesley, 1983); John L. Hazard, *Transportation: Management, Economics, Policy* (Cambridge, Md.: Cornell Maritime Press, 1977); Jan Owen Jansson, *Transportation System Optimization and Pricing* (New York: John Wiley & Sons, 1984); Adib Kanafani and Daniel Sperling, *National Transportation Planning* (The Hague, Boston, and London: Martinus Nijhoff, 1982); Harvey A. Levin, *National Transportation Policy: A Study of Studies* (Lexington, Mass.: Lexington Books, 1978); Richard M. Michaels, ed., *Transportation Planning and Policy Decision Making: Behavioral Science Contributions* (New York: Praeger Publishers, 1980); P. Nijkamp and S. Reichman, eds., *Transportation Planning in a Changing World* (Hants, England, and Brookfield, Vt.: Gower Publishing Company, 1987); Patrick O'Sullivan, *Transport Policy: Geographic, Economic, and Planning Aspects* (Totowa, N.J.: Barnes & Noble Books, 1980); Wilfred Owen, *Transportation and World Development* (Baltimore: The Johns Hopkins University Press, 1987); J. B. Polak and J. B. Van Der Kamp, eds., *Changes in the Field of Transport Studies: Essays on the Progress of Theory in Relation to Policy Making* (The Hague, Boston, and London: Martinus Nijhoff, 1980); Boris S. Pushkarev and Jeffrey

M. Zupan, *Public Transportation and Land Use Policy* (Bloomington and London: Indiana University Press, 1977); Donald F. Wood and James C. Johnson, *Contemporary Transportation,* 2nd ed. (Tulsa, Okla.: Penn Well Publishing Company, 1983).

Studies of energy and environmental implications of automotive transportation have proliferated since the oil crisis of 1973. Representative English language works in this area in the 1980s include Alan Althuser et al., *The Future of the Automobile: The Report of MIT's International Automobile Program* (Cambridge, Mass.: The MIT Press, 1984); George H. Daniels and Mark H. Rose, eds., *Energy and Transport: Historical Perspectives on Policy Issues* (Beverly Hills, London, and New Delhi: Sage Publication, 1982); Ralph Gakenheimer, ed., *The Automobile and the Environment: An International Perspective* (Cambridge, Mass., and London, England: The MIT Press, 1978); International Energy Agency, *Fuel Efficiency of Passenger Cars* (Paris: Organization for Economic Co-operation and Development (OECD), 1984); OECD, *Environmental Effects of Automotive Transport* (The Compass Project) (Paris: OECD, 1986); Office of Technology Assessment, *Increased Automobile Fuel Efficiency and Synthetic Fuels* (Washington, D.C.: U.S. Government Printing Office, 1982); Society of Automotive Engineers, *Motor Vehicle Pollution Control—A Global Perspective* (Warrendale, Pa.: Society of Automotive Engineers, 1987); and Paul J. Werbos, *Oil Dependency and the Potential for Fuel Cell Vehicles,* Technical Paper Series (Warrendale, Pa.: Society of Automotive Engineers, 1987).

More generally, discussions on transport-related energy and environmental issues in the 1980s and beyond may be found in Deborah Lynn Bleviss, *The New Oil Crisis and Fuel Economy Technologies: Preparing the Light Transportation Industry for the 1990s* (New York: Quorum Press, 1988); Mark A. Deluchi et al., ''A Comparative Analysis of Future Transportation Fuels,'' Institute of Transportation Studies (University of California, Berkeley, October 1987); and Michael Renner, ''Rethinking Transportation,'' in Lester R. Brown et al., *State of the World, 1989: A Worldwatch Institute Report on Progress Toward a Sustainable Society* (New York and London: W. W. Norton & Company, 1989), pp. 97–112.

General works on urban transportation and policy problems include Alan Altshuler with James P. Womack and John R. Pucher, *The Urban Transportation System: Politics and Policy Innovation* (Cambridge, Mass., and London: The MIT Press, 1979); Tom Rallis, *City Transport in Developed and Developing Countries* (New York: St. Martin's Press, 1988); Gabriel Roth and George G. Wynne, *Learning from Abroad: Free Enterprise Urban Transportation* (London: Transportation Books, 1982); World Bank, *Urban Transport, Sector Policy Paper* (Washington, D.C.: World Bank, May 1975).

The transformation of the modern law of the sea in the 1970s was met by a proliferation of political, legal, economic, and scientific works about national and international maritime shipping policies in the 1970s and 1980s. Non-country-specific works in this area include Bernard J. Abrahamsson, *International Ocean Shipping: Current Concepts and Principles* (Boulder, Colo.: Westview Press, 1980); Ademuni-Odeke, *Protectionism and the Future of International Shipping: the Nature, Development and Role of Flag Discriminations and Preferences, Cargo Reservation and Cabotage Restrictions, State Intervention and Maritime Subsidies* (Dordrecht: Martinus Nijhoff, 1984); David Bess, *Marine Transportation* (Danville, Ill.: Interstate Printers, 1976); Alan E. Branch, *The Elements of Shipping,* 4th ed. (London: Chapman and Hall, 1977); Hans Ludwig Beth, Arnulf Hader, and Robert Kappel, *Twenty-Five Years of World Shipping* (London: Fairplay, 1984); Hans Bohme, *Restraints on Competition in World Shipping,* Thames Essay

No. 15 (London: Trade Policy Research Centre, 1978); Alan W. Cafruny, *Ruling the Waves: The Political Economy of International Shipping* (Berkeley, Los Angeles, and London: University of California Press, 1987); Rodney P. Carlisle, *Sovereignty for Sale: The Origins and Evolution of the Panamanian and Liberian Flags of Convenience* (Annapolis: Naval Institute Press, 1981); Ignacy Chrzanowski, Maciej Krzyanowski, and Krzystof Luks, *Shipping Economics and Policy—A Socialist View* (London: Fairplay, 1979); B. M. Deakin, *Shipping Conferences: A Study of Their Origin, Development, and Economic Practices* (Cambridge: Cambridge University Press, 1973); European Commission, *Progress Towards a Common Transport Policy: Maritime Transport* (Brussels: European Community, March 1985); European Parliament, *Working Documents on the Community Shipping Industry: An Interim Report Drawn Up on Behalf of the Committee on Economic and Monetary Affairs* (Brussels: European Community, December 1976); European Parliament, Ad Hoc Merchant Shipping Committee, *EEC Shipping Policy—Flags of Convenience* (Brussels: European Community, 1979); Karl Fasbender and Wolfgang Wagner, *Shipping Conferences, Rate Policy, and Developing Countries: The Argument of Rate Discrimination* (Hamburg: Weltarchiv GMBH, 1973); Sidney Gilman, *The Competitive Dynamics of Container Shipping* (London: Gower Publishing Company, 1983); Edgar Gold, *Maritime Transport: the Evolution of International Marine Policy and Shipping Law* (Lexington, Mass., and Toronto: Lexington Books, 1981); R. O. Goss, ed., *Advances in Maritime Economics* (London: Cambridge University Press, 1977); Amos Herman, *Shipping Conferences* (Deventer: Kleur, 1983); Olav Knudsen, *The Politics of International Shipping* (Lexington, Mass.: D. C. Heath, 1973); R. Michael M'Gonigle and Mark W. Zacher, *Pollution, Politics, and International Law: Tankers at Sea* (Berkeley and Los Angeles: University of California Press, 1979); Noel Mostert, *Supership* (New York: Alfred A. Knopf, 1974); Organization for Economic Co-operation and Development Maritime Transport Committee, *Maritime Transport* (Paris: OECD, annual); M.B.F. Ranken, ed., *Greenwich Forum VI: World Shipping in the 1980s* (Guildford: Wertbury House, 1981); Thorsten Rinman and Rigmer Linden, *Shipping: How It Works* (Gothenburg, Sweden: Rinman and Linden, 1979); Harvey Silverstein, *Superships and Nation States—The Transnational Policies of IMCO* (Boulder, Colo.: Westview Press, 1978); Gunnar K. Sletmo and Ernest W. William, *Liner Conferences in the Container Age* (New York: Macmillan, 1981); Stanley G. Sturney, *The Code—The Next Five Years* (Bremen: Institute of Shipping Economics and Logistics, 1980); United Nations, *Review of Maritime Transport* (Geneva: United Nations, annual); and World Bank, *The Developing Countries and International Shipping* (Washington, D.C.: World Bank, November 1981). Comparative national statistics on merchant fleets are found in U.S. Department of Transportation Maritime Administration, *A Statistical Analysis of the World's Merchant Fleets, January 1, 1983* (Washington, D.C.: U.S. Department of Transportation Maritime Administration, 1984). Other sources of statistical information on international maritime shipping include the American Bureau of Shipping and Lloyds Register.

Studies of common transportation problems among European Community members are prepared for discussion by the European Conference of Ministers of Transportation (ECMT). Such studies and discussions are found in, chronologically, *Infrastructure Capacity Problems Raised by International Transport,* Round Table 45 (Paris: ECMT, 1979); *Possibilities and Limits of Regulation in Transport Policy,* Round Table 42 (Paris: ECMT, 1979); Leo W. Chimi, *Competitive Position and Future of Inland Waterway Transport,* Round Table 49 (Paris: ECMT, 1980); *The Evaluation of Past and Future*

Policy Measures (Paris: ECMT, 1980); *Transport and the Challenge of Structural Change* (ECMT, 1980); *Review of Demand Models,* Round Table 58 (Paris: ECMT, 1982); *Ninth International Symposium on Theory and Practice of Transport Economics,* Nov. 2–4, 1982 (Paris: ECMT, 1983); R. Balat and B. Peguilan, *The Network of Air Passenger Service in Europe* (Paris: ECMT, 1983); *The Interface between Air and Land Transportation in Europe* (Paris: ECMT, 1983); Michel Frybourg, *The Cost of Combined Transport,* Round Table 64 (Paris: ECMT, 1984); A. Tarrino, *Public Transport in Rural Areas: Scheduled and Non-scheduled Services,* Round Table 65 (Paris: ECMT, 1984); *Regulations of International Transport* (Paris: ECMT, 1985); and *International Road Haulage: Taxation Systems,* Round Table 71 (Paris: ECMT, 1986). The Organization for Economic Cooperation and Development (OECD) has also occasionally conducted studies on transportation problems common to its members. Their recent studies include *Airports and the Environment* (Paris: OECD, 1975) and *The Future of European Passenger Transport* (Paris: OECD, 1977). See, as well, Jurgen Erdmenger, *The European Community Transport Policy: Towards a Common Transport Policy* (London: Gower Publishing Company, 1983; originally published as *EG unterweg-Wegezur Gemeinsamen Verkehrspolitik,* Baden-Baden: NOMOS, Verlagsgesellschaft, 1981).

Transportation problems as they relate to economic development in the developing countries are discussed in I. J. Barwell, et al., *Rural Transport in Developing Countries,* a Study Prepared for the International Labour Office within the Framework of the World Employment Programme (London: Intermediate Technology Publications, 1985); R. T. Brown, *Transport and the Economic Integration of Latin America* (Washington, D.C.: Brookings Institution, 1966); United Nations, Department of International Economic and Social Affairs, Office of Programme Planning and Co-ordination, *Main Issues in Transport for Developing Countries During the Third United Nations Development Decade (1981–1990)* (New York: United Nations, 1982); and United Nations, *Multimodal Transport and Containerization: Guidelines on the Introduction of Containerization and Multimodal Transport and the Modernization and Improvement of the Infrastructure of Developing Countries* (Geneva: United Nations, 1982).

BRAZIL

As the country chapter on Brazil demonstrated, a general understanding of the nation's historical background is crucial to adequately appreciate the problems associated with public transportation development in Brazil. A good introduction to Brazil's history is found in E. Bradford Burns, *A History of Brazil,* 2nd ed. (New York: Columbia University Press, 1980). Brazil's socioeconomic background is briefly introduced in Brazil, *Survey of the Brazilian Economy* (Washington, D.C.: Embassy of Brazil, 1965). More critical studies of Brazil's economic development are available in Stefan Robock, *Brazil: A Study in Development* (Lexington, Mass.: D. C. Heath and Co., 1975) and Hilario Torloni, *Estudos De Problemas Brasileiros* [Studies of Brazilian problems], 16th ed. (Sao Paulo: Livrara Pionera Editora, 1983).

There are many studies of economic and political development in Latin America, including Brazil. A representative sample includes David Collier, ed., *The New Authoritarianism in Latin America* (Princeton, N.J.: Princeton University Press, 1979); Rawle Farley, *The Economics of Latin America, Development Problems in Perspective* (New York: Harper and Row, 1972); Alan Gilbert, *Latin American Development: A Geographical Perspective* (Baltimore, Md.: Penguin, 1974); Albert O. Hirschman, *A Bias for Hope: Essays on Development and Latin America* (Boulder, Colo. and London: Westview Press, 1985); Inter-American Development Bank, *Economic and Social Progress in Latin America, Economic Integration* (Washington, D.C.: IADB, 1974); and Inter-American Development Bank, *Economic and Social Progress in Latin America, The External Sector* (Washington, D.C.: IADB, 1982).

Statistics on transportation in Brazil can be found in *Anuario Estatistico dos Transportes* [Annual statistics of transportation] (Brasilia: Empresa Brasileira de Planejamento de Transportes, 1978, 1980, and 1984) and Armin Ludwig, *Brazil: A Handbook of Historical Statistics* (Boston: G. K. Hall & Co., 1985).

The federal administration organization and its functions are described in *Perfil: Administracao Federal, 1985* [Profile: Federal administration] (Sao Paulo: Editora Visao, 1985). The performance of the national bureaucracy in Brazil in public policy making and implementation is critically examined in Robert Daland, *Exploring Brazilian Bureaucracy: Performance and Pathology* (Washington, D.C.: University Press of America, 1981).

A comprehensive study of Brazil's public transportation system and policy is provided in J. C. De Macedo Soares Guimaraes, *Transportes No Brasil* [Transportation in Brazil] (Rio de Janeiro: Editora Lidador, Ltda., 1976). A study of maritime transportation is found in Murillo Burzel Valente, *A Politica de Transportes Maritimos do Brazil* [Politics of maritime transportation of Brazil], 2nd ed. (Brasilia: Ministerio dos Transportes, 1972). For Brazil's effort to reduce oil consumption in transportation, see Fernando Homen De Mello and Eduardo Gianetti Da Fonseca, *Proalcool, Energia E Transportes* (Sao Paulo: Livrara Pionera Editora, 1981).

The main periodicals on Brazilian transportation are *Jornal dos Transportes* and *Transporte Moderno*.

CHINA

An annual survey of major developments in China is found in Editorial Department of the PRC Year Book in Beijing, ed., *People's Republic of China Year Book* (Beijing: Xinhua Publishing House, annual). The most authoritative compilation of national statistics is found in State Statistical Bureau, People's Republic of China. *Statistical Year Book of China 1986* (Hong Kong: Economic Information Agency, 1986).

Economic development efforts and challenges in China are examined in Ma Hong and Sun Shangin, eds., *Studies in the Problems of China's Economic Structure* (Arlington, Va.: Joint Publication Research Service, Foreign Broadcast Information Service, China Report Economic Affairs, August 3, 1984); Foreign Broadcast Information Service, China Report Economic Affairs, *China in the Year 2000* (Arlington, Va.: Joint Publication Research Service, March 6, 1986); Joint Economic Committee, *Chinese Economy post Mao* (Washington, D.C.: Government Printing Office, 1978); Joint Economic Committee, *China Under the Four Modernizations* (Washington, D.C.: Government Printing Office, 1982); Joint Economic Committee, *China's Economy Looks Toward the Year 2000* (Washington, D.C.: Government Printing Office, 1986); World Bank, *China Long-Term Development Issues and Options, A World Bank Country Economic Report* (Baltimore, Md.: The Johns Hopkins University Press, 1985). These reports and studies include discussions of China's transport problems and policy goals.

More specifically, developments in China's transportation are reviewed in the occasionally published *China Transport* (Hong Kong). An excellent study of prewar railroad development in China is found in Ralph William Hueneman, *The Dragon and the Iron Horse: the Economics of Railroads in China, 1876–1937* (Ann Arbor, Mich.: University Microfilms International, 1982). More recent developments in the nation's transportation as it relates to economic development are examined in World Bank, *China: The Transport Sector,* Annex 6 to *China Long-Term Development Issues and Options* (Washington, D.C.: World Bank, 1985) and Jacques Yenny and Lily Uy, *Transport in China: A Comparison of Basic Indicators with Those of Other Countries* (Washington, D.C.: World Bank, 1985).

Current economic developments, including transportation developments, are reported in *Beijing Review, The China Business Review,* and *Far Eastern Economic Review.*

EAST GERMANY

Economic trends in East Germany in the 1980s are examined in Deutsches Institut für Wirtschaftsforschung, *Handbuch DDR-Wirtschaft* [Handbook of the economy of the German Democratic Republic], 4 Auflage, (Reinbeck bei Hamburg: Rowohlt Taschenbuch Verlag GmbH, 1985). A concise introduction to the East German economy, including some statistics on transportation is available in German Institute for Economic Research, *Handbook of the Economy of the German Democratic Republic* (Westmead, Farnborough, Hampshire, England: Saxon House, Teakfield, 1979). For more general information on East Germany, see *DDR und Osteuropa—ein Handbuch* [GDR and Eastern Europe—A handbook] (Opladen, Leske & Budrich GmbH, 1981). A good source of national statistics including transportation is *Statistisches Jahrbücher der DDR* [GDR statistical yearbooks].

A good introduction to the historical development of transportation in East Germany is found in E. Kramer, *Die Entwicklung des Verkehrswesens in der DDR* [The development of the transportation system in the GDR] (Berlin, GDR: Transpress VEB Verlag für Verkehrswesen, 1978). A concise overview of East German transportation system and policy is provided in R. Hopf, "Verkehrswesen" [The transportation system] in *DDR-Handbuch* [GDR handbook] (Köln: Bundesministerium für Innerdeutsche Beziehungen, Verlag Wissenshaft und Politik, 1985). Handy summaries of transport economy, railway transport, and transportation in general are found, respectively, in *Lexikon der Wirtschaft—Verkehr* [Lexicon of the economy—transportation] (Berlin, GDR: Transpress VEB Verlag für Verkehrswesen, 1972); *Transpress Lexikon Eisenbahn* [Transpress railroad lexicon] (Berlin, GDR: Transpress VEB Verlag für Verkehrswesen, 1981); *Transpress Lexikon Transport* [Transpress transportation lexicon] (Berlin, GDR: Transpress VEB Verlag für Verkehrswesen, 1981).

Economic studies of East German transportation are found in Autoren Kollektiv, *Ökonomie des Transports,* Bd. 1 und 2 [Transport economy, vol. 1 and 2] (Berlin, GDR: Transpress VEB Verlag für Verkehrswesen, 1977); Autoren Kollektiv, *Ökonomische Geographie der Deutschen Demokratischen Republik* [Economic geography of the German Democratic Republic] (Gotha/Leipzig: VEB Hermann Haack, Geographisch-Kartolographische Anstalt, 1977); Autoren Kollektiv, *Reproduktion und Verkehr* [Reproduction and transportation] (Berlin, GDR: Transpress VEB Verlag für Verkehrswesen, 1982); P. Franke et al., *Transportpreise* [Transportation prices] (Berlin, GDR: Transpress VEB Verlag für Verkehrswesen, 1971); K. Hofmann, *Ökonomik, Organisation und Planung der Eisenbahn* [The economics, organization, and planning of the railroad] (Berlin, GDR: Transpress VEB Verlag für Verkehrswesen, 1968). J. Günther,

Transportstatistik [Transportation statistics] (Berlin, GDR: Transpress VEB Verlag für Verkehrswesen, 1970) provides transportation statistics up to the late 1960s. More recent statistics and other data on transportation in East Germany are available in *Internationale Transport-Annalen* [International transportation annals] (Prague: NADAS; Berlin, GDR: Transpress; Warsaw: WkL, annual; appeared until the early 1980s) and G. Mieth, G. Tessman, and J. Matthäi, *Transportpreise* [Transportation prices] (Berlin, GDR: Transpress VEB Verlag für Verkehrswesen, 1981).

Problems of transport administration and planning are discussed in the monthly periodical *DDR Verkehr, Zeitschrift für Komplexe Fragen der Leitung und Planung des Verkehrswesens* [GDR transportation, (monthly) periodical for complex questions of administration and planning in the transportation system] (Berlin, GDR: Transpress VEB Verlag für Verkehrswesen, monthly). Roadway transportation is reviewed in *Die Strasse, Zeitschrift für Forschung und Praxis des Strassenwesens* [The road, (monthly) periodical for road network research and practice] (Berlin, GDR: Transpress VEB Verlag für Verkehrswesen, monthly). Transportation developments in East Germany are also often discussed in *Deutschland Archiv* (Köln: Verlag Wissenschaft und Politik, 1981); *Wochenbericht des DIW* [DIW weekly report]; and *FS-Analysen.*

The main periodical on East German transportation is *DDR-Verkehr.*

FRANCE

A general introduction to the history of economic development in France is found in François Caron, *An Economic History of Modern France* (New York: Columbia University Press, 1979) and J. J. Carré, P. Dubois, and E. Malinovash, *French Economic Growth,* trans. John P. Hatfield (Stanford: Stanford University Press, 1975).

For an overview of the transport sector in France, see Maurice Bernadet and Gilles Joly, *Le Secteur des Transports* [The transport sector] (Lyon: Economica, 1978); Michel Chesnais, *Transports et Espace Française* [Transportation and French geography] (Masson, 1981); E. R. Quinet, R. Marche, and C. Reynaud, *Les Transports en France* [Transportation in France] (Paris: Documentation Française, 1982); E. R. Quinet, R. Marche, and C. Reynaud, *La Coordination des Infrastructures de Transport* [Coordination of transport infrastructure] (Paris: Documentation Française, 1980).

The most recent transportation development plans are found in INSEE, *Les Transports en France en 1983–1984—XXIIEe Rapport de la Comptes des Transports de la Nation* [Transportation in France in 1983–1984—the 22nd report of the National Transportation Accounting Board], November 1985; Commissariat Général du Plan, *Politique des Transports, IX Plan 1984–1988* [The policy of transportation, Ninth Plan 1984–1988] (Paris: Documentation Française, 1983); and J. Villette, *Transports Décentralisations 9th Plan* [Transportation decentralization Ninth PLAN] (Paris: Documentation Française, 1986).

For examinations of roadway transportation and policy in France, see: Albert Boyer, *Les Transports Routiers* [Roadway transportation] (Paris: Presses Universitaires de France, 1973); Ministère des Transports, Ministère de l'industrie et de la Recherche, *Rapport de la Mission Transports Terrestres* [Report of the Commission on Land Transportation] (Paris: Documentation Française, 1983); and OECD Staff, *Road Binders and Energy Savers* (Paris: OECD Roads Transportation Research Service). Highway transportation is examined in Alain Fayard, *Les Autoroutes et Leur Financement* [Autoroutes and their finance] (Paris: Documentation Française, 1980); Charles Richard, *Les Autoroutes*

[Freeways] (Paris: Presses Universitaires de France, 1984); and SECAP, *Système de Gestion Autonome du Résseau d'Autoroutes et Application du Péage à son Financement* [The self-management system of the freeway network and the use of toll revenues for self-financing] (Paris: SCET-Autoroute, 1984).

For a study of roadways and railways, see Denis Broussole, *Le Rail et La Route* [Railways and roadways] (Paris: Economica, 1981) and Pierre Guillaumat, *Orientations pour les Transports Terrestres* [Objectives for land transportation] (Paris: Documentation Française, 1978). The high-speed train TGV is extensively discussed in *Les Aspects Socio-Économiques des Trains à Grande Vitesse* [The socioeconomic aspects of high speed trains], 2 volumes (Paris: Documentation Française, 1984); Jean-Francois Bozin, *Les Défis du TGV* [The challenges of TGV] (Paris: Denoël, 1981); Philippe Lorin, *Le Train à grande Vitesse* [The high-speed train] (Paris: Fernal Nulttain, 1981); and Ministère des Transports, *TGV-Atlantique (Rudeau Report)* (Paris: Documentation Française, 1984).

Air transportation is extensively discussed in Paul Funel and Jacques Villiers, *Le Transport Aérien Française* [French air transport] (Paris: Documentation Française, 1982). For the most recent air transport development plan, see Commissariat Général du Plan, *Aéronautique et Espace, IX Plan 1984–1988* [Air travel and geography, Ninth PLAN 1984–1988] (Paris: Documentation Française, 1983).

A concise description of inland waterway transportation is found in Roger Grégoire, *Le Transport Fluvial* [Waterway transportation] (Paris: Documentation Française, 1983).

For urban transportation in France, see P. Borg et al., "Paris," in *Managing Transport* (Paris: OECD, 1979) and Pierre Merlin, *Les Politiques de Transport Urbain* [Urban transport policy] (Paris: Documentation Française, 1985). For the Channel Tunnel project, see Jean-Pierre Navailles, *Le Tunnel sous la Manche* [The Channel tunnel] (Champ Varrow: Epoques, 1987).

Transportation problems in provinces are examined in Commissariat Général de Plan, *Compétênce Transferées aux Collectivités Territorials* [Delegation of tasks to territorial collectivities] (Paris: Documentation Française, 1985) and Roger Price, *The Modernization of Rural France* (New York: St. Martin's, 1983).

French transport periodicals include *Actualités Sociales des Transports; Antenne Inter Transports; Auto-Journal; Chronique du Transporteur; Bulletin Officiel* (Ministère de l'Aménagement du Territoire, de l'Équipement, du Logement et des Transports); *Information Transports; Nord-Transports; Bulletin de Documentation et d'Information* (Régie Autonome des Transports Parisiens); *Revue* (Fédération des Travaux Publics et des Transports); *Routes et Chantiers; Transport Public; Transports.*

JAPAN

A good introduction to Japanese history is found in Edwin O. Reischauer, *The Japanese* (Tokyo: Tuttle, 1977) and Mikiso Hane, *Japan: A Historical Survey* (New York: Scribner's, 1972). Japan's modern economic history is reviewed in George C. Allen, *A Short Economic History of Modern Japan* (New York: St. Martin's, 1980). A comprehensive study of Japan's current economic situation is found in Edward J. Lincoln, *Japan: Facing Economic Maturity* (Washington, D.C.: Brookings Institution, 1988).

Japanese government provides a detailed account of major developments and policy measures in public transportation in its annual transport white paper—*Unyu Hakusho* [Transport white paper] (Tokyo: Ōkurashō Insatsukyoku, annual). All major developments in Japanese public transportation, including political, economic, legal, industrial, and technological developments are summarized in the indispensable annual *Kōtsū Nenkan* [Transport yearbook] (Tokyo: Kōtsū Kyōkai, annual). Transport Policy Council, *Basic Direction of a Comprehensive Transport Policy Based on Long Term Perspectives: Laying the Groundwork for Tomorrow's Needs under Conditions of Trials and Adversity (Excerpts)* (Tokyo: Transport Policy Council, 1981) provides a summary description of the government's transportation policy goals for the 1980s. A concise summary description of Japan's public transportation is found in Edward J. Lincoln, "Transportation and Communications," in Frederica M. Bunge, ed., *Japan: A Country Study,* Area Handbook Series (Washington, D.C.: U.S. Government as represented by the Secretary of the Army, 1983), pp. 176–178 and Edward J. Lincoln, "Transportation," in *Kodansha Encyclopedia of Japan,* vol. 8 (Tokyo: Kodansha, 1983), pop. 98–104.

Extensive statistical data are included in the transport white paper just noted. Other sources of transport statistics include *Japan: An International Comparison* (Tokyo: Keizai Kōhō Center, annual); *Kōtsū Nenkan* [Traffic yearbook] (Tokyo: Kōtsū Kyōryokukai, annual); Ministry of Transport, *Annual Report of Transport Economy, Summary* (Tokyo: Printing Bureau, Ministry of Finance, annual); *Statistical Yearbook of Japan* (Tokyo: Nihon Tōkei Kyōkai, annual); Ministry of Transport, *The Current Situation of Japanese Shipping* (Tokyo: Japan Maritime Development Association, annual); *Statistical Handbook of Japan* (Tokyo: Statistics Bureau, Management and Coordination Agency, annual); and Unyushō, ed., *Nihon Kaiun no Genkyō* [The current condition of Japanese maritime shipping] (Tokyo: Nihon Kaiji Kōhō Kyōkai, 1984). Statistics on transport-related energy can be found on an annual basis in Unyushō Unyuseisakukyoku Jōhōkanribu, ed., *Unyu Kankei Enerugii Yōran* [Digest of transport-related energy] (Tokyo: Unyushō Unyuseisakukyoku Jōhōkanribu, annual).

Organizational structure of the Japanese government, including the Ministry of Transport, is presented in Administrative Management Bureau, Management and Coordination Agency, Prime Minister's Office, *Organization of the Government of Japan, 1984* (Tokyo: Institute of Administrative Management, 1985). For a concise introduction to the Ministry of Transport, its history and organization, see *Unyushō* [The Ministry of Transport] (Tokyo: Kyōikusha, 1979) and Seisakujihōsha, ed., *Nihon no Kanchō: Sono Hito to Soshiki, 1984-nenban Unyushō* [Administrative agencies of Japan: Their people and organization, 1984, The Ministry of Transport] (Tokyo: Kokudoseisaku Kenkyūkai, 1984).

Sector-specific studies are abundant in Japanese language but very rare in English. Representative studies of railway transport in Japanese include Asahi Shimbunsha Chosakenkyushitsu, *Kokutetsu Kaikaku—Kōsha kara Minei e* [JNR reform—From a public enterprise to private operation] (Tokyo: Asahi Shimbunsha, 1982); Kichizo Hosoda, *Kokutetsu o Kataru* [Speaking of JNR] (Tokyo: Rikuun Keizai Shimbunsha, 1981); *Kokutetsu: Kōkigyō to Kōkyō Kōtsu* [JNR: Public enterprise and public transportation], Jūristo Zōkan Sōgū Tokushū, vol. 31 (1983); Kenichi Masui, ed., *Shitetsu Gyōkai* [Private railroad industry] (Tokyo: Kyōikusha, 1976); Fumio Takagi, *Kokutetsu Zakkubaran* [Speaking frankly about JNR] (Tokyo: Tōyō Keizai Shimpōsha, 1977); and Toshi Kōtsū Kenkyūjō, *Tetsudō Keiei Handobukku* [Railway management handbook] (Tokyo: Seibunsha, 1980).

Concise information on Japanese road transport can be found in Hiromi Arisawa and Shuzo Inaba, eds., *Nihon Rikuum Jūnenshi* [The ten-year history of Japanese land transport] (Tokyo: Nihon Hyōronsha, 1966) and Yukihide Okano, *Rikuun Gyōkai* [The land freight industry] (Tokyo: Kyōikusha, 1982). For a critical study of urban transportation in Japan, see Namiki Oka, *Toshi to Kōtsū* [Urban cities and traffic] (Tokyo: Iwanamishoten, 1981).

Maritime shipping has been extensively studied in Japan. A good historical introduction is R. Furuta and Y. Hirai, *A Short History of Japanese Shipping* (Tokyo: Tokyo News Service, 1967). Recent examples of studies of Japanese maritime shipping include *Japan's Shipping Policy,* JAMRI Report, no. 3 (Tokyo: Japan Maritime Research Institute, September 1984); Masao Oda, *Kaiun Gyōkai* [The maritime shipping industry] (Tokyo: Kyōikusha, 1985); George Totten, "The Reconstruction of the Japanese Shipbuilding Industry," in Robert L. Friedheim et al., *Japan and the New Ocean Regime* (Boulder, Colo.: Westview Press, 1984), pp. 130–172; and Unyushō, ed., *Nihon Kaiun no Genkyō* [The current condition of Japanese maritime shipping] (Tokyo: Nihon Kaiji Kōhō Kyōkai, 1984).

A brief introduction to Japanese air transport industry is found in Yoshimasa Yamanobe, *Kōkū Gyōkai* [Civil air industry] (Tokyo: Kyōikusha, 1985). A comprehensive, multimodal study of transport needs in the "information age" is found in *Jōhōka Jidai ni okeru Kōtsū Sangyō* [Transport industry in the information age] (Tokyo: Unyu Keizai Kenkyū Center, 1984).

For a look at the most recent sample of Japanese transportation studies in English, see *Transportation Research,* Part A: General, vol. 23A, no. 1 (January 1989), Special Issue: Transportation Research in Japan.

Japanese language periodicals on transportation include *Kaiji Kōtsū Kenkyū* [Studies of maritine transport]; *Kaijihō Kenkyūkaishi* [Organ of maritine law research association]; *Kaijishi Kenkyū* [Studies of maritime history]; *Kōsokudōro to Jidōsha* [Highway and automobiles]; *Kōtsūgaku Kenkyū* [Transport research], *Kōwan* [Ports and harbors]; *Unyu to Keizai* [Transport and economy], *Toransupōto* [Transport].

KOREA

Excellent studies of Korea's postwar economic development are found in Kwang Suk Kim and Michael Roemer, *Growth and Structural Transformation,* Studies in the Modernization of the Republic of Korea, 1945–1975 (Cambridge, Mass.: Harvard University Council on East Asian Studies, 1979); Robert Repetto et al., *Economic Development, Population Policy, and Demographic Transition in the Republic of Korea,* Studies in the Modernization of the Republic of Korea, 1945–1975 (Cambridge, Mass.: Harvard University Council on East Asian Studies, 1981); and World Bank, *Korea: Policy Issues for Long-Term Development* (Baltimore: The Johns Hopkins University Press, 1979). Recent examples of national economic development plans with important implications for public transportation are found in *Che o ch'a Kyongje Sahoe Paljon o gyenyon Kyehoek Kyoto'ongbu Sokwan Sujong Kyehoek, 1982–1986* [The fifth economic and social development five-year plan and the revised plan for the Ministry of Transportation, 1982–1986] (Seoul: the ROK Ministry of Transportation, 1983) and *National Land Development Planning in Korea* (Seoul: Korea Research Institute for Human Settlements, 1984).

Convenient sources of statistical information include *A Handbook of Korea* (Seoul: Korean Overseas Information Service, 3rd and 5th editions, 1979 and 1983); *Economic Statistics Yearbook* (Seoul: The Bank of Korea, annual); *Korean Economic Yearbook*

(Seoul: The Federation of Korean Industries); *Korean Statistical Yearbook* (Seoul: The ROK Economic Planning Board); and *Major Statistics of Korean Economy* (Seoul: The ROK Economic Planning Board, annual).

Annually updated information on public transportation and policy is provided in *Annual Yearbook of Korean Transportation* (Seoul: Kyotong Sinposa, annual); *Report on Transportation Survey* (Seoul: The ROK Economic Planning Board, annual); and *Transportation in Korea* (Seoul: The ROK Ministry of Transportation, annual).

Recent studies of Korean transportation include Moon-Suk Ahn and Chong Bum Lee, "A Network Analysis of International Relations: A Case Study of the Transportation System in Korea," in Bun Woong Kim, David S. Bell, and Chong Bum Lee, eds., *Administrative Dynamics and Development: The Korean Experience* (Seoul: Kyobo Publishing, 1985); Ho-kyu Im, *Hangukui Chonghap Susong Ch'egye* [Korean integrated transportation system] (Seoul: Korea Development Institute, 1979); "Development of Transportation and Communication," in *Long-Term Prospect for Economic and Social Development, 1977–91* (Seoul: Korea Development Institute, 1978); and Tallman Neuner, "Transport," in Parvez Hasan and D. C. Rao, eds., *Korea: Policy Issues for Long-Term Development,* published for the World Bank, Baltimore: The Johns Hopkins University Press, 1979.

Recent developments in road transportation in South Korea are discussed in *Highway Network Master Plan Study (I): Summary* (Seoul: The ROK Ministry of Construction and Korea Research Institute for Human Settlements, 1985) and *Study of Road User Charges: Final Report* (Seoul: The ROK Ministry of Construction and Korea Research Institute for Human Settlements, 1986).

Discussions of urban transport problems and policy measures are contained in Won-Yong Kwon, *Metropolitan Growth and Management: The Case of Seoul* (Seoul: Korea Research Institute for Human Settlements, 1980); Edwin S. Mills and Byung-Nak Song, *Urbanization and Urban Problems,* Studies in the Modernization of the Republic of Korea, 1945–1975 (Cambridge, Mass.: Harvard University Council on East Asian Studies, 1979); and Yung-Hee Rho and Myong-Chan Hwang, eds., *Metropolitan Planning: Issues and Policies* (Seoul: Korea Research Institute for Human Settlements, 1979).

MEXICO

On the general topic of political-economic development in Latin America, including Mexico, see David Collier, ed., *The New Authoritarianism in Latin America* (Princeton, N.J.: Princeton University Press, 1979); Rawle Farley, *The Economics of Latin America, Development Problems in Perspective* (New York: Harper & Row, 1972); Alan Gilbert, *Latin American Development: A Geographical Perspective* (Baltimore, Md.: Penguin, 1974); Albert O. Hirschman, *A Bias for Hope: Essays on Development and Latin America* (New Haven, Conn.: Yale University Press, 1971); Inter-American Development Bank, *Economic and Social Progress in Latin America, Economic Integration* (Washington, D.C.: IADB, 1984); Inter-American Development Bank, *Economic and Social Progress in Latin America, The External Sector* (Washington, D.C.: IADB, 1982); International Monetary Fund, "Mexico—Recent Economic Developments" (Washington, D.C.: International Monetary Fund, July 1, 1982); and Howard J. Wiarda and Harvey F. Kline, eds., *Latin American Politics and Development* (Boston: Houghton Mifflin, 1979). Recent economic development plans for the Mexican government are presented in Secretária de Programación y Presupuesto, "Plan Global de Desarrollo

1980–1982'' [Global development plan, 1980–1982] (Mexico City, 1980) and ''Plan Global de Desarrollo, 1983–1988'' [Global development plan, 1983–1988] (Mexico City [Ministry for Programs and Budget], 1983).

Statistical information on transportation and other socioeconomic developments in Mexico can be found in Organization of American States, *Boletin Estadistico de la OEA* [Statistical bulletin of the OAS] (various issues); Inter-American Development Bank, *Informe Annual* (Washington, D.C.: Inter-American Development Bank, annual); Secretária de Programación y Presupuesto, ''Información Fundamental de la Cuenta Pública, 1979'' [Information fundamental to the public accounts, 1979], *Programa* no. 4 (November 1980–February 1981) (Mexico City, 1981); and *Statistical Abstract of Latin America* (Los Angeles: UCLA Latin American Center Publications, various issues).

On the role of transportation in economic development, see Wilfred Owen, ''Transportation and World Development,'' *Transportation Quarterly,* vol. 39, no. 2 (July 1985), pp. 365–374; and E. J. Taaffe, R. L. Morrill, and P. R. Gould, ''Transport Expansion in Underdeveloped Countries: A Comparative Analysis,'' *Geographical Review,* vol. 53 (October 1963), pp. 503–529. The relationship between energy costs and the development of transportation is examined in Inter-American Development Bank, *The Impact of Energy Costs on Transportation in Latin America* (Bogota: IADB, 1982).

For a study of the railroad infrastructure in the 1960s, see K. J. Kansky, *Structure of Transportation Networks,* University of Chicago, Department of Geography Research Paper 84 (Chicago: University of Chicago, 1963). For more recent developments in Mexican rail transportation, see John H. Coatsworth, *Growth Against Development: The Economic Impact of Railroads in Porfirian Mexico* (Dekalb, Ill.: Northern Illinois University Press, 1981); Frank Malone, ''Rail Renaissance in Mexico,'' *Railway Age,* no. 182 (April 13, 1981), pp. 22–26, 75–77; Frank Malone, ''Mexico's Amazing Metro: Mover of Millions—And Growing,'' *Railway Age,* no. 182 (April 13, 1981), pp. 30–31; and World Bank, ''Mexico-Railway Sector Project,'' R85–165 (May 22, 1985).

SOVIET UNION

The geographical, political, and economic background of the Soviet Union can be found in Ed A. Hewett, *Energy, Economics, and Foreign Policy in the Soviet Union* (Washington, D.C.: The Brookings Institution, 1984); Jerry F. Hough and Merle Fainsod, *How the Soviet Union Is Governed* (Cambridge, Mass.: Harvard University Press, 1979); *Soviet Economy in the 1980s: Problems and Prospects,* part I, U.S. Congress Joint Economic Committee (Washington, D.C.: U.S. Government Printing Office, 1983); and A. T. Khrushchev and I. V. Nikol'skii, eds., *Ekonomicheskaya geografiya SSSR* [Economic geography of the USSR], part I, 2nd ed., (Moscow: Moscow State University Press, 1985).

Statistics on the Soviet economy and transportation are found in *Narodnoye khoziaistvo SSSR* [National economy USSR] (Moscow, annual); E. V. Petrov and I. M. Aliksieva, *Statistika avtomobil'nogo transporta* [Statistics of automobile transportation] (Moscow: Transport, 1983); *Transport i sviaz': Statisticheskii sbornik* [Transportation and communications: Statistical handbook] (Moscow: Central Statistical Administration of the USSR Council of Ministers, 1957 and 1972); and *USSR Facts & Figures Annual* (Gulf Breeze, Fla.: Academic International Press).

For historical accounts of Soviet transportation development, see Richard M. Haywood, *The Beginnings of Railway Development in Russia in the Reign of Nicholas I,*

1835–1842 (Durham, N.C.: Duke University Press, 1969); Holland Hunter, *Soviet Transport Experience: Its Lessons for Other Countries* (Washington, D.C.: The Brookings Institution, 1968); A. N. Markova, *Transport SSSR: Osnovnyye etapy ego razvitiya* [Transportation USSR: Basic stages of its development] (Moscow: Nauka, 1977); Boris Pavlovich Orlov, *Razvitiye transporta SSSR, 1917–1962: Istoriko-ekonomicheskii ocherk* [The development of transportation in the USSR, 1917–1962: Historical-economic overview] (Moscow: USSR Academy of Sciences, 1963); J. N. Westwood, *A History of Russian Railways* (London: George Allen & Unwin, 1964); *Zheleznodorozhnii transport SSSR v dokumentakh* [Railroad transportation of the USSR in documents] (Moscow: Transport, 1957); and Ernest W. Williams, Jr., *Freight Transportation in the Soviet Union* (Princeton: Princeton University Press, 1962).

For discussion of more recent and current transport trends and problems, see I. Ya Aksenov, *Edinaya transportnaya systema* [Unified transportation system] (Moscow: Transport, 1980); John Ambler, Dennis J. B. Shaw, and Leslie Symons, eds., *Soviet and East European Transport Problems* (New York: St. Martin's Press, 1985); V. A. Balakin et al., *Planovo-Ekonomicheskaya rabota v transportnom stroutel'stve* [Planning-economic work in transportation construction] (Moscow: Transport, 1984); I. A. Butin et al., *Transportnyi kompleks sotsialisticheskoi ekonomiki* [The transportation complex of the socialist economy] (Moscow: Moscow State University Press, 1984); A. G. Kovrigin, *Finansy zheleznodorozhnogo transporta* [Finances of railroad transportation], 2nd ed., (Moscow: Transport, 1984); V. G. Nikitenko and Y. G. Gutsev, *Transport v narodnokhoziaistvennom komplekse BSSR* [Transportation in the national-economic complex of the BSSR (Belorussia)] (Minsk: Nauka i Tekhnika, 1978); Holland Hunter and Deborah Kaple, "Transport in Trouble," in *Soviet Economy in the 1980s: Problems and Prospects,* part I, U.S. Congress Joint Economic Committee (Washington, D.C.: U.S. Government Printing Office, 1983); *Problemy razvitiya transporta SSSR: Kompleksnaya ekspluatatsiya* [Problems in the development of transportation in the USSR: Complex exploitation] (Moscow: Transport, 1983); S. M. Rezer, *Upravleniye transportnymi predpriyatiyami* [Administration of transportation enterprises] (Moscow: Nauka, 1982); and Leslie Symons and Colin White, eds., *Russian Transport* (London: Bell, 1975).

For discussions of railroad development in Siberia and the Soviet Far East, see L. I. Kolesov, *Mezhotraslevyye problemy razvitiya transportnoi sistemy Sibiri i Dal'nego Vostoka* [Interbranch problems in the development of the transportation system of Siberia and the Far East] (Novosibirsk: Nauka, 1982); Robert North, *Transport in Western Siberia* (Vancouver: University of British Columbia Press, 1979); and Allen S. Whiting, *Siberian Development and East Asia: Threat or Promise?* (Stanford: Stanford University Press, 1962).

Problems of automotive transportation are discussed in V. N. Ivanov, *Avtomobil'nyi transport: Problemy, perspektivy* [Automobile transportation: Problems, perspectives] (Moscow: Transport, 1981); W. H. Parker, "The Soviet Motor Industry," *Soviet Studies,* vol. 32, no. 4 (1980), pp. 515–541; E. V. Petrov and I. M. Aliksieva, *Statistika avtomobil'nogo transporta* [Statistics of automobile transportation] (Moscow: Transport, 1983); D. Velikanov, "Avtomobil'nyi transport: Zadachi ego dal'neishego razvitiya" [Automobile transport: Goals of its further development], *Kommunist,* no. 15 (1983), pp. 70–79; and Toli Welihozkiy, "Automobiles and the Soviet Consumer," *Soviet Economy in a Time of Change,* vol. 1, Compendium of Papers Submitted to the U.S. Congress, Joint Economic Committee, Oct. 10, 1979.

Information on Soviet maritime transport is found in Robert Athay, *Economics of Soviet Merchant Shipping Policy* (Chapel Hill: University of North Carolina Press, 1972); Atlantic Council of the United States, *The Soviet Merchant Marine: Economic and Strategic Challenge to the West* (Washington, D.C.: Atlantic Council, 1978); and T. B. Gluzhenko, *Morskoi transport SSSR* [Maritime transport USSR] (Moscow: Transport, 1984).

Soviet periodicals dealing with transportation include the following: *Avtomobil'noye khoziaistvo* [Automobile economy]; *Grazhdanskaya aviatsiya* [Civil aviation]; *Gudok* [Whistle]; *Planovoye khoziaistvo* [Planned economy]; *Rechnoi transport* [River transport]; *Vozdushnyi transport* [Air transport]; and *Zheleznodorozhnyi transport* [Railroad transport].

UNITED KINGDOM

For basic statistics on U.K. transportation, consult "Transport and Communications," in *Britian 1986: An Official Handbook* (London: Central Office of Information, Reference Services, 1986); European Conference of Ministers of Transport, *1982 Transport Statistical Series: Trends in Investment, Infrastructure, Rolling Stock, and Traffic* (Paris: ECMT, 1985); and United Nations, *Annual Bulletin of Transport Statistics for Europe* (New York: UN, annual). Statistical information on U.K. maritime shipping is found in General Council of British Shipping, *British Shipping Review* (annual) and Department of Industry and Trade, *General Trends in Shipping: A Report on the U.K. Merchant Fleet, World Shipping, and Seaborne Trade,* series 2, no. 6 (London: Department of Industry and Trade, November 1979).

Historical accounts of transportation development in the United Kingdom are found in Derek H. Aldcroft, *Studies in British Transport History, 1870–1970* (Newton Abbot, England: David & Charles, 1974); H. J. Dyos and D. H. Aldcroft, *British Transport: An Economic Survey from the Seventeenth Century to the Twentieth* (Leicester, England: Leicester University Press, 1969); Brian Fullerton, *The Development of British Transport Networks* (London: Oxford University Press, 1975); and Michael R. Bonavia, *The Nationalisation of British Transport: The Early History of the British Transport Commission, 1948–53* (London: Macmillan, 1987).

Discussions of current public transportation planning and management in the United Kingdom are found in John Adams, *Transport Planning: Vision and Practice* (London: Routledge and Kegan Paul, 1981); B. M. M. Barrett, "United Kingdom," in *Public Transport in Rural Areas: Scheduled and Non-Scheduled Services,* Round Table 65 (Paris: Economic Research Center, European Conference of Ministers of Transport, 1984), pp. 197–254; Brian T. Bayliss, *Planning and Control in the Transport Sector* (London: Gower Publishing Company, 1981); Malcolm Buchanan et al., *Transport Planning for Greater London* (Farnborough, England: Saxon House, 1980); James A. Dunn, Jr., *Miles to Go: European and American Transportation Policies* (Cambridge, Mass., and London: The MIT Press, 1981); Stephen Glaiser and Coriane Mulley, *Public Control of the British Bus Industry* (London: Gower Publishing Company, 1983); D. W. Glassborow, "The Constraints Imposed by Physical Planning on Regional Transport Organisation: Report on Some Aspects of British Experience in Recent Years," *The Regionalisation of Transport and Regional Planning in Practice Seminar,* Council of Europe, Strasbourg, December 5–6, 1983, pp. 107–130; Peter Hall and Carmen Hass-Klau, *Can Rail Save the City?: The Impacts of Rail Rapid Transit and Pedestrianisation on British and German Cities* (Hants, England, and Brookfield, Vt.: Gower Publishing Company, 1985); Peter J. Mackie, David Simon, and Anthony E. Whiteing, *British Transport Industry and the European Community* (London: Gower Publishing Company, 1987); Robert G. Smith, *Ad Hoc Governments: Special Purpose Transportation Authorities in Britain and the United States* (Beverly Hills, Calif.: Sage Publications, 1974); Alan Thomas and John Aldridge, *A.E.C. Builders of London's Buses* (Transport Service) (London: Ian Henry Publication, 1985); A.W.J. Thompson and L. C. Hunter, *The Nationalized Transport Industries* (London: Heinemann Educational Books, 1973); and Frances Wilkins, *Transport and Travel from Nineteen Thirty to the Nineteen Eighty's* (Batsford, England: David and Charles, 1985).

Major transport periodicals published in the United Kingdom include *Cargo Systems International; Journal of Transport Economics and Policy; Journal of Transport History; Transport; Transport Management; Transport Research; Transport Reviews;* and *Transportation Planning and Technology.*

UNITED STATES

Statistics on public transportation in the United States can be found in Federal Highway Administration, *Highway Statistics 1986* (Washington, D.C.: U.S. Department of Transportation, 1987); Mary C. Holocomb, *Transportation Energy Data Book: Edition 9* (Oak Ridge, Tenn.: Oak Ridge National Laboratory, 1987); "National Transportation Statistics: Annual Report" (Washington, D.C.: Research and Special Programs Administration, U.S. Department of Transportation, annual); *Transit Fact Book,* 1985 ed. (Washington, D.C.: American Public Transit Association, 1985); Transportation Policy Associates, *Transportation in America: A Statistical Analysis of Transportation in the United States* (Washington, D.C.: Transportation Policy Associates, annual); U.S. Department of Transportation Maritime Administration, *United States Oceanborne Foreign Trade Routes, August 1981* (Washington, D.C.: U.S. Department of Transportation Maritime Administration, 1982); and Transportation Systems Center, *National Transportation Statistics,* Annual Report (Washington, D.C.: Department of Transportation, annual).

Recent studies of U.S. transportation system and policy in general include Ann Friedlander and Robert Simpson, *Alternative Scenarios for Federal Transportation Policy* (Washington, D.C.: Research and Special Programs Administration, U.S. Department of Transportation, 1978); Paul Stephen Dempsey and William E. Thoms, *Law and Economic Regulation in Transportation* (New York; Westport, Conn.; and London: Quorum Books, 1986); James A. Dunn, Jr., *Miles to Go: European and American Transportation Policies* (Cambridge, Mass., and London: The MIT Press, 1981); Theodore E. Keeler, *Railroads, Freight, and Public Policy* (Washington, D.C.: The Brookings Institution, 1983); D. Maltby and H. P. White, *Transport in the U.S.* (London: Macmillan, 1982); James C. Miller, III, ed., *Perspectives on Federal Transportation Policy* (Washington, D.C.: American Enterprise Institute for Public Policy Research, 1975); Robert G. Smith, *Ad Hoc Governments: Special Purpose Transportation Authorities in Britain and the United States* (Beverly Hills, Calif.: Sage Publications, 1974); Kirk Steinman, *Public/Private Partnerships in Transit* (Washington, D.C.: Office of Planning Assistance, U.S. Department of Transportation, 1985).

For studies of deregulation and its impact on public transportation, see Robert W. Crandall et al., *Deregulating the Automobile* (Washington, D.C.: The Brookings Institution, 1986); Martha Derthick and Paul J. Quirk, *The Politics of Deregulation* (Washington, D.C.: The Brookings Institution, 1985); Lester B. Lave, "Conflicting Objectives in Regulating the Automobile," in Robert H. Haveman and Julius Margolis, eds., *Public Enterprise and Policy Analysis* (Boston: Houghton Mifflin, 1983); Steven Morrison and Clifford Winston, *The Economic Effects of Airline Deregulation* (Washington, D.C.: The Brookings Institution, 1986); Dorothy Robyn, *Braking the Special Interests: Trucking Deregulation and the Politics of Policy Reform* (Chicago and London: University of Chicago Press, 1987); Irene S. Rubin, *Shrinking the Federal Government: The Effect of Cutbacks on Five Federal Agencies* (New York: Longman, 1985); Stephen J. Thompson, *Deregulation of Transportation* (Washington, D.C.: Congressional Research Service, December 1984).

For studies of transport-related energy issues, see Daniel K. Boyle, *Transportation Energy Contingency Planning: Quantifying the Need for Transit Actions* (Washington, D.C.: Office of Planning Assistance, U.S. Department of Transportation, 1983) and U.S. Department of Energy, *Assessment of Costs and Benefits of Flexible and Alternative Fuel Use in the U.S. Transportation Sector—Progress Report One: Context and Analytical Framework,* (Washington, D.C.: Department of Energy, 1988).

Studies of urban transportation services and policy in the United States are contained in P. M. Allen et al., *Dynamic Urban Growth Models: Interim Report* (Washington, D.C.: Research and Special Programs Administration, U.S. Department of Transportation, 1978); Alan Altshuler with James P. Womack and John R. Pucher, *The Urban Transportation System: Politics and Policy Innovation* (Cambridge, Mass., and London: The MIT Press, 1979); John A. Bailey, *Constraints Against Introduction of New Technology or Innovative Marketing in Urban Transportation* (Chicago: The Transportation Center at Northwestern University, October 1970); Michael A. Kemp, *The Consequences of Short-Range Transit Improvements: An Overview of a Research Program* (Washington, D.C.: Urban Mass Transportation Administration, U.S. Department of Transportation, 1978); Wilfred Owen, *Transportation for Cities: The Role of Federal Policy* (Washington, D.C.: The Brookings Institution, 1976); K. H. Schaeffer and Elliot Sclar, *Access for All: Transportation and Urban Growth* (New York: Columbia University Press, 1980); Vukan R. Vuchic, *Urban Public Transportation: Systems and Technology* (Englewood Cliffs, N.J.: Prentice-Hall, 1981); Edward Weiner, *Urban Transportation Planning in the United States: An Historical Overview* (New York; Westport, Conn.; and London: Praeger, 1987); Edward Weiner, *Urban Transportation Planning in the United States: A Historical Overview* (Washington, D.C.: Office of the Assistant Secretary for Policy and International Affairs, U.S. Department of Transportation, 1983).

Discussions of rural transportation in the United States are contained in Jon E. Burkhardt, *Planning Rural Public Transportation Systems: A Section 147 Demonstration Program Technical Assistance Manual* (Washington, D.C.: Federal Highway Administration, U.S. Department of Transportation, 1979); David Chicoine and Norman Walzer, *Financing Rural Roads and Bridges in the Midwest* (Washington, D.C.: Office of Transportation and Agricultural Marketing Services, U.S. Department of Agriculture, October 1984); Fred Coldren, ed., *Rural Rides: A Practical Handbook for Starting and Operating a Rural Public Transportation System* (Washington, D.C.; Farmers Home Administration, U.S. Department of Agriculture, November 1979); Ira Kaye, "Transportation," in Don A. Dillman and Daryl J. Hobbs, eds., *Rural Society in the U.S.: Issues for the 1980s* (Boulder, Colo.: Westview Press, 1982).

Discussions of U.S. maritime transportation are found in *American Shipper* (a trade journal): Josseph H. Ball, *The Government-Subsidized Union Monopoly: A Study of Labor Practices in the Shipping Industry* (Washington, D.C.: Labor Policy Association, 1966); Ernst G. Frankel, *Regulation and Policies of American Shipping* (Boston: Auburn House, 1982); Lawrence Juda, *The UNCTAD Liner Code: United States Maritime Policy at the Crossroads* (Boulder, Colo.: Westview Press, 1984); John Kilgour, *The U.S. Merchant Marine: National Maritime Policy and Industrial Relations* (New York: Praeger, 1975); Robert A. Kilmarx, ed., *America's Maritime Legacy: A History of the U.S. Merchant Marine and Shipbuilding Industry Since Colonial Times* (Boulder, Colo.: Westview Press, 1979); James C. Barker and Robert Brandwein, *The U.S. Merchant Marine in National Perspective* (Lexington, Mass.: D.C. Heath, 1970); United States Department of Commerce Maritime Administration, *The U.S. Merchant Marine and the International Conference System* (Harbridge House Study, Washington, D.C.: U.S. Government Printing Office, 1978); H. David Bess and Martin T. Farris, *U.S. Maritime Policy: History and Prospects* (New York: Praeger, 1981); Ernest Frankel, *Regulation and Policies of American Shipping* (Boston: Auburn House, 1982); Irwin Heine, *U.S. Merchant Marine: A National Asset* (Washington, D.C.: National Maritime Council, 1976); and Clifton Whitehurst, Jr., *The U.S. Merchant Marine: In Search of an Enduring Maritime Policy* (Annapolis: Naval Institute Press, 1983).

Major professional periodicals on U.S. transportation include *Defense Transportation Journal; ITS Review* (University of California, Berkeley, Institute of Transportation Studies); *Journal of Advanced Transportation; Journal of Safety Research; TR News* (National Research Council); *Texas Transportation Researcher; Transportation Journal; Transportation Research; Transportation Science;* and *Transportation USA*.

WEST GERMANY

Transport statistics are found in The Federal Minister of Transportation, ed., *Verkehr in Zahlen 1986* [Transportation in figures 1986] (Bonn, 1986).

Discussions of federal transportation policy in general are contained in Gerd Aberle, *Verkehrspolitik und Regionalentwicklung: Integration und Evaluierung der Verkehrspolitik im Rahmen der Regionalpolitik und der regionalen Entwicklungsplanung* [Transportation policy and regional development: Integration and evaluation of the transportation policy under the framework of regional policy and regional development planning] (Bonn, 1981); Herbert Baum, "Possibilities and Limits of Regulation in Transport Policy," Report of the 62nd Round Table on Transport Economics of the European Conference of Ministers of Transport (Paris: ECMT, 1983); Brian T. Bayliss, *Planning and Control in the Transport Sector* (London: Gower Publishing Company, 1981); Walter Hamm, "Regulated Industries: Transportation," in *Zeitschrift für die gesamte Staastwissenschaft,* 1980, pp. 576–592; Walter Hamm, "Verkehrspolitik" [Transportation policy] in *Handwörterbuch der Wirtschaftswissenschaft* [Handbook of economics], vol. 8 (Stuttgart, 1980), pp. 249–257; Harald Jürgensen and Dieter Aldrup, *Verkerspolitik im europaischen Integrationstraum* [Transportation policy in the European Market] (Baden-Baden, 1968); Andreas Predöhl, *Verkehrspolitik* [Transportation policy] (Göttingen, 1958); Ulrich van Suntum, *Verkehrspolitik* [Transport policies] (München, 1986); The Federal Minister of Transportation, ed., *Bundesverkehrswegeplan 1985* [Federal transportation infrastructure plan 1985] (Bonn, 1985); Rainer Willeke, "Liberalisierung und Harmonisierung als Aufgabe einer gemeinsamen Verkehrspolitik im EG-Raum" [Liberalization and harmonization as task and chance of a common transport policy in the EC], *Zeitschrift für Verkehrswissenschaft* [Journal of transportation policy], vol. 58 (1987), pp. 71–99; and Fritz Voigt, *Verkehr* [Transportation], vol. 2, *Die Entwicklung des Verkehrssystems* [The development of the transportation systems] (Berlin, 1966).

Pricing and other economic aspects of transportation are discussed in Herbert Baum, *Staatlich administrierte Preise als Mittel der wirtschaftspolitik* [Public administered prices as means of economic policy] (Baden-Baden, 1980); Herbert Baum, "Deregulation of rates for international road haulage within the European Community," *Journal of Transport Economics and Policy,* vol. 18 (1984), pp. 23–50; Herbert Baum and Wolfgang Kentner, "Tariff Policies for Urban Transport," Report of the 46th Round Table on Transport Economics of the European Conference of Ministers of Transport (Paris: ECMT, 1980); Achim Diekmann, *Wirtschaftliche Aspekte der Verkehrssicherheit* [Economic aspects of road safety] (Stuttgart, 1972); Rolf Funch, "Stassenverkehrsteuern" [Taxes on road traffic] in *Handwörterbuch der Wirtschaftswissenschaft* [Handbook of economics], vol. 7 (Stuttgart, 1977), pp. 468–479; Werner Rothengatter, *Kosten- und nachfrageorientierte Preisbildung im Verkehrssektor* [Cost- and demand-based pricing in the transportation sector] (Karlsruhe, 1974); Kunibert Schmidt, *Verkehrsinfrastrukturinvestitionen als Mittel einer wachstumsorientierten Konjunkturpolitik* [Transportation infrastructure investments as means of a stabilization policy] (Bentheim, 1976); Hellmut St. Seidenfus et al., *Ordnungspolitische Szenarien zur Verwirklichung eines Gemeinsamen Europäischen Verkehrsmarkets, Teil A: Szenarien und ökonomische Wirkungszusammenhänge* [Regulatory scenarios on the implementation of a common European transport market, part A: Scenarios and economic issues] (München, 1986); Fritz Voigt, *Verkehr* [Transportation], vol. 1, *Die Theorie der Verkehrswirtschaft* [The theory of transportation economics] (Berlin, 1973).

Railway transportation in West Germany is discussed in Gerd Aberle and Rainer Willeke, *Wege zur Sanierung der Eisenbahn—Die Bundesbahn im internationalen Leistungsvergleich* [Possibilities of readjustment of the railways—An international comparison] (Frankfurt, 1973); Gerd Aberle and Ulrich Weber, *Verkehrswegebenutzungsabgaben für die Eisenbahn* [Paying for using the infrastructure of railways] (Darmstadt, 1987).

Discussions of the energy and environmental impact of public transportation in West Germany are contained in Rainer Willeke, ed., *Bedingungen nachhaltiger Energiesicherung für den Verkehr* [Conditions for long-term energy conservation for transportation] (Düsseldorf, 1980); Ernst-Albrecht Marburger, *Die ökonomische Beurteilung der städtischen Umweltbelastung durch Automobilabgase* [An economic assessment of the environmental impact due to automobile air pollution] (Bentheim, 1974); and Rainer Willeke and Wolfgang Kentner, *Die Kosten der Umweltbelastung durch den Verkehrslärm in Stadtgebieten* [The costs to the enviroment of traffic noise in urban areas] (Bentheim, 1975).

Main transport periodicals in West Germany include *Der Stadtverkehr* and *Transportation: Law and Legislation.*

ZAIRE

For the history of Zaire and other African countries, see Philip Curtin et al., *African History* (Boston: Little, Brown, 1978); Shafik-G Said, *De Léopoldville à Kinshasa: La Situation économique et financiére au Congo ex-Belge au jour de l'indepéndance* [From

Leopoldville to Kinshasa: The economic and financial situation of the former Belgian Congo at independence] (Brussels, 1969); Crawford Young and Thomas Turner, *The Rise and Decline of the Zairian State* (Madison: Wisconsin University Press, 1985).

For annual descriptions of economic developments in Zaire, see République du Zaire, *Conjoncture Économique* [Economic report] (annual).

For a historical account of the development of railway, roadway, and waterway transportation in Zaire, see André Lederer, *L'Évolution des Transports à l'ONATRA durant les années 1960 à 1977* [The evolution of transportation at ONATRA from 1960 to 1977] (Brussels: Académie Royale des Sciences d'Outre-Mer, 1978). Historical accounts of the development of railroads in Central and Southern Africa are contained in Rene Cornet, *La Bataille du Rail—La Construction du Chemin de fer de Matadi au Stanley Pool* [The rail war—The construction of the railway from Matadi to Stanley Pool] (Brussels: Cuypers, 1958); John R. Day, *Railways of Southern Africa* (London: Barker Limited, 1963); S. E. Katzenellenbogen, *Railways and the Copper Mines of Katanga* (New York: Clarendon Press, 1973).

The importance and impact of foreign investment and economic aid in Zairian economy is described in European Economic Communities, *EEC Zaire Assistance Report, 1985* (Brussels: European Economic Communities, 1986); Tshimuanga Muepu, ''Investissement Externe et Intégration Économique au Zaire'' [Foreign investment and economic integration in Zaire], *Geneva-Afrique* (1982), pp. 105–132; Kendall Stiles, *Structure and Process of IMF Decision-making,* Ph.D. dissertation (Baltimore, Md., 1987).

For information on Zaire's political and administrative background, see J. David Gould, *Bureaucratic Corruption in Zaire* (New York: Pergamon Press, 1980); and Mashida Ngoy-Munokowa Ngandu, *Zaire: Structures Politico-administratives et productivité de l'économie national* [Zaire: Politico-administrative structures and national economic productivity], Ph.D. dissertation (Munich, 1984).

INDEX

ABOUT THE EDITOR AND CONTRIBUTORS

TSUNEO AKAHA, Ph.D., is Associate Professor of International Policy Studies at the Monterey Institute of International Studies, Monterey, California. He is the author of *Japan in Global Ocean Politics* (1985) as well as numerous journal articles.

DAVID ANDERSON is Assistant to the Village Manager in Glencoe, Illinois. He is coauthor of "Transportation in the U.S.: An Overview of Transit Modes and Preliminary Analysis of Factors Impacting Policy" (unpublished paper).

HERBERT BAUM, Ph.D., is Professor of Economics at the University of Essen, West Germany. He is author of *Staatlich administrierte Preise als Mittel der Wirtschaftspolitik,* and numerous articles and technical reports.

GEORGE M. GUESS, Ph.D., is Director of the Transportation Studies Program and Associate Professor of Public Administration and Political Science at Georgia State University, Atlanta, Georgia. He is the author of *The Politics of U.S. Foreign Aid* and numerous journal articles.

RAINER HOPF, Ph.D., is a researcher at the Deutsches Institut für Wirtschaftsforschung (German Institute for Economic Research), Berlin, West Germany. He is the author of many books, reports, and articles on East and West Germany.

MARY KIHL, Ph.D., is Associate Director, Design Research Institute; Associate Dean for Research, College of Design; and Professor of Community and Regional Planning, Iowa State University, Ames, Iowa. She is the author of many journal articles and book chapters on transportation policy.

YOUNG WHAN KIHL, Ph.D., is Professor of Political Science at Iowa State University, Ames, Iowa. He is author of *Politics and Policies in Divided Korea,* and coauthor of many books, including *Security, Strategy, and Policy Responses in the Pacific Rim.*

DALE KRANE, Ph.D., is Associate Professor of Public Administration at the University of Nebraska at Omaha. He is the coauthor of *Compromised Compliance: Implementing the 1965 Voting Rights Act,* and author of many articles.

TROY LYONS is a teaching assistant in the Department of Political Science and the Department of German at Bowling Green State University, Bowling Green, Ohio.

FRANK McKENNA, Ph.D., is Director of the Center for Government Research and Public Service, and Associate Professor of Political Science, at Bowling Green State University, Bowling Green, Ohio. He is the author or coauthor of more than a dozen articles, numerous reports, and a book.

KENDALL STILES, Ph.D., is Assistant Professor of Political Science at Bowling Green State University, Bowling Green, Ohio. He is the author of the forthcoming *Negotiating Conditionality in the IMF* and several journal articles on international political economy.

MITCHELL P. STROHL, Ph.D., is Professor of Political Science at American University of Paris, and author of *The International Law of Bays* and *Transportation Geography of Western Europe.*

JANE P. SWEENEY, Ph.D., is Associate Professor of Political Science at St. John's University in New York. She is the author of *The First European Elections: Neo-Functionalism and the European Parliament,* and several articles on European politics and women's rights.

WILLIAM L. WAUGH, JR., Ph.D., is Associate Professor of Public Administration and Political Science at Georgia State University, Atlanta, Georgia. He is the author of *International Terrorism: How Nations Respond to Terrorists,* and numerous book chapters, articles, and reports.

JOHN P. WILLERTON, JR., Ph.D., is Assistant Professor of Political Science at the University of Arizona, Tucson, Arizona. He is the author of journal articles dealing with Soviet domestic politics and foreign policy.

JACQUES YENNY, Ph.D., has been a project economist at the World Bank for over twenty years. Between 1980 and 1987 he served as principal transport economist on Chinese transportation.